2001

W9-ACL-134

www.wadsworth.com

wadsworth.com is the World Wide Web site for Wadsworth and is your direct source to dozens of online resources.

At *wadsworth.com* you can find out about supplements, demonstration software, and student resources. You can also send e-mail to many of our authors and preview new publications and exciting new technologies.

wadsworth.com
Changing the way the world learns®

From the Wadsworth Series in Mass Communication and Journalism

General Mass Communication

Shirley Biagi, *Media/Impact: An Introduction to Mass Media*, 4th Ed.

Shirley Biagi, *Media/Reader: Perspectives on Media Industries, Effects, and Issues*, 3rd Ed.

Louis Day, *Ethics in Media Communications: Cases and Controversies*, 3rd Ed.

Robert S. Fortner, *International Communications: History, Conflict, and Control of the Global Metropolis*

Kathleen Hall Jamieson and Karlyn Kohrs Campbell, *The Interplay of Influence*, 4th Ed.

Paul Lester, *Visual Communication*, 2nd Ed.

Cynthia Lont, *Women and Media: Content, Careers, and Criticism*

Joseph Straubhaar and Robert LaRose, *Media Now: Communications Media in the Information Age*, 2nd Ed.

Ray Surette, *Media, Crime, and Criminal Justice: Images and Realities*, 2nd Ed.

Edward Jay Whetmore, *Mediamerica, Mediaworld: Form, Content, and Consequence of Mass Communication*, Updated 5th Ed.

John D. Zelezny, *Communications Law: Liberties, Restraints, and the Modern Media*, 2nd Ed.

Journalism

Dorothy Bowles and Diane L. Borden, *Creative Editing*, 3rd Ed.

Robert L. Hilliard, *Writing for Television, Radio & New Media*, 7th Ed.

Lauren Kessler and Duncan McDonald, *The Search: Information Gathering for the Mass Media*

Lauren Kessler and Duncan McDonald, *When Words Collide*, 5th Ed.

Alice M. Klement and Carolyn Burrows Matalene, *Telling Stories/Taking Risks: Journalism Writing at the Century's Edge*

Fred S. Parrish, *Photojournalism: An Introduction*

Carole Rich, *Writing and Reporting News: A Coaching Method*, 3rd Ed.

Carole Rich, *Workbook for Writing and Reporting News*, 3rd Ed.

Photojournalism and Photography

Fred S. Parrish, *Photojournalism: An Introduction*

Marvin Rosen and David DeVries, *Introduction to Photography*, 4th Ed.

Public Relations and Advertising

Jerry A. Hendrix, *Public Relations Cases*, 4th Ed.

Jerome A. Jewler and Bonnie L. Drewniany, *Creative Strategy in Advertising*, 6th Ed.

Eugene Marlow, *Electronic Public Relations*

Barbara Mueller, *International Advertising: Communicating Across Cultures*

Doug Newsom and Bob Carrell, *Public Relations Writing: Form and Style*, 5th Ed.

Doug Newsom, Judy VanSlyke Turk, and Dean Kruckeberg, *This Is PR: The Realities of Public Relations*, 7th Ed.

Juliann Sivulka, *Soap, Sex, and Cigarettes: A Cultural History of American Advertising*

Gail Baker Woods, *Advertising and Marketing to the New Majority: A Case Study Approach*

Research and Theory

Earl Babbie, *The Practice of Social Research*, 8th Ed.

Stanley Baran and Dennis Davis, *Mass Communication Theory: Foundations, Ferment, and Future*, 2nd Ed.

Sondra Rubenstein, *Surveying Public Opinion*

Rebecca B. Rubin, Alan M. Rubin, and Linda J. Piele, *Communication Research: Strategies and Sources*, 5th Ed.

Roger D. Wimmer and Joseph R. Dominick, *Mass Media Research: An Introduction*, 6th Ed.

Creative
Editing Third Edition

Dorothy A. Bowles

University of Tennessee–Knoxville

Diane L. Borden

San Diego State University

Wadsworth
Thomson Learning™

AUSTRALIA ■ CANADA ■ DENMARK ■ JAPAN ■ MEXICO ■ NEW ZEALAND ■ PHILIPPINES

PUERTO RICO ■ SINGAPORE ■ SOUTH AFRICA ■ SPAIN ■ UNITED KINGDOM ■ UNITED STATES

Journalism Editor: Karen Austin
Associate Development Editor: Ryan E. Vesely
Editorial Assistant: Dory Schaeffer
Executive Marketing Manager: Stacey Purviance
Marketing Assistant: Ken Baird
Print Buyer: Barbara Britton
Permissions Editor: Susan Walters
Project Manager: Gary Palmatier, Ideas to Images
Interior and Cover Designer: Gary Palmatier
Copy Editor: Cathy Baehler
Technical Illustrator: Ideas to Images
Cover Photographer: Tom Farrington
Compositor: Ideas to Images
Printer: West Group

For permission to use material from this text, contact us:

Web: www.thomsonrights.com
Fax: 1-800-730-2215
Phone: 1-800-730-2214

Printed in the United States of America

2   3   4   5   6   7   03   02   01   00

Library of Congress Cataloging-in-Publication Data

Bowles, Dorothy A.
    Creative editing / Dorothy A. Bowles, Diane L. Borden. — 3rd ed.
        p.   cm.
    Rev. ed. of: Creative editing for print media. 2nd. c1997.
    Includes bibliographical references and index.
    ISBN 0-534-56178-0
    1. Journalism—Editing.   2. Editing.   I. Borden, Diane L.
II. Bowles, Dorothy A.   Creative editing for print media.
III. Title.
PN4788.B75   1999
070.4'1—dc21   99–33126

For more information, contact:

Wadsworth/Thomson Learning
10 Davis Drive
Belmont, CA 94002-3098
USA
www.wadsworth.com

International Headquarters
Thomson Learning
290 Harbor Drive, 2nd Floor
Stamford, CT 06902-7477
USA

UK/Europe/Middle East
Thomson Learning
Berkshire House
168-173 High Holborn
London WC1V 7AA
United Kingdom

Asia
Thomson Learning
60 Albert Street #15-01
Albert Complex
Singapore 189969

Canada
Nelson/Thomson Learning
1120 Birchmount Road
Scarborough, Ontario M1K 5G4
Canada

Contents

Chapter 5   Checking Facts   141

Chapter 6   Legal Concerns   167

Preface

THEY now bear titles such as database producer, technical director, informational designer, Internet strategist and Web technologist. They can earn between $45,000 and $110,000 a year, and the market for their talents gets stronger each year. They are the copy editors of the 21st century, and their jobs reflect the ubiquitous changes in communication technologies at the end of the millennium.

No matter what their titles, modern copy editors are at the very heart of any print or online media organization, supplying the lifeblood for healthy existence and serving as gatekeepers of news and entertainment for the public. More than at any previous time in history, senior editors recognize and appreciate the value of good copy editors. This praise makes even better an already excellent employment picture for copy editors, who are rewarded at many organizations with higher salaries than those of reporters or writers with comparable experience.

Journalists with the personal attributes and word and visual skills explained in this book will have no trouble finding stimulating and rewarding careers as copy editors. In addition, those who aspire to become managers will discover that the copy desk is a fertile training ground for learning the intricacies of the print or online production process and is a frequent path to management positions.

This third edition of *Creative Editing* recognizes and addresses the impact that technological, lifestyle and competitive changes have brought to traditional media industries, particularly as they affect the roles of copy editors. At the same time, the book emphasizes traditional and still highly valued editing skills: using correct grammar, punctuation, style and vocabulary; fact checking; writing headlines; handling photographs and informational graphics; using typography; and designing and laying out pages.

A special feature of *Creative Editing* is the extensive collection of in-book exercises, which allows students to test their understanding of the material in each chapter and to practice their editing skills. New exercises have been added to almost every chapter, and students may now download exercises from a Web site to practice electronic editing and layout. For instructors, an answer booklet is available upon adoption of the text.

Many other new features mark this third edition. New material about electronic editing, with a strong emphasis on the World Wide Web, is integrated throughout the book. The authors believe that the Internet and online publishing offer great potential as an expanding job market for copy editors. Thus, new material focuses on how to edit copy for Web sites; how to access Internet discussion groups of interest to communicators; how to use Internet search and fact-checking tools; and how to design and lay out Web pages.

Chapter 4 on editing stories is expanded to include editing copy for Web sites and copy from news services. Sections on how to edit stories based on public opinion surveys and how to handle copy laden with numbers have been updated and expanded. Chapter 5 on checking facts is completely revised. It teaches students how to find information in both printed and electronic versions of standard reference works and how to use Internet search tools, discussion groups and commercial databases. The chapter includes extensive lists of reference materials and Web URLs useful for fact checking.

This edition also expands and updates material on journalism ethics, including new discussions about media credibility, media convergence, online ethics, and recent incidences of ethical lapses by journalists at large media organizations. Chapter 10 on editing pictures and infographics includes expanded information about digital photography and about matching the appropriate type of graphic to the information to be communicated. Many new examples of effective infographics also are included. Chapter 11 on layout and design has new sections on magazine and Web site layout and design, including many new and updated illustrations from professional and university publications.

Most chapters in the third edition include an end-of-chapter essay written by a professional journalist to help students understand the work of copy editors. A short biographical sketch and a small photo accompany each of these essays so students can see the career path of the professional. Of particular note in this edition is an essay by an online journalist at <u>washingtonpost.com</u> and an essay by two recent college graduates on the importance of internships.

As in prior editions, the organization of *Creative Editing* remains logical and progressive. Chapter 1 explores how media convergence is making the role of copy editors even more important now than in the past, explains the organization of a typical print-media organization and discusses career opportunities for copy editors.

Chapters 2, 3, 4 and 5 focus on the copy editor's tools: the proper use of grammar and punctuation; the importance of precision and consistent style when editing words, sentences and paragraphs; the importance of editing leads and making news judgments when editing stories, whether in print or online; and the need to check facts, including how to use both standard reference materials and electronic databases.

Chapter 6 offers a detailed treatment of legal concerns that affect editors—including libel, invasion of privacy and copyright infringement—and suggests ways that editors can help their publications avoid lawsuits. Chapter 7 examines ethical situations of specific concern to editors, including online ethics, and suggests ways to frame discussions that should prove useful in ethical decision-making. This chapter also offers a sampling of behavioral codes from professional journalism organizations, including the Society of Professional Journalists, as well as a section on how to edit with good taste and sensitivity.

Chapter 8 discusses typography, particularly type sizes, widths, styles, weights and families, and is a necessary precedent to Chapter 9, which focuses on the art of writing headlines. This chapter discusses the function and characteristics of headlines, increasingly important in the online environment, and offers rules for writing, counting, placing and styling headlines.

Chapters 10 and 11 launch a discussion of visual journalism, focusing particularly on editing pictures and infographics, including digital photographs, and on designing and laying out pages, both for print publications and on the Web. Chapter 11 also discusses pagination, personal computers and laser graphics.

Chapter 12 explores the growth of public relations as a career choice for students majoring in mass communication programs and suggests ways to create public relations materials such as fliers, brochures and newsletters.

An appendix provides an extensive list of frequently misused words.

Throughout the book, we have adhered to the most commonly used journalistic style and have sought to avoid sexism, racism, ageism, homophobia and other discriminatory language.

We would like to thank Rebekah Bromley for updating her chapter on creating fliers, brochures and newsletters. We also would like to express our heartfelt gratitude to the professional journalists across the nation who helped supply materials and insights for this book. Special thanks go to our end-of-chapter essayists: Gina Acosta, Peter Bhatia, Sharon Bibb, Cole C. Campbell, J. Ford Huffman, Matthew Lee, Michele Medley, Lynne Perri and Amanda Traughber.

Others who deserve our utmost appreciation are Wynne Brown, Rob Heller, Bill Lee and Tom Farrington for help with photos; Sally Guthrie for suggestions about Web sites; Christa Carter for research help; and Carol Goodhue and the staff of the *San Diego Union-Tribune* for allowing us to photograph editors at work.

It was a real pleasure to work with the highly professional production-management specialist Gary Palmatier of Ideas to Images and with copy editor Cathy Baehler. The people at Wadsworth also deserve our thanks: Deirdre E. Cavanaugh, executive editor for communications; Ryan E. Vesely, associate development editor; and Hal Humphrey, production project editor.

We also offer our special thanks to those who read the manuscript at various stages and gave us many valuable suggestions, including James D. Whitfield, Northeast Louisiana University; Jon M. Smith, Southern Utah University; and Bob Gassaway, University of New Mexico.

Diane L. Borden
San Diego State University

Dorothy A. Bowles
University of Tennessee

Deadlines do not wait for inspiration.

—*Charles M. Schulz, "Peanuts" creator*

The Copy Editor's Role in the Newsroom

CONVERGENCE. That was the buzzword in mass-media circles at the turn of the century. Convergence of technologies, convergence of job responsibilities, convergence of content. They burst onto the stage of journalistic debate at warp speed and with little regard for consequences. The name of the game was, and is, content.

What does convergence mean? And how will it affect the role of copy editors in the 21st century? To some, convergence means the merging of the technologies of communication—calling up the Internet on your cable television screen, or accessing a television news broadcast on your home computer. For others, convergence means mergers of media companies into mega-media companies—telephone companies that buy cable television companies that buy computer companies that buy newspaper companies that buy television networks, etc.

Convergence also may mean redefinition and marketplace relocation—newspapers becoming "information organizations," partnering with other local media or organizations within the community to produce online city guides, such as Boston.com, Cox's Access Atlanta and Knight-Ridder's Real Cities sites.

Others see convergence as the intertwining of job responsibilities—reporters who conjure up photo illustrations for their stories, or copy editors who perform the tasks formerly performed by printers and typesetters. For others, convergence means the erasing, or at least blurring, of the lines between news and entertainment, between fact and opinion, between truth and fiction. Which is the "real" news program, ABC Nightly News with Peter Jennings or Hard Copy? Which is the "real" entertainment program, Entertainment Tonight or NBC News with Tom Brokaw? Which is truth and which is fiction, Boston Globe columns by Mike Barnicle or Tom Berendt's novel, *Midnight in the Garden of Good or Evil?*

At the 1997 Catto Conference on Journalism and Society, set in the breathtaking mountain landscape of Aspen, Colo., noted journalist and author Robert MacNeil explored these issues. He said the news media are treading on dangerous ground if they remain isolated from these trends.

"The compartments between ours and other segments of the media are not colorfast," he said. "Our products are tossed in the same frenzied laundromat of competition for the public's attention and dollar, and the fabrics bleed into one another. The ravishing colors of entertainment media bleed into the necessary black, white, and grey of journalism … in print and video and on the Internet.

"The range of media activities now resemble the electromagnetic spectrum. All human activities, from a Mozart opera to pornography, to war on Saddam Hussein, to a learned article in a scientific journal … are reducible to digital bits and bytes, evermore tightly compressed, evermore quickly flashed … around the globe in the blink of any eye…."

MacNeil was talking about convergence, especially in media content. For journalists, and particularly for copy editors, at the beginning of a new millennium, the production of content will be, as it always has been, an essential ingredient in any media company's success. Companies that supply content to those who control the technological means to transmit it will benefit most in the new age, according to 52 percent of senior industry executives polled at a 1998 Global Convergence Summit presented by Business Week magazine and Price-Waterhouse-Coopers accounting firm. Newspapers, magazines, broadcast stations, public relations firms, advertising agencies and World Wide Web sites will be competing for bright, energetic, talented people who understand this brave new world of content convergence.

The often-unspoken theme that underlies these discussions is the need for good editing and for good editors. Copy editors in the 21st century will be less likely than their 20th century counterparts to perform media-specific tasks or to think in narrowly defined media boxes. They will perform all the tasks discussed in this book—copy editing, headline writing, layout and design, etc.—and they will perform them in a variety of media forms. Editors will prepare a story for a print publication, for example, then later in their workday, add video and audio for a broadcast version or an online version. At places like MSNBC (a media organization put together by Bill Gates' Microsoft Corp. and the National Broadcasting Co.), editors already perform this multitasking and find it's an exciting new world.

How we got here

It became commonplace in the mid-1990s for reporters and editors of the print media to go online—to retrieve information from government documents, to gather information from online discussion groups and chat rooms, and to publish information in many formats, including electronically, for their readers. According to the Poynter Institute, a journalism education facility in St. Petersburg, Fla., 702 U.S. daily newspapers offered Web sites in 1997, more than triple the number only a couple of years earlier. In addition, thousands of magazines, newsletters, newswires and television and radio transcript services had created online products (see Figure 1-1).

The immediacy and the relatively easy access to electronic information has lured millions of people to the Internet, but for journalists and copy editors, in particular, the beauty of the new resources may be a beast as well. The media marketplace has become increasingly competitive, and many forms of traditional mass media are struggling to maintain their market share. Both newspapers and network news programs have shown declines in the last two decades. Total daily newspaper circulation had declined to 56.7 million in 1997, and only 48 percent of those surveyed in a 1995 Times Mirror Center poll had watched a network news program the night before, down from 60 percent in 1993. More than 150 dailies have folded in the last 30 years, as have countless magazines and newsletters.

Many new print media outlets have been created, of course, as have a plethora of online news and information services. But for print media journalists, the challenge to relate to readers in new and exciting ways is stronger than ever (see Figure 1-2). Traditional concerns about core journalism values such as accuracy and balance also have come under renewed scrutiny as more and more journalists use the emerging online technologies to gather and analyze news and information (see Chapter 7 on ethics).

Even with the headlong rush into the new technologies, most news publications in the new millennium probably will not look much different from those of today. They simply will be better organized, concentrate more on their primary geographic communities, use more color and attempt to squeeze more information into less space.

Figure 1-1
Collage demonstrates the importance of content and the similarity in appearance of World Wide Web sites from several different forms of news media—newspapers, magazines, broadcast networks and content companies, such as Microsoft.

Figure 1-2
World Wide Web site of the student newspaper at Indiana University in Bloomington, Ind., won first place in the 1998 Best of the Net contest, sponsored by Associated College Press and NetGuide. The Indiana Digital Student is located at http://www.idsnews.com.

Whatever form they take, their future is certainly secure. Print news products are likely to be around well into the 21st century and beyond. However, they may look more like a medium that blends text, sounds, still pictures and video through technological advances in fiber optics and computers. Such a format will make the verbal and visual skills of good copy editors even more valuable in newsrooms of the future.

Witness the following scenario from a 1989 American Society of Newspaper Editors report on technology and the future. The incident takes place as the closing credits of a movie scroll up the wide screen of the high-definition television set:

> The viewer points her remote channel selector at a newspaper symbol in the lower right corner of the screen, and then the movie dissolves into an electronic version of a front page, with typographically attractive headlines and a couple of still photos.
>
> She points to a headline about a surgeon general's warning on the impact of high-salt diets on children's health. The screen fills with a detailed report of the surgeon general's press conference. She begins to read, then moves her pointer to position a small arrow over the first word of the surgeon general's statement. Immediately the text is replaced with a short video showing highlights from the press conference.
>
> Returning to the text, she reads further, until she reaches a reference to the relative risks of sodium and potassium salts. Pointing the arrow to the word "potassium" calls up a listing of brand names for sodium substitutes, as well as a listing of popular packaged foods that have recently replaced sodium salts with potassium salts.

This kind of multimedia product is available now, and the people who produce the newspaper or magazine or multimedia product of the future—editors, reporters, designers, photographers and artists—are the ones likely to be affected most by technological changes. Copy editors, key bridges between information gatherers and information consumers, will be called on to perform all the traditional copy editing tasks plus some duties that are now the domain of other news personnel (see Figure 1-3).

Figure 1-3
Mercury Center in San Jose, Calif., one of the first newspaper World Wide Web sites in the United States, is part of the Knight-Ridder company's "Real Cities" network, which partners with other organizations in the community to publish online city guides.

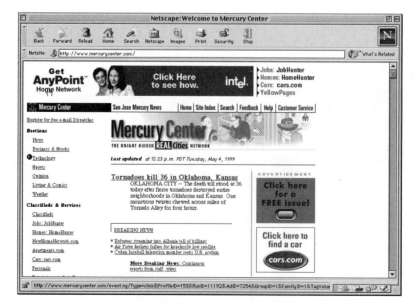

The importance of good copy editing

Good newspapers, good magazines, good news broadcasts all have one thing in common: They all have good teams of editors. Although bylines give reporters name recognition copy editors do not have, the strength of the copy editing staff is one of the most important predictors of the strength of the news organization.

Perhaps more than at any previous time in newspaper history, senior editors are recognizing the value of good copy editors, an appreciation that makes an already excellent employment picture even better for copy editors. Linda Grist Cunningham, chair of an ASNE committee that conducted a survey of copy editors, said: "As the literacy skills of even our better writers decline and as the demands of technology complicate our production schedules, editors will be forced to pay attention to the needs of copy editors if we are to improve our newspapers."

Copy editors are a rare breed, and they are scarce. Just ask any editor or publisher trying to hire one. And they are dedicated, intelligent individuals whose love of language and penchant for precision make many reporters look good. Copy editors are the very heart of the organization, supplying the lifeblood for healthy existence and serving as gatekeepers of the news for the public. In this regard, their place in the future of the news and information industry is assured.

The importance of copy editors is recognized and rewarded at many small newspapers with salaries higher than those of reporters with comparable experience. Yet, in the latest survey of pay levels for newsroom staff members, copy editors showed smaller salary gains than reporters. Mervin Aubespin, vice chair of the American Society of Newspaper Editors Human Resources Committee in 1995, said this problem must be addressed. "Some newspapers report they are having difficulty recruiting and retaining copy editors, but they don't seem to be doing much in compensation for the technological responsibilities, the pagination and the photo editing, that are being added," he said. Aubespin, associate editor/development at the Louisville (Ky.) Courier-Journal, added that increased salary levels would be helpful in attracting younger staff members to copy editing (see Figure 1-4).

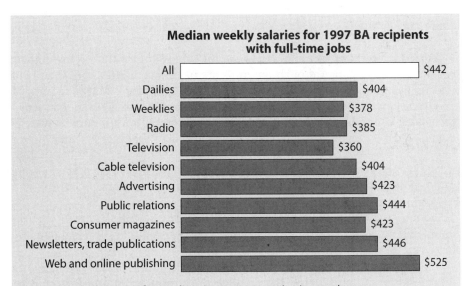

Median weekly salaries for 1997 BA recipients with full-time jobs

All	$442
Dailies	$404
Weeklies	$378
Radio	$385
Television	$360
Cable television	$404
Advertising	$423
Public relations	$444
Consumer magazines	$423
Newsletters, trade publications	$446
Web and online publishing	$525

Source: Annual survey of journalism & mass communication graduates

Figure 1-4
To determine the median weekly salaries for 1997, the Henry W. Grady College of Journalism and Mass Communication at the University of Georgia conducted a survey of journalism and mass communication graduates during the 1996-97 academic year. The survey included responses from students at 450 colleges and universities across the United States and Puerto Rico, which offer programs in journalism and mass communication.

Online editors, on the other hand, seem to be garnering good salaries. According to "Online News Salaries and Staffing," a study published by Interactive Publishing Surveys in January 1998, experienced online editors were making between $45,000 and $75,000 a year. A typical entry-level salary in North America was $25,000 a year. In addition, job satisfaction seemed high: Nearly half of all Web sites reported no employee turnover in the preceding year, and, among those sites that did lose people, most only lost one or two employees.

Journalists who possess the personal attributes and verbal and visual skills described in this book will have no trouble finding stimulating and rewarding work as copy editors. In an earlier era, few copy editors were without reporting experience; desk work was seen as a promotion from reporting. However, those in charge of hiring today no longer insist that reporting be a prerequisite to working on the copy desk. Also, journalists who aspire to management positions will learn that the copy desk is a good place to learn the intricacies of print production and is a frequent path to management jobs.

The duties of a copy editor

Great reporting alone will produce, at best, a mediocre newspaper. Good editing is the difference between a great publication and a mediocre one.

The chief duties of the copy editor include the following:

▶**Improving copy by making dull or verbose copy interesting and concise.** Copy editors can transform halting stories into ones that sing. Creativity is essential. However, as long as the information has been expressed clearly, the aim of the copy editor is to preserve as far as possible the words of the reporter and to retain the tone of the story as it was written.

▶**Correcting errors of grammar, spelling and style in all copy, including informational graphics.** Too many reporters, triumphantly bringing in stories that were difficult to pry loose, refer to minor errors as "just typos." Yet even the smallest error or inconsistency can cause readers to wonder whether that carelessness extends to the reporting as well.

▶**Correcting errors of fact and emphasis.** An expert copy editor is invariably a walking compendium. Although reporters are better acquainted with their beats and their sources, the copy editor can supply a context—other stories, the city, the county, the nation, the world—that the reporters, whose single-minded focus is their story, almost inevitably fail to comprehend. Copy editors unfamiliar with the context must be adept at using many reference sources for quick research.

▶**Judging news value.** Copy editors must be alert to the flow of current affairs and understand how a single item integrates with the stream of news.

▶**Guarding against libel and other legal problems.** The copy desk is usually the last line of defense against legal concerns that are costly to a publication in money and in lost time.

▶**Protecting and enhancing the publication's reputation and image.** Most newspapers would like to have a reputation for accuracy and thoroughness in news coverage. It is up to copy editors to build and preserve that reputation. The personality or image of the publication—conservative or breezy, formal or informal, for example—is also largely in the hands of the copy desk.

▶**Writing headlines that summarize stories and capture readers' attention.** Copy editors' skill with words and ability to work quickly are especially valuable in this aspect of the job.

▶**Selecting, cropping and sizing photographs and other art.** Section editors, along with the photography and graphics staff, handle much of this work, but copy editors frequently are involved in the process.

▶**Writing illustration captions.** The idea that "a picture is worth a thousand words" may become meaningless unless the picture is accompanied by a carefully crafted caption.

▶**Using computer codes to designate the headline and body type style, size, width and leading.** As print media became computerized during the 1970s, copy editors assumed many of the production tasks previously performed by others. With expert knowledge of the publication's computer system, a copy editor can, with just a few keystrokes, do much of the work that previously was performed by teams of production specialists.

▶**Laying out pages.** Many decisions about how the publication will look each day are in the hands of copy editors. Designers and other graphics experts determine the basic look of the paper, but copy editors work within the overall design pattern to lay out individual pages.

▶**Exercising news judgment.** Expert news judgment is also essential as copy editors, working with other editors, make decisions about which stories will go on the front page or an inside page and how much emphasis to give individual stories.

▶**Keeping up with the newest technology.** Computer graphics, computer pagination and digital photography are rapidly changing. Editors knowledgeable about the most recent versions of software for graphics, layout and digital-image enhancement can produce better quality work faster and more efficiently. Such technical expertise is especially valuable for editors working at online publications.

The characteristics of a good copy editor

In a report from the Associated Press Managing Editors Writing and Editing Committee, William G. Connolly Jr., an editor of The New York Times Week in Review section, offered this checklist of the qualities of an outstanding editor:

▶**Confidence.** Good editors have confidence in their own intelligence, knowledge and writing skills. They know the publication's style, production capabilities and politics. They know the system—and use it.

▶**Objectivity.** Editors have an extra obligation to be objective. They must be able to put the material in a broader context and stand back from the person who wrote it. Every newsroom has problem people, but great editors have the ability to look beyond the person.

▶**Awareness.** Editors must be aware of the readers and of the personality of the publication. Layout, selection of stories, art, graphics and headlines should all come together to reinforce the publication's personality. Look at products that are in trouble, and you'll find a personality problem. Good taste and knowing what's important are the essential elements of personality.

▶**Intelligence.** Good editors must have a broad background that enables them to bring to every story a sense of why it is important and what it means in a broader context. They must be instinctively aware of what is right or wrong with a story.

▶**Questioning nature.** Good editors know there is no such thing as a stupid question. They question everything. Editors know that if they have doubts, so will the reader.

▶**Diplomacy.** Editing is a confrontation. Writing is both an intellectual and emotional experience, and good editors try to minimize the inevitable tension that arises between an editor and a writer. They understand the reporter's problems. Nevertheless, although civility and diplomacy are important, neither can be permitted to overwhelm the need to edit.

▶**Ability to write.** Editors should be better writers than reporters are, but they still must be able to retain a writer's style and ideas. A great editor's work is invisible to both the writer and the reader.

▶**Sense of humor.** Good editors are able to laugh at the absurdity of some aspects of the business—bad hours, bad tempers, bad deadlines, bad copy—and plunge ahead.

Another editor, speaking at a journalism educators' seminar at the American Press Institute, said the following attributes would produce an "almost-perfect" copy editor:

- Has a college education.

- Has newspaper experience, including reporting and editing.

- Is well-read, in both fiction and nonfiction.

- Is familiar with the news and its background.

- Has hobbies, enjoys cultural events and is well-traveled.

- Is quick and thorough when editing copy.

- Has a healthy skepticism that leads to the questioning of information in stories and a desire to release no story with unanswered questions.

- Is familiar with the rules of grammar, with punctuation and spelling and with style.

- Appreciates good writing and knows what to do with it.

- Is able to listen to the rhythm of a story.

- Has a sense of wit and pathos and the ability to discern the difference.

- Has an orderly and well-balanced mind, which implies judgment and a sense of perspective and proportion.

- Knows the laws of libel, contempt and copyright.

- Has a team spirit.

The copy desk in a modern newsroom

The traditional copy desk physically resembled a horseshoe. The chief copy editor, called the "slot editor" or simply the "slot," sat at the center of the inside curve of a semicircular desk. Copy editors sat along the outside curve of the horseshoe, known as the "rim," and were thus known as "rim editors." Although the terms *slot editor* and *rim editor* persist, the computerization of editing has changed the physical arrangement of the copy desk. Modern copy desks are arranged in a rectangular shape and generally include separate stations with an electronic editing terminal for each editor.

To help speed the flow of copy, many small and medium-sized newspapers have instituted a system of centralized editing called the "universal copy desk." Universal desk copy editors work on copy for all sections of the newspaper. Conversely, most metropolitan newspapers have specialized desks that process copy for particular categories of news: local, state, national, international, business, sports, opinion, lifestyle or entertainment.

In the 1990s, many newsrooms were experimenting with teams or clusters of journalists who would work together in small groups to conceive, report, edit and illustrate stories. Such clusters often would comprise a team leader, usually someone from the city desk; a copy editor; a reporter or several reporters; and a photographer or graphic artist. Frequently, the stories each team produced were enterprise packages, in-depth articles about issues of significance in the local community.

Some metros also have separate reporting and editing staffs for "zoned" editions, those pages or sections that target news and advertising geographically for a particular circulation area. In many newspaper markets, zoned editions have proved successful with both readers and advertisers. Subscribers receive the individual section containing news and advertising focusing on their neighborhood, along with the rest of the metropolitan newspaper. Some newspapers publish as many as 24 different zoned editions a week; others publish several zoned sections each day.

The fast pace of editing often allows little time for reflection. In today's newsrooms, where editors are asked to perform more and more of the production functions previously handled by composing-room personnel, editors increasingly find that their time is at a premium.

An age of rapid technological advances in the publishing industry has introduced computer-generated copy and computer-activated layout and pasteup (pagination). The copy editor's job, therefore, has become at once more complex, more exciting and more vital to the quality of the final product.

Pagination, some say, is the vital link to a grander scheme for automation. It calls for the end of the composing room, the place where the publication is mechanically produced. Partial pagination, now used at many newspapers and magazines, allows editors to create pages on computer terminals with all the text in place, eliminating the need for pages to be pasted up. Devices that permit the digitization of photographs, a step necessary to achieve total pagination, allow editors to produce an entire page on computer terminals. When total pagination is in place, most of the work now done in the composing room, a department that accounts for perhaps 25 percent of the total newspaper payroll, will be unnecessary. (Pagination is discussed further in Chapter 11.)

Clearly, newsroom editors and managers of the future must be ready to meet the challenges of incorporating new technology into newsroom processes.

Figure 1-5

Today's newsroom is organized hierarchically. This chart illustrates the organizational plan at a large metropolitan daily, which has separate copy desks for general-interest news, business, sports, features and the zoned editions. Many newspapers have a universal copy desk, which edits stories for all sections of the paper.

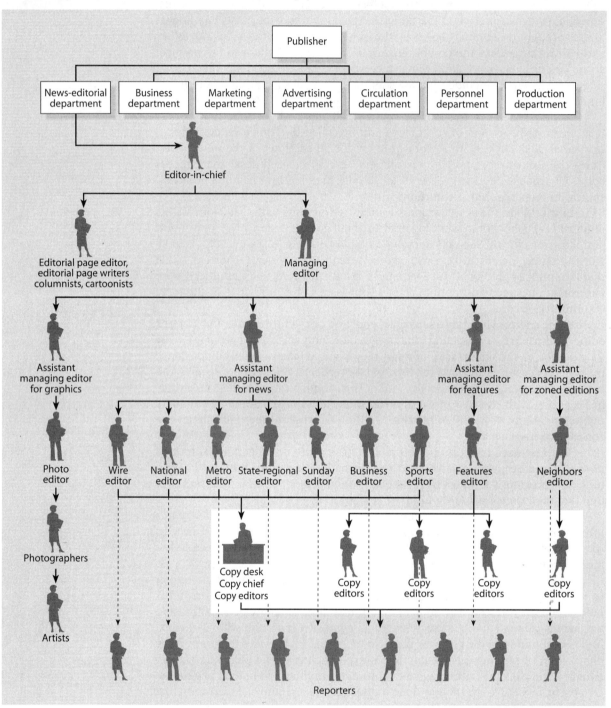

The organizational structure of newsrooms of the future may look quite different. Today most newsrooms are organized in a hierarchical structure like the one shown in Figure 1-5. That is, the organization looks like a pyramid, with the editor at the apex and the reporters, copy editors and photographers—the workers— forming the base.

Newsrooms of the future may require a more circular structure, in which job functions rather than titles determine the organization and in which jobs are interrelated rather than separated. Copy editors, many believe, will be at the center of this new newsroom because of the breadth of their job functions.

The editing process

Video display terminals (VDTs) linked to computers have greatly changed the newspaper production process. The computer revolution has simplified some aspects of the copy editor's job but has also added duties. Many production functions are now performed at the copy desk instead of in the composing room.

Copy editors not only perform more functions but are now also the last people to process copy before the final pasteup stage. Typesetters and proofreaders no longer exist as a final check to prevent errors from being published. Electronic layout will soon eliminate the physical pasteup stage as well.

To demonstrate the editing process, let's track a newspaper story from idea to publication. First, before a story is assigned to a reporter or accepted from a beat or general assignment reporter, an editor has to decide the story is newsworthy. A knowledge of the newspaper's audience is the key to determining which news values to emphasize, and many newspapers today periodically conduct sophisticated surveys to help editors stay abreast of readers' interests.

In exercising news judgment, editors evaluate the extent to which each individual story contains one or more traditional news criteria, which include

▶**Timeliness.** Something that happens today has more reader impact than something that happened yesterday. Timeliness means that up-to-the-minute information is valuable.

▶**Proximity.** Something that happens nearby physically or geographically is important to readers, but so is information about others who share a common interest, such as those who participate in the same online discussion groups.

▶**Prominence.** People who are well-known or hold positions of authority, such as the president of the United States, often are newsmakers. But others in the community often have interesting stories, too.

▶**Relevance.** A story often has an impact on its audience, whether emotional or rational. The more people who are affected by the consequences of a story, the more significant the story will be.

▶**Unusualness.** It's not usually big news if it snows in Colorado in January. But snow in Colorado in July could be newsworthy because it would be out of the ordinary.

▶**Conflict.** Whether personal or institutional, we all deal with conflicts in our daily lives, from minor fender-bender accidents to labor strikes to courtroom trials, and conflicts often are newsworthy. But journalists should always remember that conflicts involve more than two extreme positions. Many different views can be represented.

▶**Human interest.** Stories that touch readers' lives and may help them improve their lives are newsworthy.

Thus, the editing process begins before a story is ever written. Despite the idea of news teams discussed earlier, it is not usual that a copy editor is involved at this stage. Rather, it is an editor, sometimes called an ***assigning editor***, in charge of a newspaper section or category of news. Types of assigning editors vary with the organization and size of the paper, but typical examples are city, state, sports, lifestyle and entertainment editors. Whether the assigning editor conceives the idea for a story or accepts an idea generated by a reporter, he or she then helps direct the reporter's work by suggesting angles that the story might examine, sources to interview and questions to ask. The assigning editor, often in consultation with other editors or with the reporter, also determines whether the story should be accompanied by photographs or other artwork. If so, a photographer or graphic artist is assigned to begin working on the story. As in many business settings, more and more internal communication is occurring via computers, particularly through e-mail (see Figure 1-6).

Once the story is written, the assigning editor reads it, primarily for content rather than style or tone. If substantial content changes are needed—for example, if obvious questions remain unanswered—the editor generally sends the story back to the reporter for additional work. If the editor is satisfied with the overall content of the story, he or she decides where it will be placed in the newspaper, how long it will be, and what size and style of headline will accompany it. Sometimes a story is sent to the copy desk with an *HTK* ("headline to come") notation, meaning that the headline form has not yet been determined. Decisions about story placement and headline specifications are made by the person who lays out the page, which may be the assigning editor, the copy desk chief, a copy editor or perhaps a layout editor or graphics specialist.

Figure 1-6
To make it easier to express emotions while communicating over the Internet or through e-mail, a series of symbols known as emoticons has been created. To better understand these symbols, look at them sideways.

Emoticons

:-D	Big smile
:-c	Bummed out
:'-(	Crying
>:->	Devilish
:-e	Disappointed
<:-I	Dunce
:-(	Frowning
:'->	Happy and crying
:-S	Incoherent
:-I	Indifferent
>:<	Mad
:-*	Oops
:->	Sarcastic
:-@	Screaming
:-/	Skeptical
:-)	Smile
:-o	Surprised
:-&	Tongue-tied
:-0	Uh-oh
:-\	Undecided
;-)	Winking

The story is then sent to the copy desk chief, who may edit it loosely before passing it along to one of the copy editors sitting on the rim. In assigning copy, the copy desk chief often considers the special knowledge or ability of each rim editor. Like reporters, some copy editors are experts in certain fields, and this expertise can be useful in editing particular stories. Others are especially talented at handling stories of a statistical nature, writing bright or clever headlines for feature stories, or editing stories of exceptional difficulty or length.

In modern newsrooms, all of this shuffling of stories is done electronically from computer terminal to computer terminal. But as recently as the mid-1970s, the staff at many newspapers still edited paper copy with pencils, used scissors and glue for reorganizing paragraphs, and physically moved copy from person to person.

A rim editor edits the story carefully, perhaps cutting it to fit a specified length for the page layout. Copy editors, even experienced ones, should read each story at least three times. During the first reading, the copy editor analyzes the thoroughness of the content and the appropriateness and effectiveness of the lead and organization of the story. The copy editor should make few, if any, changes during this first reading.

Next the copy editor rereads the story to make changes where needed. For example, a buried or uninteresting lead may be rewritten, the overall organization of the story may be rearranged, facts are verified, and style, grammar, punctuation and spelling errors are corrected. In addition, the copy editor addresses questions of ethics, taste and sensitivity, as well as legal problems with the story.

Finally, the copy editor reads the story a third time to be sure all errors have been corrected and everything possible has been done to produce a clear, concise, accurate and well-organized story. During the copy editing process, the editor may need to talk to the reporter about unclear passages or to ask for details. Often the copy editor uses standard reference books or makes telephone calls to verify information or fill in gaps in the story.

When the copy editor is satisfied with the story, he or she writes the headline according to the specifications assigned by the editor. Computer codes are inserted so the body and headline type will be set (or ***output***, as it is expressed in computer jargon) in the desired style, size, width and leading (space between the lines of body type). If an informational graphic or photograph is to accompany the story, the copy editor edits it and writes a caption for it (processes that are discussed in Chapter 10).

Then the copy editor sends the story back to the chief copy editor for approval. If the copy chief finds fault with the editing or the headline, the story may be bounced back to the copy editor to make still more changes. If the copy and the headline meet with the copy chief's approval, the computer command is given to send the story to the composing room.

Before the advent of pagination, the story was printed on a long strip of photosensitive paper that emerged from a mainframe computer in the composing room. Following a sample layout prepared by an editor, composing room personnel trimmed excess paper and pasted the type onto a page. Most newspapers today use offset printing. In this process, after all elements for the page are pasted into position, the entire page is photographed, and a printing plate, made of plastic or metal, is made from the resulting negative. This plate is then placed on the printing press.

Gene Foreman, former deputy editor and vice president of the Philadelphia Inquirer, is a strong supporter of copy editors in the newsroom. As part of an examination of the state of copy editing in U.S. newspapers a few years ago, he wrote that although the copy desk maintains a relatively low profile in most newsrooms, it is much more important today than it was earlier.

Today's copy editors still perform the traditional tasks of refining grammar, punctuation and spelling; tightening and straightening prose; and crafting headlines and captions with reader appeal. With their computers, they also have absorbed the functions of yesterday's legions of blue-collared compositors. If the technological revolution had not drastically reduced production labor costs, many newspapers would be unprofitable now.

The technological revolution included pagination, a computerized layout program that continues to have a major impact on a newsroom's copy editing staff. A joint project sponsored by the American Society of Newspaper Editors and the Poynter Institute found that pagination tops the list of concerns of the nation's copy editors. They argue that pagination requires editors to pay more attention to computer coding schemes and production processes, formerly performed by composing-room personnel, than they had previously. Many believe, as a result, they have less time to perform their primary job function, which is to edit copy.

Most metropolitan daily newspapers print several editions of each day's issue. A good newspaper, not satisfied with merely rearranging stories or rewriting headlines, continually updates its editions to reflect the latest developments in the news. New page layouts may require that stories be edited and headlines be written as many as three or four times.

As the editions are updated, copy editors assume responsibility for rechecking material from earlier editions. Although practices vary from paper to paper, the job of reading a story already in print differs markedly from the job of handling a story before it is set in type. Between editions, copy editors read to update old information and to correct errors of fact or omission rather than read for grammatical and stylistic errors. Updates are handled quickly by making the required changes on the computer screen and outputting the entire story again. In addition to saving time, this method reprocesses the new version of the story in one clean piece and reduces the chances of error.

The copy editor's work, day or night, is usually marked by roller-coaster fluctuations in activity. At newspapers, most of the action comes in the last few hours before press deadline, regardless of whether the newspaper is distributed to readers in the morning or in the afternoon. Editors often process breaking news on deadline or incorporate new developments into stories they have already worked. They weigh the news values of stories competing for space and make last-minute calls to verify facts. Editors also match stories with accompanying late-breaking photos or graphics and then pull together all the elements of the daily miracle that is a newspaper.

A modern editor looks to the future   **By Sharon Bibb**

THE newspaper industry is more a bottom-line business than the labor of love I believed it to be when I enlisted years ago. The newspaper today competes directly with television, radio and the Internet for attention within the constraints of our harried lives. And what the newspaper is about has as much to do with marketability as it does with what the public wants and needs to know.

However distasteful that may be, the reality is that people need news and information in a new way. Newspapers have adapted some to the new market—with online services that supplement the printed word and collaborative, promotional relationships with local TV and radio affiliates. But our *attitude* as newspeople has adapted too slowly, either unwittingly or unwillingly, to our own detriment. If people are finding radio, TV and online news more desirable, more accessible, more suitable to their lifestyles, we can't blame anyone but ourselves. And no matter how clever and enterprising we think we are, we cannot hope to serve and inform an absent public. Our challenge is to respond to the new age of accelerated, mobile lifestyles. We must somehow create a product consumers can't live without.

It is no longer enough to inform. We must enlighten and fascinate and even intrigue—and in ways not possible through any other medium. What USA Today set out to do in the 1980s wasn't visionary so much as it was the right thing at the very right time. It's still right today, more than 15 years later. And in that time, papers across the nation have tried to mimic what USA Today does so well, but we haven't grasped this modern philosophy of content and form. We have aped the "look" in high style, but we haven't grasped the philosophy. All the accolades bestowed within our industry for writing and design mean nothing if we don't serve the consumer, whose loyal patronage should be our highest honor.

Even as more newspapers fold, we can expect papers that truly respond to consumers to survive—indeed, thrive. It is the format that has lost readers; the mechanics, not the vehicle, that must be more convenient.

That's where editors, particularly copy editors, enter the picture. No paper that intends to survive will be content to invest in copy editors who are simply the best professional proofreaders money can buy. The editor of the next century will have a vision—not of the future, but rooted in the here and now, with a clear and precise view of what's important to everyday people in everyday affairs.

Today's editor is one who can be what I call an "antijournalist." In our complicated world, when events are sometimes too ominous to ponder, readers are becoming more average, more ordinary in the sense that what's most important to them is how to survive. We editors must identify with that need and relate to everyday survival as they do. Remember that readers out there are just like you, with one key exception: They don't have at their disposal all the information and resources that you do. So, first and foremost, your job is to think as they do. Your job is to absorb information not as a journalist, but as another citizen in the world community; think about how you'd share that information with your best friend, your neighbor, your relatives; *then* apply your training as a professional journalist to conceptualize how to turn that information into pro-active/interactive news.

It sounds simplistic, but too frequently we edit labored stories that serve only to showcase how much we know—how talented we are as journalists—rather than what readers want and need to know. Too often you'll hear reporters and editors talking about their working stories, sharing interesting anecdotes and little-known facts, yet little of what was so interesting winds up in the story. It's as if they are prisoners of some archaic newswriting regimen learned in school—as if journalists aren't allowed to communicate with people normally, neighbor to neighbor.

Editors who crusade for readers—the "antijournalists," if you will—will be indispensable in the newsroom. They will ask the same questions readers ask: Why should I care? What can I do about it? What should I do about it? How can I help? How can I get help?

The indispensable editor will suggest answers to those questions, in ways that perhaps TV and radio can't. With sidebars or "breakouts," with charts and maps, with "FYI" boxes of names and numbers.

It all comes back to what USA Today started, but it is a true belief in the philosophy that will deliver meaningful results. It's turning long, complicated stories into digestible, understandable parts—what have been called "points of entry." If readers don't have the time or inclination for 50 inches of text, maybe they'll read a shorter mainbar with a sidebar pulled out on a more interesting aspect of the story. Maybe they'll read a "how to" portion broken out as a box. Maybe the copy editor's cutline will be as intriguing—and differently focused—as the headline. And maybe the alert editor will flag a story that cries out for a particular kind of photo, graphic, list or map.

The responsible editor will exhaust every option to break down stories into usable forms, not to diminish them but to enhance them—to give people every possible invitation to read. The points of entry should be seen as interdependent elements, not repetitious highlights of the main story.

And like USA Today, the progressive editor will remember that our society is more mobile than ever; that in every major city and even small towns, there are newcomers

Sharon Bibb

Editor Sharon Bibb received her bachelor's degree in 1975 and her master's degree in 1977, both in communications from the University of Washington in Seattle. She interned as a reporter and as a copy editor at the Tacoma (Wash.) News Tribune, where she discovered she preferred copy editing. She enjoyed the challenge of polishing stories and writing the kind of headlines that would sell those stories. She was hired as a full-time staff member by the News Tribune and performed such copy-desk duties as slotting, layout and makeup.

Three years later, Bibb was hired by the Oakland (Calif.) Tribune, where she served as the night Lifestyle section editor, Sunday Lifestyle section editor and Travel section editor. She saw a need for more newsroom efficiency and sold her editors on a job description that allowed her to write the newspaper's stylebook, redesign the Sunday TV magazine, and improve systems formats and guides.

Her increasing interest in new technology took her to the Philadelphia Inquirer, where she served as an assistant news editor and where she became involved in paginating the News, Style and Sunday sections of the newspaper.

Later, Bibb was hired by USA Today as a Life section layout editor. Her interest in new technology continued, and she eventually moved into the systems editor role at USA Today, developing pagination and training layout editors on the system.

She later returned to the Bay Area, where she served as the night news editor for the San Francisco Examiner, then moved to the Miami Herald, where she now works on the news desk. She has also served as a co-coordinator and lecturer at the Howard University High School Urban Journalism Workshop and as a faculty member for the Institute for Journalism Education's copy editing program at the University of Arizona.

unaware of very basic information—local history, tradition, laws and common practices. A good rule of thumb: If there's something you don't know or understand, chances are there will be readers out there who won't either.

All this requires a copy editor to see the big picture, to see all the possibilities within one story, and to see all the stories within one edition as they connect to others. The copy editor with the big picture will be reporter, photographer, graphic artist and layout editor all at once, seeing news as packages tied together for convenience, meaning and perspective. That editor will take an ordinary story and find ways to make it extraordinary, without changing words or tone, but perhaps simply suggesting a different presentation. The successful copy editor will be the instigator of information rather than a passive conduit through which seemingly unconnected text is proofread.

It is as much the reporters' as the assignment editors' responsibility to conceive how stories can be presented and packaged with various elements. It is no less the copy editor's job to do the same. In the current atmosphere of newsroom downsizing, the copy editor with a broader view of the finished product may well have an edge over one who would be content to edit a story and top it with a crisp headline, however meticulously.

New technology has helped elevate the goal of creatively packaging news, and editors have been required to learn new methods and new machines. It hasn't been without resistance, as various tasks have merged and shifted between editorial and production departments. Many editors working with area composition (elements typeset and aligned as they will appear in the paper) and pagination believe their jobs indeed have been reduced in some way to those of compositors who paste up type or engravers who process photos. On top of editing, they now must know elaborate coding for stories and be user-friendly with PCs and other systems that produce text, graphics and art.

Pagination is a fact of newsroom life now for papers that can afford the technology (some can't afford not to have it). There is an overwhelming benefit: The new technology rewards us with more control over the final product. Editors should welcome any new methods that allow them to see stories and pages exactly as they were planned. Any editor who becomes an expert in emerging technological systems has a more secure future in the newsroom, as even today they would be regarded as among the pioneers.

In many ways, neither the technology nor the challenge of our new times has changed the copy editor's role. In profound ways, though, it has changed. Copy editors remain the "last line of defense." But a new line has been drawn, in a battle for immediate relevance. The new battle demands we make what we publish required reading—news that captures and captivates readers, connects with them and connects them to the larger world.

Suggestions for additional reading

American Journalism Review Web site, http://ajr.org.

American Society of Newspaper Editors Web site, http://asne.org.

Borden, Diane L. and Kerric Harvey. *The Electronic Grapevine: Rumor, Reputation, and Reporting in the New On-line Environment.* Mahwah, N.J.: Lawrence Erlbaum Associates, 1998.

Columbia Journalism Review Web site, http://cjr.org.

Editor & Publisher Interactive Web site, http://mediainfo.com.

Jones, Stephen G. *Cybersociety: Computer-Mediated Communication and Community.* Thousand Oaks, Calif.: Sage Publications, 1995.

Newspaper Association of America Web site, http://naa.org.

Poynter Institute for Media Studies Web site, http://poynter.org.

Society of Professional Journalists Web site, http://spj.org.

Newman, Edwin. *Strictly Speaking: Will America Be the Death of English?* New York: Warner Books, 1975.

Newspaper Design: 2000 and Beyond. Reston, Va.: American Press Institute, J. Montgomery Curtis Memorial Seminar, 1988.

Weaver, David H., and G. Cleveland Wilhoit. *The American Journalist in the 1990s: U.S. News People at the End of an Era.* Mahwah, N.J.: Lawrence Erlbaum Associates, 1996.

Exercises

1. Observe the copy editors at your campus newspaper. How does their work compare with the work of professional copy editors, as described in this chapter? Make notes on the differences so you can discuss them in class.

2. Draw a chart to explain the copy desk arrangement at your school or local newspaper.

3. Discuss the relationships of, and explain the differences in job duties performed by, assigning editors, slot editors and copy editors.

4. Try to get an interview with a copy editor at your local newspaper and ask about his or her role and responsibilities in the newsroom. From your discussion, develop your own list of the virtues of a good copy editor.

5. On weekends, large metropolitan dailies contain inserts that are not produced locally but are transported in and inserted in the mailrooms as newspapers come off the presses. Find a Sunday edition of the largest daily in your region and identify inserts that were not produced by the newspaper's regular staff. What characteristics suggest these are out-of-town products? Does this Sunday edition also contain inserts that were produced by the newspaper's regular staff? How can you tell?

6. Review the news values listed in this chapter. Applying those news values, plus others that your instructor may add to the list, consider whether each of the following items is suitable for publication in the news section of your hometown newspaper. Tell which news values apply for each item.
   a. After a successful run on Broadway, the cast of an award-winning musical is beginning a tour of the United States. The nearest performance to your hometown will be in a city 200 miles away. (wire story)
   b. Scientists working in Washington, D.C., think they may have made a breakthrough in cancer research. The National Science Foundation awarded them a $2.5 million grant this week. (National Science Foundation press release)
   c. This is the right time for gardeners in your area to get their tulips and other bulbs into the ground. (material from local agricultural agent)
   d. Business analysts expect a bullish market for mining stocks in the next few months. (business wire story)
   e. "Tiger," a German shepherd owned by a local woman, won "best in show" yesterday at the annual dog show in Madison Square Garden. (wire story)
   f. A student from the local junior high school placed second in the national spelling bee, conducted yesterday in Washington, D.C. (story from education beat)

g. A train derailed 30 miles away. Emergency rooms at local hospitals were crowded with injured passengers. (story from police beat)

h. Fashion designers say that unisex clothes will be in vogue next year. (wire story)

i. The local school board decided last night to build a new high school in town. (story from education beat)

j. A city official says that property taxes will increase dramatically to pay for the costs of building a new high school in town. (story from city government beat)

k. A 75-year-old man was the first customer at a new bungee jumping attraction that opened yesterday on the outskirts of town. (story from business beat)

l. To mark its 100th anniversary, the Metropolitan Opera in New York City performed the classic "Madama Butterfly," and thousands of opera fans attended.

m. The local museum announced it would receive a traveling exhibit of ancient Chinese stone warriors from the Denver Museum of Natural History next month.

n. Environmentalists warned owners of new beach homes along the North Carolina coast that the structures were built too close to the sea and would not withstand another hurricane season.

o. The local chapter of the League of Women Voters announced yesterday that it would sponsor the first presidential debate between Republican candidate Elizabeth Dole and her Democratic challenger.

7. Conduct an online search for World Wide Web sites created by different news media. Locate a newspaper Web site, a magazine Web site and a broadcast network Web site. Compare the news selections, the layout and design, the amount of advertising and the way headlines are written.

> [Writing] should be treated like a precision instrument:
> It should be sharpened and it should not be used carelessly.
>
> —*Theodore M. Bernstein*

Using Correct Grammar and Punctuation

LANGUAGE is the copy editor's fundamental tool. Knowledge of correct grammar, spelling and punctuation rates as the most important skill for copy editors, according to a random sample of newspaper editors in a 1994 national survey. The same editors, representing a cross-section of large, medium-sized and small dailies, as well as weekly newspapers, ranked accuracy and fact-checking a close second in importance. Editing stories for wordiness, clarity and sentence structure was next on the editors' list of important expectations for copy desk personnel. A survey of corporate communicators and magazine editors likely would reveal similar expectations for copy editors. Figure 2-1 presents the ranking of 26 expected knowledge areas and skills for copy editors.

Students often enter beginning newswriting courses with the mistaken idea that they are embarking on a kind of writing that bears little resemblance to what

Common pitfalls in grammar and usage

Punctuation

Editing with computers

Traditional copy editing symbols

Editors' ranking of expected knowledge and skills areas

Rank	Knowledge or Skill
1	Grammar, spelling and punctuation
2	Accuracy and fact checking
3	Editing wordiness, clarity and sentence structure
4	General knowledge
5	Story structure, organization and content
6	Ethical concerns
7	Headline writing
8	Analytical/critical thinking
9	Associated Press style and usage
10	Cutline writing
11	News judgment and story selection
12	Legal concerns
13	Understanding numbers
14	Mechanics of computer editing
15	Layout and page design
16	Photo and art editing and sizing
17	Newsroom procedure and organization
18	Working with wire copy
19	Specific section editing (e.g., Sports)
20	Coaching/working with reporters
21	Software for layout/pagination
22	Typography
23	Information graphics/visual editing
24	Use of color
25	Software for graphics/Computer photo editing

Figure 2-1
This ranking of skills that copy editors are expected to have comes from a 1994 nationwide survey of newspaper editors. The research was conducted by Assistant Professors Ann E. Auman of the University of Hawaii and Betsy Cook Alderman of the University of Tennessee at Chattanooga and was presented at a national convention of journalism and mass communication educators in Washington, D.C., in 1995.

they have been taught in English courses. This is a false notion. Proper word usage and correct grammar and punctuation are important for all forms of communication. The inverted pyramid organization of news stories differs from the traditional narrative pattern, and paragraphs are kept artificially short in news stories, but most other conventions of good writing are unchanged.

Some claim that the constant stress on proper English usage is merely a form of snobbery and has no place in the fast-paced, widely circulated daily press. But a newspaper, magazine, public relations agency or online news source cannot be casual about language usage, for precision of language sharpens the meaning of fact. In addition, improper usage damages credibility. Readers question the accuracy of information in a publication containing frequent errors in spelling or use of the language.

News stories, in general, are directed to all readers, whatever their level of education. Because of the extremely diverse audience, simplicity and clarity are important. Newspaper writing must convey its message to a wide range of readers, from the fringes of illiteracy to maximum literary competence. English used in newsrooms, therefore, should be the language familiar to all educated persons. Of the four basic types of language—literary, common, colloquial and slang—common is preferred.

In recent years, the idea of "math phobia" has received much attention. Quite a few people have said they don't understand math, have never understood it and don't really think an understanding of math is essential to their lives. "Grammar phobia" hasn't been discussed as much, but it does exist. Some students attribute their grammar phobia to inadequate or unskillful instruction in grammar during grade school or high school.

Some native English speakers say they never understood English grammar until they studied the grammar of a different language. Perhaps that is because little can be accomplished in learning a foreign language without careful attention to its grammar rules and conventions. Some people who grow up in an English-speaking home or country can write and speak the language with some skill without giving careful attention to its grammar. Their understanding of grammar just seems to come naturally, although it is accompanied, in many cases, by incorrect usage, colloquialisms and slang. Most people can get by with this casual knowledge of English grammar, relying to a great extent on "what sounds right," but one who aspires to become a professional writer or editor needs more specific knowledge.

A professional writer or editor uses language to enhance communication. Journalists aren't particularly interested in being able to label the parts of speech or to diagram sentences. But to use grammar, punctuation and words correctly, they need to understand the parts of speech and how sentences are constructed. Trying to get by on what sounds right is insufficient in the world of professional journalism. So put aside your grammar phobia or, at the other extreme, the notion that you already know everything you need to know about English grammar.

Common pitfalls in grammar and usage

English is not a simple language, and unfortunately, many professional communicators have never mastered it. Mistakes common to all copy—from a beginning reporter's weather report to a nationally syndicated column—are those of grammar, punctuation, spelling, word usage and style.

Some of these common pitfalls are listed and explained in the following pages. The items are numbered so you and your instructor can refer to each item as you work on the exercises at the end of this chapter.

Subject and verb agreement

The basic rule is that the subject and predicate (or main verb) must agree in number. To apply this rule, first determine the subject of the clause, then determine whether the subject has a singular or plural meaning. Here are some rules concerning subject-verb agreement:

▶**1.** When two or more subjects are connected by the conjunction *and*, use a plural verb:

> An introvert and an extrovert rarely **make** good partners.

Use a singular verb, however, when two parts of a compound subject refer to a single person or thing:

> His friend and partner **is** very patient.

▶**2.** A noun or pronoun joined to the subject by phrases that act as prepositions rather than conjunctions is not part of a compound subject. Examples of such phrases are *along with, together with, accompanied by, as well as, including, in addition to* and *no less than.* Identify the subject and then apply the basic rule that the subject and predicate must agree in number:

> John, as well as Jim, **is** going to play on the team.
> The order form, in addition to a money order, **is** required.
> Mary, as well as her mother, **is** on the guest list.

▶**3.** When two or more subjects are joined by *or* or *nor,* the verb should agree with the nearest subject:

> Mary or her sisters **are** going to keep the appointment.
> Mary or her sister **is** going to keep the appointment.
> Neither John nor his children **are** required to attend.
> Neither John nor his son **is** going fishing today.

If both subjects are singular, the verb is singular:

> Either Jim or Jack **is** to be at the stadium by 1 p.m.

If both subjects are plural, the verb is plural:

> Neither the boys nor the girls **are** doing well on the
> agility test.

▶**4.** Don't let words before or between the subject and the verb mislead you. First find the subject of the sentence, then make its predicate agree:

> The last two innings of the game **were** dull.

In this sentence, the prepositional phrase *of the game* comes between the plural subject *innings* and the predicate *were.*

▶**5.** The prepositional phrase between fractions and percentages used as subjects influences the verb:

> Three-fourths of the students **are** prepared for college.
> Three-fourths of a cup of water **is** needed in the recipe.

▶**6.** These pronouns, when used as a subject, always take singular verbs: *it, each, either, anyone, everyone, much, no one, nothing, someone, such.* For example:

```
Each student has lunch money.

Everyone has lunch money.

No one has money for lunch.

Much has been written about grammar.

Someone is going to meet us at the airport.

It seems like years since we last met.
```

Pay special attention to the placement of *each* in a sentence. As a subject it takes a singular verb. But as an adjective in apposition with a plural subject, it needs a plural verb:

```
John and Mary each are scheduled to meet with
the president of the company.
```

▶**7.** Collective nouns take a singular verb when used in the sense of a single unit operating in agreement but take a plural verb when the collective operates as individual units or in disagreement. These are some collective nouns: *jury, team, army, audience, family, faculty, couple, group, staff, club, class, committee, crowd.* Treat the names of organizations as collective nouns as well: *National Association for the Advancement of Colored People, National Council of Churches, National Organization for Women.* For example:

```
The team is going to compete for the championship.
```

The individuals are working together as a single unit operating in agreement, so you would use a singular verb.

The combination of a plural verb with a singular-sounding noun sounds unnatural, although it is technically correct:

```
The team were arguing about their individual playing assignments
and the selection of a captain.
```

The plural verb is used because the team is in disagreement; the individuals are not working as a unit. To avoid the strange sound, most people would probably write or say "The team members were arguing ..." or "Members of the team were arguing ..." Another example:

```
The couple were married yesterday and left on their honeymoon.
They will return home next week.
```

Couple takes a plural verb in this example because the word refers to two people. But:

```
Each couple is going to buy a ticket.
```

In this example the word *couple* refers to a single unit. Some authorities say to use the singular form if the meaning is "the couple" and the plural form when the meaning is "a couple."

```
The couple is planning to attend the banquet.
A couple are planning to attend.
```

▶ **8.** *Number, majority* and *total* are singular if preceded by *the* but plural if preceded by *a:*

```
The number of convictions is increasing.
A number of people were convicted on those charges.
The majority has voted for Jones.
A majority of citizens agree that the laws should be enforced.
```

▶ **9.** Deciding whether a collective noun is singular or plural is relatively easy, but no similar rule consistently applies for "non-countable" nouns. Most of the non-countable nouns end in *s*, which makes them appear to be plural, but they are not all plural.

These non-countable nouns ending in *s* always take singular verbs: *apparatus, aesthetics, athletics, civics, economics, linguistics, mathematics, measles, mumps, news, shambles, summons, whereabouts.* Some other non-countable nouns that take singular verbs are *advice, courage, fun, health, information, jazz* and *remainder.*

These non-countable nouns need a plural verb: *assets, earnings, goods, kudos, manners, odds, pants, proceeds, scissors, shears, tactics, thanks, wages.*

These non-countables are either singular or plural, depending on context: *politics, series, gross, headquarters, statistics, ethics, species.* As a study or a science, *politics, statistics* and *ethics* take singular verbs:

```
Statistics is a required course for business majors.
Politics is not an exact science.
```

When in doubt, consult a dictionary to see which words ending in *s* need a singular verb or can be either singular or plural.

Exercise 4 at the end of this chapter tests your understanding of subject and verb agreement.

Noun and pronoun agreement

The basic rule concerning noun and pronoun agreement is that pronouns agree with their antecedents in person (first, second, third), number (singular, plural) and gender (masculine, feminine, neuter). Let's consider each idea separately.

▶ **10.** Pronouns are substitutes for nouns or other pronouns—their antecedents. Be sure that every pronoun has an antecedent and that, if other nouns or pronouns come between the pronoun and its antecedent, readers are not confused: "John introduced Mary to his mother, whom he planned to marry." In this example, the clause beginning with *whom* is misplaced, because John planned to marry Mary, not his mother. The sentence should be written this way:

```
John introduced Mary, whom he planned to marry, to his mother.
```

▶ **11.** Pronouns should agree with their antecedents in person:

```
I asked for my money.
He asked for his money.
```

▶**12.** Pronouns should agree with their antecedents in number. Singular nouns take singular pronouns (*he, she, it, him, her, his, hers, its*):

> **John** lost **his** books.
>
> The **woman** said **she** would compete in the race.

Plural nouns take plural pronouns (*they, them, their, we, us, our*):

> The **men** said **they** would go on strike.
>
> **John and Mary** received **their** new bicycles today.
>
> The **women** asked that **they** be given equal pay for equal work.

Pronouns and collective nouns that take singular verbs (see Rules 6, 7 and 8) also take singular pronouns:

> The **team** defended **its** championship.
>
> The **National Organization for Women** announced **its** position on the proposed legislation.
>
> **Either** of the boys should receive **his** prize.
>
> The **faculty** expressed **its** displeasure with the salary proposal.
>
> **Each** of the girls received **her** invitation in the mail.

The position of *each* in a sentence determines whether a later noun is singular or plural (see the comment about *each* in Rule 6). If *each* is in apposition with a plural subject, the later noun is plural. But if *each* is the subject, the noun should be singular. For example:

> The girls **each** receive **invitations**.
>
> **Each** of the girls receives an **invitation**.

Pronouns and collective nouns that take plural verbs (see Rules 7 and 8) also take plural pronouns:

> **All** of the students have **their** pencils.
>
> A **majority** of voters cast **their** votes for Jones.

▶**13.** Pronouns should agree with their antecedents in gender. If the antecedent is male, the pronoun should be masculine (*he, him, his*); a feminine pronoun (*she, her, hers*) is used for female antecedents; a neuter pronoun (*it, its*) is used for neuter antecedents.

This rule is straightforward, but problems arise with *either ... or* and *neither ... nor* constructions where one subject is masculine and one is feminine. In that situation, the pronoun should agree with the antecedent that follows *or* or *nor:*

> Neither Mary nor **John** has applied for **his** visa.
>
> Neither John nor **Mary** has applied for **her** visa.

In this example, the plural pronoun *their* would be incorrect, because *neither* is singular. However, the phrase *for a visa* would be better in both cases.

Another consideration in choosing pronoun gender is to attempt to avoid sexism in journalistic writing. Traditionally, masculine pronouns have been used to refer to a singular antecedent that included both males and females, but most newspapers now try to avoid sexist terms (as well as racist and ageist terms). One way to avoid excluding women is to use the expressions *he or she* and *his or her*. A better way is to use plural forms and plural pronouns. Compare the following:

> A **journalist** should edit **his or her** copy carefully.
>
> **Journalists** should edit **their** copy carefully.

Reflexive and intensive pronouns

Reflexive and intensive pronouns, the *self* pronouns, are used when a noun acts on itself or when a noun must be emphasized.

▶ **14.** Reflexive pronouns should not be used alone without referring to a noun or pronoun earlier in the sentence:

```
The store manager himself waited on customers.

I myself don't mind working hard.

John injured himself.
```

The following usage is incorrect: "Sarah and myself will work hard"; "He divided the work between John and myself."

Pronoun case

Case refers to the use of a pronoun in a sentence. Nominative case is used for subjects of sentences and as predicate nominatives. Objective case is used for objects, such as direct objects, indirect objects, objects of prepositions, participles, gerunds and infinitives. The objective case is also used as the subject of an infinitive. Possessive case shows ownership.

▶ **15.** Pronouns agree with their antecedents in person (first, second, third), number (singular, plural) and gender (masculine, feminine, neuter), but they take their case from the clause in which they stand.

Figure 2-2 shows the person, number, case and gender of personal pronouns. The relative pronoun *who* also has a different form for each case: *who* is nominative case, *whom* is objective case, *whose* is possessive case.

People have little problem distinguishing the proper case in simple sentences. But as sentence structure becomes more intricate, more effort is required to determine the role of each pronoun in each clause. The relative pronouns *who*, *whom* and *whose* are generally the most troublesome. In the following example, the relative pronoun is used as the subject of the sentence and thus needs the nominative case:

```
Who is coming?
```

| Person | Case | | |
	Nominative	*Objective*	*Possessive*
Singular			
First	I	me	my, mine
Second	you	you	your, yours
Third			
Masculine	he	him	his
Feminine	she	her	her, hers
Neuter	it	it	its
Plural			
First	we	us	our, ours
Second	you	you	your, yours
Third	they	them	their, theirs

Figure 2-2
The choice of personal pronoun depends on the person, number and gender of the antecedent and on the case indicated by the pronoun's position in the clause.

In this example, the object of the preposition takes the objective case:

```
To whom should we address the letter?
```

The following example is more complicated:

```
He gave advice to whoever asked for it.
```

The subject of the dependent clause is *whoever,* although the entire dependent clause is used as the object of the preposition *to.* Here, again, the nominative case is correct:

```
Jones, who I always thought was unapproachable, gave me advice.
```

Who is the subject of the dependent clause *who was unapproachable.*

In this case, *whom* is the object of the preposition:

```
We tried to discover to whom the gun belonged.
```

The final example clearly calls for the possessive case:

```
Whose gun is this?
```

Exercise 5 at the end of this chapter tests your understanding of the pronoun cases.

▶**16.** Unlike all other subjects, which are in the nominative case, the subject of an infinitive is in the objective case. Doubt about the correct form usually can be erased by transposing the sentence. In the first example, the pronoun *him* is the subject of the infinitive *to be:*

```
They declared the culprit to be him.
```

If you transpose the sentence, you can clearly see that *him* is the direct object:

```
They declared him to be the culprit.
```

▶**17.** Do not confuse *who's,* the contraction for *who is,* with the possessive form *whose.* The contraction for *it is* is *it's;* the possessive form is *its.* For example:

```
Who's going to ride in our car?
It's unusually warm today.
```

An analysis of how the relative pronoun is used is the best way to determine the correct case. However, you can also try substituting *he* for *who* and *him* for *whom* to see whether the substitute sounds right. With intricate sentences, this system is not foolproof.

Exercise 6 at the end of this chapter tests your understanding of noun-pronoun agreement and pronoun case.

Essential and nonessential clauses

Both *that* and *which* are relative pronouns used to introduce clauses that refer to an inanimate object or an animal without a name. The use of *that* or *which* depends on whether an essential or a nonessential clause is being introduced. A nonessential clause gives additional information about the noun or pronoun it modifies. Because a nonessential clause could be eliminated from the sentence without altering its meaning, the clause is set off with commas. An essential clause, on the other hand, is necessary because it gives the sentence the intended meaning; thus, it is not set off from the rest of the sentence.

▶**18.** *That* should be used to introduce an essential clause; *which* is correct for nonessential clauses. In the following example, the clause is essential because it restricts or identifies the car:

```
This is the car that won the race.
```

In the next example, the clause adds nonessential information:

```
John Smith's 1991 Ford, which won the race last weekend,
is for sale.
```

The car that is for sale is sufficiently identified or restricted by the modifiers *John Smith's 1991 Ford*. Note that commas set off the nonessential clause.

Exercise 7 at the end of this chapter tests your understanding of essential and nonessential clauses.

Possessive nouns

The possessive form of a noun is used to show ownership.

▶**19.** Most nouns form their possessive by adding an *'s* to the singular form:

```
girl's book     John's glove     horse's saddle
```

▶**20.** If a noun ends in an *s* sound and is followed by a word that begins with *s,* form the possessive by adding an apostrophe alone:

```
for appearance' sake     for conscience' sake
```

▶**21.** If the singular form ends in *s,* add *'s* unless the next word begins with *s,* in which case just add an apostrophe to the singular form:

```
the hostess's invitation    the hostess' standards
the witness's testimony     the witness' story
```

▶**22.** To form the plural possessive, first make the noun plural; then add an *'s* if the plural noun does not end in *s:*

```
woman (singular)   women (plural)   women's (plural possessive)
```

▶**23.** If the plural form ends in *s,* add only an apostrophe:

```
boy (singular)   boys (plural)   boys' (plural possessive)
```

▶**24.** For compound words, add an *'s* to the word closest to the object possessed:

```
the major general's decision (singular)
the major generals' decisions (plural)
```

▶**25.** To show that two people own something jointly, use a possessive form after only the last word. If the objects are individually owned, use a possessive form after both nouns:

```
John and Mary's home (joint ownership)
John's and Mary's projects (individual ownership)
```

▶**26.** For descriptive phrases, no apostrophe is needed for a word ending in *s.* To determine whether the word or phrase is used in a descriptive sense, try using *for* or *by* rather than *of.* The following is correct:

```
New York Yankees pitcher
```

In this case, the phrase *New York Yankees* is descriptive, meaning that the person is a pitcher for the New York Yankees.

▶ **27.** Use *'s* for a plural word that does not end in *s:*

> **women's** hospital, **men's** team

▶ **28.** For corporations or organizations with a descriptive word in their name, use the form that the group uses:

> **Writer's** Digest   the **Veterans** Administration   **Diners** Club

Journalistic style cautions against excessive personalization of inanimate objects. Often a phrase referring to an inanimate object is clearer if an *of* construction is used instead of a possessive form:

> mathematics' rules   the rules of mathematics

Personal pronouns and relative pronouns have separate forms for the possessive and do not need an apostrophe: *my, mine, our, ours, your, yours, his, her, hers, its, theirs, whose.* The exception is *one's,* the possessive form for *one.*

Exercise 8 at the end of this chapter tests your understanding of plurals and possessives.

Sequence of tenses

The tense of a verb describes the time of the action. Newswriting commonly uses past tense to report what has already happened. But confusion about the proper verb tense often arises when journalists paraphrase and attribute information.

▶ **29.** The basic rule is to select the verb tense that describes the time of the action and to stick with that tense unless a shift is needed to show a change in time. Do not shift tenses unnecessarily. In this example, all actions are in the past tense:

> The Senate **passed** the tax bill, **defeated** the food
> stamp proposal and **sent** the defense measure back to
> the appropriations committee.

Now let's shift the tense from past to past perfect to indicate that the House action took place before the Senate action:

> The Senate **defeated** the food stamp proposal,
> which **had been approved** by the House of Representatives.

A shift from past to future tense again indicates different timing of the action:

> The Senate **sent** the defense measure back to the committee,
> where it **will be amended.**

▶ **30.** Grammarians agree on the basic rules for consistency in verb tenses, but neither grammarians nor newspaper editors agree on the importance of a rule governing the sequence of tenses in reported speech. That rule states that when reported speech is used, the verb of attribution governs subsequent verbs in the sentence.

To a great extent, journalistic work involves reporting what has happened in the recent past and what sources have said, so journalists commonly use reported speech, which can be distinguished from direct speech and parenthetical speech:

> "I **disagree** with the mayor's policies, but I **don't confront** him
> about them," Jim said. (direct speech)

> Jim **disagrees** with the mayor's policies, he said, but he **doesn't confront** him. (parenthetical speech)

Note that, in parenthetical speech, the quote is paraphrased and the attribution is in the middle of the paraphrase. In reported speech, in contrast, attribution is at the beginning of the sentence:

> Jim **said** he **disagreed** with the mayor's policies, but he **didn't confront** the mayor about them. (reported speech)

In this example, the verb of attribution is in the past tense, so other verbs are in the past tense as well.

It can be argued convincingly that reported speech confuses readers. Does Jim still disagree with the mayor, or is the disagreement a thing of the past? Strict proponents of following the sequence of tenses in reported speech can argue that the job of the newspaper is to report what the source said at the time the reporter received the information ("Jim disagrees with the mayor") rather than being concerned about whether the source changed his mind between the time he said it and the time the article was published. Of course, one way to avoid the problem is to use a present-tense verb of attribution ("Jim *says* he disagrees"), but typical usage in news stories calls for past-tense attribution.

The rule for sequence of tenses in reported speech requires that the verb used in direct speech should be changed one degree: from present to past (*disagrees* to *disagreed*), from past to past perfect (*disagreed* to *had disagreed*), from future to future perfect (*will disagree* to *would disagree*).

Some grammar books omit entirely the sequence-of-tenses rule for reported speech, and many editors pay no attention to it. Other editors are rigid in their adherence to the rule. The late Theodore M. Bernstein, for many years a wordsmith at The New York Times, devoted six pages to an explanation of sequence of tenses in his book *Watch Your Language*. He ended his discussion with this suggestion: "Normal sequence of tenses is desirable except when it produces obscurity or ambiguity." So even Bernstein, who stood firmly by the rules of sequence of tenses for reported speech, would allow a variation for perpetual truths, referred to as "exceptional sequence." Thus, this sentence would be correct:

> She **said** that the earth **revolves** around the sun.

Irregular verb forms

Irregular verbs change the middle of the word to create the past tense instead of adding *ed*, *t* or *en* at the end, as is the pattern for regular verbs.

▶**31.** Check a dictionary when you are uncertain about forming the past and past participle forms of a verb. These are the principal parts (present, past, past participle) for some of the irregular verbs that are frequently misused:

> awake, awoke, awakened
> be (am, is, are), was (were), been
> bear, bore, born
> bite, bit, bitten
> broadcast, broadcast, broadcast
> burst, burst, burst
> catch, caught, caught
> cling, clung, clung
> do, did, done
> drink, drank, drunk
> drive, drove, driven
> drown, drowned, drowned

eat, ate, eaten
find, found, found
fly, flew, flown
fly, flied, flied *(for a baseball)*
forsake, forsook, forsaken
get, got, got (gotten)
go, went, gone
hang, hanged, hanged *(as in "execute someone")*
hang, hung, hung *(as in "hang a picture")*
hide, hid, hidden
hit, hit, hit
know, knew, known
lay, laid, laid *(transitive verb meaning "to place")*
lead, led, led
leave, left, left
lie, lay, lain *(intransitive verb meaning "to recline")*
mean, meant, meant
pay, paid, paid
ring, rang, rung
rise, rose, risen *(not to be confused with transitive verb raise)*
say, said, said
set, set, set *(transitive verb meaning "to place")*
shake, shook, shaken
shine, shone, shone
show, showed, showed (shown)
shrink, shrank, shrunk
sit, sat, sat *(intransitive verb)*
spring, sprang, sprung
steal, stole, stolen
strive, strove, striven
swear, swore, sworn
swim, swam, swum
swing, swung, swung
tear, tore, torn
weave, wove, woven
wring, wrung, wrung
write, wrote, written

Pay particular attention to the correct meanings and principal parts of *lie/ lay, sit/set* and *rise/raise. Lie* and *lay* are particularly troublesome because the past tense of *lie* is the same as the present tense of *lay. Set, lay* and *raise* are transitive verbs and need direct objects.

Exercise 9 at the end of this chapter tests your understanding of troublesome verb tenses.

Subjunctive mood

Some usage experts (Rudolf Flesch, for one) argue that the subjunctive mood is dead or is dying and has little practical use. Other grammarians (Theodore M. Bernstein, for example) say that the subjunctive mood is alive and necessary.

▶**32.** Use the subjunctive mood to express a condition that is either contrary to fact or is purely hypothetical:

```
If I were president of the company, I would give
workers a salary increase.
```

Were is used instead of *was* because the condition is contrary to fact; I am not president of the company.

Except for forms of *to be*, the present tense of the subjunctive mood is the infinitive without the *to*. That verb form is the same as the indicative mood for the first and second persons but not for the third-person singular:

Indicative	Subjunctive
I run	*I run*
you run	*you run*
she runs	*she run*

```
If Jennifer were in shape to run faster, the coach would
not have asked that I run the final leg of the relay.
```

Misplaced and dangling modifiers

Modifiers are used to make writing more descriptive and interesting. To avoid confusion, modifiers should refer clearly and logically to some specific word in the sentence. Modifiers that aren't attached grammatically are called "misplaced" or "dangling" modifiers. They can bring a humorous picture to mind, as in this example:

```
Running down the road, my nose got cold.
```

You have a couple of options for correcting this dangler:

```
Running down the road, I felt my nose getting cold.
As I ran down the road, my nose got cold.
```

▶ **33.** Modifiers must be attached grammatically to the word they modify to avoid reader confusion. Consider this sentence: "*To grow strong, good diet* is important." What is to grow strong? Not the diet. The infinitive phrase has no word to modify in this sentence. Give it a logical noun or pronoun to modify:

```
To grow strong, children need a good diet.
```

Prepositional phrases often cause problems when misplaced or left dangling. Here's an example of the problem: "*As a member of Congress,* I want to get your views on alleged ethics violations by some of your colleagues." The reporter is not a member of Congress. The sentence could be written correctly in several ways. Here are two:

```
Because you are a member of Congress, I want to get your views
on alleged ethics violations by some of your colleagues.

I want to ask you, a member of Congress, about your views on
alleged ethics violations by some of your colleagues.
```

The word *only* as a modifier is frequently misplaced in sentences, leading to ambiguity. An omitted article (*a/an* for indefinite reference, *the* for definite reference) often causes the confusion with *only*. In these examples, the placement of *only* has a considerable effect on the meaning:

```
She was only a lawyer.
She was the only lawyer.
He gave the hungry children only money.
He gave only the hungry children money.
He gave the hungry children the only money.
```

Double negatives

A negative word is one that expresses *no*. The rule prohibiting the use of double negatives—two negative words in a row—has been drilled into us since elementary school. It is so fundamental that the Associated Press Stylebook and Libel Manual does not even include it.

▶**34.** Avoid double negatives. "He *don't* know *nothing*" is a construction that no journalist would use. Still, a double negative sometimes slips past, particularly in long sentences and especially when the adverbs *hardly, rarely* and *scarcely* are used. Consider the following pairs of examples:

> She **never hardly** studies.
> She **hardly ever** studies.
> The store **doesn't** have **but** one brand.
> The store **has but** one brand.

But, when used as an adverb, is also a negative.

Negative adjectives (those with the prefixes *im, in, ir, non* and *un*) may be used with negative adverbs. Therefore, the following are correct:

> It is **not impermissible** to use negative adjectives with negative adverbs.
> It is **not incorrect** to say it this way.

Authorities have mixed opinions on usage of the phrase *cannot help but*, as in

> Workers **cannot help but feel** the effect of the wage freeze.

Bernstein, Flesch and the *American Heritage Dictionary* accept this usage; the *Random House Dictionary* says it is common usage but frowned on. To avoid the argument, omit *but* and use the present participle:

> Workers **cannot help feeling** the effect of the wage freeze.

Exercise 10 tests your understanding of misplaced modifiers and double negatives.

Parallel construction

Lack of parallel construction is another common pitfall in writing. Parallelism helps give a sentence balance, rhythm and symmetry.

▶**35.** Use the same grammatical patterns to express equal ideas in a sentence. Here, along with improved versions, are examples of sentences that hinder understanding because they lack parallel construction. The first set demonstrates that the objects of a preposition should both be either gerunds or nouns:

> Cardiovascular health is promoted by **exercising** frequently and a good **diet**. *(not parallel)*
> Cardiovascular health is promoted by frequent **exercise** and a good **diet**. *(parallel)*
> Cardiovascular health is promoted by **exercising** frequently and **eating** a good diet. *(parallel)*

Don't mix two kinds of verbals:

> Velcro is popular for **fastening** shoes and **to keep** compartments in handbags shut. *(not parallel)*

> Velcro is popular for **fastening** shoes and **keeping** compartments in handbags shut. *(parallel)*

Avoid shifting from active to passive voice; consistency in voice speeds reading and aids comprehension:

> Congress **passed** the tax-reform legislation, but the minimum-wage increase **was defeated**. *(not parallel)*

> Congress **passed** the tax-reform legislation but **defeated** the minimum-wage increase. *(parallel)*

In a series, don't mix verbals and nouns:

> He was charged with drunken **driving, carrying** a weapon, **resisting** arrest and **possession** of cocaine. *(not parallel)*

> He was charged with drunken **driving, carrying** a weapon, **resisting** arrest and **possessing** cocaine. *(parallel)*

Not only should be followed by *but also:*

> She **not only** sold some of her possessions, she took a second job to earn money to pay the hospital bills. *(not parallel)*

> She **not only** sold some of her possessions, **but** she **also** took a second job to earn money to pay the hospital bills. *(parallel)*

Don't mix nouns and a dependent clause in a series:

> They elected him because of his **knowledge, honesty** and **because** he was personally appealing. *(not parallel)*

> They elected him because of his **knowledge, honesty** and **personal appeal**. *(parallel)*

Exercises 4 through 10 at the end of this chapter will test your understanding of fundamental grammar principles. Unless your instructor directs you otherwise, use the copy editing symbols at the end of this chapter to complete the exercises.

Punctuation

A good copy editor, knowing the purpose for each punctuation mark, never relies simply on "what sounds right." Understanding the rules of punctuation requires a good knowledge of grammar and sentence structure. After studying the grammar section in this chapter and completing the related exercises at the end of the chapter, you should be ready to review the basic punctuation rules presented here. If you need a more thorough study of punctuation, consult a basic grammar and punctuation book or a reference guide such as the AP Stylebook.

Correct punctuation is essential for clarity. Consider the potential for confusion in this sentence:

> Go to the parking lot and get on the second bus that displays "stadium" as its destination.

Following those directions, one might walk past many buses before arriving at the second one with the "stadium" designation. Change the punctuation, and it becomes clear that the second bus in the parking lot is the one to board. The information after the comma is simply additional information.

```
Go to the parking lot and get on the second bus, which displays
"stadium" as its destination.
```

Punctuation in these sentences makes clear how many doctors are in the house:

```
The doctor, who is my sister, will see you now.
(only one doctor who happens to be my sister)
The doctor who is my sister will see you now.
(more than one doctor; one of them is my sister)
```

The most common punctuation marks are the ampersand, apostrophe, colon, comma, dash, exclamation point, hyphen, parentheses, period, question mark, quotation marks and semicolon.

▶**Ampersand.** Do not use the ampersand (&) in place of *and* in body copy or in headlines, except when it is part of a company's formal name.

▶**Apostrophe.** Use an apostrophe to form the possessive. Refer to Rules 19 through 28 in this chapter for information on using apostrophes to make nouns possessive.

Use an apostrophe to indicate omitted letters in contractions: *I'm, doesn't, rock 'n' roll, it's* (*it is,* not to be confused with the pronoun *its*). Contractions reflect informal speech and should be used only in that context in journalistic writing.

Use an apostrophe to indicate omitted figures: *the celebration of '90, the '20s* (no apostrophe needed before the *s*). Also use an apostrophe to make the plural of a single letter: "She made 3 *A's* and 2 *B's* on her report card," "The Oakland *A's* won the World Series."

Do not use an apostrophe with multi-letter plurals or with the plurals of numbers: "This is the section for *VIPs,*" "The company ordered new *747s.*"

▶**Colon.** Use a colon at the end of a sentence to introduce lists, tabulations or texts: "These bills passed during the legislative session:" (the list follows, often in separate paragraphs, each introduced with a dash, bullet or some other typographical device).

The part of the sentence before the colon should be an independent clause. It is incorrect to use a colon after a *to be* verb or words like *such as* or *including.* Avoid this use of the colon: "The items stolen were: a television set, ring and watch."

The word after a colon should *not* be capitalized unless it is a proper noun or the beginning of a complete sentence: "The police report listed these stolen items: a television set, ring and watch." But: "She told her students this: If you work hard, you will succeed in this class."

Use a colon to introduce a direct quotation of more than one sentence that remains in one paragraph:

```
The coach said in his resignation letter: "It is with
regret that I leave this university. We've had a long,
successful run, and I expect that my successor will
maintain the winning tradition of this great institution.
It's time for me to turn to other opportunities."
```

When used with quotation marks, a colon goes outside the quotation marks unless it is part of the quotation itself.

Use a colon to introduce a single item for emphasis: "His thoughts were concentrated on one thing: revenge."

Use a colon in time designations, except for the even hour: *1:30 a.m., 2:15 p.m.* (but *7 a.m.*).

Use a colon to separate the main title and subtitle of a book or an article, a chapter and verse in the Bible, and sections of statutes: *The Truth Hurts: A Critique of a Defense of Defamation; John 3:16; Tennessee Code 5:2.*

Use a colon in a headline to replace a verb of attribution if the speaker is at the beginning of the headline:

Jones: 'Taxes are too high'

▶ **Comma.** The comma is the most misused mark of punctuation, probably because of its frequency.

Use commas to separate the elements in a series. But note that news-service practice, observed on most U.S. newspapers, omits the comma before the conjunction in a simple series: "She ordered a hamburger, fries and orange juice." But use a comma before the conjunction in a series if an integral element of the series requires a conjunction: "She ordered orange juice, toast, and ham and eggs."

Use a comma to separate a series of equal adjectives. If the adjectives can be separated by *and* without changing the sense, they are equal: *an old, bent tree; a slow, deliberate manner.*

Use commas to set off nonessential phrases and clauses:

```
His mother, on the other hand,
lived in New York City. (nonessential phrase)
His mother, who is an artist,
lives in New York City. (nonessential clause)
```

Nonessential phrases include such items as hometowns, ages and political affiliation. All should be set off with commas.

Use a comma to set off a dependent clause that introduces a sentence:

```
Because of his appeal to elderly voters, he was
considered a sure bet to win re-election to the Senate.
```

Use a comma to set off a long introductory phrase. But no comma is needed after a short introductory phrase unless its omission would slow comprehension:

```
In the morning she will feed her cats.
Across the street, lives my sister. (comma helps comprehension)
```

Use a comma before the conjunction in a compound sentence: "The mayor unveiled her plan for redevelopment of a downtown park, but each member of the city council expressed concern about the estimated cost of the project."

Use a comma to set off a direct quotation from its attribution. For quotations that are more than one sentence long within a single paragraph, use a colon to set off the attribution:

```
He said, "Let's go now."
"Let's go now," he said.
He said: "Let's go now. It will be dark soon, and the headlights
on my car are not working properly."
```

A comma setting off attribution after a direct quotation always goes inside the quotation marks.

Commas are not used to set off attribution in paraphrased quotations or partial quotations:

```
He said he wanted to leave immediately.
He said that it was "of upmost importance" that they leave.
```

Use a comma to set off nouns of direct address and *yes* and *no* at the beginning of a sentence: "James, please pay attention"; "Yes, I will pay the bill."

Set off the name of a state if the state name follows a city; separate the names of the city and the state: "Nashville, Tenn., is a music publishing center." Note that newspaper style is to abbreviate state names when they are used with a specific city but not when they stand alone in a sentence: "Nashville, *Tenn.,* is a book and music publishing center"; "Tourism is a major source of state revenue in *Tennessee.*"

Use commas to set off conjunctive adverbs: "It is essential, *therefore,* that we pay the bill"; "*However,* we could ask the company to extend the time period."

News services and most newspapers use commas for figures of 1,000 or more because the comma speeds comprehension. This rule would not apply for figures of more than 1 million or those that are part of a street address, room number, serial number, telephone number or year.

▶ **Dash.** Most typewriters do not have a separate key for a dash. Instead, two hyphens are typed to represent a dash. Some computers do have a dash key, eliminating the need to strike the hyphen key twice.

Use dashes in a sentence to denote an abrupt change in thought or an emphatic pause: "His selection as chairman—*much to the surprise of the committee*—was based on political favors rather than merit." Also use dashes to set off a list or parenthetical material that contains commas: "The notice listed the qualifications—*80 wpm typing speed, knowledge of computers, good writing skills*—that the successful applicant must have."

Use a dash in a headline to replace a verb of attribution if the quotation comes before the name of the speaker:

'Taxes are too high'—Jones

Use a dash before an author's or composer's name at the end of a quotation:

```
"Despite its cost, the children need the
school lunch program."—Mayor Jane Doe
```

Use a dash after the dateline at the beginning of a story:

```
KNOXVILLE, Tenn. (AP)—A $75 million complex opened ...
```

▶ **Exclamation point.** Use an exclamation point after an expression of surprise, incredulity or other strong emotion, but avoid overuse. A comma rather than an exclamation point is used after mild interjections, and mildly exclamatory sentences should end with a period.

When used with quotations, the exclamation point goes inside the quotation marks when it is part of the quoted material:

```
"Stop!" he shouted.
```

The exclamation mark goes outside the quotation marks when it is not part of the quoted material:

```
We loved the movie "Batman"!
```

▶**Hyphen.** Hyphens are used to join words that form a single idea. Use a hyphen between two or more words that form a compound modifier placed before the word they modify:

> She took a photograph of the **moss-covered** tree.
> **Out-of-date** merchandise was on sale.
>
> He is a **part-time** teacher.
>
> He teaches part time. *(no hyphen; modifier comes after the word it modifies, **teaches**)*

As in the last example, combinations that are hyphenated before a noun are not hyphenated when they come after the noun. However, after a form of the verb *to be*, such combinations are generally hyphenated to avoid ambiguity: "His second novel was *second-rate*"; "They are *top-notch*." Do not use a hyphen after adverbs that end in *ly* or after the adverb *very*.

Some publications use a hyphen to designate dual heritage: *Japanese-American, Mexican-American*. Not all stylebooks agree on this point, however, so follow the style used at the publication where you work. These terms do not refer to dual heritage and are therefore not hyphenated: *Latin American, French Canadian*.

For the use of hyphens in prefixes, consult a dictionary. The general rule is that a hyphen is used if a prefix ends in a vowel and the word that follows begins with the same vowel: *re-elect, pre-election, anti-intellectual, pre-empt, pre-exist.* Use a hyphen to attach a prefix to a proper noun: *anti-American*.

Use a hyphen, not the word *to*, between numbers that express odds, ratios, scores, some fractions and some vote tabulations:

> The odds of her winning are **5-4.**
>
> The ratio of water to sugar is **2-1.**
>
> The Yankees beat Boston **3-2.**
>
> **Two-thirds** of the books were sold.

Use a hyphen to spell out two-word numbers when the first word ends in *y: forty-five, twenty-two, fifty-one*. The usual newspaper style is to use figures rather than spell out numbers greater than nine, but numbers that begin a sentence should be spelled out.

Two prefixes may be linked to one word by using suspensive hyphenation: "She accepted the deal on a *one- to three-month* trial basis"; "Those selected had a *50- to 90-vote* margin."

▶**Parentheses.** Parentheses are used to set off an aside, information that explains or qualifies but is not essential to the sentence. Journalists use parentheses sparingly. The AP stylebook indicates that the temptation to use parentheses is a clue that the sentence is becoming contorted; suggested solutions are to rewrite the sentence or, if the sentence must contain incidental material, to use commas or dashes.

If the material enclosed in parentheses comes at the end of a sentence but the enclosed material is not a complete sentence, put the period outside the closing parenthesis. If the enclosed material is a complete sentence, include the period at the end of the sentence within the closing parenthesis:

> She is an excellent reporter (and a fine writer).
>
> (If you don't know French, you might not like the movie.)

▶**Period.** Use a period at the end of a declarative sentence and at the end of a mildly imperative sentence:

> She is coming to the party. *(declarative)*

> Please come here. *(mildly imperative)*

Use a period in many abbreviations—B.A. degree; Baton Rouge, La.; U.N. headquarters; U.S. military—and as a decimal point in figures—$1.8 million, 4.6 miles, $3.25.

Periods, like commas, always go inside quotation marks:

> The speaker told the crowd, "Our government should help us."

Three spaced periods are used to form an ellipsis, which is used to indicate the deletion of one or more words in condensing quotations, texts and documents. If an ellipsis comes at the end of a sentence, put the required mark of punctuation—period, question mark or exclamation point—and then a space before typing the ellipsis: "My administration will uphold the law...."

▶**Question mark.** Use a question mark at the end of an interrogative: "Who is responsible for this mess?" Do not use a question mark to indicate the end of indirect questions: "He asked who was responsible for the mess."

Question marks go inside or outside quotation marks, depending on the meaning. If the quotation is a question, the question mark is included within the quotation marks. But if the quoted material is not a question, the question mark goes outside the quotation marks:

> She asked, "Are you ready to go?"
> Who wrote "War and Peace"?

Do not use a comma before the attribution in a direct quotation if a question mark is needed to end the quoted material:

> "Are you ready to go?" she asked.

▶**Quotation marks.** Surround the exact words of a speaker or writer when reporting them:

> "I think it is important to finish quickly," Jones said.

Running quotations—those that continue for more than one paragraph—should not have a close-quote mark at the end of the first paragraph if the quoted material is a complete sentence. However, open-quote marks are needed at the beginning of the second paragraph to indicate that the quotation is continuing:

> Jones said, "I think it is important to finish quickly
> to make up for unavoidable delays caused by bad weather.

> "Our credibility is at stake here because we promised
> to have the job finished before July 1."

If the first paragraph of a continuing quotation ends with a partial quotation, close-quote marks should be used at the end of the partial quotation and open-quote marks should be used at the beginning of the next paragraph:

> Jones attributed the delays to "bad weather."

> "Our credibility is at stake here because we
> promised to have the job finished before July 1."

Do not use quotation marks with a question-and-answer format. Each speaker's words should start a new paragraph:

Q: Who was responsible?
A: John Smith.

Use quotation marks around a word or phrase that is used in an ironic sense or that is unfamiliar on first reference:

The "doctor" treated people for two years
before being exposed as a fake.

To save space, single quotation marks are used for direct quotations in headlines:

**'I will campaign
for re-election,'
Rep. Jones says**

Use single quotation marks around a quotation within a quotation:

She testified, "John never told me
specifically, 'I plan to kill my boss.'"

Note that three quotation marks—a single quote and double-quote marks—are used when, as in the last example, two quoted elements end at the same time.

Follow the style used by your publication regarding the use of quotation marks with titles of books, plays, movies, television shows, poems, songs and works of art. Some publications have switched from quotation marks to italics for such titles. Electronic typesetting equipment allows newspapers and magazines to use italics with relative ease, whereas insertion of italics was time-consuming with previous typesetting technology.

News-service style is to put quotation marks around the titles of all books, movies, operas, plays, poems, songs, television programs, lectures, speeches and works of art—except for the Bible and books that are primarily catalogs of reference material, including almanacs, directories, dictionaries, encyclopedias, gazetteers, handbooks and similar publications.

The period and comma always go within the close-quote marks. Other punctuation marks go within the quotation marks when they apply to the quoted matter only. They go outside the quotation marks when they apply to the whole sentence.

▶ **Semicolon.** In general, use the semicolon to indicate a greater separation of thought and information than a comma can convey but less than the separation that a period implies. In a compound sentence, for example, a comma is insufficient separation between the two independent clauses. A comma and a coordinating conjunction can be used between the two clauses, or a semicolon alone can be used:

The city has committed $500,000 to the project,
and private developers will also put money into it.

The city has committed $500,000 to the project;
private developers will also put money into it.

The city has committed $500,000 to the project;
however, private developers will pay most of the cost.

Use semicolons to separate elements of a series when individual segments contain material that must also be set off by commas:

```
Club members elected Jane Smith, president; Robert Blake, vice
president; Sam Brown, secretary.
```

Be sparing with semicolons. To many readers, a semicolon signals a difficult passage and becomes a point at which to exit the story.

Exercises 11 through 14 at the end of this chapter will test your punctuation skills. Your instructor may want you to complete the end-of-the-chapter exercises by using either traditional copy editing symbols or by using a computer and word-processing software. These two topics—computers and copy editing symbols—are discussed in the following sections of this chapter.

Editing with computers

Reporters and editors at newspapers, magazines and online news sources, as well as corporate communicators, write and edit copy at video display terminals linked to a central computer or at personal computers that are part of a network. In this modern process, a writer enters a story into the computer system. Then editors retrieve the story from the computer files.

Once the story is on the screen at the copy editor's desk, changes are typed directly into the system (see Figure 2-3). The copy editor formats the copy by entering computer codes for the type style, size, leading (the amount of space between lines of type) and column width. The copy editor types the headline at the top of the story and codes it for type style and size.

Figure 2-3
An editor works at a video display terminal. When she finishes editing the story and writing a headline for it, she will insert computer codes that specify the desired type style, size, width and amount of leading. Production personnel will paste the computer-generated type into place, according to an editor's layout. (Photograph by Tom Farrington, San Diego State University/ courtesy of the San Diego Union-Tribune)

Finally, the copy is sent electronically to a phototypesetter, which produces a hard copy that can then be pasted onto a page. As an alternative to manual pasteup, many news organizations and public relations firms now use layout software to transfer computer files directly into page layouts. This paperless process, called pagination, is expected to become the print-media norm during the next decade.

Computerized typesetting eliminates the retyping of stories to set them in printer's type, a redundancy that allows new errors to be introduced. Because re-keyboarding is unnecessary, the proofreader's job no longer exists at most newspapers. Nor does electronic typesetting require some of the copy editor's old tools: reams of copy paper, soft-lead pencils, scissors and glue.

In addition to helping with typesetting, computers provide reporters and editors with almost instant access to information stored in databases. Without leaving their desks, reporters and editors can use personal computers to search the newspaper's or magazine's own morgue (files of previously published stories) or to get information from commercial or academic databases anywhere in the world. By the early 1990s, fax machines, personal computers for data gathering and analysis, electronic news libraries, database searching, and online access to public records were becoming routine at news organizations, opening the way for new career opportunities for journalists facile with the new technology.

Traditional copy editing symbols

Today's computerized world has little need for traditional copy editing symbols, but knowledge of the symbols continues to have some practical application because not all journalism schools, publications, public relations firms and advertising firms are fully computerized. Some editing jobs are still done the old-fashioned way with paper and pencil. In addition, occasions for using traditional proofreading symbols still arise.

When preparing copy that is to be re-keyboarded by a typist, writers should always double- or triple-space. Such wide spacing allows copy editors to write corrections between the lines of type.

Copy editors write parallel to the lines of type, instead of writing in the margins, to avoid causing confusion and difficulty for the typesetter. If there is insufficient room between lines of type to write a correction, copy editors use scissors and paste to insert clean paper on which corrections can be written. If the correction is long, copy editors type it and then paste the correction in its proper place.

All notations on the copy that are not to be set as part of the story—such as indications of column width, typeface, point size and other instructions to the typesetter—are circled. Copy editors avoid using lines and arrows to vertically transpose paragraphs or sentences within a story. Such markings are difficult to follow, so copy that needs rearranging is cut and pasted into the story at the proper place.

An experienced copy editor never blacks out, pastes over, or destroys a word, phrase or guideline. To delete the copy, the editor simply draws a line through it, in case the information is needed later for checking purposes or needs to be restored to the copy.

Figure 2-4
Copy editing symbols are written within or above a line of copy that has not yet been typeset.

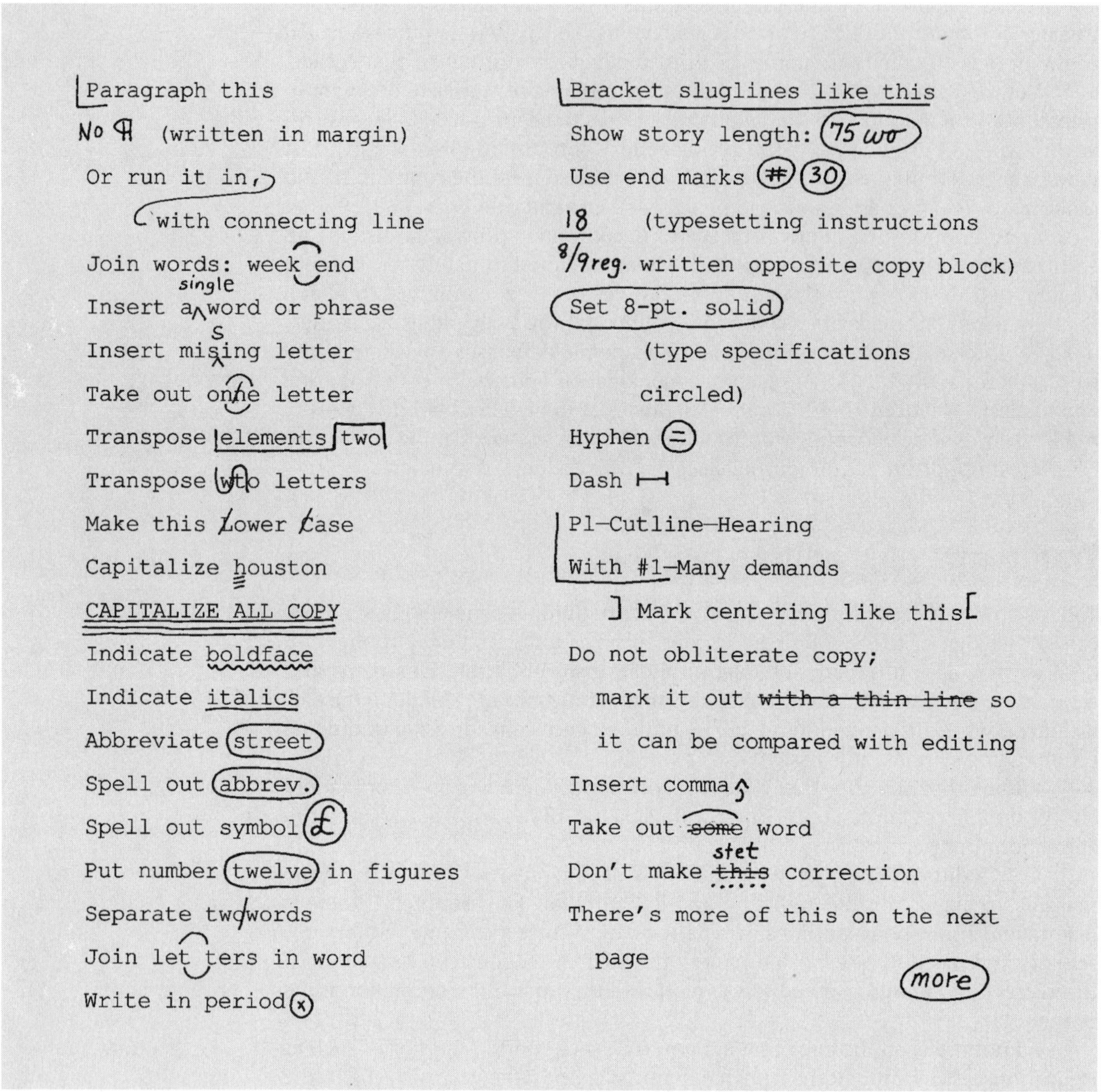

```
⌐Paragraph this                      ⌐Bracket sluglines like this
No ¶ (written in margin)              Show story length: (75 wo)
Or run it in,⌐                        Use end marks (#) (30)
    ⌐with connecting line             18      (typesetting instructions
                                      ⁸/9reg. written opposite copy block)
Join words: week⌣end
          single                      (Set 8-pt. solid)
Insert a∧word or phrase
              s                            (type specifications
Insert mis∧ing letter                      circled)
Take out on⌣e letter
                                      Hyphen (=)
Transpose ⌐elements⌐two⌐
                                      Dash ⊢⊣
Transpose ⌐tw⌐o letters
                                      ⌐Pl—Cutline—Hearing
Make this /Lower /Case
                                      ⌐With #1—Many demands
Capitalize houston
═════                                      ] Mark centering like this⌐
CAPITALIZE ALL COPY
════════════════════                  Do not obliterate copy;
Indicate boldface
         ∿∿∿∿∿∿∿∿                         mark it out with a thin line so
Indicate italics                                   ───────────────
         ───────                          it can be compared with editing
Abbreviate (street)
                                      Insert comma∧
Spell out (abbrev.)
                                      Take out ⌣some⌣ word
Spell out symbol (£)
                                                  stet
Put number (twelve) in figures        Don't make this correction
                                                 ∙∙∙∙∙∙
Separate two⌐words
                                      There's more of this on the next
Join let⌣ters in word
                                          page
Write in period⊗
                                              (more)
```

Copy editing symbols (see Figure 2-4), which indicate changes in copy without using words, are easy to learn. Lack of consistency in the use of copy editing symbols may confuse the typist and slow the re-keyboarding process.

Proofreading symbols, on the other hand, are used after the copy has been set in type (see Figure 2-5). Substantive changes are not made at this point in the production process, because the purpose of proofreading is to catch typographical errors. There isn't room on the typeset version, or pasteup copy, for errors to be marked within the line or paragraph, so proofreading symbols are placed in the margins of the copy, with a line drawn to indicate the exact place of the error.

Exercise 15 at the end of this chapter tests your knowledge of copy editing symbols.

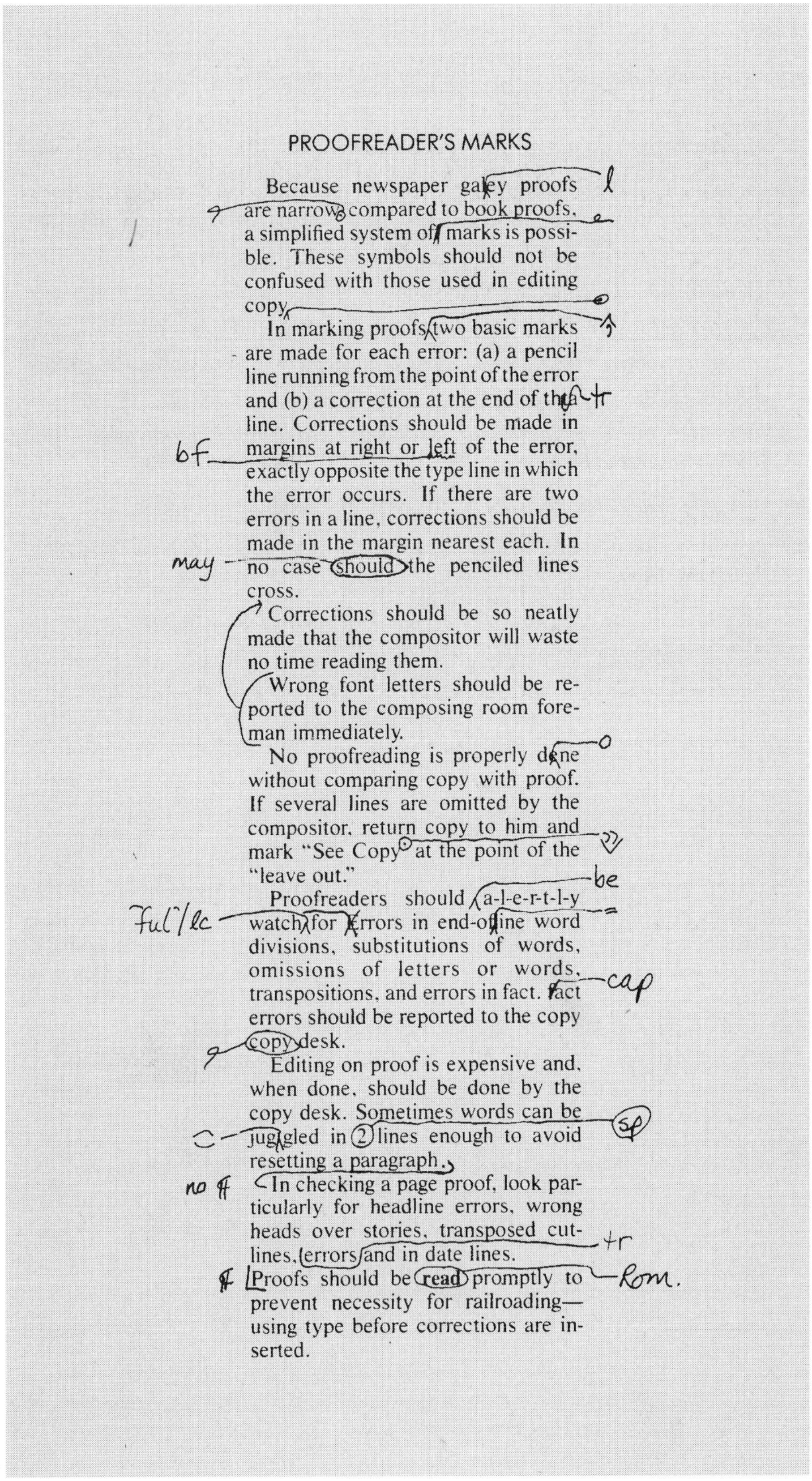

PROOFREADER'S MARKS

Because newspaper galley proofs
are narrow compared to book proofs,
a simplified system of marks is possible. These symbols should not be
confused with those used in editing
copy.

In marking proofs two basic marks
are made for each error: (a) a pencil
line running from the point of the error
and (b) a correction at the end of the
line. Corrections should be made in
margins at right or left of the error,
exactly opposite the type line in which
the error occurs. If there are two
errors in a line, corrections should be
made in the margin nearest each. In
no case should the penciled lines
cross.

Corrections should be so neatly
made that the compositor will waste
no time reading them.

Wrong font letters should be reported to the composing room foreman immediately.

No proofreading is properly done
without comparing copy with proof.
If several lines are omitted by the
compositor, return copy to him and
mark "See Copy" at the point of the
"leave out."

Proofreaders should a-l-e-r-t-l-y
watch for errors in end-of-line word
divisions, substitutions of words,
omissions of letters or words,
transpositions, and errors in fact. Fact
errors should be reported to the copy
copy desk.

Editing on proof is expensive and,
when done, should be done by the
copy desk. Sometimes words can be
juggled in 2 lines enough to avoid
resetting a paragraph.

In checking a page proof, look particularly for headline errors, wrong
heads over stories, transposed cutlines, errors and in date lines.

Proofs should be read promptly to
prevent necessity for railroading—
using type before corrections are inserted.

Figure 2-5
Proofreading symbols are written in the margins of typeset copy. This method of proofreading applies to newspapers. A slightly different approach is used in book publishing.

Suggestions for additional reading

Bernstein, Theodore M. *The Careful Writer: A Modern Guide to English Usage.* New York: Atheneum, 1978.

———. *Watch Your Language.* New York: Pocket Books, 1965.

Brooks, Brian S., and James L. Pinson. *Working with Words: A Concise Handbook for Media Writers and Editors,* 3rd ed. New York: St. Martin's Press, 1996.

Goldstein, Norman (ed.). *The Associated Press Stylebook and Libel Manual.* Reading, Mass.: Addison-Bacon, 1998.

Gordon, Karen Elizabeth. *The Well-Tempered Sentence: A Punctuation Handbook for the Innocent, the Eager, and the Doomed.* New Haven, Conn.: Ticknor & Fields, 1983.

Kessler, Lauren, and Duncan McDonald. *When Words Collide: A Journalist's Guide to Grammar and Style,* 4th ed. Belmont, Calif.: Wadsworth, 1995.

Rogers, James. *The Dictionary of Clichés.* New York: Ballantine Books, 1987.

Strunk, William, Jr., and E.B. White. *The Elements of Style,* 3rd ed. New York: Allyn & Bacon, 1995.

Zinsser, William Knowlton. *On Writing Well: The Classic Guide to Writing Nonfiction,* 6th ed. New York: Harpers, 1998.

Exercises

1. Label each word in the following sentences according to its part of speech.

   a. Marty Hudson has not eaten since Monday.

   b. Hudson is on a hunger strike in the Roanoke City Jail.

   c. Hudson, 32, is a United Mine Workers of America strike organizer.

   d. The study found that teachers want to receive broadcasts from other networks.

   e. Completing the story about the council meeting moments before deadline, the reporter took a break to get a cup of coffee.

   f. Stop! You can't go in there.

2. Identify the subject, verb, direct object or complement in each clause in the following sentences. Draw one line under the subject, two lines under the verb, and three lines under the direct object or complement. Mark whether the verb is completed by a direct object, predicate nominative or predicate adjective.

   a. In some rural areas, people believe the devil makes them sick.

   b. They dose themselves with turpentine to cure worms and tie a dirty sock around their neck to treat a sore throat.

   c. Doctors should know about these cultural and religious beliefs of their patients.

   d. The American Bar Association has said it will not rate future judicial candidates on ideology or politics, but the ABA's critics say the advisory group could still kill the nominations of qualified conservatives.

   e. A young woman wanted to tell the invading soldiers that they were unwelcome in her city.

   f. Thinking they wouldn't shoot a woman, she walked fearlessly toward their lines.

   g. They fired. She fell. A bullet wound turned her white shirt scarlet.

   h. Although some people buy three or four pairs of sunglasses at a clip, the average number of sunglasses purchased per person is 1.3 pairs, according to Ray-Ban research.

   i. Thomas Edison had 400 species of plants in the garden of his winter home on the Caloosahatchee River in Fort Myers, Fla.

j. With intentions of revising his travel book annually, Arthur Frommer tells
   of travels that are politically oriented, vacations on campuses and at
   dance camps, and digs with archeologists.

3. Label each sentence in Exercise 1 according to sentence type: simple, compound, complex, compound-complex.

4. Choose the correct verb in these sentences. To show that you understand the rules of subject-verb agreement and are not relying only on what sounds right, write the number of the rule (as numbered in this chapter) that applies to each choice.

   a. Five passengers on the plane and a farmer working in the field [was, were]
      killed.

   b. Like other produce wholesalers on the three-block-long market, she [know,
      knows] the ultimate follower of seasons [is, are] the farmer.

   c. Each of the children [is, are] enrolled in music lessons.

   d. Neither John nor his brothers [know, knows] what to expect when election
      day [come, comes].

   e. The final hours of the legislative session [was, were] chaotic.

   f. Two-thirds of the protesters [was, were] arrested before noon.

   g. Club members [was, were] scheduled to vote for new officers.

   h. The committee, composed of three members of the board of directors, [is,
      are] going to plan the annual convention.

   i. A number of animals [was, were] trapped in the burning barn.

   j. The majority [is, are] in favor of the legislation limiting immigration,
      which [is, are] to be voted on today.

   k. Politics [was, were] interesting when I studied it in college, but the
      courses [has, had] little effect on my personal politics, which [was,
      were] firmly fixed.

   l. Good manners [is, are] best learned when young.

   m. The mayor's delegation, as well as several Chamber of Commerce members,
      [was, were] scheduled to meet with the executives visiting from Japan.

   n. Everyone [hope, hopes] that the contract will be awarded to this company.

   o. The National Council of Churches [is, are] planning a convention in
      Washington, D.C., this year.

p. The company's earnings [was, were] greater this year than last year because new products [was, were] popular.

q. The total sold [was, were] 450, but a total of 10 [was, were] returned because of faulty construction.

5. Mark each pronoun in the following sentences, and tell whether it is in the nominative, objective or possessive case.

a. An offshore intake pipe sucked up a scuba diver and pulled him 1,650 feet through the duct before depositing him at a nuclear power plant.

b. "I thought I was dead," said William Lamm, 45, who was spear-fishing when he was pulled into the 16-foot diameter, barnacle-studded pipe off Florida Power & Light's St. Lucie nuclear plant on the Atlantic Coast.

c. Lamm said the suction pulled off his mask and diving gloves and ripped his mouthpiece out several times as he moved through the pipe at 7 feet per second.

d. Lamm, a scuba diver for five years, says it will be a long time before he dives again, if at all.

6. Indicate correct noun and pronoun agreement by crossing out the incorrect pronoun choices in these sentences.

a. Jeff Mayer bills [hisself, himself, themselves] as the most expensive maid in the nation. Business executives pay [his, him] $1,000 so [he, him] will tell [they, them, it] how to clean off [they, them, their, there, its] cluttered desks.

b. Some financially strapped cities can't make across-the-board purchases of semiautomatic pistols, [that, which] cost from $350 to $550. But police departments frequently permit officers to buy [they, them, there, their] own sidearms.

c. Each male officer was required to buy [his, him, its, their, them] own uniforms.

d. Uniforms were expensive, but [they, them, it] lasted for several years if [they, them, their, its] owners kept [their, its] weight constant so the uniforms fit properly.

e. Listen carefully to those [who, whom, whose] you have reason to believe know how to express [theirselves, themselves] well.

f. I will exchange letters with [whoever, whomever] writes.

g. [Who, Whom] shall you choose as captain?

h. The company needs to know [who, whom] it is insuring.

i. I thought [she, her] to be my friend.

j. [Who, Whom] do you suppose [he, him] to be?

k. Between you and [I, me], I think [she, her] previous boyfriend was friendlier.

l. None but [I, me] was able to complete the work.

m. Some of [we, us] editors think students need to know much more about grammar.

n. The editors decided to hire the student [who, whom] scored highest on the English usage test.

o. The newly married couple went to a resort in the Smoky Mountains on [their, its] honeymoon. [They, It] will return home next week.

p. The women's basketball team is in [their, its, it's] first season of competition.

7. Cross out the incorrect pronoun choices in the following sentences. Add commas where needed to set off nonessential clauses.

a. Three victims were members of a Delaware Army National Guard unit [that, which, who] had just completed [their, its] first week of training.

b. Officer Glenda Jones [who, whom] has been coordinating police patrols in housing developments plagued by drugs, gangs and gambling said most of the problems stem from non-residents.

c. Widely publicized safety breakdowns at the government's nuclear weapons plants are rooted in a perverse devotion to secrecy and poor management, congressional investigators said in a report issued Sunday. The safety problems [that, which] came to light during the past two years were aggravated by a lack of outside scrutiny and effective oversight from the Energy Department [that, which] pays private companies to run the facilities, the report said.

d. He criticized the students [who, whom, that, which] led the demonstrations [that, which] were crushed by army assaults.

e. Eight-year-old Chad Brenner said he would have liked to use the $39,541.55 tax refund check [that, which] was mistakenly mailed to him to buy a new bicycle.

8. Complete this list of nouns and pronouns to show the plurals and possessives:

	Singular	Singular possessive	Plural	Plural possessive

a. Smith _____

b. girl _____

c. man _____

d. attorney general _____

e. church _____

f. Jones _____

g. army _____

h. monkey _____

i. mouse _____

j. piano _____

k. oasis _____

9. Use the correct verb and verb tense in each of the following sentences.

Lie or lay

a. The gun _____ in the street.

b. The gun had _____ in the street for several hours before it was recovered by police.

c. The police officer _____ the gun on the table.

d. The officer thought that he had _____ the gun on the table, but his supervisor could not find it.

e. The woman _____ on the beach to get a suntan.

f. She had _____ there for several hours before she noticed that she was getting sunburned.

g. _____ the baby in the crib.

h. The twin babies were _____ in the crib.

i. _____ her books aside, she spoke to him.

Sit or set

    j. We were _____ on the swing when Bill began crying.

    k. She _____ the books on her desk.

    l. The fat man _____ on the chair and broke it.

    m. She had _____ the alarm clock for 6 a.m.

    n. They had _____ in the car for two hours.

Rise or raise

    o. Please _____ the flag.

    p. He _____ from the water and surprised me.

    q. The dough has _____ sufficiently.

    r. The student _____ her hand.

    s. He had _____ his hand several times, but the teacher did not call on him to respond.

    t. The stage was designed to allow the orchestra to _____ from the orchestra pit.

10. Rewrite or edit the following sentences to correct misplaced or dangling modifiers and double negatives.

    a. Police described the suspect as a burly, white, middle-aged male with brown hair and a beard, more than 6 feet tall. _____

    _____

    _____

    b. Accused of making errors on telephone bills for the past four months, students living in residence halls will receive a refund from the phone company for long-distance calls. _____

    _____

    _____

    _____

    c. AIDS in New York City is becoming the most common cause of death for women under the age of 35. _____

    _____

    _____

    d. An anti-government coalition staged the protest march in an attempt to force the ouster of Panama's Gen. Manuel Noriega yesterday afternoon.

    _____

    _____

    _____

    e. After training the tiger cub to walk on a leash, it could be used in the zoo director's presentations to schoolchildren. _____

    _____

    _____

    f. Still searching for an incinerator site, a previously rejected location is getting a second look by the city council.

    _____

    _____

    g. The baby kitten doesn't have scarcely any hair. _____

    _____

    h. The jail is the first in the state to be operated by a private management firm that accommodates 100 inmates. _____

    _____

    _____

    i. A Manchester woman, on the pretense of searching for someone, allowed a man to enter her home and was assaulted. _____

    _____

    _____

    j. The zoo doesn't have but one gorilla, but the director says another one will be added next year. _____

    _____

    _____

11. Edit the following sentences to punctuate them correctly. Use correct copy editing symbols. Pay particular attention to the correct use of apostrophes, colons and commas.

    a. Down's syndrome has been linked to a defect on a tiny slice of one of the human chromosomes an important step toward prevention and treatment of the disorder researchers said Saturday.

    b. "By mapping a gene you can find it isolate it and develop new means of therapy" said Dr. Frank Ruddle of Yale University one of the organizer's of the conference.

c. At the Ninth International Gene Mapping Workshop two years ago in Paris scientist's had mapped about 1000 human gene's.

d. The announcement of 400 new genes Saturday brings the total to nearly 2000 an increase of more than one-fourth over what it was two weeks ago.

e. Meanwhile the Immigration and Naturalization Service has proclaimed the law a clear success but the current administration has yet to put it's own stamp on immigration policy.

f. "The legislation bought time for everyone and made the problems more manageable for a while" said Leonel J. Castillo former I.N.S. commissioner.

g. The law offered legal status to aliens who had lived in the United States continuously since before Jan. 1 1982 and imposed penalties on employers who knowingly hired illegals.

h. He said that he had but one thing on his mind sleeping.

i. Gardeners who wear broad brimmed hats, coveralls, and heavy duty gloves while using an electric hedge clipper to trim bushes are displaying common sense—but not enough of it says the American Optometric Association.

j. The garb protects the face from the sun and clothing and hands from the wear and tear of yard work but the eyes are left exposed and vulnerable to flying twigs leaves and other debris.

12. Edit the following sentences to punctuate them correctly. Use correct copy editing symbols. Pay particular attention to the correct use of dashes, exclamation points and hyphens.

a. She announced that newly developed tests would be used during the upcoming tournament to detect drug using athletes.

b. A 4 foot boa constrictor a scary tarantula and a baby Bengal tiger gave Joey Black a front line education about zoos.

c. "Bring back tax incentives" Jones [headline]

d. Every state has reported influenza activity except New Hampshire and Rhode Island with three states New York Connecticut and New Mexico listing widespread outbreaks.

e. Bob Woodward wrote "VEIL The Secret Wars of the CIA, 1981-1987.

f. Gosh It will be a 15 to 20 minute procedure and I don't think I can lie still that long.

13. Edit the following sentences to punctuate them correctly. Use correct copy editing symbols. Pay particular attention to the correct use of parentheses, periods, question marks, quotation marks and semicolons.

   a. "We don't know how much longer we can wait before beginning it (the Dexter Bridge project the mayor said.

   b. It was identified as a Russian plane but US planes were in the area also Maj Gen Larry Jones said.

   c. Did the Maryville Tennessee Daily Times win the photography award.

   d. Dustin Hoffman won an Oscar for Rainman he also appeared in Midnight Cowboy.

   e. The inmate said to the parole board "Jones should not be released from prison. He is a dangerous man. He has told me several times, I will kill again if I get a chance.

14. Use the copy editing symbols in Figure 2-4 to punctuate the following sentences:

   a. Davis who is usually soft spoken talked in loud tones yesterday.

   b. Eisenhower who was commander of the national force refused to attack.

   c. The 1000 word story had a pro American tone and a definite anti Communist slant.

   d. The Manning who used to live here was returned to England.

   e. The Iron Building which is a 40 story structure is owned by Pat Maffery Jr.

   f. The home office is in Los Angeles which is one of Americas largest cities.

   g. The 25 member board held a five day conference.

   h. Headlines which are fashioned to summarize the stories are also used to display the news.

   i. Citizens who voted for the new law now are regretting their lack of knowledge about its impact.

   j. Durham shot his father in law with a 12 gauge shotgun and received a 15 year sentence when the 12 man jury recommended mercy.

15. Use the correct copy editing symbols to make changes in this story:

While performing such simple tasks as brushing-teeth or tossing back a drink, Young adults have suffered strokes by causing trauma to one of 4 main arterys supplying blood to the brain doctors reported.

A 32 year old woman recently suffered a stroke after playing a drinking game in which she tossed back several shotsof whiskey, according to a lettter published today by the New England Journal of Medicine.

"It was not only the alcohol but the manner in which she consumed it said Dr. Richard Trosch, a neurology resident at the yale university School of Medicine.

Knocking back a shot of whiskey shouldbe include among a list of potential stroke-causing "trivial traumas," including old whip lash injuries, child birth, lifting heavy, brushing teeth and diving into water Trosch wrote.

Trosch said young adults was particularly prone to damageing the extracranial carotid artery a vein through which bloood is pumped from the heart to teh brain

> Every misused word revenges itself forever upon a writer's reputation.
>
> —*Agnes Repplier*

Consistent Style and Correct Words

CONSISTENCY and precise word usage are important in communication. Research indicates that readers are irritated when they find, for example, *advisor* in one paragraph and *adviser* in another or *street* spelled out in one address and abbreviated in another. Readers notice when writers and copy editors confuse *effect* with *affect* or write *biannual* when they mean *biennial*.

Readers wonder whether a publication careless about style and proper language usage can be trusted to be accurate and fair about its more substantive content. This chapter will introduce you to common style conventions used by most U.S. newspapers and the AP stylebook. Then, the second half of the chapter will call to your attention some words that are frequently misused, both in written and spoken English.

Consistent style for carefully edited publications

All good news publications and even most mediocre ones adopt consistent style, and all reporters and editors are expected to adhere to that style. The same applies for magazines, newsletters, brochures and other printed materials.

Thomas W. Lippman, director of personnel/news of The Washington Post, wrote this about style:

> We are a medium of mass communication. The need to communicate clearly and quickly with a vast and diverse audience imposes its own restrictions. We have little room for Joycean experimentation or 800-word, punctuation-free Faulknerian paragraphs. We strive for consistency of presentation not because we adhere pedantically to inflexible rules, but because we want to enlighten our readers without confusing them or diverting their attention from the material at hand. In addition, we recognize that the newspaper is read every day by educated people who expect us to uphold a high standard of English usage. Consistency of style is part of the high quality they have a right to demand.

Although some publications have compiled their own stylebook, most use the one published by The Associated Press. In addition, newspapers generally develop a supplementary style guide to incorporate spellings, titles and other matters peculiar to their city and state. Besides a guide for capitalization, abbreviation, punctuation, spelling, numerals and other usage, the AP stylebook has evolved into a valuable reference source.

Your reporting and editing teachers are likely to require you to use the AP stylebook or some other style manual. Don't panic, thinking that you can never learn everything in the book. Even experienced copy editors haven't committed the entire volume to memory, but, through study and frequent use, they have memorized basic style points commonly encountered in news stories. In addition, experienced copy editors are familiar with the types of information contained in the stylebook so that they can find specific facts and style points quickly. Working under deadline pressure, copy editors lack time to look up routine style matters, and they don't waste time consulting a variety of reference books if the stylebook contains the information needed for the story they are editing.

This chapter focuses on some style matters that you should learn because they appear in many stories in a typical edition of a newspaper, as well as in press releases and other materials produced by public relations practitioners. You should not have to refer to the stylebook each time you encounter these style matters.

What information do the following news leads have in common?

A city council committee approved pay raises of up to 28 percent for council members and some other elected officials yesterday. Under the proposal, a council member's base salary would go to $70,000, from $55,000, and the mayor's salary would rise to $165,000 from $130,000.

———————

Joe Blow, 31, a New York police officer linked to the 30th Precinct corruption scandal, pleaded guilty yesterday to selling more than a kilogram of cocaine that he took from Harlem drug dealers while in uniform.

———————

Fred Smith, 521 Oak Ave., won the high-point trophy in the Holiday Masters Open Swimming Championships yesterday. The 74-year-old Smith took first place in the 50, 100, 200 and 500 freestyle events and the 50-yard backstroke.

———————

Undefeated Austin-East, down 40-39 at halftime, came back for a 69-63 victory Saturday night over previously unbeaten Chattanooga Brainerd. Andrea Fenderson's 21 points led the way for the 8-0 Roadrunners.

———————

Fountain City Post Office employees contributed $200 to the Empty Stocking Fund to help buy toys for needy children.

———————

Just nine days before Christmas, fire destroyed a warehouse containing an estimated $1 million worth of goods meant to be distributed by one of the city's largest charities.

More than 100 firefighters battled the blaze Friday night at the four-story building at 4400 Western St. Crews were still pouring water on the persistent flames at noon Saturday, some 17 hours after the fire was first reported.

———————

Tommy McGruder, 35, who once weighed 800 pounds, lost half his body weight on his own, but he needed help taking off 75 more pounds. So surgeons Friday took them off for him—all in skin.

———————

A man trying to escape a speeding ticket plunged into an icy river and refused to come out for 40 minutes.

———————

```
Police stopped Stephen Coleman, 25, at about 1:30 a.m. Saturday.
Police said he was going 56 mph in a 25 mph zone.
```

———————

```
Both Republican and Democratic legislators are planning $1,000-
a-ticket dinners on Jan. 8, the day before a new ban on
political fund raising goes into effect.
```

The common ingredient in these leads is numbers, including numbers used in addresses, ages, dates, distances, dollar amounts, sports scores, speed and time. Numbers are used in most stories and should be used in a consistent pattern throughout the publication. The following section explains some of the AP stylebook rules regarding the use of numbers.

Numerals

Generally, spell out the numbers one through nine; use numerals for 10 and higher: "The couple has four cats and two dogs"; "She needs 10 more tickets to win."

Use numerals for:

- Addresses and streets numbered 10 and higher: *15th Avenue, 12th Street*

- Ages of people and things: *the 11-year-old prodigy, in their '60s, the car was 3 years old*

- Dates and time: *June 1, 1992; 7 p.m.*

- Decimals and percentages: *cost of living rose 5 percent, unemployment down 0.5 percent, $2.5 million*

- Decisions, rulings and votes: *The Supreme Court ruled 5–4*

- Dimensions and measurements: *a 4-foot fence*

- Exact dimensions and measurements: *The star player is 6 feet 4; The puppies each weighed 2 pounds, 5 ounces; The rug is 9 by 12 feet*

- Fractions contained in numbers greater than one: *5 1/2 inches*

- Geographical and political districts: *5th Congressional District*

- Monetary units: *5 cents, $5, $500, $5 million*

- Numerical ranking: *No. 1 choice*

- Recipe amounts: *2 cups of flour*

- Speeds: *5 mph*

- Sports scores, standings and odds: *5–3 victory, 2–1 odds*

- Temperatures except zero: *70 degrees; minus 5 degrees; The temperature stood at zero at midnight*

Use words for:

- Addresses and streets below 10: *Fifth Avenue*

- Distances below 10: *five-mile race*

- Fractions smaller than one: *one-half inch*

- Indefinite or approximate figures: *Thanks a million; We walked about five miles; A thousand times no!*

▪ Numbers used at the start of a sentence, except for a numeral that identifies a calendar year: *Five hundred people protested; 1990 was a good year*

Abbreviations

Abbreviations are used to save space, especially in headlines, and to improve readability. They should not be overused or used if they are unfamiliar or confusing.

Most all-capital abbreviations are spelled without periods: *FBI, CIA, ABC, AFL-CIO, NASA*. But all-capital abbreviations of places and of the United Nations take periods: *U.S., U.N.* Most other abbreviations take periods: *c.o.d., Inc.* An exception: *55 mph.* Abbreviations should not be used at the beginning of a sentence.

▶**Acronyms.** Acronyms may be used after the first reference if they are well known. Some commonly used acronyms may be used on first reference: *NASA, radar, NATO, AIDS.* Do not follow an organization's full name with an abbreviation or acronym either in parentheses or set off by dashes. If an abbreviation or acronym would not be clear on second reference without this arrangement, do not use it.

▶**Addresses.** Use the abbreviations *Ave., Blvd.* and *St.* only with numbered addresses: *1600 Pennsylvania Ave.* Spell them out and capitalize when they are part of a formal street name without a number: *Pennsylvania Avenue.* Do not abbreviate *Circle, Court, Drive, Highway, Lane, Road, Place* and so on.

▶**Businesses and organizations.** Abbreviate *Co., Corp., Ltd.* and *Inc.* when used at the end of a business's name: *The New York Times Co.* Spell out *Association, Bureau, Department* and *Division.*

▶**Dates and times.** Abbreviate *Jan., Feb., Aug., Sept., Oct., Nov.* and *Dec.* only when they are used with specific dates: *Jan. 25, 1947.* Spell out *March, April, May, June* and *July. A.D., B.C., a.m.* and *p.m.* take periods; *PDT, MDT, EST* and the like don't.

▶**Military.** Abbreviate military ranks before names on first reference (*Gen. Irene Smith*); do not use rank after the first reference (*Smith*). Some common abbreviations are *Gen., Col., Maj., Capt., Lt., Sgt.* and *Pfc.* See the complete listing of military ranks in the AP stylebook.

▶**States.** Spell out *United States* when used as a noun; abbreviate *U.S.* as an adjective: "The U.S. plan failed."

Most state names are abbreviated when they follow the name of a town or city. The correct abbreviations are

Ala.	Ga.	Minn.	N.J.	Tenn.
Ariz.	Ill.	Miss.	N.M.	Va.
Ark.	Ind.	Mo.	N.Y.	Vt.
Calif.	Kan.	Mont.	Okla.	Wash.
Colo.	Ky.	N.C.	Ore.	Wis.
Conn.	La.	N.D.	Pa.	W. Va.
D.C.	Mass.	Neb.	R.I.	Wyo.
Del.	Md.	Nev.	S.C.	
Fla.	Mich.	N.H.	S.D.	

Do not abbreviate Alaska, Hawaii, Idaho, Iowa, Maine, Ohio, Texas or Utah. Use two-letter Postal Service abbreviations only with full addresses, including ZIP codes.

▶**Titles.** Abbreviate *Gov., Lt. Gov., Sen., Rep., Dr.* and the *Rev.* before a name on first reference. Do not use titles after the first reference. Do not abbreviate *Attorney general, Controller, Detective, District attorney, Officer, Professor* or *Superintendent*.

▶**Other abbreviations.** *AWOL, GI, POW, SOS* and *TV* are acceptable on first and succeeding references. Academic degrees take periods: *B.A., M.S., Ph.D.* Do not use periods in plane or ship designations: *USS Enterprise, SST.*

Capitalization

In addition to capitalizing the first word of a sentence, you should capitalize the following:

▶**Academic degrees.** Capitalize the abbreviation for but not the formal names of degrees: *B.A., M.S.,* but *bachelor of arts, master of science.* Lowercase general references: *bachelor's degree, master's degree.*

▶**Geography.** Capitalize regions: *West Coast, East Coast, the South, the West, Pacific Coast, the Northwest.*
  Capitalize natural features: *Blue Ridge Mountains, Gulf Stream, Continental Divide.* Capitalize popular names of natural features: *Deep South, Bible Belt, Texas Panhandle.* But lowercase plurals and general directions: *western, the coasts, boat on the bay.*

▶**Government.** Capitalize full names and short forms: *the U.S. Postal Service, Postal Service; the Federal Reserve Board, the Fed.* Lowercase general terms: *delayed at customs, the post office.*
  Capitalize city as part of a formal name: *Kansas City.* Lowercase city elsewhere: *the city of Seattle, a Missouri city.*
  Capitalize formal names of committees: *the Senate Appropriations Committee.* Lowercase informal names of legislative committees and names of subcommittees.

▶**Politics.** Capitalize political organizations or movements: *the Democratic Party, Republicans, Communists.* Lowercase political philosophies: *socialism, communism, democracy.*

▶**Religion.** Capitalize all recognized faiths and their members: *Protestants, Catholics, Jewish faith.*

▶**Titles.** Capitalize official titles before names, unless they are simply job descriptions: *Pope John Paul III* (but *the pope*), *Professor Catharine Stimpson, Officer Jay Brown, engineer Mary Jones, coach Barb Smith.*

▶**Trade names.** Capitalize trade names when their use is necessary: *Kleenex, Jell-O, Band-Aid.* Generic references are preferred: *tissue, gelatin, bandage.*

▶**Other capitalization.** Capitalize the names of official and historical documents, doctrines, legal codes and laws. Capitalize designating terms before figures and letters: *Room 222, Section 8, Title 9, Channel 60.* Lowercase the seasons: *winter, spring, summer, fall.* Lowercase academic departments unless they are proper nouns or adjectives: *journalism department, department of journalism; English department, department of English.*

Time

A specific time should precede the day, and the day should precede the place: "The production will begin at 8 p.m. Friday at the Opera House."

Use *noon* and *midnight,* not *12 a.m.* and *12 p.m.*

Avoid redundancies: *5 p.m. tomorrow,* not *5 p.m. tomorrow night.*

Use *today, this morning, tomorrow* and the like as appropriate. Use the day of the week elsewhere. Use *Monday, Tuesday* and so on for days of the week within seven days before or after the current date. Use the month and a figure for dates beyond this range. Avoid redundancies, such as *last Thursday* or *next Friday;* the verb tense should denote usage. Always spell out days of the week.

Use an apostrophe for omitted figures in years: e*vents of '89.*

Use figures for decades, with an apostrophe for omitted figures: *the 1990s, the '90s.*

For centuries, lowercase the word *century* and spell out century numbers below 10: *the third century, the 20th century.*

Cities and datelines

The general rule is that names of towns and cities in the United States should be followed by the abbreviation of the state: Norman, Okla.; Salem, Ore. Exceptions are the names of states that should never be abbreviated: Alaska, Hawaii, Idaho, Iowa, Maine, Ohio, Texas, and Utah. Thus, cities and towns in those states are followed by the unabbreviated name of the state: Athens, Ohio; Austin, Texas; Provo, Utah; Bangor, Maine.

Cities and towns within the state where a newspaper is published generally stand alone. For example, a newspaper published in Tennessee would not follow the name of a city within Tennessee with the abbreviation *Tenn.*: Morristown, Franklin, Chattanooga. If, however, it is not clear from the context of the story that a home-state city is meant instead of an out-of-state city with the same name, then use the name of the state: Athens, Tenn. (to distinguish from Athens, Ohio).

Another exception to the general rule is the list of cities designated by the Associated Press as standing alone without the name of the state. Generally, these are large cities that appear frequently in the news and are not likely to be confused by readers. These are the U.S. cities that can stand alone:

Atlanta	Indianapolis	Pittsburgh
Baltimore	Las Vegas	St. Louis
Boston	Los Angeles	Salt Lake City
Chicago	Miami	San Antonio
Cincinnati	Milwaukee	San Diego
Cleveland	Minneapolis	San Francisco
Dallas	New Orleans	Seattle
Denver	New York	Washington
Detroit	Oklahoma City	
Honolulu	Philadelphia	
Houston	Phoenix	

These foreign cities stand alone:

Beijing	Kuwait	Panama City
Berlin	London	Paris
Djibouti	Luxembourg	Quebec
Geneva	Macau	Rome
Gibraltar	Mexico City	San Marino
Guatemala City	Monaco	Singapore
Havana	Montreal	Tokyo
Hong Kong	Moscow	Toronto
Jerusalem	Ottawa	Vatican City

Stories that do not originate locally should have a dateline at the beginning. A dateline should contain a city name, entirely in capital letters, followed in most cases by the name of the state, country or territory where the city is located. The style at many newspapers is to follow the dateline with the abbreviation of the news service in parentheses, followed by a dash and then the lead paragraph of the story.

```
TULSA, Okla. (AP)—Heavy winds and rain ...
WASHINGTON (AP)—The cost of living rose ...
```

See the *dateline* entry in the AP stylebook for the correct style for island nations, territories and overseas territories. It includes information about date selection and how to cite other cities within the body of a datelined story.

Other style issues

In addition to knowing correct style for numerals, abbreviations, capitalization, time, cities and datelines, copy editors must know correct style for the following:

▶ **Long titles.** Avoid their use before a name. Use *John Jones, assistant undersecretary for the interior,* rather than *Assistant Undersecretary for the Interior John Jones.*

▶ **Time zones.** Capitalize the names of time zones in formal usage: *Eastern Standard Time, Pacific Daylight Time, EST, PDT.*

▶ **Weather terms.** A *blizzard* has winds of 35 mph or more and considerable falling or blowing snow, with visibility near zero. A *cyclone* is a storm with strong winds rotating about a moving center of low atmospheric pressure. A *funnel cloud* is a violent, rotating column of air that does not touch the ground. *Gale winds* are sustained winds within the range of 39 to 54 mph (34 to 47 knots). A *hurricane* is a warm-core tropical cyclone in which the minimum sustained surface wind is 74 mph. A *tornado* is a violent rotating column of air forming a pendant and touching the ground. A *knot* is one nautical mile (6,076.10 feet) per hour. To convert knots into approximate statute miles per hour, multiply knots by 1.15. Always use figures to express the result: "Winds were at 7 to 9 knots."

▶ **Temperatures.** Use figures for all except zero: "The day's low was minus 10." Temperatures get higher or lower; they don't get warmer or cooler. The temperature scale generally used in the United States is Fahrenheit rather than Celsius. In the Fahrenheit scale, the freezing point of water is 32 degrees and the boiling point is 212 degrees. To convert a Fahrenheit temperature to Celsius, subtract 32 from the Fahrenheit figure, multiply by 5, and divide by 9 ($77 - 32 = 45$; $45 \times 5 = 225$; $225 \div 9 = 25$ degrees Celsius).

In addition to the frequently used style matters discussed in this chapter, the AP stylebook is crammed with useful information for reporters and copy editors. Keep it handy. Use it often.

Exercises 1 through 4 at the end of this chapter test your knowledge of style points summarized in this chapter. Exercises throughout the remainder of this textbook will require you to use these style points, as well as many others in the AP stylebook.

Correct word usage

The English language, particularly the U.S. version of it, changes constantly. New words, many associated with evolving technology, enter the language, and some words and phrases once reserved for spoken but not written language eventually become commonly accepted for both forms of communication. Copy editors and other wordsmiths should recognize the evolutionary nature of the language but at the same time work to protect it from barbarisms that detract from clear, concise communication.

Students often balk at grammar and word usage drills, arguing that incorrect usage should stand, on the basis that "it's the way people say it." A purist might ask *What people?* and question why professional communicators should let nonprofessionals assume the role of experts. Spoken English is not the same as written English, and even the most careful and graceful writer may lapse into imprecision when speaking extemporaneously.

The remainder of this chapter will consider a few of the word usage problems that copy editors must guard against. A list of other frequently misused words is included in the Appendix.

▶ **Words to eliminate.** If these words are part of either your written or spoken vocabulary, quit using them: *alright, irregardless, towards, wreckless.* The correct version is *all right. Regardless* or *irrespective* should be used in place of *irregardless.* Unless you are writing for a British publication, *toward* is the correct word. One might have occasion to use *wreckless* in the sense of a place where wrecks do not occur—a *wreckless* intersection perhaps—but the intended meaning is generally *reckless*, as in *reckless* behavior.

▶ **Crutch words.** These words seem to run in cycles. A few years ago, *hopefully* was a crutch word, seemingly used to steady a speaker or writer who was about to launch into a thought. "Hopefully, our team will win the big game." "Hopefully, I will make an A on the exam." The correct phrase in these example sentences is *I hope. Hopefully* is an adverb, so it should modify verbs, adjectives or other adverbs, not nouns or pronouns. "He looked into her eyes hopefully as he proposed marriage."

More recently, the adverb *basically* has become a crutch word, misused in the same way as *hopefully* was a few years ago.

▶ **Redundant phrases.** Eliminating a few dozen redundant phrases in each issue of a newspaper provides space for another story. Perhaps enough space could be saved to run another obituary if the redundancies *funeral service, autopsy to determine the cause of death, died suddenly* and *fatal killing* were eliminated from obits.

Copy editors should use the delete key on these redundant expressions:

acute crisis	commute *back and forth*	consensus *of opinion*
bald-*headed*	*completely* destroy	*dead* body
basic essentials	(eliminate, empty, full,	depreciate *in value*
climb *up*	finished, true)	

entirely new (original, complete)	*kept* watch	rise *up*
end result	large *in size*	*self*-confessed
few *in number*	*new* record	*sworn* affidavits
first *annual*	*noon* luncheon	*total* operating costs
follow *after*	*pair of* twins	*underground* subway
free gift	plan *for future (ahead, in advance)*	*very* unique (*really* unique, *most* unique)
general public	*possibly* might	whether *or not*
hot-water heater	reason is *because*	*12* noon (midnight)
invited guest	*regular* weekly meeting	8 a.m. *this morning*

▶**Wrong words.** Experienced police reporters know that *burglary, robbery* and *theft* must not be used interchangeably. It is common newspaper practice, however, to assign rookie reporters who may not know the precise meanings of these words to the "cop shop." As always, copy editors must be on guard.

Burglary, as defined by common law, means forcible entry with intent to commit a crime. *Robbery* means stealing with force or threat of force; *theft* means stealing without force or threat of force. A holdup is a robbery; shoplifting is theft.

Alleged and *allegedly* are other misusages common to police stories. These words do not afford the legal protection that some reporters associate with them. In addition, production errors could lead to the word being dropped. Rather than writing, "Jones allegedly assaulted the woman," it is better to write, "Jones has been charged with assault."

In the sense of killing, reserve the word *execute* for the taking of life by due process of law. Terrorists or gangsters do not execute people, although they may engage in execution-style murder.

Although some usage experts have abandoned efforts to preserve the distinctions, *feel, believe* and *think* have different meanings. *Believe* is used to express ideas that are accepted on faith: "She said she *believes* in God." Use *think* when mental processes and reason, rather than emotion, are used to form an opinion: "Researchers said they *think* their studies will lead to medical advances." To describe emotional or physical sensations, *feel* is the correct word: "She said she *feels* sad." "He said he *felt* the prick of the needle."

Two other words that should not be used interchangeably are *if* and *whether*. To introduce a condition, use *if*, as in, "*If* it rains, the picnic will be canceled." To express an alternative, use *whether*, as in, "He asked *whether* the picnic had been canceled." The word *whether* includes the idea that something may or may not exist, so it is redundant to say *whether or not*.

Refute is another troublesome word in that it is sometimes mistakenly used to indicate disagreement as a synonym for *deny, contradict, reject, rebut* or *dispute*. For something or someone to be refuted, it must be proved to be false or mistaken. If there is any question about the success of the argument, *refute* is not the proper word. *Disprove* is a correct substitute for *refute*.

Convince and *persuade* have different meanings. People are *persuaded* to do or believe something; they become *convinced*, meaning they feel secure about a decision of principle. *Convince* should not be followed by an infinitive but by *that* or *of*. "She *persuaded* her father to allow her to attend the party." "He was *convinced* that it was the right thing to do."

For spatial relationships, *over* is the word to use, as in, "The boy jumped *over* the wall." For figures, *more than* is the preferred usage: "*More than* 40,000 attended the football game."

A person's ability to use language, either spoken or written, is referred to as *verbal* skill. *Oral* skills are spoken, not written. A person who gives a speech makes an *oral* presentation.

Two other words that are often misused are *figuratively* and *literally*. The former is an adverb describing an action that is not in its usual or exact sense or is metaphorical, as in *a figure of speech*. *Literally* means exactly, actually, precisely as stated. When used to mean a display of great emotion or anger, it is incorrect to say he *literally* hit the ceiling. He did not actually hit the ceiling. What is meant is that he *figuratively* hit the ceiling.

In comparing quantities, use *fewer* if the items can be counted or separated easily: *fewer* dollars, *fewer* inches of rain. Use *less* for items that cannot be counted or separated easily: *less* money, *less* rain.

Like and *as* are often misused. If a conjunction is needed to join two parts of a sentence, *as* is the correct word. In this sentence a conjunction is needed to link the two clauses: "The women look *as though* they might be sisters." Use *like* if a preposition is needed: "The women look *like* sisters."

Because and *since* are not interchangeable. Use *because* to denote a specific cause-effect relationship: "They canceled the company picnic because it rained." *Since* is acceptable in a causal sense when the first event in a sequence led logically to the second but was not its direct cause: "They wore casual clothes to work since a company picnic was scheduled for the afternoon."

▶**Words that sound alike.** Writers and editors sometimes misuse words that sound alike and are spelled similarly but have different meanings. Following are some examples:

- **all together, altogether:** The two-word expression means in a group; *altogether* means thoroughly or entirely. "Let's go *all together* in one car." "It is an *altogether* ridiculous idea."

- **allude, elude, illusion:** To refer indirectly to something is to allude to it; *elude* means to escape a pursuer. "The author *alluded* to his previous bouts with alcoholism." "The criminal *eluded* the police." The word *illusion* comes from the Latin, meaning "to mock." An illusion is a false idea or conception, as *illusions of grandeur*.

- **carat, caret, carrot, karat:** *Carat* is the unit of weight (200 milligrams) for measuring precious stones and metals. *Carat* is also spelled *karat*. *Caret* is an editing mark used to indicate an insertion. *Carrot* is a vegetable.

- **compose, comprise:** The parts compose the whole; the whole comprises its parts. The consensus among usage experts is the expression *is comprised of* should be avoided. "The U. S. government *comprises* the executive, legislative and judicial branches." *Comprised* is a transitive verb, so it needs a direct object. These usages are correct: "Nine players *compose* the team." "The team *is composed of* nine players." "The team *comprises* nine players."

- **credible, creditable, credulous:** Something that can be believed is credible, as *a credible story*. *Creditable* means deserving credit or praise. "His service to the community was *creditable*." A *credulous* person is one who tends to believe too readily, is gullible.

- **eminent, imminent:** *Eminent* is an adjective describing something that is high, lofty, prominent, renowned. "An *eminent* person will be the best candidate for the university presidency." Something that is likely to happen without delay, that is impending, can be said to be imminent. "The appearance of the sky indicates that a storm is *imminent*."

- **farther, further:** Use *farther* to refer to physical distances. "She can run *farther* than I can." *Further* means to a greater extent or degree, as *investigate the matter further. Further* also can mean in addition. "*Further,* I will not do as you ask because your plan is unethical."

- **imply, infer:** The speaker or writer *implies;* the listener or reader *infers.* "In her speech, the company president *implied* that major policy changes were forthcoming." "After listening carefully, I *inferred* that the policy changes would not involve my department."

- **incidence, incidents:** *Incidence* refers to the rate of occurrence, as in *the incidence of a particular disease in the United States.* An *incident* is an occurrence. The word does not mean attack or violence, although those adjectives might apply to an incident. "It was an *incident* that he would remember fondly for the rest of his life."

- **levee, levy:** A *levee* is an embankment to prevent a river from flooding bordering land. "They stood on the *levee* to watch the barges float downstream." *Levy* as a noun is an imposed tax or fine; as a verb it means to impose a tax or fine. "The state legislature will *levy* an income tax." "The amount of the *levy* has not been determined."

- **naval, navel:** *Naval* pertains to a navy. *Navel* is the small scar on the abdomen where the umbilical cord was attached to the fetus; also *navel orange.*

- **pore, pour:** *Pore* as a transitive verb means to study carefully, to ponder. It is used with *over,* as *to pore over books.* Used as a noun, *pore* is a tiny opening, as in skin and plant leaves, for absorbing or discharging fluids. Neither meaning is related to the verb *pour,* which means to cause to pour in a continuous stream. "I will *pour* the milk from the bottle."

- **stationary, stationery:** An object that does not move is *stationary.* One uses *stationery* when writing a letter.

- **tortuous, torturous:** *Tortuous* means full of twists and turns, crooked, deceitful or tricky, as *a tortuous act* or *tortuous path. Torturous* pertains to torture.

Still other frequently misused words are explained in the Appendix.

Common spelling errors

Most word-processing programs for computers now have spell-check functions, but, as the following poem shows, they are far from foolproof.

```
Spell Checker Blue It
I have a spelling checker;
It came with my PC.
It plane lee marks four my revue
Mistakes I cannot sea.
I've run this poem rite threw it.
I'm sure your pleas to no,
Its letter perfect in it's weigh.
My checker tolled me sew.
```

As useful as computerized spell-checker programs are, they are not designed to catch correctly spelled but misused words, so a good copy editor would never rely entirely on such an aid. Following are a few commonly misspelled words. Keep in mind that in some cases there are alternative correct spellings (*advisor, good-bye*) but that these are the preferred ones.

a lot	disappoint	likable	recur
acceptable	discipline	loose	referee
accessible	doughnut	lose	religious
accidentally	drowned	lovable	repetitious
accommodate	drunkenness	mantel	resistance
accumulate	eighth	mantle	responsibility
acknowledgment	embarrass	marshal	rhyme
across	employee	medicine	rhythm
adviser	envelop	mischievous	ridiculous
alleged	envelope	misspell	sacrilegious
allotted	equipped	naive	schedule
already	erroneous	necessary	scissors
Alzheimer's disease	exaggerate	nickel	seize
anoint	experience	niece	seizure
apparent	familiar	ninth	separate
appearance	February	occasion	sergeant
appellant	fierce	occurred	sheriff
arctic	financial	offered	siege
argument	foreign	omitted	signaled
assistant	fortunate	ordinarily	similar
attendance	forty	parallel	sincerely
bachelor	fraudulent	pastime	sizable
beggar	gauge	percent	skier
beginning	good-bye	personal	skiing
broccoli	grammar	personnel	soldier
business	grievance	physician	sophomore
caffeine	guarantee	pigeon	succeed
calendar	harass	possession	successful
canceled	height	potato	superintendent
cancellation	heir	potatoes	supersede
category	illegitimate	practically	surprise
cellar	immediately	prairie	surveillance
cemetery	inevitable	preferred	tendency
chief	innocence	preparation	thoroughly
Cincinnati	inseparable	pretense	tobacco
commemorate	jewelry	prevalence	tournament
commitment	judgment	preventive	truly
committee	knowledgeable	professor	ukulele
comparable	laid	quantity	usable
compatible	legitimate	questionnaire	vacuum
conceive	leisure	readable	veterinary
criticize	liaison	receipt	villain
desirable	lieutenant	receive	weird
dilemma	lightning	recommend	wherever
			X-ray

Exercises 5 through 12 at the end of this chapter test your knowledge of word usage discussed in this chapter and the list in the Appendix of frequently misused words.

How to be a hit as an intern

By Amanda Traughber and Gina Acosta

COPY editing can be a rewarding career, both financially and professionally. But many aspiring journalists never consider it because, let's face it, Woodward and Bernstein were reporters, not copy editors.

It may not be a high-profile job, but there are many reasons why you should consider copy editing and why, if you choose that career path, getting an internship should be your first priority. If you want a job that pays you to read the publication before it hits the newsstands, you have to be a hit as an intern first.

Why should you consider copy editing? Copy editors usually are paid more than reporters. In addition, while your reporter colleagues are chasing stories at all hours, you will not be forced to take work home with you.

Copy editing makes you a better writer. Understanding the mechanics of clear, well-formed sentences, grammar and story organization in other people's work will enhance your own.

If you want a newspaper job, being a copy editor gives you a perspective that many don't receive: how the production of a newspaper works. Often, you will be called upon to work with reporters, graphics planners, assignment editors and page designers or print-shop composers as the paper moves toward the finish line. As you consult with all of these people, you will have the opportunity to make decisions AND to witness the making of important decisions.

The market for copy editors is a good one. Because many journalists who are just starting out overlook copy editing as a career move, newspapers have a harder time finding people to fill their openings on the copy desk. This makes it easier to get a job as a copy editor and drives up the price the paper is willing to pay for your skills.

Not only is it easier for you to get a job at some papers if you want to be a copy editor, but also starting out as one can give you a leg up on promotions to higher levels of responsibility.

So we've talked you into becoming a copy editor. Before you make a decision, also consider that a successful copy-editing career requires a few basics:

- You must be detail-oriented.

- You must be a grammar and spelling expert or have the willingness to learn to be an expert.

- You must have an interest in computers and technology because the newsroom is an ever-changing place.

- You must know basic newspaper design and computer programs such as QuarkXPress because page layout is a copy desk responsibility at many newspapers.

- You must love to learn about new subjects.

Amanda Traughber

Amanda Traughber is a copy editor on the National Desk of The Washington Post. She holds a bachelor of science in journalism from the University of Kansas and has been an intern on The Kansas City (Mo.) Star's universal desk and The Washington Post's Metro, National, Foreign and Financial desks. She is working on a project for the American Copy Editors Society to encourage students to pursue careers in copy editing and is compiling a nationwide listing of paid copy-editing internships. The list is available at http://www.copydesk.org/internlist/htm.

Gina Acosta

Gina Acosta is a recent journalism graduate of Florida A&M University and a copy editor on The Washington Post's Metro Desk. She has interned at The Miami Herald, the Tallahassee Democrat, The Hartford Courant and The Washington Post. She is a member of the National Association of Hispanic Journalists and the American Copy Editors Society, where she serves on an education committee. She can be reached at acostag@washpost.com.

■ You must be a people person in order to tell someone diplomatically that his story would be better if it were reorganized.

■ You must be a night owl or adaptable to night hours because most copy editors begin work around 4 or 5 p.m. and stay until midnight or later. (Some people see these hours as a benefit: Working nights enables some people to run errands before work and have their weekends to play.)

Once you have developed skills and made contacts at school and gatherings of journalism organizations, use those contacts to land an internship.

Internships are necessary to get a copy-editing job at a newspaper, and they are valuable to you for many reasons.

You can't get a job without experience, and you can't get experience without a job. Avoid this trap with internships, which don't require heavy experience to obtain. School training and work on a school publication will only get you so far, but they will be enough to land you an internship, which you can use as a springboard into a job. We can't stress enough how key an internship is to getting a first job.

Working as an intern gives you experience in the trenches. You will learn from people who have been working as copy editors every day for years and years. Their experience and guidance will teach you far beyond what you've learned in college survey courses.

Internships give you an opportunity to prove to yourself whether you are cut out to be a copy editor. After a summer of learning about the copy desk and the workings of a newspaper, you should have an idea of how well you can perform the job and whether you want to pursue copy editing as a career.

Better to decide after a summer spent at a newspaper while you're in college than after you've left school.

In addition to trying out copy editing as a career, an internship will give you an opportunity to take the newspaper for a test drive. If you like editing but don't feel comfortable in a particular newsroom, don't give up. Each paper has its own style and office politics, and it's better to decide whether you feel comfortable there after having an internship, before you accept a job and feel stuck there for a year or two. (It can reflect poorly on you if you hand another potential employer a resume with frequent job changes.)

Being an intern also provides an opportunity to network with other interns, who one day will be in leadership positions at newspapers nationwide. Fellow interns will give you advice and an outlet for comparing notes about varied experiences.

And the best part of many internships is that as you're gathering experience to list on your resume and contacts to help you get your first job, you'll probably also be drawing a paycheck. Many internships pay, and copy-editing internships often pay better than reporting internships.

Suggestions for additional reading

Brooks, Brian S., and James L. Pinson. *Working with Words: A Concise Handbook for Media Writers and Editors*, 3rd ed. New York: St. Martin's Press, 1996.

Kessler, Lauren, and Duncan McDonald. *When Words Collide: A Journalist's Guide to Grammar and Style*, 4th ed. Belmont, Calif.: Wadsworth Publishing, 1995.

Miller, Casey, and Kate Swift. *Handbook of Nonsexist Writing*, 2nd ed. New York: Harper & Row, 1988.

Semmelmeyer, Madeline, and Donald O. Bolander. *The New Webster's Grammar Guide*. New York: Berkley Books, 1991.

Zinsser, William. *On Writing Well*, 6th ed. New York: Harpers, 1998.

Exercises

1. Unless your instructor tells you otherwise, use the style rules given in this chapter and the AP stylebook to circle the correct style in each of the following sets. All are first reference unless otherwise noted.

a. 4th and Iowa streets
4th & Iowa
Fourth and Iowa streets
Fourth and Iowa Streets

b. 5 cents
five cents
5¢
$.05

c. The Supreme Court ruled eight to one.
The Supreme Court ruled 8-1.
The Supreme Court ruled 8 to 1.
The Supreme Court ruled 8/1.

d. *(news story)*
she is 5 feet 8 inches
she is 5-8
she is five feet eight
she is 5 feet 8

e. 12 noon
noon
12:00 p.m.
12:00 noon

f. 8 p.m. tonight
8 P.M. tonight
8 tonight
8:00 tonight

g. 1999 A.D.
1999 AD
A.D. 1999
AD 1999

h. Number One choice
Number 1 choice
No. 1 choice
No. one choice

i. Joe Jones, 7
Joe Jones, seven
seven-year-old Joe Jones

j. the '60s
the '60's
the 60s
the 60's

k. The odds were 5-4.
The odds were five to four.
The odds were 5 to 4.
The odds were five-four.

l. The baby weighed 8 pounds, 13 ounces.
The baby weighed 8#13.
The baby weighed 8 lbs., 13 oz.
The baby weighed eight pounds, 13 ounces.
The baby weighed eight lbs., 13 oz.

m. The boy is nineteen.
The boy is 19.
The man is 19.
The man is nineteen.

n. The girl is nineteen.
The girl is 19.
The woman is 19.
The woman is nineteen.

o. I owe you three dollars.
I owe you $3.
I owe you $3.00.
I owe you 3 dollars.

p. She represents the 8th Congressional District.
She represents the Eighth Congressional District.
She represents the 8th congressional district.
She represents the eighth congressional district.

q. the 9-by-12 rug
the nine-by-12 rug
the 9 by 12 rug
the nine by 12 rug

r. Queen Elizabeth 2nd
Queen Elizabeth Two
Queen Elizabeth the Second
Queen Elizabeth II

s. $1,200,000
1.2 million dollars
1,200,000 million dollars
$1.2 million

t. Fifth Armored Division
5th Armored Division
Fifth Armored Div.
5th Armored Div.

u. from $6 to $7 million
from $6-$7 million
from $6 million to $7 million
from six to seven million dollars

v. 10 knots
10 knots per hour
ten knots
ten kph

w. Her sons are 15, 12, and seven.
Her sons are 15, 12 and 7.

x. They have 12 chairs, five tables and four lamps.
They have 12 chairs, 5 tables and 4 lamps.

y. Act 1, Scene 3
act 1, scene 3
Act One, Scene Three
Act I, Scene 3
Act I, Scene III

z. The incumbent beat King 11,101 to 9,706.
The incumbent beat King 11,101-9,706.
The incumbent beat King 11.1 thousand to 9.7 thousand.

2. Unless your instructor tells you otherwise, use the style rules given in this chapter and the AP stylebook
to circle the correct style in each of the following sets. All are first reference unless otherwise noted.

a. Go to Cumberland Avenue
Go to Cumberland Ave.

b. 123 9th St.
123 Ninth St.
123 9th Street
123 Ninth Street

c. Captain Mary Brown
Capt. Mary Brown
Mary Brown, Captain

d. Chancellor Marvin Smith
Dr. Marvin Smith, Chancellor
Chancellor Dr. Marvin Smith
Chanc. Marvin Smith

e. *(second mention)*
Chancellor Smith
Chan. Smith
Smith
Dr. Smith

f. Carol Bass, Vice-Chancellor of Student Affairs
Vice Chancellor for Student Affairs Carol Bass
Carol Bass, vice chancellor for student affairs
Carol Bass, vice-chancellor of student affairs

g. *(second mention)*
Vice Chancellor Bass
Bass
V-C of student affairs Bass

h. *(second mention)*
Attorney General Herman
Att. Gen. Herman
A.G. Herman
Herman

i. *(second mention)*
Dr. Smith
Mary Smith
Ms. Smith
Smith
Mary

j. from Jan. 22-25
from January 22 to 25
from Jan. 22 to Jan. 25
from Jan. 22 to 25

k. Marilyn Jones, dean of law
Law School Dean Marilyn Jones
Marilyn Jones, dean of the School of Law

l. the English Department
the Department of English
the English department

m. the History Department
the History department
the history department
the Department of history
the Department of History

n. Grade Point Average
GPA
grade point average
g.p.a.

o. National Organization for Women
National Organization of Women

p. His birthday is in Feb.
His birthday is in February.

q. His birthday is Feb. 8.
His birthday is February 8.
His birthday is 8 February.
His birthday is the eighth of February.

r. It is a large Corp.
It is a large corporation.
It is a large corp.
It is a large Corporation.

s. She is an executive at the Hanover Corp.
She is an executive at the Hanover Corporation.
She is an executive at the Hanover corp.
She is an executive at the Hanover corporation.

t. 35 m.p.h.
35 mph

u. Mount Everest
Mt. Everest

v. *(in a sports story)*
first base
First Base
1st base
1st Base

w. the television show "Jeopardy"
the television show Jeopardy

x. The New York Times
the New York Times
the "New York Times"

3. Unless your instructor tells you otherwise, use the style rules given in this chapter and the AP stylebook to circle the correct style in each of the following sets. All are first reference unless otherwise noted.

a. Dorothy Bowles, professor of journalism
Prof. Dorothy Bowles, journalism
Professor of Journalism Dorothy Bowles
Dorothy Bowles, prof. of journ.
Prof. Dr. Dorothy Bowles

b. *(second mention)*
Prof. Bowles
Professor Bowles
Bowles
Dr. Bowles

c. Carmen Jones, asst. prof. of history
Asst. Prof. Carmen Jones
Carmen Jones, assistant professor of history
Carmen Jones, assistant professor in history

d. 7 a.m.
7 A.M.
7:00 a.m.
7:00 A.M.

e. the Tennessee River
the Tennessee river
the Tenn. River
the Tenn. river

f. 17th Century
Seventeenth Century
17th century
seventeenth century

g. *(second mention, mid-sentence)*
Coach Hufford
coach Hufford
Coach Bonnie Hufford

h. They traveled through the West Coast states.
    They traveled through the west coast states.

i. The oil spill was along the East Coast.
    The oil spill was along the east coast.

j. Knox County District Court
    Knox County district court
    district court of Knox county

k. the Mississippi and Ohio Rivers
    the Mississippi and Ohio rivers
    the Miss. and Ohio rivers

l. He drove northwest.
    He drove Northwest.
    He drove north west.

m. Philippine islands
    Aleutian islands
    Pacific islands
    Mediterranean Islands

n. Department of Defense
    defense department
    department of defense
    Defense department

o. Western Texas
    western Texas
    W. Texas
    West Texas

p. Knox County jail
    Knox County Jail
    Knox Co. jail

q. Knoxville Fire Department
    Knoxville fire department
    Knoxville Fire Dept.

r. The town has no Fire Department.
    The town has no fire department.

    s. U.S. House of Representatives
         United States House of Representatives
         US House
         U.S. House of Reps.

    t. Gen. Colin Powell
         General Colin Powell
         general Colin Powell
         Colin Powell, General

    u. National Anthem
         National anthem
         national anthem

    v. National guard
         national guard
         National Guard

    w. Pacific Ocean
         Pacific ocean
         pacific ocean

    x. He is the Pope.
         He is the pope.
         He is the Pontiff.

    y. the State of Texas
         the state of Texas
         The State of Texas

4. Unless your instructor tells you otherwise, use the style rules given in this chapter and the AP stylebook to circle the correct style in each of the following sets. All are first reference unless otherwise noted.

    a. Tuesday at 7 p.m. in 127 University Center
         In 127 University Center Tuesday at 7 p.m.
         7 p.m. Tuesday in 127 University Center
         7 p.m. Tuesday night in University Center room 127

    b. Detroit, Mich.
         Detroit
         Detroit, MI
         Detroit, Michigan

c. El Paso, Texas
   El Paso
   El Paso, Tex.
   El Paso, TX

d. Paris, France
   Paris, Fr.
   Paris

e. Liverpool, Great Britain
   Liverpool, England
   Liverpool, United Kingdom
   Liverpool

f. San Juan, Puerto Rico
   San Juan, P.R.
   San Juan

g. Temperatures fell 5 degrees.
   Temperatures fell five degrees.
   Temperatures fell 5°.

h. *(standing alone in sentence; not a title)*
   Chief Justice of the Supreme Court
   Chief Justice of the United States
   chief justice of the United States
   chief justice of the Supreme Court

i. We will play this coming Saturday.
   We will play Saturday.
   We will play next Saturday.

j. U.S. Congress
   U.S. congress
   United States Congress
   United States' Congress
   United States congress

k. daylight-saving time
   daylight savings time
   DST
   daylight-savings time

l. 62 degrees Fahrenheit
62F.
62 Fahr.
Fahrenheit 62
F 62

m. Flags ashore sometimes fly at half-mast.
Flags ashore sometimes fly at half mast.
Flags ashore sometimes fly at half-staff.
Flags ashore sometimes fly at half staff.

n. The dentist committed suicide; he hung himself.
The dentist committed suicide; he hanged himself.
The dentist committed suicide; he was hanged.
The dentist committed suicide; he was hung.

o. hydrogen bomb
H-Bomb
H-bomb
Hydrogen Bomb

p. T-shirt
Tee-shirt
t-shirt
T shirt

q. catsup
ketchup
catchup
Ketchup

r. K Mart
K-Mart
K mart
K-mart
Kmart

s. held High Mass
held high mass
sung High Mass
celebrated high Mass

t. mid-semester
   mid-term
   mid-life
   mid-America
   mid-wife

u. 12 midnight
   12:00 midnight
   12 a.m. midnight
   12 p.m. midnight
   midnight

v. The team is ranked No. 1.
   The team is ranked number one.
   The team is ranked Number One.
   The team is ranked #1.

w. King George III
   King George 3d
   King George 3rd
   King George the Third

x. 1 1/2%
   1.5%
   1 1/2 per cent
   1.5 percent
   1.5 per cent

y. She is a pom-pom girl.
   She is a pom pom girl.
   She is a pompom girl.
   She is a pom-pon girl.

z. The Rev. James Jones
   Rev. James Jones
   Reverend James Jones
   the Rev. Mr. James Jones

Note: **Exercises 5 through 12** are based on the material on correct word usage in this chapter, as well as on the list of frequently misused words in the Appendix.

5. Mark through the incorrect choices in the following sentences.

a. [A while, awhile] before he came to the party, refreshments were served.

b. As mayor, she hoped to [affect, effect] change.

c. Because of the [adverse, averse] weather conditions, we must [altar, alter] our plans.

d. Her status as a celebrity was an [allusion, illusion].

e. It is [alright, all right] for you to paint it green.

f. My dream of becoming a film star was an [allusion, illusion].

g. She [alluded, eluded] to her past glory as an actress.

h. The fall [aggravated, irritated] his knee injury.

i. The new drug has a powerful [affect, effect], but it may not be [affective, effective] for treating cancer.

j. Has he been [appraised, apprised] of the situation?

k. The teacher's [advice, advise] to her was to study harder.

l. We mailed 150 invitations [all together, altogether].

m. Were you able to get her to [ascent, assent] to our proposal?

n. He didn't seem to understand the [affect, effect] of his actions.

o. A [burro, burrow] has sure footing on mountain trails.

p. After all the monthly bills were paid, the family had a [balance, remainder] of [fewer, less] than $50.

q. After careful consideration, I [believe, feel, think] I should accept the job offer.

r. Beef [bouillon, bullion] was used in the recipe.

s. She retired to her [birth, berth] on the train.

t. He enjoys going to the horse races, and he is a big [better, bettor].

u. She seemed reluctant to [broach, brooch] the subject with her boss.

v. His explanation sounded like [baloney, bologna] to me.

w. I don't like [baloney, bologna] sandwiches.

x. It was a [bazaar, bizarre] situation.

y. Members of labor unions voted as a [bloc, block] in the spring election.

6. Mark through the incorrect choices in the following sentences.

a. Please [boar, boor, bore] holes in this piece of lumber.

b. She could hardly catch her [breath, breathe].

c. He froze the [balance, remainder] of the meat.

d. He gave his mother a beautiful [broach, brooch] for Christmas.

e. She placed the ball [beside, besides] the tennis racket.

f. The [biannual, biennial] event is in April and October.

g. The game was canceled [because of, due to] rain.

h. The judge set his [bail, bale] at $10,000.

i. The papers must be in a [bail, bale] or the recycling plant will not accept them.

j. The room was filled with smoke, making it difficult to [breath, breathe].

k. The tennis player was a [boar, boor, bore] with his frequent complaints about the referee's calls.

l. To raise money, the church sponsored a [bazaar, bizarre].

m. We used the bucket to [bail, bale] water from the leaking boat.

n. While they were on vacation, a [burglar, robber] broke in and stole a television set.

o. This would be a good [cite, sight, site] for a picnic.

p. Although she was in her mid-30s, her [childish, childlike] mannerisms made her a popular elementary-school teacher.

q. He had thick [callouses, calluses] on his feet.

r. He was [censored, censured, censered] for his unethical behavior.

s. She learned to play [chords, cords] on the guitar.

t. The [climactic, climatic] moment was when Jim met his birth mother for the first time.

u. Some NFL players receive salaries that are not [commensurate, commiserate] with their playing abilities.

v. How do NFL salaries [compare to, compare with] those of the NBA?

w. His behavior at the party shows that he is a [callous, callus] person.

x. It was [childish, childlike] for him to pull such a stunt at a formal occasion.

y. We were unable to catch [cite, sight, site] of her in the huge crowd.

7. Mark through the incorrect choices in the following sentences.

a. It was a [cement, concrete] driveway.

b. The tent was made of [canvas, canvass].

c. The truck [collided with, hit] a fence.

d. They went to the [cemetary, cemetery] to visit the grave site.

e. To [censor, censure, censer] in that manner was a violation of the First Amendment, the court ruled.

f. We admired the murals on the walls of the [capital, capitol].

g. He seemed embarrassed by her [complement, compliment].

h. When editing copy without a computer, use a [carat, caret] to show insertions.

i. I think he is too [complacent, complaisant] to be the team leader.

j. In his eagerness to please everyone, he is [reluctant, reticent] to make decisions.

k. How many sources did you [cite, sight, site] in your term paper?

l. While in the army, he was assigned to [calvary, cavalry] duty

m. We received [complementary, complimentary] tickets to the play.

n. This policy provides [comprehensible, comprehensive] coverage.

o. Although the foreign student had an excellent grasp of formal English, she sometimes did not understand the [connotation, denotation] of words.

p. Mammals, reptiles and birds [compose, comprise] the zoo.

q. The local city [council, counsel] meets every week.

r. He [counciled, counseled] the students.

s. The red tie is a good [complement, compliment] to your new suit.

t. Ask the treasurer to [disburse, dispense, disperse] payment for these bills.

u. Was she [conscience, conscious] after the accident?

v. A synonym for intermittent is [continual, continuous].

w. His story did not seem [creditable, credible, credulous] to me.

x. Because the judge seemed biased, I thought that she would not give a(n) [disinterested, uninterested] decision.

y. Salmon [croquet, croquette, coquette] was the main dish.

z. Don't talk; it might [detract, distract] the golfer.

8. Mark through the incorrect choices in the following sentences.

a. I asked the real estate agent whether she [felt, thought] the property would [deprecate, depreciate] during the next two years.

b. In the movie two men fought a [dual, duel].

c. She hit her attacker with a [cue, queue].

d. We spent a wonderful vacation in [Cypress, Cyprus].

e. The scientist spent much of his career trying to [disapprove, disprove] Einstein's theory.

f. The room has a [distinctive, distinguished] odor.

g. The [desert, dessert] was a perfect [complement, compliment] to the meal.

h. The car has [dual, duel] mufflers.

i. He hurled [epithets, epitaphs] at his opponent.

j. The new law makes a jail term mandatory for [drunk, drunken] drivers.

k. She always feels [eager, anxious] on the night before a big test.

l. The scene [evoked, invoked] memories of his boyhood home.

m. [Fliers, Flyers] were placed throughout the campus to announce the meeting.

n. After many years as a successful newspaper reporter, he became a [flack, flak] for a politician.

o. In his dealings with children in the neighborhood, he was an [erasable, irascible] old man.

p. The mother told her child to be careful at summer camp, [especially, specially] when swimming.

q. They chose this camp [especially, specially] for its musical activities.

r. As part of her physical training program, she walked at least a mile [farther, further] each week.

s. He [figuratively, literally] hit the ceiling when he heard about the ruling.

t. He [flaunted, flouted] his wealth.

u. It was a [flagrant, fragrant] foul, but the referee did not see it.

v. Please cook some [flounder, founder].

w. Please study the matter [farther, further] before deciding what to do.

x. Two [fewer, less] candidates filed for office this year.

y. His colleagues did not think his [factious, factitious, facetious] remarks were amusing.

9. Mark through the incorrect choices in the following sentences.

   a. His presence seemed to [ferment, foment] trouble.

   b. Jim is her [fiance, fiancee].

   c. The 400-pound wrestler was a [forbidding, foreboding] opponent.

   d. To accomplish the task on time, workers had to [forego, forgo] vacations.

   e. He was a [gorilla, guerrilla] in Nicaragua.

   f. The reporter became [nauseated, nauseous] when he saw the [grisly, gristly, grizzly] crime scene.

   g. [Hopefully, I hope] it will not rain on July 4.

   h. If your mother marries my father, we will become [half sisters, stepsisters].

   i. He was an [inapt, inept] carpenter.

   j. The Bible is a [holey, holy] book.

   k. The city wanted to erect a [historic, historical] marker at the site.

   l. The commander ordered that all flags on the [naval, navel] fleet should fly at [half-mast, half-staff].

   m. The temperature today will be [lower, cooler] than yesterday.

   n. After the discussion, the marriage [counselor, councilor] had a better [incite, insight] into the couple's problems.

   o. Grease is [insoluble, insolvable, insolvent] in water.

   p. Did you [elicit, illicit] a promise from the child?

   q. Have you decided [if, whether] you will attend this university?

   r. He was [impassable, impassible] during the funeral.

   s. She was [incredible, incredulous] at the sales representative's claims for the product.

   t. This was the [cite, site] of a World War II [interment, internment] camp.

u. You should be polite to John, [irregardless, irrespective] of your dislike for him.

v. It was an [ingenious, ingenuous] solution to the problem, and she wondered why no one had tried it earlier.

w. The [eminent, imminent] scientist was born in Germany but [emigrated, immigrated] to the United States.

x. He brought [elicit, illicit] drugs into the country.

y. The teachers did everything they could to [insure, ensure] the students' safety.

10. Mark through the incorrect choices in the following sentences.

a. The doctors had no explanation for the higher [incidence, incidents] of cancer in that county.

b. The family [emigrated, immigrated] to the United States in 1945.

c. The County Commission has the power to [levee, levy] property taxes.

d. The paint had the [affect, effect] of [lightening, lightning] the wood.

e. He was [judicial, judicious] in his handling of money.

f. I don't like him because he is a [leach, leech].

g. I am [loath, loathe] to go to the dentist.

h. The convicted drug lord told authorities that he simply was involved in (interstate, intrastate) commerce along the Canadian border.

i. When you talked to him, did you mean to [imply, infer] that you were unhappy?

j. The sky is dark; it looks [like, as though] it will rain.

k. Newspaper advertising [linage, lineage] has increased 10 percent this year.

l. He [lay, lain, layed] in the sun too long.

m. The recipe called for [leaks, leeks].

n. He was selected parade [marshal, marshall].

o. Newspapers are an example of (a) [mass media, mass medium].

p. The challenger was able to [marshal, marshall] his strength to defeat the reigning champion.

q. [May be, Maybe] she will run for office next year.

r. The car [motor, engine] overheated.

s. The commander asked that someone volunteer for the [odious, odorous] duty.

t. The experienced driver won the race with a [masterful, masterly] display of racing ability.

u. After taxes, her salary increase was [negligent, negligible].

v. He became [nauseated, nauseous] on the plane.

w. The parents were [negligent, negligible] in their treatment of the child.

x. [More than, Over] 2,000 attended the performance.

y. He could not get the company to honor the [oral, verbal] promises made by the sales clerk. Only written warranties were valid.

11. Mark through the incorrect choices in the following sentences.

a. An artist uses a [palate, palette, pallet].

b. He bit into the pizza, burning his [palate, palette, pallet].

c. She hoped to [parlay, parley] his fame into fortune.

d. The [burglar, robber] gained entry to her home on the [pretense, pretext] of coming there to repair the telephone.

e. The district attorney will [persecute, prosecute] the murder suspect.

f. The [councilor, counselor] was able to [persuade, convince] the students that a college education is important.

g. The senior class will [proceed, precede] the junior class.

h. He sent his son into town to [pedal, petal, peddle] the wooden toys.

i. She wanted to uphold the [principal, principle] of equality although it would cost her company more money.

j. He wore a [pendant, pendent].

k. I was flattered when the boss asked for my [perspective, prospective] of the situation.

l. My bicycle [peddle, petal, pedal] is broken.

m. Students who engage in [prescribed, proscribed] behavior will be expelled from this university.

n. The [principal, principle] shareholder spoke at the annual meeting.

o. The child slept on a [palate, palette, pallet].

p. The company announced its [perspective, prospective] earnings at the annual meeting today.

q. The fancy car was a [perquisite, prerequisite] that came with his new position at the company.

r. The guest speaker climbed the stairs to the [podium, lectern] and placed her notes on the [podium, lectern].

s. The doctor [prescribed, proscribed] medicine for my illness, but she seemed [quiet, quite] [reluctant, reticent] to do so.

t. The politician was [reluctant, reticent] during the interview.

u. We will finish the project [irregardless, regardless] of our financial situation.

v. You have made some serious errors, but I think that the situation is [remediable, remedial].

w. He is a [reckless, wreckless] driver.

x. Although the pay was good, the work was [seasonable, seasonal], and he wanted to work throughout the year.

y. The baker wanted the dough to [raise, rise].

12. Mark through the incorrect choices in the following sentences.

   a. The veterinarian suggested that the dog be [spade, spayed].

   b. The barber used a [strap, strop] to sharpen the razor.

   c. She ordered new [stationary, stationery] for the company.

   d. Magicians engage in [sleight, slight] of hand.

   e. Police erected a [stationary, stationery] barrier.

   f. She is a [tackful, tactful] person.

   g. It was a [tenant, tenet] that guided him in his business dealings.

   h. It was a [tort, torte] that could have been avoided with careful copy editing.

   i. Stained-glass windows are [transparent, translucent].

   j. She wore a [shear, sheer] blouse.

   k. Bob Hope is a [trooper, trouper].

   l. She hoped to join the state highway patrol as a [trooper, trouper].

   m. Here is the book [which, that] she ordered.

   n. This version of the computer program will [supercede, supersede] the one issued two years ago.

   o. Unexpected expenses will [wreak, wreck] havoc on my budget.

   p. Her argument was [tortuous, torturous].

   q. He used a special batter to make shrimp [tempura, tempra].

   r. He said it was a [venal, venial] sin.

   s. It is a [viral, virile] disease.

   t. Having gone without food for two days, the hunters had [veracious, voracious] appetites.

   u. He said he would [wangle, wrangle] an invitation.

   v. Let's not [wangle, wrangle] about this matter.

   w. The recipe called for three egg [yokes, yolks].

The White Rabbit put on his spectacles. "Where should I begin, please, your majesty?" he asked. "Begin at the beginning," the King said, very gravely, "and go on till you come to the end; then stop."

—*Lewis Carroll,* Alice in Wonderland

Editing Stories

ONCE **copy editors** understand their role in the newsroom, their audiences, the correct use of grammar and punctuation, style conventions, proper word usage and fact-checking procedures, they may be ready to begin the daunting task of improving the story on the computer screen before them. All writers, no matter the medium (books, newspapers, magazines, the Internet) and regardless of the level of their experience, require a good editor. Rarely does a piece of copy get set into type without being subjected to the skills of a copy editor. At the best-edited publications, policy demands that at least two copy editors examine each piece of copy.

When editing a story, copy editors not only must remember to pay attention to spelling, grammar, punctuation and style; they must also remind themselves of basic reporting techniques, such as

- is the story balanced, accurate and fair

- are there any legal or ethical implications

- is the lead appropriate and not buried later in the story

- does the story contain the essence of the event or issue and does it leave information holes or gaps

- has the writer developed the story structure properly

- does the reporter understand numbers or statistics, attribute information and use direct quotations correctly

- does the story contain redundancies or superfluous information

Editing leads

Reporters learn to write leads in one of several formats. Hard-news leads take a different form, for example, than feature or delayed leads. It is the copy editor's role to understand the difference and to balance the need for reader understanding with the writing style of the reporter. Most hard-news leads are written on the basis of a formula that incorporates the five W's and an H (who, what, when, where, why and how). Reporters learn to use the answers to some combination of these elements when crafting a hard-news or direct lead.

News judgment comes directly into play when making the decision to write these leads. For example, given the following set of facts, which of the six lead elements are the most important, and which should be included in the lead?

Facts for lead:

1. At a city council meeting tonight (Tuesday) in San Diego, council members voted unanimously to put a bond issue on next month's election ballot.

2. The bond issue will ask voters for authority to sell $33 million in bonds.

3. Proceeds from the bonds would be used to finance a performing arts complex for San Diego. Plans reviewed by the city council depict an impressive facility with two theaters, one seating 2,600 people and the other 400. Everyone is excited about the prospect for such a complex.

4. The mayor, a woman named Frances Howard, said following the council's vote: "I've lived in San Diego all my life, and this is the most exciting civic opportunity I've seen. If the good citizens of San Diego will build this center, we will become known far and wide as the biggest supporters of the arts in the state."

To determine the relative importance of the six lead elements, the reporter and the editor must bring the news values mentioned in Chapter 1 to bear: timeliness, proximity, prominence, unusualness, human interest, conflict. In this set of facts, two time elements should be considered: first is that the city council meeting was tonight (Tuesday night, if writing for a morning newspaper), and second is that the bond issue will be placed on next month's ballot. Which is more important? In this case, voters probably would want to know more about the future action (the ballot issue *next month*) than the past action (council meeting *Tuesday night*). The WHEN question, then, has just been answered and should be included in the lead.

The WHO answer could be both the city council, which took the action, and the voters, who will be affected by the action. Most often the people affected by the action should be included in the lead. The WHAT is the placing of the $33 million bond issue on the ballot. The WHERE question is not relevant for this lead, as no location is included in the set of facts and the editor assumes the story is local. The WHY is to finance a new performing arts complex. The answer to the HOW question, not included in this set of facts, is usually left for later in the story. The answers to both the WHAT and WHY questions are significant for the lead because they have an impact on readers.

Part of the direct-lead writing formula also includes using only a few of the news elements in the lead to keep it to one sentence and making certain that the number of words in the sentence is between 25 and 35. With all these rules in mind, the lead might be written this way:

```
San Diego voters will be asked next month to approve a
$33 million bond issue to build a 3,000-seat performing
arts complex.
```

If the reporter or the editor wanted to add a little color to this direct, hard-news lead, the lead could be written this way:

```
San Diego voters will be asked next month to approve a
$33 million bond issue to build a 3,000-seat performing
arts complex, which Mayor Frances Howard said could make
San Diego residents known as "the biggest supporters of
the arts in the state."
```

For a copy editor, the task is to balance the desire to satisfy the reader's need for clear and concise information with the reporter's right to write the story in a distinct, personal style. As mentioned earlier, the style for the lead also depends on the nature of the story. If the reporter is writing a feature story or an in-depth analysis of a major issue, the reporter should be allowed more freedom to pursue an individual style. The key is to make sure the copy is understandable to busy readers. Often copy editors learn the balancing act through day-in-and-day-out interaction with the reporting staff and with the news.

Including essential information

After copy editors make certain the lead is the best it can be, they next turn to the essence of the rest of the story and look for "holes" that need to be filled in for the reader, as well as make certain that numbers are accurate, that words are not misused and that redundancies are avoided. The copy editor should always ask: Is all the essential information included in this story? Does the story make sense? The copy editor should be able to spot whether a paragraph of vital background information is missing, or whether the first name of a source was left out, or whether too much jargon is left in.

Accuracy in numbers

Copy editors are charged with ensuring that all the numbers in a story make sense. So, besides a computer and a dictionary, the editor's tool kit should include a calculator. Making numbers easy to understand is part of the editor's job. For example, a city budget in the millions of dollars means little to readers. The story should provide a breakdown by budgetary categories and should report percentages allocated for major items. In reporting sources of revenue for the budget, the story should show how these numbers affect individual residents: How much are property taxes increasing? What is the percentage of increase? Based on these figures, the story should report the dollar increase for property taxes on the average-priced home in the community. Are automobile registration fees increasing? If so, how much?

Stories often need to report raw numbers, but those numbers will be more easily understood if the percentage of increase or decrease is also reported. Percentages are derived this way:

$$\% \text{ increase or decrease} = \frac{\text{New figure} - \text{Original figure}}{\text{Original figure}}$$

For example, if enrollment in the school district was 30,200 students last year and is 33,100 students this year, enrollment has increased 9.6 percent:

$$\frac{33,100 - 30,200}{30,200} = \frac{2,900}{30,200} = .0960 = 9.6\%$$

Another example: If the number of burglaries decreased this year from 3,196 to 3,005, the percentage of decline is 5.97 (which may be rounded off to 6 percent):

$$\frac{3,005 - 3,196}{3,196} = \frac{-191}{3,196} = -.0597 = -5.97\%$$

Remember, the percentage of change is based upon the original number and the change from the original number.

Percent and *percentage points* do not mean the same thing. If interest rates increase from 10 percent to 12 percent, they have increased 2 percentage points, but it is an increase of 20 percent:

$$\frac{12 - 10}{10} = \frac{2}{10} = 20\%$$

Copy editors should be especially alert in handling stories that include ages, box scores, infographics, results of opinion polls and information about property taxes.

▶ **Ages.** Use common sense in editing stories that include a person's date of birth, dates of accomplishments and ages. An alert copy editor should spot the inconsistencies, for example, in an obituary published in 1999 that reports the age of the deceased as 67 if the birthdate is listed as 1922 or that reports this person graduated from a university in 1932. Was he 77 when he died, or was he born in 1932? Did he graduate from the university at age 10, or is the graduation date a typographical error?

▶ **Box scores.** Add the number of points scored by each player to be sure that the totals for each team equal the final score.

▶ **Informational graphics.** Check the numbers. Do they add to the total reported in the graphic? Check that the percentages add to 100. If they don't, an explanation should be included in the graphic.

▶ **Property taxes.** Property taxes are expressed as mill levies. A *mill* is 0.1 cent (one-tenth of a cent, or one-thousandth of a dollar), and the *mill levy* for a community is generally expressed as the number of cents or dollars for each $100 in assessed valuation. Stories about property taxes should include an example of how much tax will be levied on a representative home in the community. For example, if the mill levy is 1.50, property owners will pay 1.5 cents tax for each $1 of assessed value or $1.50 for each $100 of assessed value or $15 for each $1,000. For a home assessed at $50,000 (note this is assessed value, not market value), the tax would be $750 ($15 × 50). If several governmental units within the community have taxing power, a story about the city tax rate should not mislead readers into thinking that this will be their total property tax bill. The story should include the rates that other governmental units have levied or note that the budget is not complete and thus the mill levy has not been determined.

Reporting survey results

A story based on a public-opinion survey should provide information that helps readers understand how to interpret the poll results correctly. Too often results from a hastily conducted survey at a shopping mall are presented in the same manner as polls conducted by scientific norms. This doesn't mean that person-on-the-street polls lack entertainment value, but readers should be told the difference.

When handling a story reporting that 53 percent of the people support one candidate for governor and 47 percent support another candidate, a copy editor should insist that the story answer these questions:

■ Who conducted the survey? (Was it a company that specializes in scientific polling, campaign workers, reporters?)

■ Who paid for the survey? (Did a news organization or some other disinterested party hire a survey-research firm, or did one of the candidates pay for it?)

■ Who was interviewed for the survey? (Respondents who aren't eligible to vote in the gubernatorial election—such as out-of-state tourists or minors—produce meaningless results for this survey.)

- How were people selected to be interviewed? (Was it a random sample? Did people from all sections of the state have an equal chance of being selected? Did the sample reflect the state's population according to demographic factors, such as race and ethnicity, gender, age, religious affiliation and occupation?)

- What was the margin of sampling error for this particular survey? (In a scientific survey, the size of the sample influences the margin of error. In this example of 53 percent versus 47 percent, a 3 percent margin of error would mean that one candidate could have as much as 56 percent or as little as 50 percent support, and the other candidate's support could range from 44 percent to 50 percent. In this case, the race is too close to call.

- How was the survey conducted? (By telephone? In private interviews? Or did respondents answer in the presence of co-workers, friends or other people?)

- When was the poll conducted? (In a political campaign, events can cause opinions to change quickly. The story should indicate whether such an event happened between the time the survey was conducted and its results were published.)

- What questions were asked during interviews, and what was the order of questions? (Unless the wording is controversial or central to issues in the campaign, the exact text does not have to be included in the story, but copy editors should be sensitive to the potential for bias.)

Accuracy in word usage

The Appendix lists words that often are misused in both written and spoken English. A few are homonyms that are unlikely to be confused except by people uneducated in the language. Others are word substitutions that literate people commonly but erroneously make. A few of these words have fallen into common misusage to the extent that even the experts debate the merits of maintaining the original distinctions. To professional writers and editors who want to say exactly and concisely what they mean, the distinctions are important.

Eliminating redundancies

Journalistic editing often requires that sentences and paragraphs be short and concise, using as few words as possible to tell the story because space (newshole) is at a premium. One way to achieve conciseness is to make each word meaningful and avoid jargon and redundancies. In his book *The Word: An Associated Press Guide to Good News Writing*, Rene Cappon said this:

> To say things clearly and concisely takes skill and, above all, vigilance. Bloated language is all around us. Government pumps gaseous bureaucratese into the environment. Other institutions, corporate headquarters, the professions and the social sciences diligently contribute to the effusion of jargon.

He goes on to illustrate his point by suggesting that a person who *resigned her position in order to replenish her financial resources* more appropriately *quit to make more money*, or that the Air Force's struggling to *minimize the aircraft's engine capability problems* could be put more concisely as struggling to *fix the plane's engine*.

Alert copy editors will spot the most frequently used redundancies. Here is a list published by the Minnesota Newspaper Association:

absolutely necessary	enclosed you will find	redo again
advance planning	fall down	refer back
ask the question	first and foremost	right and proper
assemble together	friend of mine	rise up
at a later day	gathered together	rules and regulations
attached hereto	honest truth	send in
at the present time	important essentials	small in size
canceled out	necessary requirements	still remain
carbon copy	open up	temporarily suspended
city of Chicago	other alternative	totally unnecessary
close proximity	patently obvious	true facts
consensus of opinion	plain and simple	various and sundry
continue on	postpone until later	
each and every	reasonable and fair	

Editing story structure

The most often used news story structure remains the inverted pyramid, which asks the reporter to assemble the factual information for the story in descending order of importance or significance. Unlike the telling of a fairy tale, for example, the news story begins with the climax or the most important fact, then compiles the rest of the information in a way that would allow the story to be trimmed from the bottom. In addition, an inverted pyramid story includes within the first three or four paragraphs a direct quotation from one of the sources in the story.

Here is a classic example of the inverted pyramid structure:

```
WASHINGTON—A plastic surgeon who had been jailed for more than
two years for refusing to let her daughter visit the girl's
father was released yesterday on a judge's orders.
```

The lead answers the WHO, WHAT and WHEN questions, often considered the most significant in a hard-news story, and is 29 words long.

```
Dr. Elizabeth Morgan emerged from jail wearing a prison jumpsuit
and carrying a dozen yellow roses.
    "I feel very happy and very grateful to everyone who has
helped me," she said. "I will probably cry when I say this, but
I want to thank God for every angel on Earth."
```

The third paragraph includes the first direct quotation.

```
She said she spent her 760 days behind bars thinking of "my
daughter and the people I love."
    Morgan's release was ordered by District of Columbia Superior
Court Judge Geoffrey Alprin—as directed by the district's Court
of Appeals under a law passed by Congress and signed by
President Bush last week.
```

This paragraph answers one of the WHY questions but is less important than the WHO, WHAT or WHEN and thus comes later in the inverted pyramid.

```
Morgan, 41, went to jail voluntarily in August 1987 on civil
contempt charges after refusing to produce the couple's 7-year-
old daughter, Hilary, for court-ordered visits with the girl's
father, Dr. Eric Foretich, Morgan's former husband.
```

```
     The case has received international attention and has been
adopted by a number of groups, including the National
Organization for Women, as a classic example of a mother
fighting for her child's mental and emotional well-being against
an unresponsive judiciary.
     Morgan has alleged that Foretich sexually abused the child;
Foretich has consistently denied the charges. Morgan is
Foretich's third wife. His second wife has also accused him of
sexual abuse of their daughter, Heather, 9. Foretich denies
those charges as well, and has charged that the two women have
acted in collusion.
```

These three paragraphs include background and chronology of the story, answering the HOW question and providing context and detail that can be placed after the hard-news elements.

Using transitions

Although many other forms of writing can be found within the print media, including storytelling and use of anecdotes, the inverted pyramid is still used at most newspapers as a way to structure a hard-news story. Copy editors need to be alert to the form of newstelling at their newspaper or magazine. But it is the copy editor's job to ensure that the story flows logically from one paragraph to the next, using good transitions that move the reader through the story chronologically or that take readers on a journey in search of a solution to a particular problem or puzzle.

Transitional techniques—including chronology, journey and problem solving—move readers along in this story by Don Williams, a staff writer for the Knoxville (Tenn.) News-Sentinel. The story, published on the 20th anniversary of the first human space flight to the moon, develops a local angle on that momentous event.

```
     Joan Trolinger waits for a rocket engine to speak thunder and
roll a brand new cloud into the sky.
     Few rocket tests are conducted here at the Redstone Arsenal,
where Wernher Von Braun brought a ragtag band of scientists and
a few leftover German V-2 rockets after World War II and
launched America toward the stars.
     Ever since Trolinger was a child she wanted to be part of
that movement into space, a movement rife with glamor, but also
with tedium and terror, as she would discover.
     Growing up in Morristown, the daughter of Jim and Sarah Gose,
she was 6 years old when she watched Neil Armstrong take his
small step/giant leap onto the moon.
     Later she made spacesuits for her dolls and suspended rocket
models from her ceiling. Children were doing much the same thing
throughout America.
     These days, at 26, Trolinger drives daily past real rockets
on display in Huntsville—rockets named for gods—Jupiter, Atlas,
Titan, Saturn.
     Trolinger still has a model of the Starship Enterprise
hanging from her ceiling, but her interest in space has matured.
```

The story continues, describing Trolinger's path to becoming a rocket engineer and working in the space program on the specific problem assigned to her: the space shuttle rocket nozzle, composed of hundreds of tubes, side by side. Icy cold liquid hydrogen is pumped through the nozzle so it can withstand the inferno it is built to control.

In addition to using chronology, journey and problem solving to move a story along, a writer can achieve continuity by

■ repeating a key word of the preceding paragraph

■ using a synonym to refer to a key word in the preceding paragraph

■ referring to a fact or idea in the preceding paragraph

■ elaborating details in logical sequence

■ using words and phrases as transitional devices

The first several paragraphs of this news story by Eric Vreeland of the Knoxville News-Sentinel staff illustrate the first three methods of achieving transition:

> The Knoxville Food Policy **Council** last week waded into the fray over where to locate a farmers' **market**. The **council** lobbied Gov. Ned McWherter to pick Knox County over Sevierville or White Pine.
>
> However, the **council** added a new wrinkle—advocating that, regardless of where the main **market** is built, **inner-city** Knoxville should be developed as a retail satellite **market**.
>
> The idea is that poor **inner-city** residents suffer by not having adequate food outlets near them. Since 1979, eight super-**markets** and about 30 independent grocers have closed in the **inner city**, says Bill **Powell**, a staff member with the **council**.
>
> **Powell** is a Mechanicsville resident and die-hard historical preservationist. He thinks he has the perfect candidate in mind for housing that retail **market**: the Western Avenue Market.

The technique of elaborating details in logical sequence was also evident in the remainder of the story as the reporter described the details of Powell's proposal for refurbishing and promoting the old market.

Writers can use a variety of words and phrases as transitional devices:

■ to show time: *then, meanwhile, shortly, thereafter, now, later, soon, all this time, formerly, previously, at last, finally*

■ to cite examples: *for instance, thus, for example, to illustrate, an illustration*

■ to indicate emphasis: *indeed, moreover, in particular, especially, in addition to, similarly, furthermore*

■ to show change of viewpoint: *however, but, nevertheless, of course, also, seriously, in another way, in a lighter view, in addition, in general, on the other hand*

Handling quotations

Careless handling of attribution in quotations can result in cluttered, ambiguous and awkward sentences.

One guideline is to grammatically join a direct quotation to the speaker. Don't make the reader guess about the source of the quotation:

> *Wrong:* Jones praised the workers. "You have exceeded our expectations, and I plan to give everyone a party."

Right: "You have exceeded our expectations, and I plan to give everyone a party," Jones said.

Attribution is important, but it can be overdone. A continuous quotation needs only one attribution, after the first break in the first sentence or at the end of the first sentence:

Wrong: "Our quota was 10,000 units," Jones said. "This month the company produced 50,000 widgets," he continued. "I plan to give everyone a party," he added.

Right: "Our quota was 10,000 units," Jones said. "This month the company produced 50,000 widgets. I plan to give everyone a party."

When two or more sentences of direct quotation run continuously in a paragraph, the speaker should be identified in the first sentence. Don't make the reader wonder who is talking. In the preceding example, the attribution is placed after the first sentence instead of at the end of the three-sentence paragraph. Quote blocks ordinarily shouldn't run more than two paragraphs; quote blocks should be separated by a transition.

What the speaker said is generally more interesting and important than who said it, so put the quotation first, followed by the attribution:

Wrong: Jones said, "I plan to give everyone a party. Our quota was 10,000 units. This month the company produced 50,000 widgets."

Right: "I plan to give everyone a party," Jones said. "Our quota was 10,000 units. This month the company produced 50,000 widgets."

This rule cannot be followed if a second speaker is quoted, because readers will be misled into thinking that the original speaker is continuing:

Wrong: "I plan to give everyone a party," Jones said. "Our quota was 10,000 units. This month the company produced 50,000 widgets."

"I wish the company would give everyone a pay increase instead of a party," Joe Smith, president of the union, said.

Right: "I plan to give everyone a party," Jones said. "Our quota was 10,000 units. This month the company produced 50,000 widgets."

Joe Smith, president of the union, said, "I wish the company would give everyone a pay increase instead of a party."

Start a new paragraph when a different speaker is quoted, as in the previous example. Direct quotations from two speakers should not be included in the same paragraph, even if the quotations are extremely brief.

Start the paragraph with the direct quotation; do not bury it within the paragraph. Inexperienced reporters sometimes write in *stutter* quotes; that is, they paraphrase what the speaker said and then use a direct quotation that says the same thing:

Wrong: Jones said that the workers exceeded their quota this month and had earned a party. "Our quota was 10,000 units," Jones said. "This month the company produced 50,000 widgets. I plan to give everyone a party."

Right: "I plan to give everyone a party," Jones said.
"Our quota was 10,000 units. This month the company produced
50,000 widgets."

Rarely is it necessary to tell the reader what question was asked. The question generally is obvious from the phrasing of the answer in either a direct or an indirect quotation:

Wrong: When asked about the company's production this month
and whether workers would be rewarded, Jones said, "I plan to
give everyone a party. Our quota was 10,000 units. This month
the company produced 50,000 widgets."

Just give the quotation.

In general, avoid fragmentary quotes. If a speaker's words are clear and concise, favor the full quotation. If cumbersome language can be paraphrased fairly, use an indirect construction, reserving direct quotations for sensitive or controversial passages that must be identified specifically as coming from the speaker. Unless a particular word or phrase has special significance or is used in an unusual or colorful sense, do not enclose it in quotation marks as a partial quotation:

Weak use of partial quotes: To conserve energy, Americans
began "turning off" lights and "turning down" thermostats,
the official said.

Good use of partial quotes: Referring to his quick pitching style,
the major leaguer said he pitched "like my hair was on fire."

Punctuate direct quotations correctly. Refer to the AP stylebook, a grammar handbook or Chapter 2 for rules on punctuating direct quotations.

Should a reporter or an editor correct grammatical errors in direct quotations? Many newspapers have the policy of making such corrections, unless, of course, the source's speech patterns are important to the story. The AP stylebook, however, notes that quotations should never be altered even to correct minor grammatical errors or word usage. AP style is to use ellipses to remove casual or minor slips of the tongue but only with extreme caution. AP recommends that if journalists have a question about a quote, either do not use it or ask the speaker for clarification.

Do not routinely use abnormal spellings, such as *gonna,* in attempts to convey regional dialects or mispronunciations. Such spellings are appropriate, however, when they are relevant or help to convey a desired effect in a feature story.

Space limitations usually preclude extensive use of direct quotations from an interview or speech. However, reporters should paraphrase and use sufficient background information to preserve the context of direct quotations, especially startling remarks. It isn't always possible for editors to detect out-of-context quotations that distort the speaker's meaning, but editors should question reporters about context when especially surprising or strong quotations are used. In addition, the manner of delivery is sometimes part of the context. Reporting a smile or a deprecatory gesture may be as important as conveying the words themselves.

Copy editors should pay careful attention to verbs of attribution. *Said* is the most common verb of attribution and usually the most appropriate. But reporters, in their reluctance to repeat *said,* often resort to other verbs of attribution. Note that terms such as *pointed out, noted* and *claimed* are not synonymous with *said* and convey editorial opinion. *Stated* and *declared* are too stilted for informal speech.

Pointed out and *noted* should be reserved for attribution when the speaker said something that is a fact: "'New York City is the largest city in the United States,' she *noted.*" It would be incorrect to use *pointed out* or *noted* as the verb of attribution if the speaker said, "New York City is the best city in the United States," because that statement is arguable, not generally accepted as fact. *Claimed* as a verb of attribution connotes doubt of the speaker's credibility. Reserve *claimed* for an assertion of legal rights by the speaker: "'Roger is innocent of the crime,' he *claimed.*" Or, "He *claimed* that the property belonged to him."

Verbs that describe the speaker's tone or mood more specifically than *said* may be used: "'The house is on fire,' he *yelled.*" "'I wouldn't do that for all the money in the world,' she *snapped.*" "'I love you,' she *whispered.*" But use such verbs accurately. A copy editor should question a reporter who has someone whispering that the house is on fire or hissing a greeting or groaning a profession of love.

Remember, reporters can report what sources said, not what they thought or believed or felt. Reporters aren't mind readers. They know only what the source said or did:

Wrong: The convicted murderer felt remorse.

Right: The convicted murderer said he felt remorse.

Another way to handle this idea would be to describe the convicted murderer's actions or comments that would indicate a feeling of remorse.

At his sentencing hearing, the convicted murderer sobbed as he listened to a mother describe one of his victims.

Shortening stories

Tight, fast-paced writing characterizes both the print and online versions of most publications today. Hurried readers, perhaps on the verge of information overload, want more information than broadcast newscasts typically provide, but they want it in concise packages. USA Today set the standard in this regard for newspapers, using short news stories and high-impact graphics. Online news sites demand brevity and conciseness because long passages download slowly and are tedious to read on a computer screen. An order to cut two or three inches from an already short 10-inch story is not uncommon on copy desks today. Editing stories for online publication will be discussed in a later segment of this chapter.

Estimating story length

Before copy editors begin cutting a story to fit a desired length for layout purposes, they must first estimate its current length. In most modern newsrooms, or modern public-relations firms, computers are programmed to provide story length with a simple keyboard or menu command. Programs vary from publication to publication because the width of standard columns varies from publication to publication and within single publications. Stories are measured in column inches; thus, wide columns require more copy to fill a space one column wide and one inch deep than do narrower columns.

Copy editors working without the copy-fitting aid of a computer can determine copy length by measuring at random several inch-long samples set in the desired column width and then counting the number of words in each sample. Averaging these word-count samples gives a fairly accurate idea of the number of words in a column inch of body copy. For layout purposes the editors divide this average into the total number of words in a story to derive an estimated length for that particular story.

Editing with precision

The reduction of story length generally falls within three broad categories: (1) trimming, a tightening of the story; (2) boiling, a more drastic process of paring most of the sentences and sacrificing minor facts; and (3) cutting, which eliminates all but the most important facts. Copy editors should be careful when reducing any story's length to ensure that elimination of facts or descriptions does not leave readers with a false or misleading impression.

▶**Trimming.** A mark of good writing is economy of language. This maxim is most eloquently stated in *Elements of Style* by William Strunk and E.B. White:

> Vigorous writing is concise. A sentence should contain no unnecessary words, a paragraph no unnecessary sentences, for the same reason that a drawing should contain no unnecessary parts. This requires not that a writer make all his sentences short, or that he avoid all detail and treat his subject only in outline, but that every word tell.

The duty of the copy editor is to delete all words and phrases that do not contribute to the clarity and conciseness of the news story. A carelessly written story must be pulled together to be compact and readable. By deleting nonessentials, the copy editor artfully turns an overwritten piece into a story with impact.

Strong writing depends on nouns and verbs. Deleting unnecessary adjectives and avoiding redundancies can help strengthen the story's message.

▶**Boiling.** In boiling a story with more than one angle, copy editors may be forced to remove one or more angles completely and to concentrate on developing the remaining angles fully. When a story presents several sides of an issue, however, all sides must be represented fairly.

An informational graphic might offer another possibility for copy editors faced with the need to eliminate one or more angles from a story. Consider whether a graph, chart, map or other graphic device might convey part of the story effectively and concisely. Be sure to coordinate such a move with personnel responsible for laying out the page and for executing graphics. A graphic approach to reducing copy length requires time and planning. It isn't a deadline-time option. Informational graphics are covered in Chapter 10.

▶**Cutting.** Most of the time, stories are cut because they need to fit a specified space, usually determined by a layout editor. Because surveys have shown that readers prefer short news stories and because the space devoted to news is limited, today's copy editors are often asked to cut a few long stories to accommodate more short ones.

When cutting a story, the copy editor should try to preserve the essential facts and enough detail to answer the reader's pressing questions. The copy editor should never assume that a story can be chopped off anywhere; cutting a story requires a great deal of skill. The broad outline of the story should be preserved when the story is not written in the routine inverted pyramid style. The flavor or tone of the story should be maintained.

After the copy editor completes the cuts, he or she should read the new version with care, making certain that transitions are clear and the copy flows past the cuts. For routine stories written in the inverted pyramid style, chopping the story from the bottom up is usually the easiest and quickest way to get the desired length.

However, bad editing can result. The copy editor must make sure no news story ends with a line like this: "In other action, the council decided …"

Copy editors must use common sense, as well as good judgment, in cutting stories for publication.

Editing news-service copy

In this age of mass-media marketing, editors of print media continually try to determine "what sells." That is to say, editors base their judgments about what kinds of content to publish on many factors, including results of reader surveys, demographic profiles of readers and potential readers and desires of advertisers.

Although the percentages vary from city to city, most research indicates that readers of daily newspapers want a variety of news topics from a variety of geographic locations. Some readers may be highly interested in news about transportation, science and education; others may be highly interested in news about politics, sports and business. Some read local news with vigor. Others prefer national and international news.

Selecting and publishing news that appeals to the diverse interests of readers is imperative if a media product is to survive. But only the most widely circulated newspapers and magazines can afford to situate reporters in offices outside their primary market area. Most U.S. newspapers, magazines and broadcast stations, therefore, rely on the news services to provide wide-ranging, non-local coverage.

Those who travel across the United States and notice the news products in the cities and towns they visit may note the similarities in this country's press accounts. Magazines such as Time and Newsweek often publish the same topic on their covers, network news broadcasts often announce the same stories each night and appear to use the same format, and daily newspapers resemble each other in content and design.

Some have called this important, and many would argue, disturbing insight into U.S. mass media of the last 100 years the "blanding" of American journalism. Researchers and media scholars continue to try to define the reasons why this is so. One significant reason is that the mass media are increasingly becoming part of the same huge corporations, which often dictate the ways their "products" will read and look. Others argue that the nature of journalistic "routines," such as accepting news from the same known sources (government officials, business leaders, etc.) and publishing on 24-hour cycles, creates these resemblances. Still others suggest that the uniform profile of media workers necessarily contributes to uniformity in content. One other reason for the quality of sameness is that many of the nation's media use the same reports from the primary news services.

Primary news services

Three primary news services offer broad coverage of world events, without direct governmental support. They are The Associated Press of the United States, Reuters of Great Britain and Agence France Presse of France. (Agence France Presse is not directly subsidized, but French government ministries pay handsomely to subscribe, an arrangement one AFP official admitted "could be called a disguised (governmental) subsidy.")

The Associated Press, the largest supplier of breaking news in the world, celebrated its 150th anniversary in 1998. Six New York City publishers created the wire service in 1848 to save newsgathering costs by sharing information with each

Figure 4-1
The Associated Press is a
worldwide organization
with considerable assets
for gathering and
disseminating the news.
(Source: www.ap.org
January 1999)

3,421	**Total number of employees**
144	AP domestic news bureaus
93	AP international news bureaus (in 71 countries)
237	**Total news bureaus worldwide**
1,780	**Total number of domestic newspapers**
6,000	Total radio/TV outlets taking AP
750	Total taking AP Network News (largest single radio network in the USA)
8,500	Total number of international subscribers
112	Total number of countries served by AP
43	Total number of Pulitzer Prizes (25 for photos)

other in a cooperative, not-for-profit arrangement. According to its Web page, the AP now serves 1,780 newspapers and more than 6,000 radio and television stations "a daily diet of more than 4 million words." See Figure 4-1.

Although AP is the only news service in the United States that attempts to provide a full range of coverage in the nation and around the world, many supplemental, or "designer," news services offer specialized coverage, focusing on the important stories of the day, analysis pieces, feature reports and opinion columns. Most metropolitan newspapers and national magazines subscribe to several services, while most small and mid-sized dailies subscribe only to AP and perhaps one or two of the supplementals.

United Press International, which was created in 1907 as a competing news service, no longer serves large numbers of daily U.S. newspapers but does sell its content to U.S. broadcast stations and international subscribers.

Supplemental services

The nation's mass media may also purchase content from among dozens of supplemental news services and hundreds of syndicated feature services. One of the best supplemental services, The New York Times Syndicate, has for many years focused on in-depth stories and analysis of news from around the world. Subscribers get a daily report from the news pages of The New York Times, as well as background pieces, opinion columns, sports columns, feature stories, photos and computer graphics. The information is distributed through many channels, including the service's own leased satellite channel, the Internet, computer dial-up services, faxes, telex and courier services.

In addition to its traditional content, the news service offers New America News Service, which provides stories by and about diverse Americans. The company explains the rationale behind the nontraditional content this way: "Not only is diversity a growing factor in the ethnic make-up of the country, but in its social fabric as well. Throughout our society, growing numbers of our citizens have discarded their 'left out' status and are insisting on equal rights and the dignity America has always stood for. Each week, New America News Service provides a package of five articles, appropriate for many sections of a newspaper, by and about these Americans." Here is a sample from a menu of recent offerings:

FEATURES

PUEBLO INDIANS—A recently unveiled postage stamp commemorates the 400th anniversary of European settlement in the Southwest and "celebrates the blending of Spanish and Indian cultures in northern New Mexico." But, columnist Tim Giago writes, "the people of the Indian pueblos were enslaved," and European settlement was the beginning of the end for much of their land holdings, culture and beliefs. "I see no need for us to join in on celebrations that would commemorate actions that nearly destroyed us as a people."

ECUADORAN HALL OF FAMER—Jaime Jarrin arrived in this country 43 years ago knowing little English and nothing about baseball, reports writer Ines Pinto Alicea. Last month, the native of Ecuador received America's top sports broadcasting award and will be inducted into the National Baseball Hall of Fame in Cooperstown, N.Y.

LESBIAN MOTHERHOOD—Lesbians today are getting pregnant in greater numbers than ever before, and the "gayby" boom is exploding worldwide. Reporter Dorothy Atcheson examines the innovative insemination options available to gay women.

NOT ALWAYS EQUAL—Each time columnist Bill Maxwell or any other African-American writer points out problems that seem to affect black citizens disproportionately, many white people, liberals and conservatives alike, weigh in with what he calls white equivalency—an attempt to draw parallels between black problems and similar white problems. "But it does not make whites and blacks equal, and it does not make their sins comparable," he says. "Yes, some of the problems are similar or the same. But let us not fool ourselves: Black skin and the unique problems that come with it do not have white equivalencies—and never will."

In addition to the supplemental services, more than 350 syndicated feature services sell to media clients thousands of political cartoons, comic strips, astrology columns, crossword puzzles, games and quizzes, advice and humor columns, commentary pieces, television listings, business features, entertainment and sports features, maps and charts, and computer graphics packages.

Handling copy

Most news media throw away far more news copy than they use, generally because of space limitations. In addition, a focus on local news generally requires that national and international news stories be condensed or digested. In the last decade of the 20th century, more and more editors spent their time merging news-service stories, compiling bits and pieces of information from several sources to create a unique story for their publications. To help busy editors keep pace with the vast quantity of copy, the news services have developed coding systems that enable editors to route stories easily and efficiently.

Priority codes, which appear at the top of all news-service stories, help assure that stories move over the news-service wires according to their urgency. Editors often use the codes to help decide order of importance. See Figure 4-2 for the principal priority codes used by AP.

Figure 4-2
The AP uses these priority
codes to indicate a story's
urgency.

f:	Flash, highest priority. Seldom used, except for stories of the utmost importance, such as presidential assassination
b:	Bulletins, first adds to bulletins, kill notes
u:	Urgent, high-priority copy, including all corrections. Must be used on all stories determined to be urgent; may be used on stories that are not urgent but require urgent transmission
r:	Regular priority. Used for advisories, digest stories, other late-breaking stories and special fixtures, such as People in the News
d:	Deferred priority. Used for spot-news items that can be delayed if more urgent material is available
a:	Weekday advances. Intended to be used more than 12 hours after transmission (Hold-for-release stories transmitted for use in less than 12 hours carry priority code **d.**)
s:	Sunday advances. Designed for use more than 12 hours after transmission
w:	Release-at-will items. Used for stories that have publishing value during and after current transmission cycle
x, y, z:	Internal routing among AP bureaus

Category codes, which also appear at the top of all news-service stories, are designed to help editors sort copy into the equivalent of electronic stacks—for example, one stack for Washington news, another for sports stories, another for entertainment and so on. Before computer editing, copy editors performed the same function by hand, separating the news stories into paper stacks to make the editorial selection process as efficient as possible. Computer systems have streamlined the process. The principal category codes used by AP appear in Figure 4-3.

In addition to using category codes and priority codes, the news services supply other information helpful to busy news editors. News *budgets*, for example, digest the stories considered the most important by the news service. The service transmits a budget at the beginning of each publication cycle; AP editors transmit the one for morning newspapers about noon Eastern time and the one for afternoon newspapers at about midnight. The AP also updates budgets during each news cycle. In addition to a budget, subscribers to The New York Times Syndicate also receive a list of the stories The New York Times plans to use on its Page One the following morning. Figure 4-4 is an example of part of an updated AP budget for morning newspapers; the sample came over the wires at a newspaper on the West Coast.

As you read through the news digest, you will notice that the news service uses other key words to tell editors more about the stories. For example, note that AP will transmit graphics with some stories, such as the one about the impeachment trial in Exhibit 4-4. Some stories are "developing" (still being reported and written); others "may stand" or "should stand," meaning the information probably won't change very much, and the news service probably won't do much updating or rewriting. Here is other information supplied by the news services to help find and sort the copy:

a:	Domestic general news items. Excludes news from Washington
b:	Special events
d:	Stories about food and diet. Primarily advance features
e:	Selected entertainment stories. Movie reviews, television reviews and columns, etc.
f:	Stories for use on business and financial pages (Editors are advised, however, that an important story of financial interest is routed to both the financial and news desks.)
i:	International news items. Includes stories from all foreign datelines, the United Nations, U.S. possessions and undated roundups keyed to foreign events
j:	Lottery numbers
l:	Selected lifestyle stories
n:	State and regional items with domestic datelines (If the dateline is foreign, the **i** category code is used. If the dateline is Washington, the **w** category code is used. If the story is written primarily for the business pages, the **f** category code is used.)
o:	Weather tables
p:	National political copy. Used only in election years
q:	Results or period scores of a single sporting event
s:	Sports stories, standings and results of more than one event
v:	Advisories about any stories or photos transmitted on the news-service wires. Designed for news digests, news advisories, lists of advance stories and indexes
w:	Stories datelined Washington, D.C. (If a subsequent lead shifts the dateline to another city, the category code changes to **a** or **b**.)

Figure 4-3
Category codes are used to indicate the type of story coming across AP wires.

▶**Key word or slug.** Names the story and is repeated on all subsequent versions. Editors use this slug throughout the editing process, including on page layouts (see Chapter 11).

▶**Cycle designator.** Indicates that morning publications have first use of the story (AM), afternoon newspapers have first use of the story (PM), or the item is available to both cycles (BC).

▶**Word count.** Estimates the length of the story.

▶**Story version vocabulary.** Reveals

- Whether the story is one of the news schedules (budgets) for that day (Bjt)

- Whether the story is the first version—first lead (1st Ld)—or a later version (2nd Ld, 3rd Ld, etc.)

- Whether the transmission is simply advising or alerting editors (Advisory)

- Whether the transmission is an advance story (Adv 01)

Figure 4-4
An AP news budget, called a news digest, is an overview of what AP editors believe are the most significant events of the day. This example is part of an updated AP budget for morning newspapers, which moved on the wires of a newspaper on the West Coast.

```
AM-News Digest, 2nd Ld-Writethru,1047
Friday AMs AP News Digest
6 p.m. Update

    The top stories from The Associated Press. The supervisor is
Stephanie Nano (212-621-1602). The photo supervisor is Scott
Braut (212-621-1900). The graphics supervisor is Justin Gilbert
(212-621-6912).
    For repeats of AP copy, please call your local bureau or the
Service Desk at 212-621-1595.


IMPEACHMENT:
    Senate takes care of formalities; up next, the tough part

WASHINGTON -- With Chief Justice William H. Rehnquist
presiding, the Senate somberly placed William Jefferson Clinton
on trial Thursday on charges of high crimes and misdemeanors
in the first presidential impeachment in 131 years. The White
House promised a ''compelling case'' for acquittal.
    Slug AM-Clinton-Impeachment. Sent as a0790.
    By David Espo. AP Photos NY116, Rep. Henry Hyde, R-Ill.,
reads the articles of impeachment; ACAP117, Sen. Jesse Helms,
R-N.C., waves as he rides his motorized wheelchair; NY122, Sen.
Strom Thurmond, R-S.C., swears in Rehnquist; AWH301, AWH302,
Clinton looks down as he waits to make remarks at an education
event. AP Graphic IMPEACHMENT TRIAL.


    Grappling with the constitutional duties

    WASHINGTON -- Leahy of Vermont took notes at a furious clip.
Gramm of Texas sat scowling at a wooden schoolhouse desk. Helms
of North Carolina, recovering from surgery on both knees,
hobbled in with a cane. ''Hear ye! Hear ye! Hear ye!'' in-
toned the sergeant at arms, demanding silence ''on pain of
imprisonment.''
    Slug AM-Impeachment-Senate Drama. Sent as a0707.
    By Mike Feinsilber.

US-IRAQ: Weapons inspection spying charge could undermine U.S.
policy

    WASHINGTON -- American weapons experts, including some from
intelligence agencies, helped U.N. inspectors hunt for Iraqi
weapons and gained information that assisted U.S. military
planners, Clinton administration officials said Thursday. But
the officials rejected suggestions that the Americans were
proxy spies.
    Slug AM-US-Iraq Inspections. Sent as a0768.
    By John Diamond. AP Graphic IRAQ RADAR. AP Photo planned.
```

HEALTH:

No long-term ill effects from birth control pills

LONDON -- Women suffer no lasting ill effects from taking
birth control pills, according to the biggest study ever on the
subject and one that some experts say finally can lay to rest
fears that have lingered since the pill was introduced in 1961.
Slug AM-The Pill. Sent as a0700. By Emma Ross.

Fidget your way to thin

WASHINGTON -- Fidgeting may be the way to stay slim. That's
the conclusion of a study in which 16 people volunteered to
stuff themselves with 1,000 extra calories a day for eight
weeks. At the end, some had gained as much as 16 pounds, while
others had gained as little as 2 pounds. The difference, says a
researcher, was the ''fidget factor.''
Slug AM-Fidgeting & Weight. Sent as a0746.
By Paul Recer.

SIERRA LEONE: Rebels apparently flushing out civilians for
shields

FREETOWN, Sierra Leone -- Plumes of acrid black smoke
billowed over eastern sections of Freetown on Thursday as
rampaging insurgents set city neighborhoods ablaze and dragged
terrified residents from their homes.
Slug AM-Sierra Leone. Sent as a0786.
By Ian Stewart. AP Graphic SIERRRA LEONE. AP Photos SLE101,
A Nigerian peacekeeping soldier stands in a helicopter; SLE103,
A Sierra Leone woman cries as she waits to leave Freetown.

With AM-Sierra Leone-Rebels

MISSING WIFE: Mountain man accused of imprisoning and killing
wife

RINGGOLD, Ga. -- Virginia Ridley's family and friends had
seen her only once after she got married in 1966. Her husband
told anyone who asked that she had left him and moved up north.
In 1997, though, it became clear that she had never left.
Instead, police say, her husband, Alvin, kept her captive in
their home for 30 years, and finally suffocated her just over a
year ago.
Slug AM-Captive Wife Trial. Sent as a0783.
By Justin Bachman. AP Photos planned.

AP-WS-01-07-99 1812EST

- How many takes (a take, or a page, usually does not exceed 450 words) the story is (2 takes)

- Whether the transmission is an addition to the first take (1st Add, 2nd Add, etc.), an insert to the story (Insert), a substitution for part of the story (Sub), a correction (Correction) or a complete rewrite of the story, including all inserts, substitutions and corrections (Writethru)

Before computer technology, news editors had to collect all these bits of information as they were transmitted—at a very slow 33 words per minute on teletype machines—and literally paste them all together into a cohesive story to send to the composing room for typesetting. Today, ultra-high-speed computers perform the cut-and-paste function, and most later versions of a story are transmitted as a write-through.

The wire editor's job

The person who oversees copy from the news services is commonly known as the wire editor, because in the years before satellite transmission, news services sent their stories by telegraph and later telephone wires. The wire editor is the news editor's link to events of the day outside the primary circulation or viewing area. The wire editor is responsible for providing the news editor with complete budgets, updated news stories and advisories on breaking news. The news editor prepares advance copy and edits stories. Communication is the key to the wire editor's job. Working closely with the news editor results in a well-packaged and informative news report.

At an afternoon newspaper with several editions, published in a metropolitan area with a competing morning paper, the job of the wire editor begins at 2 a.m. He or she reads the morning newspaper, paying close attention to the AP stories that its editors chose to use. The editor for the afternoon newspaper does not want to duplicate a wire story that has appeared in the morning paper.

Before the wire editor left the day before, he or she told a copy aide to leave that day's final afternoon edition on the wire editor's desk. Doing so helps the night news editor, who may not have seen the last edition, and also helps the wire editor refresh his or her memory about the previous day.

The news editor will mark a copy of the wire budget, which is the news service's list of stories that will be transmitted during the PM cycle. The stories selected should be processed first.

To make certain of what is in the computer system for the day, the wire editor begins to scan the *queues*, computer files of news-service stories sorted according to broad categories. The news editor also scrolls through the queues periodically. These are the broad categories used to organize the queues:

NA: National stories
FO: Foreign (international) stories
CA: California stories (this category varies, of course, with the state)
NX: New York Times and other supplemental news services
AV: Advance stories from supplemental services
AD: Advance stories from AP

The wire editor scans the queues for stories that can be killed—multiple write-throughs of the same story or versions for morning papers. The wire editor checks the morning version before killing any story in case the morning version is better than the afternoon version. The editor may decide to use a morning version if the competition hasn't already used it.

Moving through the queues, the wire editor keeps in mind the news editor's plan for the day, suggests stories that can be packaged and makes sure the news editor knows whether a story is expected to change.

The wire editor is on the lookout for stories that are important. The news editor needs to know about developing stories that will be transmitted later in the morning and about fresher versions of a story that appeared in the morning paper in another form. One way to keep the news editor informed is to use the *slug field* space at the top of the computer screen. A "good" or "wow" message there will tip off the news editor.

The news editor must have clean copy that can be sent to the copy desk with minimal effort; speed is essential. The wire editor can help reduce the time that the news editor spends with each story by doing these things:

▶ **Remove all news-service labels and numbers at the top of each story.** Anything that should not appear in print should be deleted. Only the news-service credit line, byline and dateline should remain. Many publications omit news-service bylines unless the story is a particularly important news story, a feature, an analysis or an op-ed piece. A story in which the writer exhibits personal flair usually warrants a byline.

▶ **Make certain the credit line is correct.** For example, a story transmitted by AP should not be published with the credit line for another news service.

▶ **Remove the news-service instructions at the bottom of the story.** Unless removed, these extra lines will be reflected in the total length of the story, which will cause problems when page layouts are drawn.

Increasingly, the wire editor or a copy editor rewrites news-service stories to get a better angle or, where possible, to give the story a local angle. With important international and national stories, more and more copy desks are combining stories from a variety of news services to save space and avoid duplication. For example, often stories on the Consumer Price Index and on other governmental economic or employment statistics can be combined. The publication may add local figures, as well. Stories about U.S. Supreme Court decisions, several of which may be handed down on the same day, also can be combined into one story.

John Brewer, former president of The New York Times Syndicate and now the publisher of a daily newspaper in the Pacific Northwest, says wire editing in the 1990s is "finding good stuff from the zillion news-service sources available these days and packaging it effectively." He adds that this kind of editing "takes news judgment, a good sense of design and a desire to Make It Count."

The first edition

The bulk of the stories should move to the news editor of the afternoon newspaper by 5 a.m. Late-breaking stories and Page One stories should be completed by 5:30 a.m. The afternoon weather story usually moves about this time. The AP story slugged "Nation's Weather" gives this information. If weather is particularly newsworthy—such as a tornado, a blizzard or an ice storm—AP usually moves it as a separate story. The wire editor will alert the news editor if this happens.

The first edition may be wrapped up by 8:30 a.m. Before the story conference, where chief editors and section editors discuss the day's stories and how the paper should handle them, the wire editor checks the paper to see which stories made the first edition and which stories the news editor held back.

The wire editor pays close attention to the news briefs, because many of them were prepared early the previous evening. Several items that moved across the wires too late to make the first edition are good substitutes for stale news briefs. These are shortened and passed on to the news editor.

The story conference

Wire editors usually prepare for the morning story conference, or budget meeting, while they process news-service copy for the first edition. They do this by jotting down the sluglines of stories that are expected to develop during the day. AP is good about keeping member papers advised of developing stories, and many such stories are obvious. For example, a two-sentence story at 6 a.m. about a plane crash can grow into a lead story, as information about the crash becomes available. Another key as to what is developing is the morning advisory that AP moves about 8 a.m., which lists stories the AP expects to "top"—send new leads for—during the day.

The story conference usually is attended by the managing editor, metro editor, wire editor, section editors, photo chief and perhaps others in the newsroom. Some publishers ask marketing and circulation people to sit in, as well. At this time the editors discuss stories that are ready or will be ready shortly for the day's editions and decide which stories will get Page One treatment. The news editor or wire editor may suggest local angles that staff reporters could develop as sidebars or additions to news-service stories. Decisions about the use of photographs or other art or graphics are made during this brief meeting.

During and after the crunch

The times between multiple editions of an afternoon newspaper are critical. Often the deadlines come no more than an hour apart. The wire editor must work quickly and work closely with the news editor to put out a successful follow-up to the first edition.

After the budget meeting, any stories requested by other editors are sent to the news editor. The wire editor will check frequently with the news editor to make sure that needed copy is in the queue. The wire editor will notify the news editor when stories are updated to see whether they should be re-edited. Minor changes may not be worth the trouble.

The wire editor tries to supply most of the second-edition copy to the news editor by 9:15 a.m. and the latest-breaking stories by 9:45 a.m. The wire editor will add 40 minutes to these deadlines for the third edition but will send copy earlier for inside pages.

By 11 a.m. the bulk of the wire editor's work for the day's editions is usually completed. During lulls, feature and advance copy moves to the proper departments. By noon, the wire editor should have all the queues clean, taking out advisories that are intended for editors and printing copies for the managing editor, the assistant managing editor and the news editor.

Copy editors who handle news-service material are responsible for sorting and then distributing stories to various newspaper sections and for avoiding the publication of duplicated stories, for choosing the best version of a story from among several news services and for merging several versions into one story. They also help the news editor decide the top national and international stories of the day.

The wire editor must also work closely with those responsible for the publication's computer systems to determine the most efficient way to retrieve, sort and store the vast volumes and variety of news-service material transmitted each day.

Editing for the Web

Graphics, animations and multi-media applications attract the most attention at this stage of the Web's development, but Web sites and the Internet as a whole continue to be a text-based medium. Lessons in this chapter about editing leads, including essential information in stories, handling quotations, shortening stories and editing news-service copy apply to the Web as well as traditional print-media editing. The Web's hypertext structure and the glut of information it offers, however, require copy editors to give special attention to these considerations:

- How much text will appear at any one time on the reader's computer screen

- How easy it will be for readers to get key information quickly without necessarily reading the complete text

- How the story is broken into segments

Keep it short

Web Review (http://webreview.com) quotes a "cool site" judge as saying, "If a site works, I'm going to read what they have to say," commenting further that the quality of the text was a major criteria in evaluating sites. The first part of his quote—*if a site works*—is a key to getting Web users to read the copy. Despite nifty navigational tools, the site won't work unless text is well edited and brief.

Research by Jakob Nielsen and John Morkes* indicates that Web users do not like long, scrolling pages; they prefer the text to be short and to the point. Other Nielsen research suggests that reading from computer screens is about 25 percent slower than reading from paper. Readers report that they suffer eye strain and lack of patience when reading online material. This will change in the future when high-resolution monitors become affordable; meanwhile, the lesson for copy editors is to keep Web copy brief. In *Data Smog: Surviving the Information Glut*, David Shenk writes that in an information-saturated world, journalists become consumers' first line of defense in trying to tame the information tide. Newspaper companies and journalists understand better than newcomers to the information society that "less is more" in the Internet news business. That journalistic standby, the inverted pyramid style, works well to communicate succinctly in the online environment.

Make it skimmable

For the same reasons that bulleted lists, informational graphics and other condensed information are popular in traditional media, certain factors compel their use in the online world. Such "skimmable" content, also referred to as "scannable" material, helps prevent eyes from tiring while reading from a computer screen. Additionally, Nielsen and other Internet researchers speculate that readers approach the Web with the mindset that they must be active while online, frequently moving a mouse around a page or surfing from one site to another. To sit and read a long passage seems unproductive to most Net users.

The sheer volume of Internet material—that data smog Shenk describes—compels users to move from page to page, unwilling to commit much time to any

---

*Morkes, J., and Nielsen, J., "Applying Writing Guidelines to Web Pages," Online. http://www.useit.com/papers/webwriting/rewriting.html, 1998.

single item because the next download might contain more valuable or easier-to-grasp information. These devices can help readers skim Web pages:

- Clear, informative headlines either standing alone or followed by one or two sentences with a link to the full story

- Lists of key ideas, highlighted by bullets or other typographical elements

- Paragraphs with a single idea

- Colored type to emphasize words or phrases

- Hypertext anchors, which appear on the screen in color and often underlined

- Quotes or other key passages pulled from the text and set in a different size, style or color type or highlighted by borders

- Frequent subheadings within the text

Link it

Scientists and military researchers used the Internet for a quarter of a century before Tim Berners-Lee at the CERN physics laboratory in Switzerland developed the concept of the World Wide Web in the late 1980s. The Web, based on a hypertext networked information system that made the Internet simple for everyone to use, caused Internet growth to explode, both in the number of users and the amount of information linked by computers. The term *hypertext* describes text containing links to other text. *Hypermedia* refers to the joining of a variety of media, such as text, video and sound, which the Web makes possible. HyperText Transfer Protocol (the http that forms the beginning of most Web addresses) is used by Web browsers such as Netscape and Internet Explorer to build pages held on computer servers at distant sites.

This linking capability provides writers and editors the advantages of a non-linear approach to communication. Participants in Morkes and Nielsen's Web readability study made these comments about hypertext:

"The incredible thing that's available on the Web is the ability to go deeper for more information."

"Links are a good thing. If you just want to read the page you're on, fine, you're not losing anything. But if you want to follow the links, you can. That's the great thing about the Web."

"I might be searching for one document, but I might find 15 other related things that pique my interest. It's very useful. I really enjoy that."

To determine the most reader-friendly ways to link related material, copy editors must abandon traditional linear ways of thinking. The best use of hypertext is not simply to chop a long story into separate linked pages, an online counterpart to jumping a newspaper story from Page One to an inside page. This approach discourages readers by adding to download time and complicating printing, should readers desire a hard copy of the article.

Editors must think of each story as a package of separate components and structure the package with hypertext links that readers can choose to follow or ignore according to their own needs or interests at a particular time. It is important that editors give readers specific information about what they will find if they decide to follow a link. Readers don't want a surprise after waiting for a page to download. This is not the place for teaser words or phrases.

"Hot" spots, another term for hypertext links, can be incorporated within a sentence, displayed as colored and often underlined words. In addition, links can be listed as headlines or perhaps just labels in a separate column or box alongside the main story. Each link can lead to pages with still other links about the subject. Material published on previous days can likewise be linked into an archive of stories, allowing readers to review the unfolding of a particular news story. A section about Web page design in Chapter 11 further describes how hypertext links are used.

Figure 4-5 shows how ESPN.com [http://ESPN.SportsZone.com] handled links to its package of stories about Mark McGwire's 70th homerun in the 1998 baseball season. The lead item on the home page gives basic information (too long at four sentences, some might argue) with two highlighted and underlined hyperlinks: "Big Mac launched Nos. 69 and 70" and "Making History: The home run chase." A mouse click on the first link leads to a game-day story that contains multiple links to other story angles about the momentous homerun accomplishment. The "Making History" link takes readers to a graph charting each homerun by both McGwire and Sammy Sosa, his closest competitor in the '98 homerun derby. Each homerun indicated in the graphic is linked to a separate Web page describing the circumstances for that particular homerun.

This segment of an ESPN.com home page shows links to stories about the 1998 baseball season's record-breaking 70th homerun.

Figure 4-5
This segment of an ESPN.com home page shows links to stories about the 1998 baseball season's record-breaking 70th homerun.

Online journalism: Tradition weds technology   **By Matthew Lee**

T is simply too convenient to view newspaper Web sites as the demise of the traditional print medium. Instead, Web sites should be looked upon as the next evolutionary phase of print journalism and a way for newspapers to compete on equal footing with television as the public's dominant source of information. The Web is a medium that can move beyond the practice of placing text around static images on a page with a 24-hour lag time. It allows news organizations to cover events in greater depth and with even greater speed than ever before and allows them to employ multimedia to tell the story in a way neither television nor newspapers, individually, can.

To say online journalism is without its own unique set of perils would be naive. Breaking news deadlines no longer are determined by the printing press, and accuracy is threatened in the rush to post a story 15 seconds before a competitor. But just who is the competition on the Internet? The answer is: everybody and anybody.

How does a newspaper organization deal with these issues? There is no right answer, yet, but the way in which The Washington Post and its online counterpart, washingtonpost.com, covered a shooting at the Capitol in 1998 illustrates the middle ground that has been reached at many newspaper organizations.

Most are familiar with The Washington Post newspaper but the Web site that bears the same name is in its infancy when compared to the decades the newspaper has had to establish an identity. At times, washingtonpost.com resembles a wire service; breaking news from the major wire services (Associated Press, Reuters) converge, and editors continually update stories with new information from the wire services. At other times, post.com resembles a bulletin board; all of the content from that day's print edition is posted on the site. At still other times, post.com strives to be a resource of information that is not ordinarily found, and sometimes cannot possibly be found, in the print editions. Finally, post.com also resembles a traditional print newspaper. When an event merits attention and people power, post.com will send reporters out to write stories that are only going to appear online.

An insider's view of a typical day

At washingtonpost.com, it's hard to make a distinction between the ending and beginning of a day. Typically, the office is empty during only a three-to-four-hour period—usually between the time the last of the breaking news staff goes home and 6 a.m., when the dayside shift takes over.

People who work for the breaking news unit, or pod, occupy five work-stations in the center of the office. Their main responsibility is the home page—the front page of the Web site, the very first thing readers see when they type in http://www.washingtonpost.com. They also monitor the wire services.

Dayside responsibilities vary slightly from those on the night shift. The dayside shift in the news pod begins at 6 a.m. and on normal news days ends at 6 p.m. The news cycle is such that breaking stories usually erupt between late morning and early evening, which means that the dayside shift gets the brunt of breaking news work.

The day a lone gunman fired shots in the Capitol Building, Friday, July 24, 1998, began like any other "typical day": At about 6 a.m., the dayside news pod shift begins. Any unfinished business or minor maintenance left from the previous night is taken care of, and the monitoring of the news continues.

By mid-morning the online newsroom is now near full capacity. Each section is monitoring the wires for any news that may arise. Each is also working on long-term projects or maintenance of individual sections. The post.com Business and WashTech sections, for example, are putting the finishing touches on a news package covering the Y2K computer problem. The Post newspaper Business section has planned a series of articles scheduled to run on A-1 of the print edition and to get heavy play in the main news section of the paper. In addition to housing the Post print copy, post.com's package will have related links to past articles, a huge section of additional copy generated by post.com staff writers and updates on what companies and local government agencies are doing to comply with the Y2K problem. The Post series will point to the post.com coverage. The Post and post.com business editors have been coordinating the project for several weeks.

The post.com politics section is constantly awaiting the next Clinton scandal development, sorting through the never-ending minutiae of Special Prosecutor Kenneth Starr's investigation and whatever else may come from the White House and Congress. Key documents related to the Starr investigation, and later, the Starr investigation itself, are scanned into the computer and incorporated into the news package that has taken up a life of its own. Audio of key interviews and/or testimony is recorded, digitized and included in the online news package. Any viewer with the right software attached to a Web browser (easily downloadable from any number of other Web sites) can listen to sound bites from key players in the Clinton scandal.

In the post.com sports department, several big projects loom. Reporters and editors prepare for the day Cal Ripken Jr. decides to end "the Streak" and the day Michael Jordan announces his second retirement. A windfall of copy, endless tributes and the opinion of every sports columnist will accompany both events.

These packages will also include audio clips, streaming video highlights, interactive photo galleries and a long archive of past articles chronicling the key moments of their careers—stories written on the day Jordan played in his first NBA championship or audio of the radio announcer who called the game in which Ripken broke the record for most

Matthew Lee

Matthew Lee is an assistant online sports producer at washingtonpost.com, the online version of The Washington Post. He helps keep the online sports section updated and works on long-term projects. Before being hired full time, he served as an intern in both the sports and business sections of post.com.

In 1998, Lee received a bachelor of arts degree in communication from George Mason University in Fairfax, Va. He served as the managing editor of new media for the George Mason campus newspaper, the Broadside, and was a sports stringer for the Potomac News in Woodbridge, Va. As a student, he also worked as a freelance Web designer for the American Society of Newspaper Editors and as an online producer for both the ASNE and the Asian American Journalists Association.

Lee has received several awards and honors for his journalistic talents. He won first place in sports photography (Northeast region) in the 1996 Society of Professional Journalists Mark of Excellence contest, and he received the Kevin Athari Memorial Scholarship in recognition of his service to student publications at George Mason University. He was also inducted into the campus chapter of Lambda Pi Eta, the national communication honor society.

Lee is a native of Queens, N.Y.

consecutive baseball games played. Any one of these projects must be thought about in addition to the updating of daily articles.

In midafternoon—at about the same time the first Post budget meeting is ending and the post.com budget meeting convenes—a gunman enters the Capitol Building and opens fire.

Several things happen immediately: The editor, the managing editor-news, news pod; the politics, metro and international sections; and the photo and graphics department converge. After a brief conference, a loose game plan is formulated. The news pod keeps on top of the AP stories and updates the home page as new information comes over the wire.

At the same time, the editor is on the phone with his counterparts at the Post, constantly getting updates on what information the Post print reporters are getting and how the situation is going to be covered.

The editor keeps the post.com politics section up to date on this information, even as the politics section is pushing to pull together a special-report package that will eventually encompass the breaking news developing at the moment and follow-up stories sure to come in the following days. Also part of the special-report package infrastructure will be a photo gallery/essay online, consisting of AP and Post photos put together by the photo department. The library/research department at the print Post begins tracking down other times a shooting like this happened (in fact, there were several violent incidents in the Capitol Building) and back at post.com, searches of the online archives begin.

The post.com photo department is on notice to pull photos of the incident off of the AP wire as well as photos from the Post. These will later construct the online photo gallery. The post.com graphics department begins to construct infographics of the Capitol Building and a map of the surrounding area in addition to what the Post graphics people are putting together. The post.com graphics department also has to create graphics for use in the special-report package. Part of the post.com graphics department's responsibility will also be to adapt for the Web whatever their counterparts at the Post are doing, which involves sizing and resolution of the art, among other technical things.

At 6 p.m., back in the news pod, fragmented AP stories continue to come over the wire. By this time, the Post has had a legion of reporters on the scene and their copy is coming in. The post.com news pod begins to filter out AP stories that aren't consistent with information relayed from Post reporters on the scene. The danger post.com looks to avert is falling prey to television fallacies of reporting speculation and partial information in the rush to get information out.

By 7 p.m., information coming from authorities and sources begins to solidify, and the deadline for the first edition of the Post is fast approaching. As soon as the Post copy is edited, it is sent to a computer file with other special-report package material put together by the post.com politics section. The Post copy now replaces all of the AP stories used up until this time and is surrounded by related links, additional information and graphics, all put together by the post.com staff. As the initial furor begins to subside and just before the Post copy is set to complete its journey through the editing process, the post.com news pod dayside shift begins to hand off to the night crew. The shifts have overlapped for at least the previous two hours so everyone is up to date on the situation and how it will be handled.

The news pod night crew will now fulfill its primary responsibilities to place the rest of the day's Post news section onto the site as well as keep on top of new developments of earlier incidents. The Post content that makes the first edition of the paper is always subject to change—either further copy editing or updated information is added to a story. The news pod is sure to replace the earlier versions of the story with the new copy. Every section is affected by the incident.

Over in post.com's WashTech and Business sections, the intensive labor to prepare the Y2K package in time for the series of articles that was set to run over the weekend is now on hold to make way for the Capitol-shooting coverage that will continue through the weekend.

Deadlines for every section will be earlier than usual, and the pressure to meet those deadlines will be up another notch. The paper has to hit the streets with the coverage of the shootings as soon as possible; it won't be held back from going to press on time by any of the other sections. The earlier print deadlines mean that Post content is available earlier than normal for posting on the Web site.

At around 10:30 p.m., the first edition comes off the presses. At post.com, things have settled. The night news pod is in place, taking Post content and putting it online. The only other section in place at this time is sports. As Post game stories are edited, they are put on the site.

The coverage of the Capitol-shooting incident demonstrates the complexity of the relationship between the print and online worlds, yet at the same time illustrates the benefits of this marriage between tradition and technology. If nothing else, it provides a glimpse of things to come.

Suggestions for additional reading

Berner, R. Thomas. *Language Skills for Journalists*, 2nd ed. Boston: Houghton Mifflin, 1984.

Bernstein, Theodore M. *Dos, Don'ts and Maybes of English Usage.* New York: New York Times Books, 1977 (scheduled to be reissued in 1999).

———. *Watch Your Language.* New York: Atheneum, 1965.

Biagi, Shirley. *Media/Impact: An Introduction to Mass Media*, 4th ed. Belmont, Calif.: Wadsworth Publishing Co., 1999.

Brooks, Brian S., and James L. Pinson. *Working with Words: A Concise Handbook for Media and Editors*, 3rd ed. New York: St. Martin's Press, 1996.

Desmond, Robert W. *Windows on the World: World News Reporting 1900-1920.* Iowa City: University of Iowa Press, 1980.

Emery, Edwin, and Michael Emery. *The Press and America: An Interpretive History of the Mass Media*, 6th ed. Englewood Cliffs, NJ: Prentice-Hall, 1988.

Folkerts, Jean, and Dwight L. Teeter, Jr. *Voices of a Nation: A History of Mass Media in the United States*, 2nd ed. New York: Macmillan College Publishing Co., Inc., 1994.

Gans, Herbert J. *Deciding What's News: A Study of CBS Evening News, NBC Nightly News, Newsweek and Time.* New York: Vintage Books, 1980.

Morkes, J., and Nielsen, J. (1998). "Applying Writing Guidelines to Web Pages," Online. http://www.useit.com/papers/webwriting/rewriting.html, January 10, 1999.

Murray, Donald Morison, and Donald M. Murry. *The Craft of Revision.* New York: Harcourt Brace, 1997.

Rosewater, Victor. *History of Cooperative News-Gathering in the United States, 1865-1935.* New York: Appleton-Century-Crofts, 1930.

Schudson, Michael. *Discovering the News: A Social History of American Newspapers.* New York: Basic Books, 1979.

Schwarzlose, Richard A. *The Nation's Newsbrokers—Volume 1: The Formative Years, from Pretelegraph to 1865.* Evanston, Ill.: Northwestern University Press, 1989.

———. *The Nation's Newsbrokers—Volume 2: The Rush to Institution, from 1865 to 1920.* Evanston, Ill.: Northwestern University Press, 1989.

Shenk, David. *Data Smog: Surviving the Information Glut.* New York: HarperCollins, 1998.

Tuchman, Gaye. *Making News: A Study of the Construction of Reality.* New York: Free Press, 1978.

Exercises

1. Supply the missing numbers in this exercise. Use the style outlined in Chapter 3 to express your answers unless your instructor directs you to use a different style guide.

   a. The number of faculty members increased from 752 in 1991 to 767 in 1992, an increase of _____ percent.

   b. The number of students receiving scholarships was 1,520 last year, as compared with 1,432 this year, a decrease of _____ percent.

   c. During his career, the coach has had a record of 405 wins and 110 losses, a win/loss ratio of _____ to _____ .

   d. The United Way campaign has raised $136,000, _____ [fraction] of its goal of $185,000.

   e. The number of companies contributing to the United Way campaign increased _____ percent, from 67 last year to 82 this year.

   f. He deposited $3,260. At an annual interest rate of 6.4 percent, his deposit will earn _____ during the next 12 months, giving him a total of $_____ .

   g. The grade distribution this term for freshmen at the university was 157 A's, 203 B's, 436 C's, 179 D's and 124 F's. The percentage of freshmen making A's was _____; B's, _____; C's, _____; D's, _____ and F's, _____ .

   h. The monthly subscription rate for cable television went from $11.95 for basic service to $13.97, an increase of _____ percent.

   i. Among football players at the university who had been in school for four years, four of 18 graduated last year and three of 20 graduated this year, a decrease of _____ percentage points.

   j. Census data indicate that 578 women in the county said they had been sexually assaulted last year, but the number of sexual assaults reported to all law enforcement units in the county was 265, indicating that _____ [fraction] of the alleged sexual assaults went unreported to police agencies.

k. Here are the mill levies for three taxing units: city, 42.2; county, 32.5; school district, 75.7. Property is assessed at 8.6 percent of market value. The owner of a house with a market value of $70,000 would pay property taxes on an assessed value of $_____ for a total of $_____. The city would receive $_____, the county would receive $_____, and $_____ would go to the school district.

2. Edit this story. Be on the lookout for errors in numbers as well as grammar, punctuation, spelling and style.

The state Bureau of Investigation released crime statistics yesterday which cover the first six months of 1999. According to those statistics, crime in the state dropped 5.7 per cent during the first six months of 1999 from the same period during the previous year but 9.2% more rapes were reported.

Violent crimes (murder, rape, robbery, aggravated assault) decreased over all 3.6% from the first half of 1998. Property crimes, including burglary, larcany, motor-vehical theft and arson dipped 5.7%.

Crime bureau statistics that were released yesterday indicate violent and property crimes in the state dropped for the tenth consecutive quarter. Rape is the only violant crime on the upswing in the last 5 quarters bureau director J. A. Kelly said.

Among violent crimes, rapes (at least those reported) increased from 276 in the first half of 1998 to 304 during the comparable period in 1999.

Homocides showed the biggest drop at 47.6%. 62 murders were recorded in the first half of 1998 but only 42 murders through June of 1999.

Robbery dropped 16.1 per cent while aggrevated assault was up less than one per cent.

Arson was down 12.5% with 392 cases reported in the first half of 1999, compared with 441 in 1998.

The most frequent crime commited was larcany, with 31,756 cases reported during the first half of 1999.

3. Edit the following sentences to eliminate redundancies:

a. The humane society director said she would postpone her decision about computer identification for pets until later.

b. The car skidded a total distance of 100 feet before the driver managed to resume control.

c. College students sometimes think editing exercises are totally unnecessary and the answers are patently obvious.

d. When we break camp, we must promise to assemble our lively little group together again next summer.

e. At 6 a.m. Monday morning, the networks broadcast the first news reports that Prince would begin a national tour in the fall.

f. The decision to increase funding for education became clear after the mayor asked the council for a consensus of opinion.

g. Suddenly the lawyers began to argue over whether the testimony referred back to the original crime or to the pretrial hearing.

h. The freshness of the spring rain still remains, although each and every cloud has disappeared from the morning sky.

i. A happy song advises that if you fall down, you should pick yourself up and start all over again.

j. The football player said he wouldn't turn pro at the present time but might consider the option next year.

4. Combine each pair of sentences into one sentence. Make certain each new sentence has the same meaning as the original sentences.

a. Music shouted from a stereo.

Music drifted out to the dark garden and quiet street.

_____

_____

b. Brownies had been baked.

Brownies had been stacked high on paper plates.

_____

_____

c. An awkward couple lazed to the center of the floor.

An awkward couple disappeared in a clump of bodies starting to dance.

_____

_____

d. The soft drink seeped into the carpet.

The soft drink dried to a sticky patch on the floorboards.

_____

_____

e. The sound of a ringing telephone cut through the blend of music and voices.

The sound of a ringing telephone continued and continued until someone picked up the receiver.

_____

_____

5. In hard-news stories, reporters try to make their leads as simple and as short as possible. Some of the following leads contain unnecessary attribution, redundancies, opinions of the reporter, excess wordage, unimportant quotations, too many statistics or imprecise information. Tighten the following leads:

a. Blue-collar rocker Bruce Springsteen won three American Music Awards Monday for his 18-month-old *Born in the USA* album, and nine other artists or groups won two awards each at ceremonies that ended with a stirring anniversary salute to "We Are the World."

b. The space shuttle Challenger's solid-fuel rockets were not equipped with sensors that could have warned of trouble because designers thought the boosters were "not susceptible to failure," William Graham, acting administrator of the National Aeronautics and Space Administration, said Tuesday.

c. A 14-year-old boy fired three shots into a third-floor apartment at 91 Monmouth St. Wednesday to climax an argument with a 39-year-old mother who had defended her 9-year-old daughter against an attack by the boy.

d. Four French and two Canadian women have started a ski trek from Norway's Spitsbergen Island about 690 miles across the Arctic, aiming to reach the North Pole by Jan. 1, the Norwegian NRK television reported Thursday.

e. A federal grand jury indicted former Philippine President Ferdinand Marcos and his wife, Imelda, Friday in a racketeering case that includes charges they embezzled more than $100 million from the Philippine government and used the money to buy millions of dollars' worth of New York real estate.

6. Edit this story, which has a variety of problems.

wild pigs

Titusville, Florida—AP—The wild pigs which have been giving Kennedy Space Center officials headaches for years are now ending up on the menu at the Bravard County jail.

Sheriff Jake Miller says the pigs are "goodies from heaven". "I'm constantly looking for food sources for that jail Miller said.

The plan to trap the animals is the latest of several ideas by Miller to cut down on the food bill for the jail's two hundred and fifty inmates. His efforts are apparently paying off.

The jails meal budget for the upcomming fiscial year is $260 thousand dollars, the same as in the current fiscial year. Its the first time anyone can remember the food bill not going up. The National Auronautics and Space Administration gave Miller permission about 2 months ago to trap the porkers whose population was estimated recently at over 5000 and multiplying fast.

NASA officials are afraid the pigs could threaten the space shuttle and other craft by wandering onto the space center's runway. In addition, the porkers cause traffic accidents dig near under ground cables and endanger other wild life by hogging food supplies.

The piggs began multiplying after they were abandoned by home owners displaced in the 1960's when NASA bought their property to build the space center. At first Millers traps came up empty when he tried baiting them with corn which the wild pigs barely noticed. Once trappers switched to leftovers from the jail and other goodies to give the bait an odor the hogs couldn't resist the sheriff said. About 6 hogs were slaughtered last week and are in the jails freezer waiting to be cooked. Jail Administrator Frank Billings says he hopes eventually to keep about twenty-five or thirty porkers at the prison farm to serve as a constant suply of meat.

7. Edit this story, which has various problems.

mouse trap

HIPASS, Ca (AP)—A sound so shrill that it drives rodents wild, flattens cock roaches, and sends fleas flying is whistling up a fortune for Bob Brown, a guitar player disabled by polio who retired in 1980 on a $235 a month social security check.

In his garage one day 6 years ago Brown was putting together a electric guitar when he tangled some wires. He saw rats scatter. He crossed the wires again and the rodents ran again.

Brown, 51 built what he called a "rat repellant box". Since then 18000 of the boxes have been produced in Los Angelas and TiJuana Mex

A chicken farmer North of San Diego bought the first repellant box when according to Brown "about 10000 mice were bothering the chickens every night".

"It cleared his place in 4 or 5 days" Brown said.

The Venezualan government recently bought three hundred of the boxes to kill cock roaches in food stores in Caracus and 1000 were sent to spanish graneries in Barcelona.

Brown plans to fly to New York city next week to talk to Department of housing and urban Development officials about placing 9000 units in government housing.

"The box'es frequency is over a million cycles per second Brown said. The human ear can hear up to about 20000 cycles per second.

"We're jaming the sensory systems of rats, cock roaches, and even ants" Brown said. "We've got a vibration high enough to jam 'em like a foreign broadcaster jams our radio Brown said. We discovered that the antenna on roaches just folds up when they hear that sound he said. "They're on there backs, out of touch, and without any balance"

8. Edit this story.

trooper

RICHMOND, VA.—(AP)—The star of Virginia's court ordered campaign to recruit women state troopers has been fired for "insubordination" after refusing a short notice, out of town assignment she claims gave her no chance to find a babysitter.

The state's first woman trooper, Cheryl Petska, was notified at 4 p.m. Friday that she would be dismissed at midnight for "insubordination"—her refusal to accept a two week tuor of duty in the strike troubled Virgininia coalfields.

Petska, 31, claims she was give only 48hours notice of the assignment at the CONSUL, Inc. mines and couldn't accept it because she was unable to find a babysitter for her two daughters, Tracy 10 and shannon 5.

Her husband, Mark, works as an undercover trooper for the Highway Patrol and was scheduled to be away on assignment at the same time. The Petska's live in Frdericksburg, Va.

"They told me one Friday to be at the coalfields on Monday," Petska said. "I thought the short notice was unjustified."

"My kids are in school," she said. "In the summer I can send them to my mothers, but that's not possible now."

"Everybody recognizes an emergency," her attorney, Joesph Duvall, said. But this was no emergency; this was sexy discrimination."

"TRhe coal strikes have been going on for years, and as I understand it, some divisions already have their work schedules planned thru December."

The Jonestown coal fields, site of occasional strike related violence, are an 8-hour, 400 mile drive from Cheryls home," Duvall said.

Duvall said next week he would file a request for a state police arbitration hearing of the case. If Petska is not reinstated, he said, they will take the matter to court.

Petska joined the state police in Oct. 1988. She made 500 arrests in her first year on the job, and was filmed recently in a state police promotional film that may air soon.

Only eight of the 1000 Virginia state troopers are woman.

Petska worked special coalfield duty during the Pitston Coal Company strike two years ago and said she was given almost two weeks notice then.

"It makes you a little resentful when you go out there and you do a goood job and risk you life just like everybody else. And they still won't accept you," she said.

"They want women in here, but noathing has been done to help women get thru this."

Petska was hired when the Virginia Supream Court forced the highway patrol to begin hiring women in 1988. She was one of several women who had filed a class action suit against the highway patrol, charging it with sex discrimination.

9. Edit this story.

skivvies

WASHINGTON (AP)—American taxpayers have spent more than a million dollars to help one of Japans biggest underwear makers pitch it's skivvies in Japan.

Gunze is just one of over a hundred foreign firms that have benefited from taxper-financed advertising in Europe and Asia worth $20,000,000, according to USDA documents obtained by The Associated Press.

The promotions feature home furnishings and clothing—from baby wear and boxer shorts to Scottish knits and Italian bluejeans—made over seas by foreign workers in mostly foreign-owned plants using U.S. cotton.

Gunze, the Japanese underwear manufacturer, benefited from advertising worth $1. 15 M in 1992 and 1993, the USDA reported.

Sheets and sweaters made by Benetton, a trendy Italian clothing maker that has annual sales of two billion dollars, were promoted in advertising worth another $1.3 million.

"Why should we promote sales of Japanese underwear, manufactured by Japanese companies for sale to the Japanese, in Japan? Give me a break!" said Rep. Peter H. Kostmayer, (D-Pa.). who's investigation of the USDA's Market Promotion Program turned up the list of foreign participants.

Under the program, USDA gives $200 million a year to industry associations and private companies for overseas promotions of products containing U.S. comodities.

In the case of cotton, the industry's Cotton Council International has received about $64 million since 1990 for overseas promotions. Another $15.8 M is set aside for 1994.

No money actually changes hands between the cotton Council and the individual textile and apparrel manufacturers. Instead, the cotton Council spends its money on ads touting U.S. cotton. Some mention specific products.

In return, the firms mention U.S. cotton in there own advertising and display the cotton USA trademark. Featured items must be made from at least 50% U.S. cotton.

"We give them some recognition, but its more self-serving—to identify and link in the consumers mind products that use American cotton so that we can build market share," said Adrain Hunnings, Executive Director of Cotton Council Internatl.

He said USDA's figures show the entire value of an advertising campaign, when mention of a company may only amount to a few seconds of broadcast time or 1" on a magazine page.

"Never was payment made to Benetton, never did we put any money into their ad campaign," Hunnings said.

One ad begins like this" "Ingredients for a lazy morning: Fresh coffee from Brazil. Relaxed cat from Persia. Sheets from Benetton. Cotton from America."

The next 3 paragraphs tout the fresh crisp comfortable feel of cotton, especially cotton from America. Pictured is a square-inch Benetton logo and the Cotton USA mark.

A current Benetton add pictures a dying A. I. D. S. victim. Earlier ads showed a black woman nursing a white baby and a priest and nun kissing.

Kostmayer and Sen Patrick Leahy, D-Vt., chairperson of the Senate Agriculture Cte., say it is wrong to spend tax payer money to help foreign companies advertise.

"our textile market is hurting terribly in this country. There are clothing products, textile products being manufactured in the United States by American workers that now are having to compete overseas with foreign products getting U.S. subsidies," Kostmeyer said.

A USDA official, however, said the purpose of the program is to move U.S. commodoties off the farm.

"We have not discriminated between U. S. and foreign companies and big companies and little companies. If they have a project that appears to move the product, we've treated them all equally," said Phil Mackie, Assistant Administrator for commodity and Marketing Programs at USDA's Foreign Agricultural Service.

Mackie, however, conceedes that its hard to measure the success of the cotton promotion program, as with any advertisingampaign.

Total exports of U.S. cotton have jumped from 6.7 million bails in 1990, when the cotton Council received it's first grant, to a high to 7.8 bails in 1992. Exports are expected to fall to six point eight million bails in the 1994 marketing year, which ends July 31.

10. Edit this story.

ozone

NEW YORK (AP)—Alarm over a new report that shows the ozone is deteriorating faster than scientists thought has focused attention on what consumers can do to ease the depletion.

While aerosol cans get much of the attention, the real villan is the auto air airconditioner, environmentalists say.

About a hundred fifty million air-conditioned cars and trucks travel Americas roads. Each carries about two and a half lbs. of ozone-depleting chloroflurocarbons, or CFC's. Thats about 5 times as much as the typical home refrigerator, which contains 6-8 oz.

"Nearly 20% of all the CFCs in the United States is coming from car air conditioners," said David Doniger, director of the ozone project at the Natural Resources Defence Council in Washington, D.C.

CFC's contain molecules of chlorine monoxide and bromine monoxide, which react in sunlight and deplete the protective layer.

The discovery that the ozine layer is thinning at an accelerating rate prompted President Clinton to announce today a quicker pace for phasing out ozone-depleting chemicals in the U.S.

The destruction is allows more of the sun's harmful ultra violet radiation to reach earth, raising the incidence of skin cancer and cataracts. It also can weaken the body's defenses against infection and can damage crops and marine life.

Edie Tshering of the Council on Economic Priorities said the most important thing consumers can do to help stop the release of CFC's is to have there air conditioners and refrigerators serviced regularly by technicians who capture and recycle CFCs.

"When you get rid of an old air conditioner or refrigerator, look into opportunities to have it recycled rather than just throw it away," Tschering said. "There are companies that will do that."

The New York-based council published "Shopping for a Better World," which calls itself a "guide to socially responsible supermarket shopping."

But smart action by consumers will not come close to solving the problem. The ozone threat won't pass until CFC-cased coolers and refrigerators are replaced, and that will be expensive.

Cathy Andriadis, a spokesperson for DuPont, said $135 billion worth of equipment in the United states is dependent on CFCs. DuPont is one of 15 manufacturers of CFCs worldwide.

In the meantime, the council's shopping guide has a few words to sat about those misunderstood aerosol cans.

In 1978, the U.S. government banned the use of ozone-depleting chemicals in most aerosol spraycans. Deodorants, hair sprays and many household spray cleaners are now powered by air pumps or by such chemicals as propane or butane, which doesn't contain chlorine and, therefor, won't damage the ozone layer.

But not all aerosol cans were covered by the ban. "We did a survey by cruising the shelves of supermarkets, drug stores and shoe-care stores, those sorts of places," Doniger said. "We found 150 products with 1,1,1-trichloroethane," or methyl chloroform.

The products containing methyl chloroform include bug sprays, fabric protectors, waterproofing sprays and spot removers.

Methyl chloroform is among a newer generation of chemicals that are safer for the ozone, but not entirely safe. Many belong to the class of substances called hydrochlorofluorocarbons. The are now used in refrigerators and other cooling equipment.

"It's like hitting the ozone layer with small-arms fire instead of artillery shells," Doniger said. "Its still not good for it."

The propane and butane used in some houshold products are the only propellants that are entirely safe for the ozone layer. But they have another drawback: they contribute to the greenhouse affect.

11. Edit the following wire story so it conforms to AP style. Eliminate errors of style, punctuation, spelling, grammar and fact. Trim the story from 411 words to 300 or fewer.

```
condom recall

NEW YORK, N.Y. (AP)—The city denied today it acted irresponsibly in delaying

public announcement for nearly two weeks' of the recall of faulty condoms

supplied to nearly 300 public agencies for free distrubution.

     Under fire at a news conference this morning for tardy disclosure of the

recall of 750,000 Saxon condoms, New York City Health Commissioner Woodrow

"Woody" Myers, Jr., M.D., told reporters he felt his department had acted

properly "by contacting all organizations to whom we supply condoms" by Oct.

14.

     The rubber recall became public knowledge Friday when news of it

apparently was leaked inadvertently to a writer for The New York Times by a

health department employee and was reported in the press.

     The employee, who asked not to be named, said, "The department told us to,

uh, you might say, 'keep a hat' on this information."

     Dr. Myers news conference was hastily organized this morning at New York

City Health Dept. headquarters.

     He explained the health department was informed by Safetex Corporation of

Colonial Hts., Virginia, on October 2 that 15 lots of Saxon spermicidal

condoms may exceed the four per 1,000 pinhole leakage rate allowed by federal

FDA standards.

     He said Safetex asked for recall of these lots and promised replacement.

Since the health department did not know to whom condoms from these lots had
```

been distributed, the entire distribution of 750,000 Saxons was recalled, even though some had already been distributed to the public.

"We don't know how many have been distributed or how many remain at the agencies we serve, waiting to be picked up and returned to Safetex," Myers said.

"To suggest that every Saxon condom we distributed was defective would be wrong. They were not, there was pretty low risk of pregnancy or transmission of disease. but it is a higher risk than we find acceptable."

"The agency that has the formal reponsibility in this situation is the FDA."

Meyers said only 22% of the condoms distributed by his department come from Safetex. The other 88 percent comes from from Ansell, a N.J. firm, which has taken a new order for 500,000 condoms to be delivered in 30 days to help replace the recalled rubbers.

The health department has been supplying 50 A. I. D. S. and teen-age pregnancy prevention agencies under contract for free condoms, the New York City Schools, and 250 other organizations that receive condoms on request as they need them.

12. Define the following news priority codes:

a. f _____

b. b _____

c. u _____

d. r _____

e. s _____

13. Define the following news category codes:

    a. i _____

    b. a _____

    c. n _____

    d. f _____

    e. w _____

14. Explain the differences among primary news services, supplemental news services and syndicated feature services. Describe the offerings of one of each.

15. Almost 90 percent of U.S. newspapers receive their national and international news from one news service. Discuss in a short essay either the pros or the cons of this fact.

16. Choose an important local news story from a daily newspaper. Discuss in class why it should or should not have been picked up by a news service.

17. Edit the following story from The Associated Press:

By the Associated Press

High medical bills-a burden shared by most Americans-are due in part to a relatively few ill people. And, people who generate much of the nation's medical expenses are often suffering from the effects of smoking, alcoholism, and obesity.

Few are burdening the many, in terms of medical bills. And researchers in Boston suggest that perhaps it's time for those few to pay a cost more like their share. The researchers' work, published last week in the "New England Journal of Medicine," turned up the finding that less than one and a-half percent of the nation's population may use half the hospital resources in a year.

The scientists suggest that these people should have to pay higher insurance premiums, or higher taxes, if national health insurance ever becomes a reality, after all, the doctors say, these people are ill because of harmful personal habits. Food, drink and cigarettes—carried to excess—have landed them in the hospital.

Naturally, many people with big medical bills may not have been able to prevent their illnesses. They may develop some kind of illness that could not have been predicted and that's tough to cure.

Some insurance companies already offer lower premiums for those who don't smoke—but the problem remains, proving that you don't smoke when you ask for that lower rate.

Blue Cross-Blue Shield is also encouraging subscribers to cut costs. It's promoting same-day surgery, procedures done on an outpatient basis instead of those requiring an overnight or longer stay. Among those procedures are biopsies some methods of sterilization, removal of the tonsils, and maybe some oral surgery.

Blue Cross says this not only saves money—it also shortens the nerve-wracking waiting period, and gets you back to work quicker.

And, you can seek a second opinion, which may save not only money but also the pain and trauma of surgery. At least one citizens Watchdog group feels there are too many unnecessary operations done, many of them paid for by taxes. The group, the Better Government Association (of Chicago), says that perhaps a third of all operations may not be medically necessary.

The association, which took many of its figures from House Subcommittee Hearings, also says major elective surgery in the U-S is increasing at four times the rate of the population.

Accuracy, accuracy, accuracy.

—*Joseph Pulitzer*

Checking Facts

"**IF your mother says she loves you**, check it out!" This adage has been around newsrooms for decades, serving as a reminder of the importance of journalistic accuracy and the role skepticism plays in achieving accuracy. Another newsroom notion holds that the ideal copy editor knows everything about something and something about everything. Language is the "something" that a perfect copy editor would know "everything" about. Reference materials provide the sources for editors to know "something about everything."

Assigning editors should detect gross inaccuracies and holes in a story and return it to the reporter who wrote it instead of sending it forward to the copy desk. Yet, copy editors must always be alert to errors, discrepancies and illogical statements in copy. Much of the skill in checking facts exists in sensing which specific facts to question because the sheer volume of copy a newspaper editor handles under deadline pressure does not allow the luxury of checking every single fact in each story. Editors at online newspapers, where Web sites are revised frequently each day, face even greater deadline pressure. Editors at public relations firms and magazines, where the pace tends to be less hectic, should double-check each fact in every story, and magazines typically hire fact-checkers for this purpose. The most frequent errors in news stories are in names, dates, locations and descriptions of past events.

When copy editors question facts in a story, four courses are open to them:

1. If the question can be answered by a reference source, the verification or correction can be made rather easily, provided the copy editor is facile at using reference materials.

2. If the writer is readily available, the question can be referred to that person.

3. If it is a question of company policy, taste or consistency, copy editors should know the policy, but if they do not, they must consult the chief copy editor or a managing editor.

4. If the fact is not vital and cannot be checked before deadline, it can be deleted from the story. Of course, this is the last resort, not merely an easy way out of a difficulty. A fact that is essential to the story must be checked at all costs, even if the story is held until a later edition.

To achieve the goal of being 100 percent accurate, copy editors need a librarian's working knowledge of reference materials in both printed and electronic format. This chapter provides overviews and lists of printed and electronic reference

---

The Teaching Library Internet Workshops at the University of California, Berkeley http://www.lib.berkeley.edu/TeachingLib/Guides/Internet/WhatIs.html offers a good starting point for students unfamiliar with the general concept of the Internet, the World Wide Web or other services available through the Internet. An excellent collection of Internet guides, tutorials and training information, plus a list of Internet glossaries is on the Web at http://lcweb.loc.gov/global/internet/training.html. The Library of Congress compiled this extensive list of Internet resources.

materials on general and specialized topics, emphasizing those most useful for quick fact-checking common to copy desk work.

To work efficiently, editors need to know when to consult a standard reference work, probably within reach on the copy desk or just a few keystrokes away on the Internet, and when a specialized book or electronic database is needed. Here is a sampling of questions that regularly send copy editors scrambling for answers:

- Was the architect for the General Motors Building in Detroit Albert Kahn or Louis Kahn?

- When did Pakistan become a republic?

- What is the name of the highest point in Australia?

- Is it Southwestern or Southwest Baptist Theological Seminary? Is it in Dallas or Fort Worth?

- Is the drawbridge across the Industrial Canal in New Orleans a vertical lift or a swing bridge?

- In what year was Hillary Rodham Clinton born?

- Is the seating capacity of the King Dome in Seattle really more than twice that of the Los Angeles Forum?

- How many stars does the flag of Honduras have?

- What were the top five U.S. companies in terms of advertising expenditures in 1997?

- Who is the mayor of Omaha, Neb.?

- According to the Bureau of Labor Statistics, what two occupations were projected to be the fastest growing during the next decade?

Experienced copy editors recognize that an up-to-date copy of *The World Almanac and Book of Facts* answers all these questions. Many other standard and specialized sources, including Internet locations where available, are listed at the end of this chapter. With practice, copy editors and other fact-checkers gain enough familiarity with these sources to know where to go for specific types of information and how to find it fast.

Reliability of reference sources

Journalists must exercise good judgment before relying on any information source, whether it comes from a personal interview or a printed or electronic document. This caution applies particularly to materials posted on the World Wide Web. Many documents floating around cyberspace are the electronic equivalent of "over-the-transom" anonymous notes. Anybody with a rudimentary knowledge of HTML (HyperText Markup Language) or Web authoring software and access to space on a server can post documents to the Web. Editors must decide what is reliable and what is junk. Publishers of standard reference works listed at the end of this chapter have established over many years reputations for accuracy and can be trusted to maintain similar rigor in their online publications and electronic databases.

No foolproof method exists to distinguish reputable Internet publishers from untrustworthy amateurs, but understanding Internet domains and recognizing the purpose of individual Web pages can help editors assess the accuracy of online information. To determine the domain, examine the URL (Uniform Resource Locator) of the particular information. This illustration explains how to break down e-mail and Web site addresses:

HOW TO UNRAVEL A WEB ADDRESS

HyperText Transfer Protocol. This tells your browser a Web page is coming up, rather than an FTP or gopher site.

This period is used instead of space to separate address elements on the Internet.

High-level domain. This identifies the kind of organization or country of origin. Common HLDs include com=commercial, edu=university, gov=government, ie=Ireland, us=United States.

Directory where the Web page is stored.

http://www.scholastic.com/instructor/index.html

A flourish of unnecessary punctuation that has become standard

Subdomain. Most World Wide Web servers use www, but some use tags such as web3 or w3.

Unique domain. This is the name an organization gives its Internet site. Domain names must be registered with InterNIC, at 703.742.4757, and it's a good idea to get there first with the name you want.

The Hypertext Markup Language (HTML) file that your browser uses to display the Web page.

NOTE: Some Internet addresses are more case-sensitive than others. Copy addresses exactly, and only use capital letters when they're called for.

High-level domains are as follows:

- **mil** = military agency (U.S)

- **gov** = government institutions (U.S.)

- **edu** = educational institutions

- **org** = non-profit organization

- **com** = commercial

- **net** = networks

- **de**, **uk**, etc. = two-letter, nation-specific designations (for example, **de** is Germany, **uk** is United Kingdom)

Fact-checkers can learn the name, address and phone number for owners of unique domains for non-military and non-U.S. government top-level domains by contacting the InterNIC Registration Services at http://www.networksolutions.com/cgi-bin/whois/whois. Generally, information in the .gov and .edu domains is considered more reliable than that in other domains, but this is not a hard-and-fast rule. After all, many educational institutions provide server space to all faculty, staff and students with no peer review or other attempts at verifying what is posted.

When assessing the reliability of online information, also consider the purpose of the Web site on which the information is found. Web pages usually fall into one of these categories:

▶**Personal,** a page published by an individual who may or may not be affiliated with a larger institution. Personal pages may reside on any of the domains; the most common are .net or .com, and .edu for students and faculty members. A tilde (~) is frequently embedded somewhere in the URL. Personal pages may be a useful source for personal opinion, but they aren't reliable as sources of factual information.

▶**Advocacy,** a page promoting ideas, trying to sway public opinion. These typically reside in the .org domain. As with printed materials, editors must consider the source and know the agenda of the organization sponsoring the page.

▶**Informational,** pages for the purpose of presenting factual information. The URLs frequently end in .edu or .gov, because many of these pages are sponsored by educational institutions or government agencies, but commercial information brokers using a .com domain also post material on the Web.

▶**Marketing,** pages created to sell products and services. These exist primarily on the .com domain and their sponsors range from Fortune 500 companies to scam artists.

▶**News,** pages with the primary purpose to provide current information. News organizations generally sponsor these pages, with URLs also used in the .com domain.

Jim Kapoun, a university librarian, suggests these considerations and questions for evaluating the content of Web pages:*

- **Accuracy.** Does the page list the author and institution that published the page and provide a way of contacting the author?

- **Authority.** Does the page list the author's credentials and is its domain a preferred domain (.edu, .gov, .org, or .net)?

- **Objectivity.** Does the page provide accurate information with limited advertising and is it objective in presenting information?

- **Currency.** Is the page current, and is the date of the most recent update indicated on the page? Are links (if any) also up to date?

E-mail is a tool more helpful to reporters than to copy editors working under deadline pressure. E-mail discussion lists can be good sources for opinions, but better electronic sources exist for fact-checking. Discussion lists and those of special interest to journalists and public relations practitioners will be discussed later in this chapter.

Indexes

Copy editors most frequently need books or Web pages for quick fact-checking. Generally, copy editors have neither the time nor the need to consult indexes or Internet search engines (assuming that URLs for basic reference works are already bookmarked). If a story lacks sufficient background information or otherwise requires significant additional information, it needs to go back to the reporter, perhaps with a note about a specific index that could lead to articles in magazines or academic journals with information to fill holes in the reporter's story. Many such indexes are available in both printed and CD-ROM versions.

Indexes are first-stage tools in a two-stage search process. They help compile bibliographies about a topic. The second step is to find the particular periodical that published the desired article. Even major research libraries cannot afford to subscribe to every existing academic journal, many of which cost hundreds of dollars for an annual subscription. Often interlibrary loan services are the only way to secure a particular article, so reporters and their editors must be prepared for

---

*Jim Kapoun, "Teaching Undergrads Web Evaluation: a Guide for Library Instruction," College & Research Libraries News 59(7) (July/August 1998): 522-523. Online. http://www.ala.org/acrl/undwebev.html.

the delays inherent in seeking material from an out-of-town library. Editors should heed two cautions when consulting indexes:

- Use the index most appropriate for the subject matter.

- Try a variety of key words related to the subject.

College students sometimes report to their instructors that they searched at the library and found no articles about a particular topic. Upon questioning, these students often reveal that they gave up after finding nothing in the *Magazine Index* or *Reader's Guide to Periodical Literature.* These are excellent indexes for finding articles published in general magazines but not for articles published in scholarly journals specializing in a particular subject. It is essential to use a specialized index to find articles in academic journals focusing on a single subject area.

After selecting the best index, students often struggle to come up with key words that will lead to specific articles. Students, as well as reporters who are not knowledgeable about a subject they plan to write about, should read enough about the subject to get a feel for the special terminology or jargon associated with it— words that the indexer may have used. Specialized thesauri exist in some fields to help researchers isolate subject headings related to a topic. In addition, indexes generally include a listing of subject headings used within the volume.

Dozens of indexes are available, covering topics ranging from art to zoology. Most large university libraries make available one- or two-page guides to using these various indexes, and reference librarians genuinely enjoy working with patrons who need help compiling bibliographies. Ask them for help. Here are several widely used periodical indexes, most available in both print and electronic versions:

Reader's Guide to Periodical Literature. Indexes general and popular magazines, not scholarly journals, but often a good starting point for researching a topic before going to more specialized indexes and academic journals.

Humanities Index. Supplies author and subject references to more than 300 journals covering language and literature, performing arts, philosophy, religion, history and related subjects.

Social Sciences Index. Published quarterly; covers approximately 300 periodicals.

PAIS International. Covers social scientific fields, including political science, sociology, international relations, economics and law; indexes more than 800 English-language journals, as well as many newspapers and a selection of books and government documents.

Index to Legal Periodicals. Indexes articles published in legal journals in the United States, Canada, Great Britain, Ireland, Australia and New Zealand.

General Science Index. Indexes about 150 of the most prominent journals in the physical, life and health sciences.

Business Periodicals Index. Covers approximately 300 business periodicals, including popular and research journals as well as trade magazines.

Education Index. Provides a cumulative subject index to a selected list of education periodicals, proceedings and yearbooks.

▶**MLA International Bibliography.** Indexes articles about literature, language, linguistics and folklore from more than 3,000 journals, as well as books, book chapters, book series and dissertations.

▶**Index to United Nations Documents and Publications.** Indexes official records, mimeographed documents and periodicals of the United Nations. Includes the full text of U.N. resolutions and decisions and of plenary meetings of the General Assembly and the Security Council.

▶**CIS/Index.** Indexes all congressional publications, hearings, reports, documents and public laws; includes a legislative history section.

Internet search tools

The Internet is like a gigantic research library without a card catalog and a shopping mall without locator maps or directional signs. The World Wide Web simplifies Net navigation, and search tools help users find what they need, but, thus far, no single search can ferret out everything on the Internet about a particular topic. The search is a process, requiring several stages, much like using reference books in a library.

Many of the search tools use Boolean logic, a way to combine terms using AND, OR, AND NOT and sometimes NEAR. AND requires that all terms appear in a record. OR retrieves records with either term. AND NOT excludes terms. Parentheses may be used to sequence operations and group words. Almost all search tools on the Web display a "help" icon, and the few minutes it takes to read the search tips for that particular tool will speed the search in the long term.

These are three types of Internet search tools:

- Search engines
- Meta-search engines, also called all-in-one searches or parallel searches
- Lists of databases or hypertext links indexed by subject, sometimes called "webliographies" to correspond with bibliographies of printed resources

Search engines

These typically use computer programs called spiders to continually scan the Internet, but engines vary widely in their range of search features and in the way they index and present their search results. Some index complete Web pages or page titles; others add material selectively and review sites based on content; still others present subject indexes for users to browse by keywords. Some engines also search Usenet postings, Gopher and Telnet sites. These are several popular search engines:

▶**Infoseek,** http://www.infoseek.com

▶**Alta Vista Advanced Search,** http://www.altavista.com

▶**Northern Light,** http://www.nlsearch.com

▶**Hotbot,** http://www.hotbot.com

▶**Lycos,** http://www.lycos.com

▶**WebCrawler,** http://www.Webcrawler.com

▶**Galaxy,** http://www.einet.net/cgi-bin/wais-text-multi?

These search engines present hierarchial subject headings:

▶**Yahoo,** http://www.yahoo.com

▶**Librarians' Index to the Internet,** http://sunsite.berkeley.edu/InternetIndex

▶**e-Blast from the Encyclopaedia Britannica,** http://www.ebig.com

▶**Excite,** http://www.excite.com

Meta-search engines

These query several search engines at one time. Some experts recommend using one of these all-in-one engines at the beginning of your search; other experts like to begin with a single engine before conducting a meta-search. Drawbacks of meta-searches are the slight increase in retrieval time and the lack of precision in syntax allowed on individual search engines.

▶**Inference Find,** http://www.infind.com

▶**MetaFind,** http://www.metafind.com

▶**MetaCrawler,** http://www.metacrawler.com

▶**Dogpile,** http://www.dogpile.com

Lists

These services may search databases available on the Web or they may be lists of hypertext links compiled by subject-area experts. To determine whether a specialized database is available for a particular subject, try these three services:

▶**Internet Sleuth,** http://www.isleuth.com

▶**All-In-One Search Page,** http://www.allonesearch.com

▶**Special Search Engine,** http://www.nut.edu.sg/library/specialcat.htm

Here are several lists compiled especially for journalists and public relations practitioners or students preparing for communications careers:

▶**WWW Virtual Library: Journalism,** one of the earliest and most extensive Internet resources for journalists. This site, covering all forms of journalism, broadcasting, communications, media and news, is maintained by John Makulowich, senior writer for a business newspaper published by Post-Newsweek Business Information, Inc., http://www.cais.com/makulow/vlj.html.

▶**A Journalist's Guide to the Internet,** by Christopher Callahan, assistant dean of journalism at the University of Maryland College of Journalism, http://reporter.umd.edu/.

▶**Power Reporting Bookmarks,** compiled by Bill Dedman, Pulitzer Prize-winning director of computer-assisted reporting for The Associated Press, http://powerreporting.com/

▶**Megasources,** compiled by Dean Tudor, professor at the School of Journalism, Ryerson Polytechnic University, Toronto, Canada, http://www.ryerson.ca/journal/megasources.html

▶**The Writers' Well,** sponsored by Ink Magazine, http://www.hellskitchen.com/well.htm

Many professional associations, foundations and institutes host Web sites with content related to communications, and most contain links to related sites. Here is a sampling:

▶**American Copy Editors Society,** http://www.copydesk.org

▶**American Society of Newspaper Editors,** http://www.asne.org

▶**Investigative Reporters and Editors,** http://www.ire.org

▶**National Association of Broadcasters,** http://www.nab.org

▶**National Press Club,** http://npc.press.org

▶**National Press Photographers Association,** http://metalab.unc.edu/nppa

▶**Public Relations Society of America,** http://www.prsa.org

▶**Public Relations Student Society of America,** http://www.prssa.org

▶**Society for News Design,** http://www.snd.org/

▶**Society of Professional Journalists,** http://spj.org

▶**Society of Publication Designers,** http://www.spd.org

▶**The Poynter Institute,** http://www.poynter.org

▶**The Freedom Forum,** http://www.freedomforum.org

In addition, many mass communication programs at universities have Web sites with material of interest to students and professionals.

Just as printed periodicals alter their content from issue to issue and occasionally alter their formats, the Internet changes constantly. More individuals, organizations and commercial enterprises create new Web sites and add pages each day; existing Web pages undergo frequent revision. Editors shouldn't assume an Internet search conducted yesterday will remain unchanged today. New material about a particular topic may have been added; existing documents may change URLs. This continual state of flux makes the Internet an exciting place to explore again and again and an invaluable resource for communicators.

Internet discussion groups

Although more useful for reporters in gathering information for stories than for editors, Internet discussion groups, also called "listserves" and "mailing lists," can be helpful for fact-checking when copy editors aren't facing immediate deadlines. Members of discussion groups exchange opinions and information via e-mail with people who share common interests. With an e-mail account established, it is simple to join such a group. First, decide which group or groups are of interest, and then send an e-mail message to the central computer serving those particular groups.

To communicate with other group subscribers, send an e-mail message to the list address (not the same as the subscription address), and the message will be circulated automatically to all members. The list of discussion groups numbers in the thousands, dealing with almost every subject imaginable. Some groups discuss highly specialized academic-related topics; others focus on popular culture, such as individual television shows or musicians; others concentrate on sports, recreational activities or hobbies.

Keep the initial return message from the listserve that acknowledges a subscription and explains how that particular list operates. This information includes instructions about how to quit the group temporarily or permanently. It will also explain whether the list has a digest or index feature or is archived. Some discussion lists generate multiple messages each day, rather quickly filling electronic mailboxes. It's wise to "unsubscribe" from lists that turn out to be uninteresting or that generate too many messages.

The initial acknowledgment message also may include important notes about proper etiquette observed by members. Despite a sense of anonymity offered by the Net, segments of the Internet, including discussion groups, operate like social or professional gatherings and individual communities. One doesn't want to become an unwelcome presence in the community. Newcomers to a discussion group should "lurk" awhile, meaning that they should read mail from other members for at least a few days before sending their own messages.

Another caution: Many, if not most, messages posted to discussion lists are opinions, not facts. Don't accept material from discussion lists as factual without verifying the information. In addition to real experts, these lists attract self-proclaimed experts who may transmit inaccurate statements.

Here's another piece of advice, particularly for students: Don't post questions to a discussion group that can be answered by using readily available reference sources. Members who buy access to e-mail through commercial vendors often pay according to the amount of time they spend online or the number of messages they send and receive. No member wants to spend time or money reading a message from someone who appears too lazy to go to a library or to conduct online searches. A request to discussion group members for help on a term paper or other research project is appropriate only after other resources have been exhausted. Summarize sources already consulted and information already known about the topic, and then frame a specific, narrow question for members to address.

To find discussion lists and addresses for subscribing, use an Internet browser to search these sites:

▶ **InterLinks,** http://alabanza.com/kabacoff/Inter-Links/listserv.html

▶ **Liszt,** http://www.liszt.com

▶**The Directory of Scholarly and Professional E-Conferences,** http://n2h2.com/KOVACS/Sindex.html

▶**TILE.NET/LISTS, The Reference to Internet Discussion & Information Lists,** http://tile.net/lists/

The names of some groups of particular interest to journalists and public relations practitioners and the wording of the subscription message are shown in Figure 5-1.

Figure 5-1
Here are some of the discussion groups of interest to journalists and public relations practitioners, along with information on how to subscribe to them.

Discussion Lists for Journalism and Public Relations

AGJOUR-L: Agriculture Journalism Topics
E-mail to: listproc@lists.missouri.edu
Body of Message: subscribe agjour-l

AIRWAVES: Daily digest of newsgroup
E-mail to: majordomo@jibboo.com
Body of Message: subscribe airwaves

AMEND1-L: First Amendment Issues
E-mail to: listserv@uafsysb.uark.edu
Body of Message: subscribe amend1-l <your name>

BONG-L: Burned-Out Newspaper Guild. Newsletter with journalism happenings, text cartoons
E-mail to: majordomo@majordomo.netcom.com
Body of Message: subscribe bong-l

BRDCST-L: Broadcasting and cable including management, sales and public relations
E-mail to: listserv@CRCVMS.UNL.EDU
Body of Message: subscribe brdcst-l <your name>

CABLEREG-L: Cable Regulation Digest
E-mail to: majordomo@majordomo.netcom.com
Body of Message: subscribe cablereg-l <your name>

CARR-L: Computer-Assisted Reporting and Research
E-mail to: listserv@ulkyvm.louisville.edu
Body of Message: subscribe carr-l <your full name>

COPYEDITING-L: Discussions about editing material for all sorts of publications
E-mail to: listproc@cornell.edu
Body of Message: subscribe copyediting-l <your full name>

FOI-L: Freedom of Information list
E-mail to: FOI-L-request@listserv.syr.edu
Body of Message: subscribe foi-l <your name>

HSJOURN: High School Scholastic Journalism
E-mail to: listproc@latech.edu
Body of Message: subscribe hsjourn

IRE-L: Investigative Reporters and Editors
E-mail to: listproc@showme.missouri.edu
Body of Message: subscribe ire-l <your full name>

JHISTORY: Academic and professional issues relating to journalism history
E-mail to: listproc@lists.nyu.edu
Body of Message: subscribe jhistory <your name>

JOURNET-L: Journalism education at the university level
E-mail to: listserv@american.edu
Body of Message: subscribe JOURNET-L <your name>

MAGWRITE: Magazine Writers Discussion List is an unmoderated discussion list created to help freelance magazine writers, both published and unpublished, find markets, brainstorm on articles, receive critiques of their work, and share their thoughts on all aspects of magazine article writing
E-mail to: listserv@maelstrom.stjohns.edu
Body of Message: subscribe magwrite <your full name>

MU-EPJ: Missouri University Electronic Photojournalism forum
E-mail to: listproc@lists.missouri.edu
Body of Message: subscribe mu-epj

NFICTION: Non-Fiction Writers Workshop
E-mail to: lists@psu.edu
Body of Message: subscribe nfiction

NICAR-L: National Institute for Computer-Assisted Reporting
E-mail to: listproc@showme.missouri.edu
Body of Message: subscribe nicar-l <your name>

NPPA-L: National Press Photographers Association, including news photographers and editors, system operators and graphics editors. Includes print and electronic media
E-mail to: listserv@cmuvm.csv.cmich.edu
Body of Message: subscribe nppa-l <your name>

PRFORUM: Public Relations Forum
E-mail to: listserv@iupui.edu
Body of Message: subscribe prforum <your name>

SHOPTALK: Fitzpatrick and Associates in San Francisco publishes a five-day newsletter on job changes, newspaper article reprints, ratings, jobs and letters to the editors all about TV
E-mail to: listserv@listserv.syr.edu
Body of Message: subscribe shoptalk <your name>

WRITER-L
E-mail to: majordomo@nicar-org
Body of Message: subscribe writer-l

Usenet newsgroups

Usenet newsgroups have been called the watercoolers of the Internet. They are similar to discussion groups in that they contain messages from people worldwide and are grouped by interest, but users gain access to groups and read messages via the World Wide Web instead of e-mail. Newsgroups tend to be much less scholarly than discussion lists, but content varies according to academic disciplines. Thousands of Usenet newsgroups exist and new ones are created daily.

Newsreaders, a feature of Internet browsers and most Internet service providers, provide access to newsgroups, although ISPs usually narrow the list somewhat instead of trying to carry all of them. Online files accompany browsers and ISP newsreader programs to help users configure their computers to the specifications of individual newsreaders. The next step is to determine which newsgroups to read. Here one needs to understand how newsgroups are organized in hierarchies.

Newsgroup hierarchies begin with the major subject area, followed by several words, each separated by a dot, describing subareas. For example, *rec.sports* is a newsgroup about sports; *rec.sports.basketball.women* is a more specialized rec.sports group about women's basketball. The following are the major newsgroup hierarchies:

▶ **alt** (alternate). Anything goes in this category and almost any one person can add a newsgroup to the alt group. Some ISPs don't carry the alt newsgroup because of the huge number of them and because the content of many is objectionable to ISP customers.

▶ **comp** (computers). These range from highly technical "geekspeak" to discussions of the merits of individual computer manufacturers.

▶ **misc** (miscellaneous). These are the topics that either don't fit in any of the other hierarchies or that are too general to fit a specific one.

▶ **rec** (recreation). Here people discuss topics such as sports, hobbies, outdoor activities, games and television. Each hobby, game and television show may spawn a separate newsgroup.

▶ **sci** (science). Discussions here get fairly technical. The group is subdivided into various scientific disciplines such as sci.physics.

▶ **soc** (social). All sorts of societal and cultural issues are aired here. Social topics may subdivide further to focus on an individual country, state or city, for example.

▶ **talk.** Here the talk is frequently about controversial, often emotional topics such as politics and religion.

The search engines listed earlier in this chapter can lead to newsgroups. This full-text search tool is easy to use:

▶ **DejaNews,** http://www.dejanews.com

Gopher

Gopher is an early (1991), text-only method for accessing Internet documents. To a large degree, gopher has been subsumed in the World Wide Web, so it won't get much attention in this book. You might think of gopher as "go for" because it is an easy-to-use, menu-driven tool that goes in search of information located on thousands of Internet sites. Just as four-legged gophers burrow through the ground, gopher software tunnels through the Internet, allowing users to find information without knowing addresses for specific sites.

Gopher files are presented in simple-to-understand menus, which are sometimes linked to in Web pages. Instead of using the http:// prefix for a Web page address, gopher sites may be accessed on the Web by the gopher:// prefix in the address. Gopher Jewels is a searchable Web site that leads to gopher files, including topics in journalism, communication and broadcasting.

▶ **Gopher Jewels,** http://galaxy.einet.net/GJ/index.html

Commercial electronic databases

Much of the information on the Internet is free, particularly most databases containing government records, but fees for information are more common as news organizations and other information brokers attempt to recoup their expenses and as mechanisms for online financial transactions become widely accepted. The 1998 edition of the *Gale Directory of Databases* reported that from 1975 to 1997 the number of electronic databases increased by a factor of 34, from 301 to 10,338. During that 22-year period, the number of database records (the smallest unit in electronic databases) grew by a factor of 217, from 52 million to 11.27 billion. Many of these are commercial, value-added databases, accessible either online or in CD-ROM format. Some database vendors have been in the information-selling business for many years and recently adapted their services to electronic technology, offering duplicate services in both print and electronic versions. Other vendors concentrate solely on computerized databases.

Costs of many electronic databases, based on a fee plus charges per minute for online time, are prohibitive for most individuals and small publications or public relations firms. DIALOG, Nexis and Dow Jones News/Retrieval are three of the large commercial electronic database providers used by university libraries and major publications. Each offers search services and full-text articles from hundreds of newspapers, magazines and other publications. To minimize search time and online fees for using these services, many publications now hire librarians trained to use electronic databases rather than allow reporters and editors to conduct their own searches. Likewise, college students typically funnel requests to librarians who know how to go online and find materials quickly.

CD-ROMs have become an increasingly popular medium because of the vast amount of information contained on easily portable discs. University and municipal libraries provide computer terminals for patrons to view indexes and other reference materials on CD-ROMs. As thousands of compact discs enter the marketplace, printed directories have emerged to catalog these products. In addition to the previously mentioned *Gale Directory of Databases*, another database directory is *CD-ROMs in Print: An International Guide to CD-ROM, Multimedia & Electronic Book Products*, published by the Meckler Corporation.

Standard reference works

The standard reference works described in this section will help editors find information quickly. They are listed by subject categories with Web addresses supplied for those available on the Internet. A separate subcategory for Web resources is included for some topics.

Current events sources

▶**Congressional Record.** The daily record is set into type a few hours after the House and Senate complete the legislative day and is available the next morning online at http://lcweb.loc.gov/global/legislative/congrec.html.

▶**CQ (Congressional Quarterly) Weekly Report.** This weekly summary of the actions of the U.S. Congress includes lists of legislation voted on or under consideration and of Senate and House votes.

▶**Facts on File.** Published weekly, this source gives a summary of international information on news events and domestic developments.

▶**Urban Affairs Abstracts.** This is a weekly abstracting service of the National League of Cities. It includes abstracts of articles related to urban affairs. Topics range from aging to solid waste disposal.

Factual data, statistics

▶**American Statistics Index.** This is a master guide and index to statistical publications of the U.S. government. Publications are listed by title, subject and other categories.

▶**Census of Population: General Population Characteristics.** Published for each general census period, this multi-volume set summarizes census data for the nation. Available online at http://www.census.gov.

▶**Columbia Encyclopedia.** This one-volume edition contains a wide range of information.

▶**County and City Data Book.** This provides statistical information on counties and cities throughout the country.

▶**Demographic Yearbook.** The United Nations publishes this volume, which gives world population data and statistics on such topics as mortality, marriage and divorce.

▶**Guide to Economic Indicators.** Non-expert's guide to frequently cited economic indicators in finance, inflation, labor, supply and demand and more.

▶**Guinness Book of World Records.** This book is the final authority on world records in a variety of fields. It is updated each year.

▶**Historical Statistics of the United States.** This publication gives comparative historical statistics for the country in areas such as agriculture, labor, migration and population. Available online at http://www.ucl.ac.uk/Library/ELIB/services/histatus.htm.

▶**Regional Economic Information System.** Contains personal income and employment estimates for states, counties and MSAs. Data ranges from 1969, with projections to 2045.

▶**Standard Education Almanac.** This book includes statistics on education in the United States.

▶ **Statistical Abstract of the United States.** Published by the Government Printing Office, this is a digest of data collected by all the statistical agencies of the U.S. government and by some private agencies. It has been issued since 1878. Similar statistical abstracts are available for individual states. Available online at http://www.census.gov/prod/2/gen/96statab/96statab.html.

▶ **Statistical Yearbook.** It includes world statistics on population, agriculture, industry, communications, health, culture and many other areas of economic and social affairs. A shortcoming is that no index is included.

▶ **Survey of Current Business.** Published biannually by the U.S. Department of Commerce, this book gives data on national income and production.

▶ **World Almanac and Book of Facts.** This handbook of miscellaneous information includes such subjects as copyright law, presidential elections, weights and measures, and flags of the world.

▶ **World Factbook.** The World Factbook is produced annually by the Central Intelligence Agency for use by U.S. government officials. The Factbook contains information about the geography, people, economy, industry, government, transportation and defense of the countries of the world. Some editions include country maps and photographs of flags. Available online at http://www.odci.gov/cia/publications/factbook/index.html.

ELECTRONIC RESOURCES

▶ **American Community Network.** This site contains detailed profiles of every city, county and metropolitan area in the United States. It is searchable by state, education level, demographics and more. Available at http://www.acn.net.

▶ **Acronym Finder.** This site contains information about common acronyms and abbreviations about all subjects, but focuses on computers, technology, commerce and the military. Available at http://www.mtnds.com/af.

Biographical information

▶ **American Men and Women of Science.** This volume contains information about the lives and professional activities of the people most instrumental in shaping science in America.

▶ **Biographical Dictionary of Musicians.** This work contains short biographical pieces on musicians of the past and present.

▶ **Biography and Genealogy Master Index.** This indexes more than 350 Who's Who and other current works of collective biography. It is a good place to begin a biographical search.

▶ **Congressional Directory.** This is a good source for biographical information on members of Congress, along with their committee assignments, addresses and press representatives.

▶ **Contemporary Authors.** Restricted to living authors, it includes those who have written relatively little and those who have written in obscure fields.

▶**International Year Book and Statesmen's Who's Who.** This work contains information on international and national organizations, including brief biographies of world leaders in commerce, education, industry, government and religion.

▶**Who's Who.** This biographical dictionary, published annually, gives sketches of prominent people.

▶**Who's Who Among African-Americans.** This is a biographical dictionary of notable living African-Americans. It includes a geographical and occupation index.

▶**Who's Who in America.** This is another biographical dictionary of notable living people.

▶**Who's Who in American Art.** This dictionary includes living artists, critics, dealers and other people active in art.

▶**Who's Who in American Politics.** This includes biographical sketches and current addresses of people in national, state and local government.

▶**Who's Who in Rock Music.** This volume contains biographical data on popular rock musicians, including individual performers and groups.

▶**Who's Who in Television and Cable.** This work includes information about more than 2,000 people in the field.

▶**Who's Who in the Theatre: A Biographical Record of the Contemporary Stage.** This volume provides biographical sketches of those involved with modern theater, including players, dramatists, composers, critics, managers, scenic artists, historians and biographers.

▶**Who's Who of American Women.** This volume includes biographical sketches of American women of achievement.

ELECTRONIC RESOURCES

▶**Biography and People Finder.** Contains biographical information about more than 20,000 people, past and present. Available at http://www.biography.com/find/find.html.

Book reviews

▶**Book Review Digest.** This publication condenses published reviews of fiction and nonfiction. It is also an index to reviews published in selected British and American periodicals.

▶**Technical Book Review Index.** Reviews of new books dealing with technical, scientific and medical subjects are indexed in this monthly publication.

Directories of newspapers and magazines

▶**Directory of the College Student Press in America.** This information is similar to that in the Editor and Publisher International Yearbook, except that it pertains to college newspapers and magazines.

▶**Editor and Publisher International Yearbook.** This annual reference provides information about U.S. and foreign newspapers as well as other information about the industry.

▶**Ulrich's International Periodicals Directory.** This is a subject guide to periodicals published throughout the world.

ELECTRONIC RESOURCES

▶**Publist.** This Web site contains a comprehensive directory of more than 150,000 publications and 800 newspapers, and gives information about status, subject, frequency and publisher's address and phone. Data comes from Ulrich's International Periodicals Directory. Available at http://www.publist.com.

Dictionaries and manuals of language and style

▶**The American Thesaurus of Slang.** This book covers general slang and colloquialisms.

▶**The Dictionary of Bias-Free Usage: A Guide to Nondiscriminatory Language.** Author Rosalie Maggio provides advice on how to avoid language bias concerning race, gender, sexual orientation, ethnic background, religion or belief system, age and class.

▶**A Dictionary of Modern English Usage.** This classic by Henry Watson Fowler provides definitions, pronunciations, spellings of plurals, and essays on the use and misusage of words in the English language.

▶**The Elements of Style.** Generations of journalists have learned the rules of usage and composition from studying this guide by William Strunk and E.B. White. Available online at http://www.columbia.edu/acis/bartleby/strunk/index.html.

▶**The Handbook of Nonsexist Writing.** Written by Casey Miller and Kate Swift, this book is valuable for writers and speakers who are trying to free their language from semantic bias.

▶**The Nonsexist Communicator: Solving the Problems of Gender and Awkwardness in Modern English.** This book by Bobbye D. Sorrels provides help for eradicating sexist communication.

▶**The Nonsexist Word Finder: A Dictionary of Gender-Free Usage.** This is another reference book by Rosalie Maggio that promotes gender-free speaking and writing.

▶**Oxford English Dictionary.** The most authoritative English-language dictionary, a 13-volume work, attempts to show the history of each word in the English language. Available online at http://www.oed.com/.

▶**Roget's Thesaurus of English Words and Phrases.** This aid to word selection can be especially valuable to headline writers. It provides categories of words classified by ideas. Available online at http://www.thesaurus.com/.

ELECTRONIC RESOURCES

▶**A Web of Online Dictionaries.** This site contains a reference point to dictionary search engines, thesauri and multi-lingual dictionaries. Available at: http://www.facstaff.bucknell.edu/rbeard/diction1.html.

Business and advertising

▶**Demographics USA.** This book lists information on consumer buying power including detailed market, population, household and retail sales by location.

▶**International Directory of Company Histories.** This directory includes information on the development of about 2,000 of the world's largest and most influential companies.

▶**Simmons Study of Media and Markets.** This multi-volume set provides data about buying habits in the United States.

▶**Standard & Poor's Register.** This book lists 45,000 major corporations and their addresses, officers, directors, stock, annual sales and number of employees. Indexed by SIC codes, geographic location and corporate family.

▶**Standard Directory of Advertisers.** Included are more than 17,000 companies that use national or regional advertising. The amount of money spent on advertising is broken down by media type.

▶**Standard Rate and Data Services.** Advertising rates, specifications and circulation data about mass media are included in separate monthly publications for each type of media, including business publications, consumer magazines, direct mail lists, newspapers, radio and television.

ELECTRONIC RESOURCES

▶**CompaniesOnline.** This site contains brief information on more than 100,000 public and private companies and provides their addresses, ticker symbols and ownership information. It is indexed by company name and has a browse-by-industry function. Available at http://www.companiesonline.com.

Broadcasting and film

▶**Broadcasting Yearbook.** This directory to the broadcasting industry includes current information about the Federal Communications Commission, advertising, equipment and many other aspects of the industry.

▶**Television Factbook.** This guide for advertising, television and electronics industries covers television organizations, market rankings, cable television, manufacturers and educational opportunities.

▶**Television News Index and Abstracts.** Published by Vanderbilt University since 1972, this monthly volume is a summary of the evening news broadcasts of the three major television networks.

Religion

▶**The Bible.** This is the sacred book of Christianity, and the Old Testament portion of the Bible comprises the Holy Scriptures of Judaism.

▶**A Dictionary of Comparative Religion.** This volume defines religious terms and examines their variations in meaning from one religion to another.

▶**Encyclopedia Judaica.** This book gives comprehensive coverage of aspects of Jewish life, learning and history.

▶**Encyclopaedia of Religion and Ethics.** This volume contains articles about world religions, the great systems of ethics, philosophical ideas and religious customs.

▶**New Catholic Encyclopedia.** This work contains information about the history and activities of the Roman Catholic Church from its beginnings to the present.

▶**Religions in America.** This book provides theological explanations for all religious groups in the United States, from the major established groups to smaller, charismatic groups. Part one contains descriptions of each group. Part two contains an almanac with social data, facts and figures on religion in America. It also contains a glossary of religious terminology.

ELECTRONIC RESOURCES

▶**Virtual Christianity.** This site contains multiple translations of the English Bible, plus many foreign language translations including Spanish, French, Dutch, Swahili, Polish and Farsi. Available at: http://www.internetdynamics.com/pub/vc/bibles.html.

Government, politics and law

▶**The Almanac of American Politics.** This book provides state-by-state political background, census data, voter characteristics, election results and information about senators, representatives and governors.

▶**America Votes.** This work contains election statistics for all U.S. states in presidential, gubernatorial and congressional races.

▶**Black's Law Dictionary.** Now in its sixth edition, this legal dictionary has been considered a standard for almost a century.

▶**Congressional Quarterly Almanac.** This annual publication gives a survey of U.S. congressional legislation, divided into subject areas.

▶**Dictionary of American Politics.** This book contains concise definitions for political terms and includes political slogans, slang and nicknames.

▶**Political Handbook of the World.** This volume gives information about world politics and lists newspapers with political affiliations.

▶**Public Affairs Information Service Bulletin.** It indexes books, documents, pamphlets and periodicals relating to public policy issues. Available online at http://www.pais.inter.net/.

▶**United States Government Manual.** The official handbook of the U.S. government describes most governmental agencies and their programs and lists key officials.

ELECTRONIC RESOURCES

▶**American Law Sources On-Line (ALSO).** This site provides a comprehensive, uniform and useful compilation of links to all online sources of American law that are available without charge. This site contains additional links to sources of commentary and practice aids that are available without charge. Available at http://www.lawsource.com/also.

▶**Findlaw.** This site contains an overview of the legal world, including constitutional, intellectual property and labor law, law schools, U.S. Supreme Court cases and much more. Available at http://www.findlaw.com.

▶**The Government by Sterby.** This site is a compilation of federal government sites, including departments within all branches of government: executive, judicial, legislative, the White House, independent agencies, quasi-official agencies, state governments, foreign governments, search engines and links, and federal jobs. Available at http://www.erols.com/irasterb/gov.htm.

▶**The Legal Information Institute.** This site holds the Internet publications of the Legal Information Institute, part of Cornell Law School. It offers a collection of recent and historic Supreme Court decisions, the U.S Code, U.S. Constitution, federal rules of evidence and civil procedure, recent opinions of the N.Y. State Court of Appeals and commentary on them. Available at http://www.law.cornell.edu.

▶**Legal List: Internet Desk Reference.** The site provides lists of law-related Internet sources and includes Internet-based legal research instruction. The instructional text describes how to locate legal materials on the Internet using the best research methods and search tools, as well as the helpful companion lists that provide references to online law-related resources in many categories. Available at http://www.lcp.com/The-Legal-List/TLL-home.html.

▶**Thomas.** This site provides information about activities in Congress, including the latest floor actions and the status of bills that are being acted upon. Also available is information on committees, the Congressional Record, and information about the legislative processes. Historical documents, such as the Declaration of Independence, the Federalist Papers, the U.S. Constitution and others are available at http://thomas.loc.gov.

Health and medical

▶**Mosby's Medical Dictionary.** This dictionary contains complete definitions of current medical terminology including drugs, diseases and disorders.

▶**Family Health & Medical Guide.** This book, published by the American Academy of Family Physicians, provides basic information about prevention, infections, the body, special health groups and emotional and behavioral problems.

ELECTRONIC RESOURCES

▶**Centers for Disease Control and Prevention.** The CDC home page contains current health news, infectious disease information, health information, travel health information and CDC data and statistics. Available at http://www.cdc.gov.

Maps and geographic information

▶**Commercial Atlas and Marketing Guide.** This work, revised annually, provides extensive state-by-state coverage of the United States, including basic business data. Coverage of the rest of the world is more limited.

▶**National Atlas of the United States.** This atlas includes detailed information on the physical features, resources and social activities of the United States. Thematic maps present statistics.

▶**World Atlas.** This basic atlas of the world covers the United States by region rather than state by state. Other maps focus on language, climate, agriculture and politics.

Quotations

▶**Bartlett's Familiar Quotations.** This famous source lists sayings and writings from 2000 B.C. to the present. It includes a key-word index. Available online at http://www.columbia.edu/acis/bartleby/bartlett/.

▶**The Oxford Dictionary of Quotations.** This collection has more than 70,000 entries and includes a key-word index.

Science

▶**A Dictionary of Agriculture and Allied Terminology.** This book provides definitions for both general and technical words in agriculture and related fields.

▶**McGraw-Hill Encyclopedia of Science and Technology.** This work covers every area of modern science and technology. Survey articles written for the general reader give introductions to basic scientific concepts.

Suggestions for additional reading

Ackermann, Ernest. *Learning to Use the Internet.* Wilsonville, Ore.: Franklin, Beedle & Associates, 1995.

Butler, Mark. *How to Use the Internet.* Emeryville, Calif.: Ziff-Davis Press, 1994.

Callahan, Christopher. *A Journalist's Guide to the Internet.* New York: Allyn & Bacon, 1999.

Gould, Cheryl. *Searching Smart on the World Wide Web: Tools and Techniques for Getting Quality Results.* Berkeley, CA: Library Solutions Press, 1998.

Kessler, Lauren, and Duncan McDonald. *Uncovering the News: A Journalist's Search for Information.* Belmont, Calif.: Wadsworth, 1992.

McKim, Geoffrey W. *Internet Research Companion.* Indianapolis: Que Education and Training, 1996.

Rubin, Rebecca B., Alan M. Rubin, and Linda J. Piele. *Communication Research: Strategies and Sources.* Belmont, Calif.: Wadsworth, 1986.

Rutten, Peter, Albert F. Bayers III, and Kelly Maloni. *Netguide: Your Map to the Services, Information, and Entertainment on the Electronic Highway.* New York: Random House, 1994.

Ward, Jean, and Kathleen A. Hansen. *Search Strategies in Mass Communication,* 2nd ed. New York: Longman, 1992.

Exercises

1. Use *The World Almanac and Book of Facts* or a similar printed or online source to answer these questions. Indicate the source and specific page number for each answer.

   a. Who was the architect for the General Motors Building in Detroit: Albert Kahn or Louis Kahn?

   b. When did Pakistan become a republic?

   c. What is the name of the highest point in Australia?

   d. Is it Southwestern or Southwest Baptist Theological Seminary? Is it in Dallas or Fort Worth?

   e. Is the drawbridge across the Industrial Canal in New Orleans a vertical lift or a swing bridge?

   f. In what year was Hillary Rodham Clinton born?

   g. How does the seating capacity of the King Dome in Seattle compare with that of the Los Angeles Forum?

   h. How many stars does the flag of Honduras have?

   i. What were the top five U.S. companies in terms of advertising expenditures in 1997?

2. Use printed or online sources to answer the following questions. Answer in complete sentences as though the information were part of a story you are editing. Cite your source for each answer. For printed sources, give the name of the reference work, page number and date published. For Web sites, give the complete title of the Web site, name of sponsor and URL.

   a. What is the population of the state where you currently reside? (Use most recent figures available.)

   b. What is the population of the county where you currently reside? (Use most recent figures available.) How does this figure compare with the state's other counties (1st, 14th, etc.)?

   c. How many total crimes against persons were there in your county during the most recent year for which figures are available? How many total crimes against property were there in your county?

   d. How many school districts are in your county? What is the total enrollment of each school district?

   e. How many residential units are in your county? How many are single-family homes or condos and how many are apartments?

3. Answer the following questions in complete sentences as though the information were part of a story you are editing. Cite your source for each answer. For printed sources, give the name of the reference work, page number and date published. For Web sites, give the complete title of the Web site, name of sponsor and URL.

   a. You are editing a story on the first ladies of the White House. In one or two sentences, give Martha Washington's full name, age and marital status at the time she married George Washington. Include the date of their marriage.

   b. You are editing a story about U.S. department store chains. Give a brief description of J.C. Penney, including the number of stores and approximate annual gross sales figures. Where does J.C. Penney rank among department store chains?

   c. Some local high school students have been working to build a house of playing cards. They have built the house 33 stories tall so far. How much higher would the house have to be for a world record?

   d. How many people have immigrated to the United States since 1880?

   e. Give the full names of the U.S. senators from your home state and the names of the Senate committees they serve on in the current session of Congress.

4. Answer the following questions in complete sentences as though the information were part of a story you are editing. Give a complete citation for your source for each answer.

   a. Who won the Pulitzer Prize for fiction in 1998?

   b. Use information from *Who's Who in America* to write several sentences about the winner of the Pulitzer Prize for fiction in 1998.

   c. Who won the Nobel Prize for physics in 1998? Briefly describe this person's major contribution to physics.

   d. Has the number of farms in your state increased or decreased since 1970? Give the specific number of farms in the current year (or the last year for which figures are available) and in 1970.

   e. Using Books in Print or another reference source, find a citation for a bibliography on television and ethics. Give the title of the bibliography, then check the card catalog (either print or electronic versions) at your local library to see whether the book is part of the library's collection. If it is, provide the call number. Don't forget to provide the citation for the source you used to find the book title.

5. Use standard reference materials to answer the following questions. Answer in complete sentences as though the information were part of a story you are editing. Give a complete citation for your source for each answer.

   a. What is the name of the academic journal that publishes articles about ethics and the mass media? Who is the editor of the journal and where is it published? Check to see whether this journal is available in your local library. If it is, provide the call number.

   b. Consult Polk's City Directory for your city (if no directory exists for your city, use one for a nearby city). What information is available about the city's mayor?

   c. Describe how Polk's City Directory can be used by reporters and editors in ways that a telephone book cannot be used.

   d. Who is currently the artistic director for the New York City Ballet Company?

   e. What motion picture won an Academy Award for best feature film of 1994?

6. Answer the following questions. Answer in complete sentences as though the information were part of a story you are editing. Give a complete citation for your source for each answer.

   a. "Maple Syrup" is part of the name of which genetic disease?

   b. Who is the mayor of Omaha, Neb.?

   c. According to the Bureau of Labor Statistics, what two occupations were projected to be the fastest growing between 1986 and 2000?

   d. Which major league baseball players won the batting title in the American and National leagues in 1998, and what was the batting average for each?

   e. Who is credited with the following quotation: "My country 'tis of thee, Sweet land of liberty"?

7. If you have access to e-mail, subscribe to one of the communications-related discussion groups listed in Figure 5-1. Print the welcoming message that you receive. After monitoring the discussion group for two or three days, write a brief summary of the topics covered by members during those days. If there's no discussion on the group during this time, subscribe to a different group.

8. Use an Internet search engine to find Web pages about any topic you wish, such as a hobby, sport or specific sports team, or a performer or group. Print or make notes on the results of your search. Then, use a different search engine to perform the same search and compare the results of the two in terms of the number of "hits" and the similarity of the two lists presented.

9. Provide a complete Web site citation for a list of public relations agencies that have Web sites. Your instructor may ask you to print the list or download it to a disk.

10. Provide a complete Web site citation for a bibliography on writing and editing. Your instructor may ask you to print the bibliography or download it to a disk.

11. Find a source for anniversaries of historical events and birthdays of famous people. Compile a list of four or five events and birthdays for a "This Day in History" newspaper column. Use tomorrow's date.

12. Go to the reference shelf on either gopher or the World Wide Web and find a source of information, including a map, about the U.S. territory American Samoa. Print a copy of the map, and answer these questions about American Samoa:

    a. Where is it located?

    b. What is the average annual rainfall?

    c. What is the dominant religion?

    d. What is the literacy rate?

    e. What is the capital?

13. Use the same or a different source from that used to find information about American Samoa. Find the literacy rate for your home state and compare it with the literacy rate of American Samoa.

14. Edit the story below. Check facts carefully, giving special attention to the years Polk served as president of the United States, the sequence of his administration (10th, 20th, etc.), where he was born and the state where he served as governor.

CHARLOTTE, N.C.—Our 12th president is taking a licking at the post office

counter. A stamp issued last month to mark the bicentennial of James K.

Polk's birth is a dud at the stamp window, where customers instead are

snapping up comic-strip characters and Marilyn Monroe.

"It's too bad, but the Polk stamp is pretty drab," said Judy Gurkin of the

U.S. Postal Service. "It's the kind of stamp if you put it out there the

customer is more likely to say, 'No, give me the flag.'"

Historians rank Polk, who served from 1847 to 1851, among the nation's 10

most effective presidents. His administration occupied Oregon, annexed Texas

and acquired the California Territory.

The small, sepia-toned portrait on Polk's commemorative stamp captures all

the earnestness for which he is known. Translation: It's dull.

Workers at several post offices said they had neither recieved the Polk

stamp nor fielded inquiries about it.

"I have not moved the Polk stamp at all, which is a shame because he was a

great man," said Postal Clerk Mary Drake, in Charlotte.

Polk was born south of Pineville, S. C., and moved to Columbia,

Tennessee., when he was 11. He served as Tennessee's governor before being

elected president.

> Congress shall make no law respecting an establishment of religion, or prohibiting the free exercise thereof; or abridging the freedom of speech, or of the press; or the right of the people peaceably to assemble, and to petition government for a redress of grievances.
>
> —*First Amendment, Constitution of the United States*

Legal Concerns

THE **First Amendment** to the U.S. Constitution provides, among other things, that the people may speak and write free of censorship from the federal government. Colonial history and subsequent Supreme Court interpretations of the First Amendment make it clear, however, that the First Amendment is not an absolute. Competing societal interests limit the unbridled exercise of free expression.

The press must abide by the lesson of the old saying that "your right to throw a punch ends where my nose begins." That is, the press's practice of its right to free expression must accommodate competing rights of the public, including the right to the reputation that one has built, the right to be left alone if one wishes to be left alone, the right to a fair trial for a criminal defendant, the right not to have obscene material forced upon one, the right to profit from one's intellectual or artistic creations, and the right not to be cheated by unfair or deceptive advertising.

Newsroom personnel are expected to understand the legal topics that directly concern the editorial process: prior restraint, libel, privacy, copyright and other issues. These topics are discussed in this chapter.

Prior restraint

Competing personal interests

Libel

Privacy

Copyright

Trademarks

Techniques for avoiding lawsuits

Prior restraint

The Supreme Court has held that raw governmental censorship in the form of *prior restraint,* or telling the press what types of information it cannot publish, is inconsistent with the guarantees of the First Amendment. Nevertheless, the court has ruled that the government, in the interests of national security, has a right to protect its secrets. Therefore, the press can be restrained from publishing information that will cause direct, immediate and irreparable harm to national security.

Determining what information falls into that category is not always clear-cut. The result is a judgment call by the highest arbiter in the land, the U.S. Supreme Court. The 1971 Pentagon Papers case is an example. The court held in that case that The New York Times and other newspapers could publish the secret Pentagon study of U.S. involvement in the war in Vietnam because the government was unable to prove that publication would cause direct, immediate and irreparable harm to the national security.

Freedom of expression is now guaranteed protection from abridgment by state laws, but it was not always protected. Earlier in U.S. history, state legislatures were not bound by the limits that the First Amendment placed on Congress. The states often passed laws that punished people for saying or printing information that might upset the prevailing social order. For example, some states in both the North and the South passed statutes punishing those who advocated the abolition of slavery. Many states had laws on the books that punished people who criticized certain government policies, such as drafting men into military service, or who advocated a different system of government, such as socialism or communism. In a 1925 ruling (*Gitlow v. New York*), the Supreme Court held that freedom of expression is among the liberties protected from state infringement by the due-process clause of the Fourteenth Amendment.

The First and Fourteenth amendments do not grant the press special privileges that are unavailable to other businesses. Communication companies, like other businesses, are subject to laws governing such matters as antitrust, labor, contracts, taxation and postal services. Reporters and copy editors are not expected to have specific knowledge of these matters, which are generally handled by corporate attorneys.

Competing personal interests

Our society places high value on freedom of expression, guaranteed by the First Amendment. But society likewise values other personal rights, such as the right to enjoy a good reputation once it has been earned and the right to be left alone. Also of value are property rights, including the right to profit from intellectual creations. As noted previously, the First Amendment is not an absolute, so laws concerning libel, privacy and copyright are not considered inconsistent with First Amendment guarantees.

Sometimes these interests clash. That is, the media may publish information that they think is protected expression, but individuals may think the published statements infringe on personal rights. Individuals who think their reputations have been damaged may choose to "suffer in silence," doing nothing to correct the perceived wrong. Or offended people may seek redress by asking the media to publish a clarification, correction or retraction.

A retraction is not a libel defense, but it may be sufficient to ward off a lawsuit or, if a lawsuit is successful, mitigate damages. A conversation with the newspaper editor or publisher or perhaps with the newspaper's attorney may persuade upset people that they would be unlikely to prevail in a libel or privacy lawsuit.

If informal attempts to resolve a conflict over rights are unsuccessful, a civil lawsuit may result. The party with the complaint files a lawsuit and becomes the plaintiff. The party being sued becomes the defendant. One of several things might happen at this point. For example, the parties might decide to settle out of court, in which case the defendant might pay some agreed-on amount of money for damages. However, most defendant news organizations are extremely reluctant to take this approach, because it could invite frivolous lawsuits.

Once the lawsuit is filed, both parties engage in discovery proceedings to prepare their cases. Attorneys for each side question the other party to ascertain the facts of the situation and to gain information about evidence that will be presented during the trial. The discovery process can involve many hours of expensive legal work. Copy editors may edit several stories about a newsworthy case during the discovery phase.

The defendant might file a motion for summary judgment on any of several grounds, and this action may also be worth a news story. In a motion for summary judgment, the defendant argues that no legal wrong has been committed. For example, in the case of a libel or privacy lawsuit, the defendant might argue that the offending statements did not constitute libel or invasion of privacy. Or the motion for summary judgment might be based on the argument that the plaintiff will be unable to meet the required burden of proof.

If the judge agrees, a summary judgment for the defendant may be granted, eliminating the need for a trial. This decision ends the lawsuit, unless the plaintiff appeals the judge's ruling to a higher court, arguing that the summary judgment was improperly granted.

If the lawsuit survives preliminary motions and goes to trial, the plaintiff will try to prove the elements necessary to the case. Those elements will vary with the nature of the complaint. The media defendant will argue that the plaintiff has not been damaged or is otherwise unable to meet the burden of proof. In addition, the defendant will argue one or more legal defenses.

The following sections look at the elements that the plaintiff must prove, and the legal defenses for libel, invasion of privacy and copyright infringement lawsuits.

Libel

Libel is a false statement that exposes people to hatred, ridicule or contempt, lowers them in the esteem of their colleagues, causes them to be shunned or injures them in their business or profession.

Generally, libel falls into one of two classifications: (1) libel per se (pronounced *per say*), words that are defamatory on their face and thus are presumed to damage reputation; and (2) libel per quod, words that are not ordinarily defamatory but that become damaging by facts or circumstances extrinsic to the story. Some states recognize a third category: statements susceptible to two meanings, one defamatory and the other not defamatory.

Examples of words that are defamatory on their face include those that falsely accuse someone of committing a crime or of having a loathsome disease.

An example of libel per quod would be to publish an incorrect date for the granting of a divorce so it appeared that someone had remarried before the divorce became final.

The Supreme Court ruled in 1974, in *Gertz v. Robert Welch, Inc.,* that states could not impose liability without fault on the part of the defendant. Since then, the distinction between libel per se and libel per quod has become less important, but many courts continue to make the distinction.

Plaintiff's burden of proof

A person who sues a newspaper for libel must prove the following:

- The statement was published.

- The plaintiff was identified in the statement.

- The statement was defamatory.

- The statement caused injury.

- The publisher was at fault in publishing the statement.

Publication is usually obvious in cases involving the mass media. Strictly speaking, publication has occurred when at least one person other than the defamed person has received the material. In media cases, courts have usually—but not always—held that publication has not occurred until the material reaches its intended audience. In other words, media personnel can discuss a potentially libelous item during the production process without fear of a successful libel lawsuit. However, in 1980 an Illinois jury found the Alton Telegraph liable for material that was never published in the newspaper. Publication resulted, the jury decided, during the news-gathering stage. In an attempt to verify accusations of wrongdoing by a local building contractor, reporters wrote a memo about the wrongdoing to a government official.

Identification may be established even though the plaintiff is not named in the story if people reasonably understand that the statement refers to the plaintiff. An address or title might be sufficient for people to identify the plaintiff.

Individuals cannot sue successfully just because they are members of a large group that has been defamed. For example, the statement "All lawyers are crooks" would not be sufficient identification for an individual lawyer to bring a lawsuit. But an attorney might be able to prove individual identification and harm by the statement "All lawyers at the XYZ Law Firm are crooks." No exact number exists for deciding how small a group must be before any single member can claim to have been libeled. A "rule of 25" grew out of a libel case during the 1950s, but subsequent court decisions allowed members of groups larger than 25 to sue when individuals were closely identified with the group.

Although published statements may identify and damage the memory of a deceased person, the dead cannot sue, and relatives may not sue on their behalf.

Defamation is another part of the plaintiff's burden of proof. The plaintiff must persuade the court that the offending statement carried a "sting," meaning that it harmed the plaintiff's reputation. Evidence about a plaintiff's reputation before and after publication is admissible. In a few instances, courts have decided that plaintiffs were "libel proof" because their reputations were already tarnished beyond the possibility of further damage.

In most cases involving the mass media, the plaintiff must also prove that the offending statement was *false.* True statements that harm someone's reputation are not actionable as libel, although they may be actionable as an invasion of privacy. Thus, the accurate claim that someone has been arrested and charged with murder is not actionable, even though the person may subsequently be acquitted of the charge. Minor inaccuracies will not defeat the defense of truth so long as the part of the statement that carries the sting is true. For example, a libel case would not be decided on inaccurately reporting the place of arrest of the murder suspect so long as the suspect was accurately identified and the charge accurately reported.

Copy editors should be particularly alert when dealing with copy containing any of the "red flag" words and expressions listed in Figure 6-1.

Fault joined the list of elements that a libel plaintiff had to prove following the 1964 Supreme Court ruling in *New York Times v. Sullivan.* The court determined that the U.S. Constitution protects defamatory statements published without fault. Before then, once a libel plaintiff had established publication, identification and defamation, the burden of proof shifted to the defendant, who then had to offer a defense.

Figure 6-1
"Red flag" words and phrases that should be avoided.

adulteration of products	cheats	hypocrite	scoundrel
adultery	collusion	illegitimate	shyster
has AIDS	corruption	illicit relations	sneak
altered records	coward	incompetent	sold influence
atheist	criminal	infidelity	sold out
attempted suicide	crook	Jekyll-Hyde personality	spy
bad moral character	deadbeat	kept woman	stuffed the ballot box
bankrupt	double-crosser	Ku Klux Klan	suicide
bigamist	drug addict	liar	swindle
blackmail	ex-convict	mental disease	unethical
bribery	fool	Nazi	unprofessional
brothel	fraud	peeping Tom	villain
buys votes	illegal gambling	perjurer	
	graft		

Defenses against libel

Media defendants attempt to persuade the court that they should not have to pay damages for a libeling statement because its publication was protected by the Constitution or by one of the traditional common-law defenses.

▶ **The constitutional defense.** A full-page advertisement in The New York Times in 1960 led to a case that profoundly altered libel law. A group of civil-rights leaders placed the ad, which criticized tactics used by police and public officials in several Southern cities to disrupt the civil-rights movement. The ad asked for contributions to pay bail for Martin Luther King Jr. and other movement leaders who had been jailed for their protest activities. The accusations made in the advertisement were true for the most part, but the copy also contained several minor factual errors. L.B. Sullivan, police commissioner in Montgomery, Ala., sued the Times for libel. Sullivan won $500,000 for damages in the state courts of Alabama, but in 1964 the Supreme Court of the United States overturned the damage award.

In *New York Times v. Sullivan,* the Supreme Court reasoned that public officials must live with the risks of a political system in which there is "a profound national commitment to the principle that debate on public issues should be uninhibited, robust, and wide-open, and that it may well include vehement, caustic, and sometimes unpleasantly sharp attacks on government or public officials." Further, the court said that "erroneous statement is inevitable in free debate, and…it must be protected if the freedoms of expression are to have the breathing space that they need to survive."

In effect, the Supreme Court was saying that the U.S. Constitution protects false, defamatory statements about public officials as long as the defendant does not recklessly or knowingly publish them. On the basis of that ruling, public officials accusing the media of libel became obligated to prove that a media defendant published with *actual malice*. Malice was defined by the court as knowledge of falsity or reckless disregard for truth.

Soon after the decision, the court determined that public figures, in addition to public officials, should have to prove that the defendant published with knowledge that the defamatory statements were false or with reckless disregard for truth.

In 1974, in *Gertz v. Robert Welch, Inc.,* the Supreme Court extended to all libel plaintiffs the burden of proving some measure of fault on the part of the defendant. The court held that state laws could no longer impose liability without proof that the defendant was at fault in publishing the offending statement. States were free to set the standard of fault to be met in their individual jurisdictions, with negligence being a minimum degree of fault. A finding of actual malice would be necessary to award punitive damages, the *Gertz* court specified.

Several states, including Colorado, Indiana, New York and Alaska, have decided that all libel plaintiffs must meet the actual malice standard for stories that are a matter of public interest. Other states allow private figures to show negligence on the part of the publisher, a less difficult standard of fault than actual malice.

Negligence is defined somewhat differently from state to state. In some states the "reasonable publisher" definition of negligence is used: Would a reasonable publisher in the same community or a similar community under existing circumstances have published the defamatory statement? Other states use a "reasonable person" definition: Would a reasonable person have published the statement under existing circumstances? In New York, if the case concerns a public matter, a private individual has to establish that the publisher "acted in a grossly irresponsible manner without due consideration for the standards of information gathering and dissemination ordinarily followed by responsible parties."

Here are examples of situations where state courts have ruled that the press was negligent:

- Relying on a source whom local police described as not having been reliable in the past

- Failing to examine a public court record when writing about a criminal case

- Publishing a negative, one-sided story about a teacher, based primarily on complaints of parents who had ill will toward the teacher

In most states, the fault standard to be used in the case depends on the status of the plaintiff. Thus, the outcome of a libel case often hinges on whether the plaintiff is considered a public official, a public figure or a private person. That determination is not always easy to make, and many libel verdicts have been overturned by appeals courts because the wrong fault standard was imposed on the plaintiff. In a series of cases debating this issue, the courts have set down guidelines for deciding the status of the plaintiff.

A *public official* is one who has, or who the public perceives to have, substantial responsibility for, or control over, the conduct of governmental affairs. A government employee does not necessarily meet this definition. Candidates and applicants for public office are also considered public officials in the context of a libel suit because the public is interested in their qualifications for the job.

The Supreme Court has distinguished two types of *public figures:*

- All-purpose public figures. These are people who achieve such pervasive fame or notoriety or who occupy a position of such pervasive power and influence that they are considered public figures for all purposes and in all contexts. An all-purpose public figure would be someone with a high degree of name recognition in the community.

- Limited public figures. These people, by their public statements and actions, have projected themselves into the arena of public controversy and into the vortex of a question of pressing public concern in an attempt to influence the resolution of an issue.

Few public figures are all-purpose public figures, involved in all aspects of public life. Instead, most are limited public figures; they voluntarily become involved in just a few, perhaps only one, controversy. For example, someone who becomes involved in the public debate about whether abortion should be legal in the United States would be a public figure in a libel lawsuit concerning that controversy. However, if that same person filed a libel lawsuit about a private matter or about a public controversy in which he or she had not become involved voluntarily, that person would be classified as a private person. Depending on the state, such a plaintiff might be able to argue that the publisher acted with negligence rather than actual malice, which is more difficult to prove. Another example: A person involved in a highly publicized divorce case was held to be a private person in a libel case that originated when a magazine misstated the grounds for granting the divorce. The court held that divorce was a private matter, not a public controversy.

Finally, a *private person* is one who may be widely known in the community but who has no authority or responsibility for the conduct of governmental affairs and has not thrust himself or herself into the middle of an important public controversy. Elmer Gertz, the plaintiff in *Gertz v. Welch,* was a prominent lawyer who was widely known in several contexts in Chicago. As a lawyer, he had represented defendants in highly publicized cases; he was an author and an amateur actor and had served on various citizens' committees in Chicago. The famous libel case that bears his name arose after Gertz took a case to represent a family in a civil lawsuit against a Chicago police officer who had been found guilty of murder in the shooting of a youth. The John Birch Society magazine then published an article falsely accusing Gertz of having a criminal record and being a "Leninist" or a "Communist fronter." Despite his prominence, the Supreme Court ruled that Gertz was a private person for the purposes of his lawsuit because he had done nothing to inject himself into the controversy surrounding the shooting and subsequent criminal trial of the police officer, which was the focus of the magazine article. In representing the family in a civil action, the court held, Gertz was just practicing his profession and acting in the capacity of a private person.

Reporting and writing techniques are examined during the discovery process and during the trial to determine whether the defendant acted with fault. Before and during the trial, copy editors, reporters and other newsroom personnel might be interrogated about procedures used to produce the story, including this information:

■ The number and credibility of sources

■ Deadline pressures involved in gathering information, writing and editing the story

■ The reasonable probability that the information was accurate

■ News personnel's doubts about the story's truth

Neutral reportage is the practice of accurately and disinterestedly reporting that a responsible, prominent person or organization has made false, defamatory statements about a public official or public figure. Neutral reportage is recognized in a few jurisdictions as having constitutional protection in a libel action. Most courts have not considered a case dealing with this defense or have refused to recognize it, and the Supreme Court has not decided the issue.

The several courts that have recognized neutral reportage as a libel defense have accepted the argument that such accusations are newsworthy and that the First Amendment does not require the press to ignore newsworthy statements just because the press cannot verify them or just because the reporter has doubts about their truth.

It is important to note that in cases in which the doctrine of neutral reportage has been accepted, the stories included denials or explanations from the defamed parties. Both legal and ethical concerns require careful adherence to this practice. Such stories should also alert readers to the fact that the defamatory charges are debatable and have not been independently verified. Copy editors working for a newspaper in a jurisdiction that recognizes neutral reportage should insist that such information be included in this type of story. Neutral reportage is not recognized as a libel defense in most parts of the country, so editors in those states should not allow such a story to be published if no other libel defense is available.

▶ **Common-law defenses.** Defendants in both criminal and civil cases typically argue every defense that potentially applies. Libel defendants advance the constitutional defense if the published statement is false but was published with insufficient fault on the part of the publisher. In addition, one or more common-law defenses—fair comment, qualified privilege or truth—might be argued.

Fair comment protects opinion about matters of public interest or things that have been put on public display. The doctrine of fair comment allows reviewers, for example, to publish scathing reviews of plays, movies, books, restaurants and the like.

Copy editors should ensure either that opinion in a story is based on generally known facts or that the factual basis for such opinion is stated in the story. The Supreme Court reinforced this principle in a 1990 decision, *Milkovich v. Lorain Journal.* The Supreme Court held that the Constitution does not provide a "wholesale defamation exemption for anything that might be labeled opinion."

Copy editors must eliminate opinion that relies for its support upon the existence of undisclosed information unless the editor knows that such information is accurate. For example, it is protected opinion to say that an actor gave a poor performance in a play, but to falsely imply that the poor performance can be attributed to the actor's use of drugs is an unprotected statement of fact. Copy editors must edit editorial page material with the same care as other stories. Expressions of opinion can often imply the existence of facts that may turn out to be false and defamatory and thus actionable.

A newspaper is responsible for what it publishes, including letters to the editor. Like editorials, the letter writer's opinions are protected, but the facts that underpin opinions are not protected if they are false and defamatory. This letter, which actually appeared in a newspaper, should not have left the copy desk (identifying names have been changed for the purposes of this illustration):

To The Sentinel:

I was stopped at the corner of Victoria and Water Streets when Officer Smith's cruiser hit my vehicle.

He hit me. The dent and blue paint on the driver's side door proves it. (He can't drive.)

Because of one cop's stupidity Jonesville just lost another cruiser (myself a car).

This is his sixth cruiser he zeroed, and I don't drive with my lights off.

Smith is a Wyatt Earp who likes to assault perpetrators (allegedly).

He muscled me with both hands handcuffed, lying in a hospital bed (a real man).

He's done it before, and will do it again to you.

Assistant City Attorney John Doe has numerous complaints on the matter of Smith.

Eh, what's happening Jonesville? Go to sleep. Don't get involved.

[Signature]

[Address]

EDITOR'S NOTE: Attorney Doe denies he has received complaints about Patrolman Smith, except from Dr. — with regard to his recent arrest.

The editor's note did little to remedy the situation. And the "letters policy" statement, which the newspaper published with its letters column, increased the potential for a libel lawsuit in connection with the letter: "The reader's column is for your opinions. … We do not publish letters we feel to be libelous … or that make allegations we are unable to verify independently."

Ed Williams, former editorial page editor for the Charlotte, N.C., Observer, gave these instructions to editorial page writers and editors at his newspaper:

- Get the facts straight.

- Be sure facts are facts and opinions are opinions.

- Read it on the page proofs.

- Talk with the paper's lawyers before publication if the subject matter is touchy.

Qualified privilege, another common-law defense, allows the media to cover privileged situations. But the privilege is conditioned on an accurate and fair account of the proceedings. Usually, to be considered privileged, the proceeding must be open to the public, or the information must be available for public inspection. Public meetings and public records are examples of privileged situations.

It is this common-law defense that allows the media to cover damaging and false statements that are made during trials, for example. Even if it is later revealed that a witness lied during testimony, the media are not held liable for repeating those lies. Copy editors must keep in mind, however, that the privilege applies only to those comments made during the proceedings, not to comments made by public officials or other parties outside the proceedings.

The reporter's account of what happened during a privileged proceeding must be a fair and accurate one. It would not be fair to report only one side of a controversy if conflicting viewpoints were presented during the meeting. To rely on the qualified privilege defense, journalists must make sure that records used as sources are indeed public records. Because reporters sometimes gain access to information that is not considered a public record, copy editors should be on guard against non-public information that is the basis for a potentially actionable story.

Truth is the best common-law defense against libel because falsity is an integral part of the definition of libel. Unfortunately, truth is not always easily proven. Where the offending statement concerns public matters, the plaintiff has the burden of proving falsity—certainly a heavy burden—but the defendant will try to convince the jury that the published statements were true.

The truth must be as broad as the charge. To support a published charge that the plaintiff is a crook, it is not enough to prove, for example, that the plaintiff once shortchanged someone. Likewise, it is not sufficient to prove that the plaintiff was convicted of a misdemeanor shoplifting charge if the published statement said the plaintiff was a convicted felon. Again, copy editors must be especially alert when handling stories that make accusations against someone.

Courts usually allow truth to stand as a defense even though the story contains minor inaccuracies that do not carry the "sting" of the statement. For example, to publish that someone was arrested on Aug. 1 instead of Aug. 2 is unlikely to defeat the truth defense unless other circumstances make the exact date important to the case.

Privacy

Privacy has been defined as the right to be left alone, the right to be free from unwarranted publicity. The information explosion, the increasing amount of personal information that the U.S. government collects about its citizens and the ease with which computers allow access to that data have all contributed to legal and ethical problems for the mass media.

Many journalists have ethical qualms about publishing some information that they have a legal right to publish. Opinion polls in recent years indicate a decline in media credibility, and to some extent the decline of public approval can be traced to the public perception that the media sometimes use unethical news-gathering techniques and often publish information about individuals that should remain private.

Difficult ethical questions arise as responsible journalists attempt to perform their "watchdog" function: How much does the public need to know about the private lives of candidates for public office to make wise voting decisions? Should people know that a co-worker suffers from AIDS or any other disease? Should the public know that the man who thwarted an assassination attempt on the president was gay? Ethical dilemmas posed by such questions are dealt with in Chapter 7; this section discusses the legal aspects of invasion of privacy.

Unlike libel laws, privacy laws do not protect reputational interests. Instead, they are meant to give legal redress for mental anguish and suffering caused by an invasion of personal privacy. Most states recognize four distinct legal wrongs under the broad heading of invasion of privacy:

- Intrusion into a person's physical solitude

- Publication of private information that violates ordinary decencies

- Publication of information that places a person in a false light

- Appropriation of some element of a person's personality—the person's name or likeness—for commercial purposes

Intrusion upon physical solitude can occur in several forms, such as trespassing upon private property and using hidden cameras or microphones to eavesdrop on private conversations. Unlike libel actions, publication is not a prerequisite for an intrusion lawsuit. The act of trespassing constitutes the legal wrong.

If the defendant observes the plaintiff in an embarrassing situation in public, no intrusion has occurred. But the defendant who invades the plaintiff's "zone of privacy," either physically or with mechanical or electronic devices, shows intent of intrusion. For example, it would be legally permissible to photograph or report that a public official engaged in adulterous behavior in a public place, but it would be intrusion to hide in a bedroom closet or to use hidden cameras to gather information about the public official's behavior in a private place.

Courts have held that property owners have the legal right to request that journalists leave public places such as restaurants when the journalists' purpose does not coincide with the primary purpose of the public place—to dine, for example.

Publication of private information involves publicizing a private matter that would be highly offensive to a reasonable person and is not of legitimate concern to the public. Published information that is embarrassing or upsetting to a plaintiff is not sufficient to support a privacy claim; the information must be highly offensive to a reasonable person in the community. This type of privacy is not designed to protect the "overly sensitive" person, and community mores may be considered in determining whether the information was highly offensive or lacking in newsworthiness. A jury would make that determination should an invasion of privacy lawsuit go to trial.

The information must be private, not public. If embarrassing and offensive information becomes a matter of public record, then a privacy action will not succeed. Embarrassing information like that sometimes published in "looking back into history" columns—for example, that a person with good standing in the community served a prison sentence years ago—usually is not actionable if based on information available in public records. Unlike the law of defamation, truth is not a defense for this type of privacy lawsuit if the offensive information is indeed private and not newsworthy.

False light is like defamation in that it involves falsity and requires showing the publisher's knowledge of falsity or reckless disregard for truth if the matter is of public concern. As in libel law, truth and privilege are defenses for this aspect of privacy. However, no damage to reputation is required. Some courts have required that the false light statement be highly offensive to a reasonable person.

Picture captions and file photographs used to illustrate stories can be particularly troublesome. For example, a couple filed a false-light privacy lawsuit against a magazine that published a picture showing their child being hit by a car. The use of the picture in the newsworthy context of an accident would have been permissible if the caption had been accurate. However, the magazine used the picture to illustrate a story titled "They Ask to Be Killed," which concerned careless or negligent actions through which people cause themselves harm. Because the accident had involved no carelessness or negligence on the part of the child or the parents, the family won the lawsuit.

Appropriation is the unauthorized use of a person's name or likeness for commercial gain—for example, using someone's name or picture in an advertisement without permission. The argument is made that such use causes the plaintiff mental anguish. A better argument may be that a "right of publicity" is involved and that unauthorized use deprives people of the right to decide how their name or picture will be used and the right to profit from such use.

It is not considered appropriation for a newspaper or magazine to solicit subscriptions by using copy or pictures that ran in earlier issues of the publication. So long as the ad does not imply that the person named or pictured is endorsing the publication, such an ad is considered a sample of the contents.

Appropriation usually concerns the advertising department of a newspaper or magazine more than the editorial department. Permission is not needed to use people's name or picture for news purposes, assuming that no illegal news-gathering techniques were used. Written consent should be obtained from people whose name or picture is used for advertising purposes.

▶**Invasion of privacy defenses.** Legal defenses for invasion of privacy lawsuits vary. Truth, for example, is a defense for false-light invasion of privacy but not for any of the other three categories of privacy cases. If truth cannot be established in a false-light case, the defendant can try to establish that the falsity was not published with actual malice.

Consent, either explicit or implied, is the only legal defense for trespass. One who allows a reporter to enter private property or who does not object to the presence of visible cameras or recorders, for example, has consented.

Consent is also the defense for appropriation. For commercial use, rather than news, the consent should be written.

Faced with a lawsuit claiming publication of private information, a defendant can argue newsworthiness and claim that the published material is not highly offensive to a reasonable person.

Copyright

Copyright law provides the right to control or profit from a literary, artistic or intellectual production. In preventing material from being copied without permission of the copyright owner, copyright law both protects and restricts the mass media.

A key principle of copyright law is that facts and ideas cannot be copyrighted. No person or news organization can "own" the facts concerning a newsworthy story or the idea of covering a particular subject. But the manner of expression used to tell the story or discuss the idea—the specific patterns of words and the pictures—can be copyrighted and thus protected from infringement by others. Plagiarism is both illegal and unethical.

Many publications may use the same article through contractual agreements with news services and other suppliers of syndicated material. Members of The Associated Press, for example, agree to send to AP all spontaneous local news stories, and AP members have the right to use such "spot news" stories verbatim.

The AP contractual agreement specifies that stories resulting from individual enterprise and initiative and copyrighted by the originating news organization cannot be used by fellow AP members without permission. For example, the collapse of an overhead walkway into a crowded hotel lobby in Kansas City, Mo., which killed more than 100 people, was a major news story. No single publication or news service owned the rights to that story. The Kansas City Star and Kansas City Times and other AP members in that metropolitan area furnished AP with much of the spot news coverage of the disaster and rescue efforts. AP members throughout the world could publish those stories and photos.

In the days and weeks after the disaster, the Times and the Star, morning and afternoon papers owned by the same company, invested time, energy and money in an investigation of the cause of the walkway collapse. The company hired consulting engineers and architects to study the blueprints and construction methods, and reporters and editors investigated the city's building inspection procedures, examined public records and conducted interviews. The series of stories produced by that initiative won a Pulitzer Prize for the Star. Those stories, unlike news about the initial collapse, could not be used without permission of the copyright owner, the Star.

Current copyright law protects original works of authorship fixed in any tangible medium of expression, now known or later developed. Categories of such works include literary works; musical works, including any accompanying words; dramatic works, including any accompanying music; pantomimes and choreographic works; pictorial, graphic and sculptural works; motion pictures; and other audiovisual works and sound recordings. According to a 1998 amendment to current copyright law, a copyright lasts for the lifetime of the owner plus 70 years, after which the work becomes part of the public domain.

Under the work-made-for-hire doctrine, unless specific contractual agreements establish otherwise, the publication, rather than an individual employee, owns the copyright on published material. Reporters and photographers who work for a publication do not own work done as part of their employment. Unless the employer gives permission, reporters or photographers cannot sell or give away copies of their work or authorize some other publication to use it. The duration of copyright protection for works made for hire is 95 years from the date of first publication or 120 years from the date of creation, whichever expires first.

Free-lance journalists retain ownership in their work unless they expressly sign away such rights. A free-lancer can agree to give or sell specific rights to a work and retain all other rights. For example, an author can sell "first serial rights," which allow a publication to publish the work one time anywhere in the world; "first North American rights" allow publication of the work one time in North America only.

The defense against copyright infringement is *fair use*. This defense allows publications to use brief quotations from a copyrighted work for the purposes of critical reviews or scholarly work. Key ideas behind the fair use doctrine are that the one who copies must add substantial independent work and that such copying should be in the public interest. Despite the protests of producers of television shows, the Supreme Court ruled that the copying of off-the-air television shows for non-commercial use is "time shifting" for the convenience of viewers rather than copyright infringement.

Because no formula exists for determining how much copying is permissible under the fair use doctrine, copy editors should give careful scrutiny to stories that contain verbatim passages from copyrighted material. Several paragraphs may be acceptable in some circumstances, whereas a single line from a poem or song may be grounds for a successful infringement lawsuit. Much depends on the amount and nature of the material that the copier adds to the original work.

These are factors that courts generally consider when deciding whether copyrighted material has been used fairly:

- The purpose and character of the use, including whether such use is of a commercial nature or is for not-for-profit educational purposes

- The nature of the copyrighted work

- The amount and substantiality of the portion used in relation to the copyrighted work as a whole

- The effect of the use on the potential market for or value of the copyrighted work

Trademarks

In addition to copyrighted works, other legally protected types of intellectual property include trademarks, service marks and trade names. A *trademark* is defined by statute as "any word, name, symbol or device or any combination thereof, adopted and used by a manufacturer or merchant to identify its goods and distinguish them from those manufactured or sold by others." The term *service mark* is used for distinctive identifiers for a service rather than a product. A *trade name* is defined by statute as "any name used by a person to identify his or her business or vocation." Proctor & Gamble, for example, is the trade name of a business that identifies its products with many different trademarks, including Ivory soap, Tide detergent, and Crest toothpaste. A single word—Sears, for example— may be used for all three purposes: to identify products and services and the name of the company that produces those products and services. Examples of trademark symbols are the peacock feathers identifying the National Broadcasting Company and McDonald's golden arches.

In addition to identifying sources of goods and services, trademarks function to warrant that goods coming from a particular source will be of consistent and desirable quality. The instant recognition value of trademarks permits companies to use shortcuts in advertising their products and services. Companies recognize the tremendous value of their trademarks and work zealously to protect them from infringement and from falling into generic use.

Some trademarks have become generic because they were used by the public to designate the genus of the products. The King-Seeley Thermos Company, for example, originated the term *thermos* for vacuum-insulated containers during the 1920s, but the term fell into general use, leaving King-Seeley unsuccessful in its attempts to prevent Aladdin Industries from referring to its vacuum-insulated products as "thermos" bottles. Other examples of former trademarks that are now generic are aspirin, cellophane and yo-yo.

To protect their marks from falling into generic use, trademark owners take steps—such as using advertisements—to educate the public that the mark should not be used in a generic sense. Companies also write warning letters to journalists and others who used trademarks incorrectly, such as using them as a noun or verb, as in "Xerox this document" or "make a Xerox." Correct usage for trademarks is as an adjective followed by a noun: Xerox copier, a Xerox copy, Kleenex tissue, Teflon coating, Jeep vehicle, Weed Eater trimmer.

Trademarks should be differentiated typographically from words around them. AP style is to capitalize a trademark, but the wire service directs that a generic term should be used unless the trademark name is essential to the story. In its alphabetical entries, the AP stylebook includes many trademarks, together with generic equivalents. Plural forms should not be used, such as "She uses Kleenexes." The correct form is "She uses Kleenex tissues." Trademarks should not take the possessive form, as in "the Jeep's windshield." Instead, write "the windshield on a Jeep sport utility vehicle."

Techniques for avoiding lawsuits

A copy editor reviewing a story for libel, privacy or copyright problems has four choices:

- Publish the story because it has no legal problems.

- Kill the story because it is libelous, invades privacy or infringes copyright.

- Skillfully edit the story to remove offending passages.

- Expect a lawsuit, but publish the story because we'll win if we're sued.

The decision to publish a dangerous-but-defensible story must not be made lightly and must not be made by a copy editor acting alone. As noted elsewhere in this book, the copy desk is the last line of defense at most publications today. No typist will retype the copy. No proofreader will read the copy after it is in type. If the copy editor lets a dangerous story leave the computer terminal, the story is likely to be published. If a dangerous story has made it through the reporter and the assigning editor to the copy desk, it is up to the copy editor to notify a supervising editor. The story may then be subjected to review by the chain of command at the publication, and attorneys may become part of the decision-making process.

Cost of a lawsuit

Most journalists would applaud the publisher who publishes an important story in the face of an expensive lawsuit, and most would have little respect for the timid publisher or the one who places greater emphasis on the bottom line of the balance sheet than on the social responsibility of the press. However, the tremendous cost of a lawsuit—even one that the publisher can win—is a factor in deciding whether to publish. Is the story worth the cost of a lawsuit? It might not be, especially for a small publication or a company with few financial reserves.

A lawsuit is an immense drain on the time and energy needed to go about the business of publishing. A small staff will be unable to meet deadlines if personnel are occupied with planning sessions with lawyers and then with sitting in a courtroom day after day during pretrial motions, jury selection, then the trial and perhaps the appeals process.

In addition to time and energy, costs are a tremendous burden. A 1986 report issued by the Gannett Center for Media Studies (now The Freedom Forum Media Studies Center) put the average cost of defending a libel lawsuit at $95,000 to $150,000. That is for legal costs alone and does not include money for damages if the publisher loses the lawsuit. The average damage award for libel now exceeds that for medical malpractice or product liability. In 1985, the average medical malpractice damage award was $650,000, and the average product liability award was $750,000, as compared with $2 million for libel.

Libel insurance isn't a complete solution either, because libel insurance premiums have tripled during the past several years. Further increases are expected, and insurance companies are now writing contracts that exclude the costs of defending lawsuits.

Complaints from the public

The most desirable outcome for the publication is to publish the important, dangerous-but-defensible story without being sued. Assuming that the story is fair and balanced, the publisher may be able to persuade the would-be plaintiff that a lawsuit is a waste of time and money.

Unfortunately, the publisher or publisher's representative may never get an opportunity to placate an angry person if newsroom personnel fail to exercise common courtesy. Anyone who calls the newsroom with a complaint, with a story tip or for any other reason should never be passed around from one person to another or treated with the "Hey-we've-got-a-crazy-on-the-line" approach.

Three professors at the University of Iowa interviewed more than 700 people who had sued the media on libel claims from 1974 to 1984. The majority of these libel plaintiffs told the researchers that they were upset about harm to their reputation and about emotional distress, rather than financial damage. They said that they sued to seek restoration of their reputation and to punish the media, not to get money.

The plaintiffs told researchers that a lawyer was not the first person they called after they became upset about something read in a newspaper or magazine or heard in a broadcast. First the distraught person contacted the offending publisher or broadcaster—either with a personal visit to the newsroom or, usually, with a telephone call. After that initial contact, however—after being treated rudely—the person was no longer just upset and hurt. The person was angry. Then came the call to a lawyer. What could have been a golden opportunity to head off a lawsuit became a golden opportunity for an attorney.

The media can't be expected to satisfy all agitated complainers, even if the publisher or station manager were willing to yield to every demand. But media personnel can be expected to refrain from rudeness. The Iowa researchers recommended that newsroom managers take the following actions:

■ Insist that everyone in the newsroom understand the great power that the press has to hurt people and that everyone give courtesy a high priority.

- Make one person responsible for dealing with complaints. Be sure that person has good human-relations skills. If financially possible, select someone who is not responsible for news coverage, because editors don't have time to handle complaints and because often the qualities and skills that make a person a good editor or news director are not the same qualities that make for good people skills.

- Develop policies and procedures for addressing complaints. Put those policies and procedures in writing, and make sure that everyone in the newsroom knows what they are.

- Deal harshly with any employee who stifles a complaint and doesn't direct it to the designated person.

Two trends during the past few years show that newspapers treat reader complaints seriously: More regularly publish corrections columns, and more have created the position of ombudsman or reader representative. At one time, newspaper editors did not want to admit that their paper made mistakes, but now many papers of all sizes publicly correct errors that have appeared in print.

Readers can talk back to their newspapers through letters to the editor, of course, but the majority are not motivated to spend time and effort writing letters. Many readers will take the time to phone the paper and report errors, and those who do seem to appreciate the opportunity to talk with someone specially designated as the reader representative. Where questions of news judgment and standard journalistic practices are concerned, the reader representative can often satisfy angry readers simply by explaining why journalists do certain things.

Smaller newspapers rarely have someone on the payroll to serve solely as a reader representative, but small papers, like their larger counterparts, often publish a regular corrections column. Newspapers vary in their policies about what kinds of errors they acknowledge and the prominence they give to corrections columns. Some give the corrections column prominent treatment in the front section; others relegate the column to a less noticeable spot in a back section.

Along with the corrections, some papers tell readers how each error was made, such as "incorrect information supplied by a source," "a reporting error" or "a copy editing error." Some papers, in addition to correcting the error, go a step further by apologizing. Regardless of specific policies on the content of regularly published corrections columns, they serve as one more quality-control device for newspapers and can help enhance credibility with readers.

Prepublication cautions at the newsgathering stage

The work of avoiding clearly libelous stories or ones that invade privacy or infringe on copyright should begin at the reporting stage, so that such stories never reach the copy editor. That's the way it should be. But in a "real-life" newsroom, the copy editor must aggressively question reporters about their newsgathering techniques and the credibility of their sources.

Reporters must understand that they can defame someone at the news-gathering stage, even before a story is written. Making a defamatory statement about someone to a third party constitutes slander, so the old reporter's ploy of pretending to know more than he or she does to gain information can be dangerous. A reporter who has no proof and is just fishing for information shouldn't tell a source, "We already know that Jones is a dishonest cop. We just want your comments." A statement like "We're looking into Jones' conduct as a police officer, and we'd like to get your comments" is far safer.

Privacy can also be invaded during the newsgathering stage. Being in hot pursuit of a story does not excuse intrusion or trespassing. Reporters have no legal right to enter private property without consent, even if the purpose of the story is to expose wrongdoing on the part of the property owner.

Journalists have no legal right to accompany protesters onto private property—a nuclear power plant, for example—to get a story. The power plant operators may legally restrict reporters and cameras to a particular "viewing" area, even though the view from that area might not result in pictures that are as good as those the photographer could get from the vantage point of the protesters.

Likewise, in some jurisdictions it is considered trespassing for a reporter or photographer to accompany public officials onto private property. Court decisions are mixed on this question. To be safe, news personnel should have permission from the property owner, preferably in writing or with witnesses to oral consent. If the property owner is present, observes the reporter or photographer and doesn't object, then "implied consent" could be argued. But journalists have little recourse if the owner asks them to leave the property. The general rule is that anything that can be seen from a public place is not private, so it is permissible for a photographer to stand in a public area to take pictures of something newsworthy on private property. Yet it would be hard to defend a photographer who climbed a seldom-scaled cliff to take pictures with a telephoto lens of activities in a fenced yard.

Another form of trespass or intrusion is surreptitious taping. Most states allow one-party consent; that is, the reporter may record an interview or telephone conversation without telling the source, but a dozen or so states require both parties to give consent for taping. Know the law in your state. Many journalists and news organizations, however, question the ethics of such newsgathering procedures. Even where surreptitious taping is legal, a reporter who has no ethical qualms about using hidden recorders should talk with supervising editors about organizational policy on the matter.

Prepublication cautions at the copy desk

Generally, an assigning editor reads stories before sending them to the copy desk, but copy editors must not assume that the assigning editor was alert to all potential legal problems. As always, accuracy is essential. In addition, copy editors should take special care to ensure that stories are fair and balanced. Stories involving reluctant sources or confidential sources, as well as stories about lawsuits, can be particularly dangerous.

▶ **Accuracy, fairness and balance.** Accuracy cannot be stressed too much, and attention to accuracy must start at the very beginning of the newsgathering process—when the idea for a story is conceived. The copy editor must be alert to stories that reporters approached with preconceived notions—for instance, that the subject of the story was a good guy or a bad guy; that corruption existed in the police department; that the school superintendent was incompetent. Copy editors shouldn't hesitate to question reporters about whether they examined all angles of a story and relied on the most credible sources.

To head off lawsuits, the copy editor must check the story for fairness and balance, ensuring that the reporter has included evidence from interviews and from record searches to support generalizations. The copy editor should ascertain that the reporter has contacted those who might be damaged by the story. Denials, if made, should be included in the story.

Remember that truth is a defense for libel but not a defense for three of the four types of privacy cases. Private information that is highly offensive to a reasonable person is actionable as an invasion of privacy, even when the information is true. Also, truth is often difficult to prove in a libel lawsuit. Although the plaintiff has the burden of proving the falsity of a story about a public matter, the publication will also present arguments to support the accuracy of the story, because the burden of proof is a distinction that is difficult for juries to make.

Literal accuracy is not always enough to defend against a libel lawsuit, because literal accuracy is not necessarily the same as truth. One newspaper was hit with a libel lawsuit when it published a story stating that a woman shot her husband when she found him in the company of another woman. The statement was literally accurate, but it wasn't entirely true, because it falsely implied adultery. The truth was that the woman entered a residence where her husband was sitting in the living room in the company of several other people, including the "other woman's" husband.

A story that accurately reports that someone made a false and defamatory statement about someone else may also be grounds for a successful libel action. Unless the charge is made during a privileged situation, such as a city council meeting, it is not safe to republish defamatory statements. For example, publishing someone else's statement that a local merchant was dishonest would be dangerous unless the newspaper had independent proof of, say, embezzlement or the newspaper was published in one of the few jurisdictions that recognizes neutral reportage as a libel defense. The general rule is that anyone who republishes a defamatory quotation is just as guilty of libel as the original defamer.

Double-check even routine facts and stories, because those are often the basis for a lawsuit. The University of Iowa study showed that more than half the libel lawsuits against newspapers were based on stories that appeared on inside pages. About 45 percent of the lawsuits were for front-page stories.

▶**Reluctant sources.** If a person who might be damaged by a story is reluctant to talk to a reporter and is avoiding phone calls, the copy editor should not let the story go with a simple "Jones was unavailable for comment."

The copy editor should work with the assigning editor to make sure that the reporter goes to extra lengths to talk with the person. Have the reporter make several calls to Jones' business, home, lawyer, family, usual hangouts. In talking to people at all these places, the reporter may also gain important information for a better story. It is also helpful to leave messages for the reluctant source.

Establish a record of attempts to get the source to talk. These extra efforts may be important if the publication is sued for libel. Repeated attempts to reach the person and obtain information from sources close to him or her may help show a lack of fault on the part of the press.

If conditions were imposed on an interview and the reporter agreed to those conditions, the copy editor should be prepared to honor them. Should the news organization decide to violate agreements that the reporter made with a source, such a decision should be the responsibility of supervising editors rather than a copy editor.

▶**Confidential sources.** Anonymous sources should be avoided in most instances. Some news organizations have adopted a policy of allowing their use only in exceptional circumstances, arguing that the public is better served if it knows the source of information. Also, the story is stronger when the source is named, and the publication has a better legal case if the story becomes the basis for a lawsuit.

Many states do not have shield laws to protect confidentiality if the defendant in a libel lawsuit uses information from a confidential source. Source credibility is one factor used in determining actual malice. If the jury does not know the identity of the source, credibility cannot be judged.

When a newspaper is faced with a story of Watergate magnitude, an anonymous source may be the only way to get the story, such as meeting "Deep Throat" in the parking garage in the dark of night. But too often the use of anonymous sources seems to readers to be an excuse for "weasel" journalism and sloppy, lazy reporting. The use of anonymous sources can be an invitation to exaggerate, embellish, slant or take a cheap shot.

Information supplied by an anonymous source should be verified independently by at least one other source, preferably more than one. If the decision is made to use an anonymous source in a story, explain to readers why the identity is being withheld. Give readers enough information to establish the source's authority to speak on the subject. Of course, this is sometimes difficult to do without revealing the source.

▶**Stories about lawsuits.** Be especially alert to libel and privacy dangers when copy editing stories about civil or criminal lawsuits. Never let a story leave the copy desk saying that someone "may" or "plans to" file a civil lawsuit. Be sure that the lawsuit has been filed and, depending on the laws of the state, that some action has been taken on the lawsuit. Make sure that the complaint is accurately quoted or paraphrased once the lawsuit is filed.

In criminal cases, double-check all key facts: the name of the accused, address, specific charge. Use middle names or initials for the suspect to avoid confusion with someone who has a similar name. Be aware that manslaughter and murder are not the same charge.

Let the court, not your publication, judge the guilt or innocence of the defendant. The word *alleged,* as in "alleged ax murderer John Jones," does not always get the publication off the libel hook. Grammatically, the description *alleged ax murderer* can be understood to mean that Jones is an ax murderer who also happens to be accused, which is hardly what the writer meant, unless the writer does not accept the innocent-until-proven-guilty principle of American jurisprudence.

Don't let defamatory out-of-court statements by police or attorneys find their way into print. If the police chief says, "We've got an airtight case against this killer John Jones," don't go to press with the statement unless the police chief says it in a privileged, public situation. When reporting what was said during an open court session or other privileged situation, be sure to restate it accurately and to present a fair account of what happened during the privileged proceeding.

In the interest of fairness, the outcome of both civil and criminal cases—especially if the criminal defendant is acquitted—should be published as prominently as the story about the defendant's arrest or indictment.

▶**Headlines and quote boxes.** The copy editor's task doesn't end with the story. Once the story is "lawsuit-proof," the editor must take care not to libel someone or invade privacy in the headline. Quote boxes can be problematic also, because quotations taken out of context may be damaging.

Suggestions for additional reading

Carter, T. Barton, Marc A. Franklin, and Jay B. Wright. *The First Amendment and the Fifth Estate: Regulation of Electronic Mass Media,* 4th ed. Mineola, N.Y.: Foundation Press, 1996.

————. *The First Amendment and the Fourth Estate: The Law of Mass Media,* 7th ed. Mineola, N.Y.: Foundation Press, 1997.

Communication Law Writers Group. Wat Hopkins, ed. *Communication and the Law,* 1999 ed. Northport, Ala.: Vision Press, 1999.

Franklin, Marc A., and David A. Anderson. *Cases and Materials on Mass Media Law,* 5th ed. Westbury, N.Y.: Foundation Press, 1995.

Gillmor, Donald M. *Mass Communication Law: Cases and Comment,* 6th ed. Belmont, Calif.: Wadsworth, 1997.

Holsinger, Ralph L., and Jon Dilts. *Media Law,* 4th ed. Dubuque, Iowa: McGraw-Hill College, 1997.

Middleton, Kent, Bill F. Chamberlin, and Matthew D. Bunker. *The Law of Public Communication,* 4th ed. White Plains, N.Y.: Longman, 1997.

Moore, Roy. *Mass Communication Law and Ethics,* 2nd ed. Hillsdale, N.J.: L. Erlbaum Associates, 1998.

Overbeck, Wayne, and Rick D. Pullen. *Major Principles of Media Law,* 1999 ed. Fort Worth, Texas: Harcourt Brace College, 1999.

Pember, Don R. *Mass Media Law,* 1999 ed. Dubuque, Iowa: McGraw-Hill College, 1999.

Tedford, Thomas L. *Freedom of Speech in the United States,* 3rd ed. State College, Pa.: Strata Publishing Co., 1997.

Teeter, Dwight L., Don Le Duc, and Bill Loving. *Law of Mass Communications,* 9th ed. Westbury, N.Y.: Foundation Press, 1998.

Watkins, John J. *The Mass Media and the Law.* Englewood Cliffs, N.J.: Prentice-Hall, 1990.

Zelezny, John D. *Communications Law: Liberties, Restraints, and the Modern Media,* 2nd ed. Belmont, Calif.: Wadsworth, 1996.

Exercises

1. Consider the legal implications as you read this account and then answer the questions that follow it.

> Shortly after the Three Mile Island nuclear plant in Pennsylvania was shut down because of an accident, a newspaper reporter was told by a former security employee at the plant that plant security was inadequate and lax. To observe the security precautions firsthand, the reporter used the name and credentials of a former college roommate to apply for a job as a guard at the plant. The reporter was hired, and after two weeks of training, he started working full time as a guard.
>
> The reporter worked two weeks at the plant, during which time he made notes about the facility and took photographs of the control room. He told no one there about his affiliation with the newspaper.
>
> After quitting the security guard job, the reporter returned to his newspaper and wrote a series of articles about his experiences and observations at the nuclear plant. Before the stories were published, the reporter revealed his true identity to his former employers and asked to interview them. They refused to be interviewed.
>
> Metropolitan Edison, operator of the plant, went to court seeking an injunction to prohibit publication of the articles. A spokesperson for the company told reporters that the company did not want the reporter to divulge anything that could be detrimental to the security of the plant and the community. The spokesperson said that publication of the articles might expose the plant to terrorist attacks, which would endanger national security.

Answer these questions about this situation:

a. This case involves prior restraint. What is meant by prior restraint?

b. If the court follows the precedent of the Pentagon Papers case discussed in this chapter, what legal test will the court use to decide whether to grant the injunction?

c. Briefly describe the argument that Metropolitan Edison would use to try to persuade the court to issue the injunction.

d. Briefly describe the argument that the newspaper would use against the granting of the injunction.

e. Given your knowledge of precedent, which argument do you think the court will accept?

2. For each of the following statements, tell which elements of libel are present, if any, and what, if any, defense is available if the item sparks a libel lawsuit.

a. The Community Theater production of "Dear Old State University" is three hours of sheer boredom. Instead of buying a ticket to this masquerade of a play, spend your $10 on something worthwhile.

b. Jane Playwright denies that she is an addict, but she must have written "Dear Old State University" during one of her frequent bouts with booze and drugs.

c. A woman, who asked that her name not be revealed, said in an interview that John Politician, local mayor, raped her last year after the Christmas party for city employees. She said that she did not report the rape to police because she was afraid that she would lose her job at City Hall.

d. Sarah Bitter, who testified yesterday, told reporters that the prosecutor did not ask the right questions when she was on the witness stand. "If he had done his job right, I could have told the jury enough to convict that murdering John Smith," Bitter said.

e. In passing sentence on John E. Smith yesterday, Judge James Hangman said, "You are a sorry excuse for a man. The lowest animal known to humankind deserves more mercy than you gave your victim. I wish this state gave me the authority to pronounce the death penalty on such dregs of humanity as you."

f. Jane X. Doe, 2468 Kingston Ave., was drunk when she raced her car through the red light at Green and Main streets and struck the pedestrian, police on the scene said.

g. Jane X. Doe, 2468 Kingston Ave., was arrested and charged with driving under the influence of alcohol after an accident at Green and Main streets last night.

h. "You are a murderer!" Sarah Bitter screamed from the witness stand as she pointed at the defendant, John E. Smith.

i. "All sorority girls are whores," the evangelist told a campus crowd yesterday. "State universities shouldn't condone the sinful activities of sororities and fraternities."

j. At a meeting of the city council yesterday, a social worker told council members that Mayor John Politician was "charging big money to poor people who rent his rat-infested hovels."

k. The Coffee Cup Cafe was ordered closed yesterday by the county health department. Records indicate that the cafe has scored below the "acceptable" rating at each of the last three inspections by health officials.

l. Unless you're in the mood for a middle-of-the-night visit to the hospital emergency room, don't eat at the Country Style Delights restaurant. The desserts are pretty good, but the rest of the food isn't fit for a dog to eat.

3. Show that you understand the legal distinction between a limited public figure and a private person by naming two people in your town and the contexts in which each would be considered a limited public figure.

4. Describe a situation in which the president of the city council would be considered a private person in a libel lawsuit.

5. Consider each of the following situations in terms of privacy. Tell which privacy category, if any, and what defense, if any, apply. Which side is likely to win if a privacy lawsuit is filed?

   a. Suzy Goodtan, movie celebrity, was sunbathing nude in her backyard, which is surrounded by an 8-foot privacy fence. A photographer stood on a 10-foot ladder to look over the fence and take Suzy's picture. The picture was never published.

   b. Mark Jones was shopping at the Super Save Supermarket yesterday when a big display of tomato soup cans fell on his head. He is now in the hospital, suffering from a head injury. A photographer who happened to be in the supermarket at the time of the accident took a picture of Mark lying on the floor awaiting the ambulance. The local newspaper published the picture with a tagline reading "Freak Accident," and the caption included Jones' name and address.

   c. If the picture caption mentioned in item b included the name and address of the Super Save Supermarket, would the owner of the market have a good chance to win a libel or privacy lawsuit? Explain.

   d. In the same edition of the newspaper that ran the picture of his accident, Mark Jones was surprised to see an advertisement with a picture of him and his cute six-year-old daughter entering the store. Copy for the ad reads: "Mark Jones and six-year-old Heather enjoy shopping at Super Save, where they can buy at the lowest prices in town."

   e. A famous actress is in town to appear in a play. The local newspaper publishes a picture of a prominent local executive, who is married, embracing the actress in a hotel lobby. The picture caption identifies both the man and the actress.

   f. The caption for the picture of the actress and the prominent executive embracing implies that the two have a romantic relationship.

   g. A magazine reveals that 25 years ago Stephen Goodman was released from prison after serving a 10-year term on a conviction of molesting children. During the past 25 years, Goodman has been an outstanding citizen in town and has been honored for his volunteer work with children. Goodman's family, friends and business associates were unaware of his past criminal conviction.

   h. A magazine reveals that 25 years ago Stephen Goodman was arrested and charged with molesting children but was acquitted after a trial.

   i. A magazine publishes a story revealing intimate, graphic details about the sex life of a famous Hollywood actor. The story is based on interviews with two long-time employees at the actor's home.

   j. To attract subscribers, a newspaper uses direct-mail advertising to all non-subscribers in town. The ad includes a page reprinted from the newspaper, showing a color picture of the star quarterback at the state university.

6. You are a photographer for a local newspaper and specialize in sports photography. A nationally circulated sports magazine contacts you about buying some of your pictures that have appeared in the newspaper. Discuss this situation in terms of copyright.

7. A local woman is the author of a new book. The newspaper wants to condense the book and publish it as a series of newspaper stories during the next month, along with a feature story about the author. Is such a series likely to qualify as fair use? Explain your answer.

The domain of the mass media today is an ethical jungle in which pragmatism is king, agreed principles as to daily practice are few, and many of the inhabitants pride themselves on the anarchy of their surroundings.

—*Hodding Carter III*

Editing and Ethics

IN the book *Drawing the Line,* Scott McGehee, publisher of the News-Sentinel in Fort Wayne, Ind., describes a significant lesson she learned when she served as the managing editor of the Detroit Free Press:

> The most difficult ethical questions, in my view, are not always the momentous ones. . . .
>
> [T]he lead story in a Sunday lifestyle section, a profile of a tennis mother, [was] thoroughly researched, beautifully written—and devastating.
>
> The reporter had spent occasional whole days for weeks with the mother and her talented, preteen, tennis-playing son. The mother had opened up—sometimes in post-midnight telephone calls to the reporter—to reveal her innermost hopes, dreams and fears. The reporter, a former tennis prodigy herself, had taken it all in.
>
> The resulting story painted in vivid detail the sad case of a mother living through her son, single-minded in her devotion to his success, suffocating in the pressure she applied. The story of this one woman and her son was skillfully constructed to illustrate the stage-mother, little-league-father syndrome, with lessons to be inferred by any caring parent.
>
> Several days after publication, I got a telephone call from a woman with a quavering voice who said she was that mother. She had already talked to her lawyer, who had convinced her she couldn't get successful legal revenge. But she wanted me to know that the reporter and I had ruined her marriage, her relationship with her son, her life. She had bared her soul to the reporter, who had used it as grist for a mean, unfair story, she said.
>
> That was all: one phone call. No face-to-face confrontation, no barrage of complaints from friends and family, no spate of canceled subscriptions, no lawsuit filed. But the pain in the woman's voice still haunts me.
>
> So do the questions I didn't ask: Did the reporter have some unresolved problems from her own tennis-playing youth that colored the story unfairly? Would the story have worked just as well without the mean tone? Did the reporter get too close, allowing the mother to assume she was a friend, not merely a reporter? Did the story unfairly take advantage of a woman who had no previous experience dealing with the press?
>
> I'll never know the answers to most of those questions, but I know the answer to the last one: Yes.

Editor McGehee suggested that, in this case, her attempt to draw the line between ethical and unethical conduct had failed, and her newspaper's lack of attention to the fairness of this story had needlessly hurt people in their private lives. Such day-to-day ethical concerns are the topic of this chapter.

We know, from observation of coverage of the presidential impeachment scandal and other stories, as well as from research conducted by the chief media organizations in this country, that a substantial credibility gap exists between the media and their audiences. This disconnection reached such crisis proportions in the 1980s that editors and publishers thought it warranted some action. Some began to respond by remembering the basics:

- Practice journalistic principles of fairness, accuracy and completeness
- Respect people's feelings
- Become aware of sensitive topics
- Broaden issues of coverage

Others, such as The Tribune in Oakland, Calif., instituted policies to handle corrections and clarifications and revised local stylebooks to include sections on how to address issues of poor taste, profanity and violence.

But many believe that the credibility "challenge," among other factors, has had a negative effect on the financial health of traditional news media. Newspaper circulation rates, for example, although increasing in raw numbers, have failed to keep up with population growth. Network news share has also continued to slip.

Nationwide surveys taken in the late 1990s revealed that the public did not appreciate or like what reporters and editors did, how they did it, or the explanations they offered for their actions.

In December 1998, the American Society of Newspaper Editors released the results of an important research study called "Examining Our Credibility: Why Newspaper Credibility Is Dropping." The survey indicated that, among other things, the U.S. public wanted the media to rein in their eagerness for the sexy story. More than 80 percent of Americans believed sensational stories got lots of news coverage because they were exciting and not because they were important. Christine Urban, who conducted the study, said, "The public believes that the reporter's job is to report the facts—completely, insightfully and without spin, and clean of any intent to sway or convince."

The study also indicated that four-fifths of the adults in the United States believed the news media were biased and the same percentage believed that powerful people or organizations could influence a newspaper to "spike or spin" a story. More than a third noticed factual, grammatical and spelling errors, which undermine perceptions of credibility; and more than three-fourths expressed concern about stories that used anonymous sources. Almost half said a story shouldn't be published or broadcast if no source was willing to go "on the record," meaning allow his or her name to be used in the story.

Today, as we begin a new millennium, media ethics must be discussed within the context of these increasingly negative perceptions of journalists, as well as within the context of emerging media technologies, such as digital photo imaging and online information sources. Should editors, for example, digitally manipulate a news photograph to delete obtrusive details in the foreground or to change the color of a person's clothing or jewelry? Should editors link, in any way, online editorial content with advertising? Should print publications report on cybergossip without checking all the facts? (See discussion of these issues later in this chapter.)

Journalists and journalism educators are pondering the role of the press in the 21st century. In the mid-1990s, newspaper journalists were forging the concept of public journalism or civic journalism. Jay Rosen, associate professor of journalism at New York University, and Davis "Buzz" Merritt, editor and senior vice president of The Wichita (Kan.) Eagle, were leaders in defining the reform movement known as public journalism, which calls on the press to "take an active role in strengthening citizenship, improving political debate and reviving public life."

In addition, a diverse group of daily newspaper editors participated in the ASNE-sponsored Journalism Values Institute, a multiyear project to define journalism values, and issued a series of reports in mid-decade that focused on how to stay true to core journalism principles—such as news judgment, balance, accuracy, leadership in the community, accessibility and credibility—in the age of new media.

Just as journalists are engaged in nationwide conversations about how to undertake a fundamental reassessment of the basic mission of the press, so, too, should journalism students enter into a robust and earnest discussion of media ethics on their campuses.

How to decide questions of ethics

The stereotypes of journalists as cynical, conniving and unprincipled hacks who believe that a scoop is sacred persist in the popular culture. But what kind of decisions do real journalists make? Here are three newsroom scenarios that editors might face:

- Your newspaper's summer intern discovers that the death of a prominent member of the community occurred because of complications associated with AIDS. You're the senior editor on duty, and your final edition goes to press in 30 minutes. Should you publish the cause of death?

- As your newspaper's sports editor, you believe your audience wants to read stories about all the games, both home and away, of the professional football franchise in your area. Your newspaper cannot afford to send you to the away games, but the owners of the football team will allow you to travel with the team, free of charge, and will grant you exclusive interviews with the star players as well. Should you accept the team's offer?

- Your newspaper's photographer returns from an assignment with a dramatic photo of an accident scene. In the foreground, a child's covered body, turned away from the camera, lies in the street; in the background, traffic stands still and passersby look on. As the editor who is laying out tomorrow's Page One, you must decide whether to use the photograph.

Those who are in the business of editing and judging the news face such ethical questions as a matter of routine. Often journalists must find answers within hours—or even minutes—because of the harsh deadlines of publication or broadcast.

What are the benefits of publishing the story about the prominent citizen dying of AIDS? Does the newspaper have a policy calling for inclusion of the cause of death in obituaries? Would a great public good be served by publication? Should respect for the privacy of the relatives and friends of the deceased be considered? What personal values do you bring to bear on your decision?

In the case of the sports editor, the question is whether traveling with the football team legitimately adds value to the newspaper's reporting or to readers' understanding of the sport. Or might the editor simply be submitting to a form of bribery and risking conflict of interest?

What news values in the accident photograph warrant its use? Is the photo a sensational exploitation of the senseless death of a child, or is it a legitimate portrayal of a newsworthy event?

Few ethical decisions are clear-cut, and many are quite complicated. Most of the time, journalists have no detailed ground rules to guide them in making such decisions.

Some groups of professionals are able to turn to rules and principles for help in solving ethical problems. Law students, for example, study the ethics of their profession along with court procedure. Medical students study the ethics of medicine along with anatomy. Both know that the ethical code of their profession is universal and that individual practitioners will be policed by their own colleagues, who have the power to take away their licenses to practice.

Journalists, on the other hand, have no such procedures or universal rules of conduct. For them, the signs are at best blurred and at worst nonexistent. Restraints are few, and a licensing and policing agency like the American Bar Association or the American Medical Association doesn't exist. Most journalists are acutely aware of the need for ethical performance, and most attempt to respect standards for responsible journalism codified by national press organizations. Still, ethics remains a trial-and-error proposition.

What is ethics?

In popular usage, one meaning of *ethics* is "a set of principles of conduct governing an individual or group." One writer said that ethics refers not only to statements about our conduct and the conduct of others but also to statements of what that conduct ought to be.

People embrace certain ethical standards of conduct because of the moral education provided by their culture—their family, school, church, friends and peers—and because of an inner commitment to culturally defined moral standards. Ethics, therefore, is personal. It is determined and enforced by each of us individually, and it can provide us with certain basic principles by which we can judge actions to be right or wrong, good or bad, responsible or irresponsible.

Because of this background, we make many moral judgments without much thought or deliberation. Most of us, for example, would not hesitate to say that we value telling the truth.

Once in a while, an ethical decision involves more than one moral rule. For example, most of us have been taught that stealing is wrong; we have also been taught that life is highly valued. What if a loved one required medication to live and we had no money to buy that medication? Would we hesitate to steal the medicine from the pharmacy? Would we be morally justified in doing so? Does the value of a life outweigh the harm done by stealing the medicine? Or is stealing always wrong, regardless of the motivation?

Philosophical principles

When we are looking for a way to balance conflicting ethical rules, we are seeking moral standards, philosophical principles we can invoke to help us justify our decision. One philosopher we might call on to help justify our decision about stealing the medicine is Immanuel Kant. Kant's *categorical imperative* is based on a conviction that as human beings we have certain moral rights and duties and that we should treat all other people as free and equal to ourselves. Our actions are morally right, then, only if we can apply our reasoning universally—that is, only if we would be willing to have everyone act as we do, using the same reasoning in any similar situation. Kant's view is an absolutist view: Right is right and must be done under even the most extreme conditions. Thus, we cannot justify stealing the medicine unless we are willing to let anyone steal medicine under similar circumstances.

The argument that a greater good would be served by saving the life of our loved one than by not stealing the medicine might be justified by John Stuart Mill's *principle of utility*. His utilitarian theory is one of the most influential in journalism today. It is based on the notion that our actions have consequences, and those consequences count. The best decisions, the best actions have good consequences for the largest number of people possible. The utilitarian principle prescribes "the greatest happiness for the greatest number." In media situations, this maxim often translates into "the public's right to know." In the example, utilitarians might argue that more good consequences would flow from stealing the medicine and thus saving the life than from any other act we could perform in that situation. Therefore, we would be morally justified in stealing the medicine.

A third philosophical principle, Aristotle's **golden mean**, holds that moral behavior is the mean between two extremes, at one end excess and at the other deficiency. Find a moderate position, a compromise, between these two extremes, and you will be acting with virtue. In this case, the moderate and ethical position between the two extremes—stealing the medicine or allowing the loved one to die— might be to offer to work for the pharmacist in return for the medicine.

The philosophical principles of Kant, Mill and Aristotle are just three among many that can be used to help justify ethical decisions. At first these three approaches may seem inapplicable to today's fast-paced newsrooms. But on closer examination we can sense how they might hold value for today's editing processes. At the very least, the use of philosophical principles allows us to step back for a moment and ponder the situation more than we might ordinarily do in the rush to publish. In addition, invoking a theory or philosophical principle helps us frame our approach toward solution of the ethical issue; in other words, it helps us see the problem in a broader light rather than isolate it from any historical, social or economic context. Unfortunately, in the day-to-day scramble to publish and broadcast, journalists rarely take time to reason carefully through a thorny ethical problem.

How to use the Potter box

In their book *Media Ethics: Cases and Moral Reasoning*, Clifford G. Christians, Kim B. Rotzoll and Mark Fackler describe a model of moral reasoning called the Potter box (see Figure 7-1). Formulated by Dr. Ralph Potter of the Harvard Divinity School, the Potter box helps dissect a situation requiring an ethical response by introducing four dimensions of analysis: definition, values, principles and loyalties. To make a decision, we move through each dimension—from defining the situation to considering values to appealing to an ethical principle to choosing loyalties— eventually reasoning our way toward a solution.

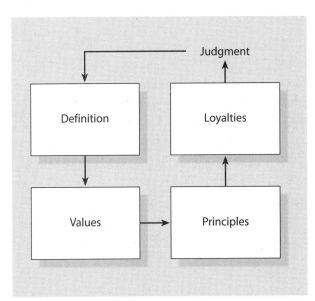

Figure 7-1
The Potter box can be used to analyze the dimensions of an ethical problem for journalists. The first step is definition of the situation. It is followed by outlining the possible values at work and determining the relevant principles to apply. The next step is choosing loyalties. After the four-stage analysis, the final step is to make an ethical decision about whether or not to publish.

To see how this method of moral reasoning works, let's return to one of the scenarios mentioned at the beginning of this chapter. You are editor of the Daily Bugle, a mid-sized newspaper in Hampshiretown. At the 4 p.m. meeting to discuss the next day's paper, you are handed a photograph showing the mangled body of a child hit by a car. The body is partially covered by a sheet, and a small pool of blood is visible in the background. Passersby look on in horror, and a soccer ball is evident in the foreground.

According to the caption information on the back of the photo and an attached story, the girl in the foreground of the photo is 7-year-old Tammy Davis, daughter of William Davis, owner of the town's biggest furniture store and president of the country club.

Tammy was playing soccer in a park after school when the ball rolled into the street. As Tammy chased the soccer ball, she was hit by a car and killed.

Daily Bugle photographer Clara Lenz came across the accident on her way to another assignment, and she took the picture. She strongly believes that the photo should be published and that it should be displayed prominently on Page One.

You know you must get some questions answered before you make a decision. You linger to talk to Mike Modular, the news editor, after the meeting.

Modular tells you that the newspaper's police reporter has learned that the driver of the car scored 0.25 on his Breathalyzer test—well over the legal limit for driving a car—and is sobering up in the city jail. Modular recommends against publishing the photo, especially on Page One.

The Potter box can help you decide whether to publish the photograph, as the photographer wishes, or to not publish it, as the news editor wishes.

▶**Step 1 is to define the situation.** Photographer Lenz might define the situation as this: The daughter of a prominent citizen of the community was run down and killed by a drunken driver, and the newspaper has a photograph of the scene. News editor Modular might define the situation as this: The newspaper has a photograph that depicts, in gruesome detail, the scene of an automobile fatality on a city street.

▶**Step 2 is to identify the values underlying the choices.** This part of the exercise asks you to define the costs and benefits of publication. What are the positive and negative values that reflect your own personal ethics?

In this case, photographer Lenz might identify these positive values as benefits of publishing the photograph:

- The photo is an accurate depiction of a very newsworthy event, an event that occurred locally, publicly and recently.

- In addition, the victim was the daughter of a prominent local citizen, adding to the newsworthiness of the photo.

- The photo also is well-composed and technically good; it has impact, one of the elements essential in high-quality photojournalism.

News editor Modular, on the other hand, might identify these negative values as the costs of publishing the photograph:

- The photo is in extremely poor taste and is too gruesome; it depicts in graphic detail the senseless death of a child.

- The newspaper's unwritten policy is not to publish photos showing dead bodies.

▶ **Step 3 is to appeal to a moral principle to help justify your decision.** If you were to agree with Lenz and decide to publish the photograph, you might call on Mill to help justify your decision. The utilitarian principle would argue that the public has a right to know about this newsworthy event and that the more the newspaper can educate the public about this problem, the more likely it is that a solution will be found. "The greatest good for the greatest number" would suggest publication.

Conversely, if you were to agree with Modular and decide not to publish the photograph, you might call on Kant to help justify your decision. The absolutist view would argue that you should follow the newspaper's policy not to publish photos of dead bodies, no matter what. Right is right, and wrong is wrong. And publishing a tasteless, gruesome photo like this one is wrong.

▶ **Step 4 is to choose loyalties.** This last step is very significant and often the most agonizing one, because direct conflicts arise among competing obligations. To whom is the highest moral duty owed? Is the first loyalty to yourself, to the newspaper, to the family of the victim, to the readers, to your colleagues or to society?

Lenz might argue that the ultimate loyalty is to society and to readers. The newspaper has a social obligation to inform and educate the public about the problem of drunken driving, and the photograph is part of that campaign. Lenz also might argue that a secondary loyalty would be to herself; publication of the photo might win the praise of her colleagues and could even win a journalistic award.

Modular, on the other hand, might argue that the ultimate loyalty should be to the newspaper and its policies regarding publication of tasteless material. Or he might argue that the highest moral duty is owed the surviving family and that the photo should not be published because it would hurt them even more than they already are hurt by their child's tragic death.

After reasoning your way through the four dimensions of the Potter box, definition, values, principles and loyalties, you should be able to reach a responsible and ethical decision. The questions become more and more focused as the discussion proceeds through each of the quadrants. In the end, bringing your own personally defined ethics to bear, what would you decide? Would you publish the photograph or wouldn't you?

Unfortunately, reporters and editors do not often use such methods to make moral judgments. They either react instinctively, hoping that they will make the right decision and that the negative consequences will not be too overpowering, or they try to find answers in a professional code of ethics.

Codes of ethics

The American Society of Newspaper Editors, the Associated Press Managing Editors and the Society of Professional Journalists have compiled generalized statements about well-known unethical behaviors. These codes of ethics provide little substantive guidance to help journalists balance conflicting moral rules. But they do provide a starting point for defining an ethical problem that needs to be resolved.

The ASNE and APME codes of ethics appear in Figures 7-2 and 7-3. The SPJ code appears in Figure 7-4.

In addition to these general codes of ethics, individual newspapers have developed their own codes or policy statements, most of which address such issues as acceptance of gifts and junkets or conflicts of interest. Here is a

Figure 7-2
The American Society of Newspaper Editors has published this "Statement of Principles." (Reprinted courtesy of the American Society of Newspaper Editors)

Preamble

The First Amendment, protecting freedom of expression from abridgment by any law, guarantees to the people through their press a constitutional right, and thereby places on newspaper people a particular responsibility. Thus journalism demands of its practitioners not only industry and knowledge but also the pursuit of a standard of integrity proportionate to the journalist's singular obligation.

To this end the American Society of Newspaper Editors sets forth this Statement of Principles as a standard encouraging the highest ethical and professional performance.

Article I: Responsibility

The primary purpose of gathering and distributing news and opinion is to serve the general welfare by informing the people and enabling them to make judgments on the issues of the time. Newspapermen and women who abuse the power of their professional role for selfish motives or unworthy purposes are faithless to that public trust.

The American press was made free not just to inform or just to serve as a forum for debate but also to bring an independent scrutiny to bear on the forces of power in the society, including the conduct of official power at all levels of government.

Article II: Freedom of the Press

Freedom of the press belongs to the people. It must be defended against encroachment or assault from any quarter, public or private.

Journalists must be constantly alert to see that the public's business is conducted in public. They must be vigilant against all who would exploit the press for selfish purposes.

Article III: Independence

Journalists must avoid impropriety and the appearance of impropriety as well as any conflict of interest or the appearance of conflict. They should neither accept anything nor pursue any activity that might compromise or seem to compromise their integrity.

Article IV: Truth and Accuracy

Good faith with the reader is the foundation of good journalism. Every effort must be made to assure that the news content is accurate, free from bias and in context, and that all sides are presented fairly. Editorials, analytical articles and commentary should be held to the same standards of accuracy with respect to facts as news reports.

Significant errors of fact, as well as errors of omission, should be corrected promptly and prominently.

Article V: Impartiality

To be impartial does not require the press to be unquestioning or to refrain from editorial expression. Sound practice, however, demands a clear distinction for the reader between news reports and opinion. Articles that contain opinion or personal interpretation should be clearly identified.

Article VI: Fair Play

Journalists should respect the rights of people involved in the news, observe the common standards of decency and stand accountable to the public for the fairness and accuracy of their news reports.

Persons publicly accused should be given the earliest opportunity to respond.

Pledges of confidentiality to news sources must be honored at all costs, and therefore should not be given lightly. Unless there is clear and pressing need to maintain confidences, sources of information should be identified.

■ ■ ■

These principles are intended to preserve, protect and strengthen the bond of trust and respect between American journalists and the American people, a bond that is essential to sustain the grant of freedom entrusted to both by the nation's founders.

This Statement of Principles was adopted by the ASNE Board of Directors, Oct. 23, 1975;
it supplants the 1922 Code of Ethics ("Canons of Journalism").

Figure 7-3
This is the "Code of Ethics" published by the Associated Press Managing Editors. (Reprinted courtesy of the Associated Press Managing Editors Association)

These principles are a model against which news and editorial staff members can measure their performance. They have been formulated in the belief that newspapers and the people who produce them should adhere to the highest standards of ethical and professional conduct.

The public's right to know about matters of importance is paramount. The newspaper has a special responsibility as surrogate of its readers to be a vigilant watchdog of their legitimate public interests.

No statement of principles can prescribe decisions governing every situation. Common sense and good judgment are required in applying ethical principles to newspaper realities. As new technologies evolve, these principles can help guide editors to insure the credibility of the news and information they provide. Individual newspapers are encouraged to augment these APME guidelines more specifically to their own situations.

Responsibility

The good newspaper is fair, accurate, honest, responsible, independent, and decent. Truth is its guiding principle.

It avoids practices that would conflict with the ability to report and present news in a fair, accurate, and unbiased manner.

The newspaper should serve as a constructive critic of all segments of society. It should reasonably reflect, in staffing and coverage, its diverse constituencies. It should vigorously expose wrongdoing, duplicity or misuse of power, public or private. Editorially, it should advocate needed reform and innovation in the public interest. News sources should be disclosed unless there is a clear reason not to do so. When it is necessary to protect the confidentiality of a source, the reason should be explained.

The newspaper should uphold the right of free speech and freedom of the press and should respect the individual's right of privacy. The newspaper should fight vigorously for public access to news of government through open meetings and records.

Accuracy

The newspaper should guard against inaccuracies, carelessness, bias or distortion through emphasis, omission or technological manipulation.

It should acknowledge substantive errors and correct them promptly and prominently.

Integrity

The newspaper should strive for impartial treatment of issues and dispassionate handling of controversial subjects. It should provide a forum for the exchange of comment and criticism, especially when such comment is opposed to its editorial positions. Editorials and expressions of personal opinion by reporters and editors should be clearly labeled. Advertising should be clearly differentiated from news.

The newspaper should report the news without regard for its own interests, mindful of the need to disclose potential conflicts. It should not give favored news treatment to advertisers or special-interest groups. It should report matters regarding itself or its personnel with the same vigor and candor as it would other institutions or individuals. Concern for community, business or personal interests should not cause the newspaper to distort or misrepresent the facts.

The newspaper should deal honestly with readers and newsmakers. It should keep its promises.

The newspaper should not plagiarize words or images.

Independence

The newspaper and its staff should be free of obligations to news sources and newsmakers. Even the appearance of obligation or conflict of interest should be avoided.

Newspapers should accept nothing of value from news sources or others outside the profession. Gifts and free or reduced-rate travel, entertainment, products and lodging should not be accepted. Expenses in connection with news reporting should be paid by the newspaper. Special favors and special treatment for members of the press should be avoided.

Journalists are encouraged to be involved in their communities, to the extent that such activities do not create conflicts of interest. Involvement in politics, demonstrations and social causes that could cause a conflict of interest, or the appearance of such conflict, should be avoided.

Work by staff members for the people or institutions they cover also should be avoided.

Financial investments by staff members or other outside business interests that could create the impression of a conflict of interest should be avoided.

Stories should not be written or edited primarily for the purpose of winning awards and prizes. Self-serving journalism contests and awards that reflect unfavorably on the newspaper or the profession should be avoided.

Adopted by the APME convention in Philadelphia, Oct. 12, 1994.

Figure 7-4
This version of the Society of Professional Journalists' Code of Ethics was adopted in September 1996.

Preamble

Members of the Society of Professional Journalists believe that public enlightenment is the forerunner of justice and the foundation of democracy. The duty of the journalist is to further those ends by seeking truth and providing a fair and comprehensive account of events and issues. Conscientious journalists from all media and specialties strive to serve the public with thoroughness and honesty. Professional integrity is the cornerstone of a journalist's credibility. Members of the Society share a dedication to ethical behavior and adopt this code to declare the Society's principles and standards of practice.

Seek Truth and Report It

Journalists should be honest, fair and courageous in gathering, reporting and interpreting information.
Journalists should:

- Test the accuracy of information from all sources and exercise care to avoid inadvertent error. Deliberate distortion is never permissible.
- Diligently seek out subjects of news stories to give them the opportunity to respond to allegations of wrongdoing.
- Identify sources whenever feasible. The public is entitled to as much information as possible on sources' reliability.
- Always question sources' motives before promising anonymity. Clarify conditions attached to any promise made in exchange for information. Keep promises.
- Make certain that headlines, news teases and promotional material, photos, video, audio, graphics, sound bites and quotations do not misrepresent. They should not oversimplify or highlight incidents out of context.
- Never distort the content of news photos or video. Image enhancement for technical clarity is always permissible. Label montages and photo illustrations.
- Avoid misleading re-enactments or staged news events. If re-enactment is necessary to tell a story, label it.
- Avoid undercover or other surreptitious methods of gathering information except when traditional open methods will not yield information vital to the public. Use of such methods should be explained as part of the story.
- Never plagiarize.
- Tell the story of the diversity and magnitude of the human experience boldly, even when it is unpopular to do so.
- Examine their own cultural values and avoid imposing those values on others.
- Avoid stereotyping by race, gender, age, religion, ethnicity, geography, sexual orientation, disability, physical appearance or social status.
- Support the open exchange of views, even views they find repugnant.
- Give voice to the voiceless; official and unofficial sources of information can be equally valid.
- Distinguish between advocacy and news reporting. Analysis and commentary should be labeled and not misrepresent fact or context.
- Distinguish news from advertising and shun hybrids that blur the lines between the two.
- Recognize a special obligation to ensure that the public's business is conducted in the open and that government records are open to inspection.

Minimize Harm

Ethical journalists treat sources, subjects and colleagues as human beings deserving of respect.
Journalists should:

- Show compassion for those who may be affected adversely by news coverage. Use special sensitivity when dealing with children and inexperienced sources or subjects.
- Be sensitive when seeking or using interviews or photographs of those affected by tragedy or grief.

- Recognize that gathering and reporting information may cause harm or discomfort. Pursuit of the news is not a license for arrogance.
- Recognize that private people have a greater right to control information about themselves than do public officials and others who seek power, influence or attention. Only an overriding public need can justify intrusion into anyone's privacy.
- Show good taste. Avoid pandering to lurid curiosity.
- Be cautious about identifying juvenile suspects or victims of sex crimes.
- Be judicious about naming criminal suspects before the formal filing of charges.
- Balance a criminal suspect's fair trial rights with the public's right to be informed.

Act Independently

Journalists should be free of obligation to any interest other than the public's right to know.

Journalists should:

- Avoid conflicts of interest, real or perceived.
- Remain free of associations and activities that may compromise integrity or damage credibility.
- Refuse gifts, favors, fees, free travel and special treatment, and shun secondary employment, political involvement, public office and service in community organizations if they compromise journalistic integrity.
- Disclose unavoidable conflicts.
- Be vigilant and courageous about holding those with power accountable.
- Deny favored treatment to advertisers and special interests and resist their pressure to influence news coverage.
- Be wary of sources offering information for favors or money; avoid bidding for news.

Be Accountable

Journalists are accountable to their readers, listeners, viewers and each other.

Journalists should:

- Clarify and explain news coverage and invite dialogue with the public over journalistic conduct.
- Encourage the public to voice grievances against the news media.
- Admit mistakes and correct them promptly.
- Expose unethical practices of journalists and the news media.
- Abide by the same high standards to which they hold others.

Sigma Delta Chi's first Code of Ethics was borrowed from the American Society of Newspaper Editors in 1926. In 1973, Sigma Delta Chi wrote its own code, which was revised in 1984 and 1987. The present version of the Society of Professional Journalists' Code of Ethics was adopted in September 1996.

sampling, culled from a report by the Associated Press Managing Editors Professional Standards Committee:

▶Gifts

Editorial employees will accept no gifts or favors of significant value offered in connection with their jobs. [Fort Worth (Texas) Star-Telegram]

We accept no business-connected gifts or gratuities. We do not accept free rooms, sample merchandise, special reduced rates for members of the press, funds provided by gaming establishments and racetracks for members of the media to use, or any other low- or no-pay arrangement. Gifts of insignificant value—a calendar, pencil, key chain or similar item sent out routinely by a corporation, for instance—may be accepted if it would be awkward to send them back. All other gifts will, however, be returned to the donor with the explanation that it is in violation of Inquirer policy to accept any gifts. Bottles of liquor or wine shall be considered gifts of more than token value and may not be retained. Where it is impractical to return a gift, it will be given to charity and the donor will be advised of the reason. (The Philadelphia Inquirer)

Junkets

The News pays all costs connected with travel by staff members on News business. This includes transportation, meals and lodging. Junkets, free trips and reduced fares are not accepted. An exception may be made when the free or subsidized transportation is the only means available to cover an event, such as a police or military flight to or over a disaster area. [Ann Arbor (Mich.) News]

Any travel for either a story or story-research is company travel. Even on chartered trips (such as accompanying a sports team) or hitchhiking on a State Police plane, we insist on being billed for our prorata share of the expense. [Louisville (Ky.) Courier Journal]

Meals

Meals and/or drinks shared with news sources should be paid for, wherever possible, by the staff member. When the cost of a meal includes an additional sum (for example, a $500-a-plate political fund-raiser) the staff member will pay the price of the meal. (Detroit Free Press)

The Star prefers to pay for meals that staff members share with news sources. (In instances where insistence on paying would be awkward or otherwise inappropriate, staff members should make it clear that the newspaper will reciprocate in the future.) (Minneapolis Star)

Connections

Employees must not use their position on the paper to their advantage in commercial transactions or for other personal gain. This specifically prohibits such practices as the use of Journal stationery for private business matters, letters of protest or similar dealings. (Milwaukee Journal)

Merchandise

Samples of any products, including but not limited to books, records and tapes, generally should be regarded as gifts, in that those not used for news purposes should be donated to charity, with a letter to the giver explaining the action. Those samples, books, records, tapes etc. that are desired for news purposes will be purchased from the sender by The Star at the standard retail price and will remain the property of The Star. (Minneapolis Star)

Free books and record albums will not be solicited. Those unsolicited books and albums received will either be given to a reviewer as compensation for the review or be sold at an employee's sale with the proceeds going for charitable purposes. (Des Moines Register)

Tickets

Free tickets or passes to sports events, movies, theatrical productions, circuses, ice shows or other entertainment shall not be accepted or solicited by staff members.

Staff members covering events which involve an admission charge shall pay for a ticket. The money for the ticket should either be obtained from The Statesman in advance or a voucher submitted for reimbursement after the event. The exception to this will be those events where separate press facilities (press box or table) are provided. In these instances where the public is not being deprived of a seat, no ticket shall be required unless deemed so by the sponsoring group.

Press box and sideline passes are to be used only by reporters or photographers assigned to cover the event.

A staff member who attends an event for background purposes shall buy a ticket and submit an expense voucher.

Season passes to movies will not be accepted.

Any expenses for nightclub admissions, cover charges, meals, refreshments and other expenses for reviewers or critics will be reimbursed. (Idaho Statesman, Boise, Idaho)

▶ Conflicts of interest

It is the policy of this company that no employee shall invest his time or money in any business competitive to this corporation. Investments of this kind usually result in divided loyalty.

Financial investments or other outside business activities by Journal staff members that could conflict with the Journal's ability to report the news, or that would create the impression of such a conflict, must be avoided. (Milwaukee Journal)

Work for a politician or a political organization, either paid or voluntary, is forbidden. Also forbidden is (1) holding public office or (2) accepting political appointment to any position for which there is remuneration other than expenses. There is no quicker source of misunderstanding and suspicion in our profession than the area of politics. We must not give any person reason to suspect that our handling of a story, editorial or picture is related in any way to political activity by a member of the staff. [The Manhattan (Kan.) Mercury]

Staff members must avoid involvement in public affairs that have the potential for a conflict of interest or could create the impression with the public of a conflict of interest. Non-conflicting community involvement is encouraged. Common sense prevails.

Participation in politics is not permitted.

This section does not preclude voting or registration in a political party for voting purposes.

Work in public relations for pay is prohibited.

Volunteer work in charitable causes is commendable, if limited to non-controversial activities.

The common sense clause requires that all parties maintain communication and understanding so that professional standards may be maintained without undue restraint on personal activities.

Staff members must not act as sports officials, scorers, judges, umpires or referees for pay or as a volunteer at professional, collegiate or high school competitions.

Any outside employment must be cleared in advance with the executive editor. Common sense prevails. [Elmira (N.Y.) Star-Gazette and Sunday Telegram]

Editing with good taste and sensitivity

Of all the copy editor's duties, eliminating passages that are in poor taste or harbor stereotypes can be the most challenging. Just as it is important to edit stories for accuracy, style, consistency, conciseness and libel, it is likewise crucial to be alert to issues of sensitivity.

Twenty years ago, most newspaper stylebooks would not have addressed issues of sensitivity. But today, many contain guidelines for handling references to age, dialect, disabilities, race, nationality, religion, gender and sexual orientation, and they outline when it is and is not acceptable to use profanity or graphic detail in a story. Here are some of the commonly adopted rules at many newspapers for these issues:

▶ **Age.** Ages of individuals should be mentioned in stories and headlines only when relevant or useful in describing them. Avoid terms such as *old, senior, senior citizen, retiree, middle-aged* and *teen-ager* unless they are specifically relevant to the story. The legal age for adulthood is 18. Persons who are 18 and older are women and men, not girls and boys. Do not refer to young children with obvious or implied adjectives, such as *tiny* or *little*.

▶ **Sexism.** The basic rule is that people of different genders should be treated the same unless their gender is relevant to the news. Physical descriptions of women or men are permissible only if relevant to the story. Generally, avoid terms that specify gender. For example, use *journalist* instead of *newsman* or *newswoman*, *firefighter* instead of *fireman* or *firewoman*. Avoid phrases, such as *male nurse* or *woman doctor*, that suggest we think there is something unusual about the gender of the person holding those jobs. When in doubt about sexist word usage, consult Casey Miller and Kate Swift's *The Handbook of Nonsexist Writing* or Rosalie Maggio's *The Nonsexist Word Finder: A Dictionary of Gender-Free Usage*.

▶ **Race and ethnicity.** Do not mention race, ethnicity or national origin unless it is clearly relevant to the story. In stories involving politics, social action or social conditions, race is not automatically relevant. Avoid terms such as *ghetto, barrio, inner city, suburbs*. They are inaccurate and stereotypical. Do not use a person's race when reporting a crime story unless the incident is racial or ethnic in nature. State the country the person is from if race or ethnic origin is relevant, rather than lumping all Africans, Asians or Central and South Americans into continental categories. Be aware of questionable connotations. *Culturally deprived* or *culturally disadvantaged* implies superiority of one culture over another. In fact, people so labeled often are bicultural and bilingual.

▶ **Disabilities.** Avoid degrading and inaccurate references to disabilities. Disabilities should not be mentioned in stories or headlines unless they are pertinent. People who are permanently disabled generally do not like to be described as handicapped. Use *disabled* or specify the nature of the disability. When a disability requires use of a wheelchair, say *uses a wheelchair*, not *confined to a wheelchair*. The word *handicapped* is acceptable in describing a temporary disability: "The baseball player was handicapped by a sprained wrist."

▶ **Sexual orientation.** Sexual orientation—or identifying places and products as being favored by those of a particular sexual preference—should be mentioned only if demonstrably pertinent. When sexual orientation is mentioned, exercise caution in word usage. *Gay* may be used as an adjective but not as a noun: *gay man*. *Lesbian* is generally preferred in reference to homosexual women, *gay* in reference to homosexual men. Use *gay-rights activist,* not *gay activist.* Avoid such terms as *admitted* or *avowed.*

▶ **Profanity, obscenity and violence.** Profanities and obscenities should not be used unless something significant would otherwise be lost. The test should be "Why use it?" rather than "Why not use it?" The simple fact that a person used profanity or obscenity is not in itself justification for printing it. However, it may be used if the term was used in public—especially by a public official or celebrity—and it reflects a mood or frame of mind that can be conveyed in no other way or if the words themselves play a role in the story (as in reports about Supreme Court obscenity rulings). Detailed descriptions of a pornographic film or an episode of violence or mayhem should not be used unless they provide significant information or understanding that would otherwise be lacking in the story.

Newspaper stylebooks cannot suggest guidelines for handling every issue of sensitivity. As both our society and our language change, the ways by which we communicate will necessarily change as well. Newspaper editors recognize that both writing styles and technical styles must adapt to those changes.

In the late 1980s, a coalition of black leaders, including two-time presidential candidate the Rev. Jesse Jackson, called for use of the term *African-American* in place of any other name for a member of the black community. Jackson argued that "*black* tells you about skin color. . . . *African-American* evokes a discussion of the world." Many newspapers and magazines adopted the new appellation, but linguists, historians, anthropologists and politicians continued to debate its propriety. William O. Beeman, a teacher of linguistic anthropology at Brown University, wrote in the Baltimore Sun:

> In linguistic matters, time is the only arbiter. If enough people begin to use the new label, nothing can stop its introduction into general American parlance. When the style sheets of major publications and news syndicates shift, it is clear that American usage has also shifted. The term Negro was dropped in favor of black in the early 1970s. When the media begin to refer to black Americans as African-Americans on a routine basis, we will know that this important linguistic change has taken roots. We will also know that in a subtle and important sense the way the African-American community is viewed in the United States has changed forever.

Sometimes, campus publications are at the forefront of style changes. Former student editor-in-chief Nora Wallace and her team of editors at the Golden Gater, a twice-weekly newspaper at San Francisco State University, added this entry about AIDS to their stylebook in spring 1989:

> Human Immunodeficiency Virus (HIV) is a disease encompassing three levels: a stage with no symptoms, AIDS Related Complex (ARC) and AIDS. HIV disease is an increasingly common way of referring to people with AIDS. In all cases, be precise and ask the source.
>   People with HIV don't necessarily have AIDS.
>   Use "people with AIDS" or "persons with AIDS" on first reference.
>   AIDS is not a gay person's disease, and it never should be implied that gay people are the only population affected by AIDS.
>   People with AIDS should not be referred to as "victims," unless the term is used as "victims of the AIDS epidemic."

Careful editors should have precision as their goal. Remaining alert to issues of sensitivity—whether handling issues of race and gender, referring to the opposing sides on the abortion debate (pro-choice? anti-abortion? pro-life?) or developing precise terminology in stories about AIDS—is a key responsibility of copy editors and one to be taken seriously.

Situational ethics

Editors face many day-to-day ethical decisions beyond remaining alert to issues of good taste and sensitivity. The kinds of ethical dilemmas that reporters face are different from those copy editors face, and copy editors face different dilemmas than managing editors or publishers do.

Reporters are likely to be concerned with questions involving the newsgathering process:

- Should confidential sources be used? Under what circumstances?

- Should classified information be used? Under what circumstances?

- Is going undercover to get the story ever justified? When?

- Is invasion of someone's privacy ever justified? When?

Copy editors are likely to be concerned with decisions involving the writing, editing and production processes:

- Is the use of profane language or obscene photographs ever justified? When?

- Are the implicit biases of the editor or the newspaper as a cultural institution evident in the selection of stories and photos? Should they be? Do certain people, groups or institutions receive more play than others? Conversely, are some people, groups or institutions ignored?

- Are headlines and captions fair and accurate?

- Are stories edited to eliminate bias and opinion? Are subjective words or words suggesting a viewpoint given thoughtful consideration?

Managing editors and other senior editors are likely to be concerned with questions of policy:

- Should victims of crimes be identified? If so, when? In stories about rape? About incest? About battering? In stories involving juveniles?

- Should suspects in crimes be identified? If so, when? At their arrest? When they are charged? At the time of trial?

- Should the cause of death be listed in obituaries involving victims of suicide or AIDS?

- Who in the newsroom should know the identity of confidential sources? Just the reporter? The supervising editor? The managing editor? The publisher? If a reporter pledges confidentiality to a source, are editors bound by the same promise?

- How involved should newsroom employees be in writing and editing special sections that promote consumer products?

- How should corrections and clarifications be handled?

Journalists face these kinds of moral and ethical decisions daily and often have little more to guide them than their own sense of justice and fair play.

Press response to criticism

In recent years, journalists have begun to heed the messages delivered by readers and viewers that indicate they want a more responsible and credible press. Many newspapers have created positions on their staffs for reader representatives, or ombudsmen. These journalists answer reader questions and investigate reader criticism, providing a necessary link between the newspaper and the public. Some large, metropolitan newspapers also employ media critics, who write about the good and bad trends in the press as an industry.

In late 1998, a group of about two dozen senior managers from major Web news sites formed the Online News Association, devoted to "tackling thorny issues of ethics, credibility and credentials faced by Web journalists." According to independent journalist J.D. Lasica, who writes a column for Online Journalism Review at the University of Southern California http://ojr.usc.edu, hopes for the new organization are high. "One hopes that the group's lofty ideals are carried out in practice," he wrote, "for the Web's mantra speaks to inclusion, not exclusion; networking, not closed doors; talent and shared experiences, not titles or private clubs."

Lasica reported that the topics heading the new group's list of concerns included credibility of the new medium, the blurring of lines between news and advertising, the instantaneous nature of Web news, and credentials for Web journalists.

In addition, the print media often provide access to their pages through consumer columns, op/ed pages, letters to the editor and online chat rooms to elicit reader response. For many years, newspapers also have encouraged readers to bring errors to the attention of the editors.

The Philadelphia Inquirer stylebook includes this policy about corrections:

> We promptly and forthrightly correct our published errors. An allegation of factual error in our news columns should be treated with the utmost seriousness and should be referred to the appropriate assigning editor immediately. . . . A "Clearing the record" notice may also be used to clarify published facts that, while technically not in error, may have been confusing or misleading.

Many newspapers "anchor" their corrections in the same place every day so readers will know where to find them. One newspaper's "Corrections & Clarifications," for example, are found on Page Two of the sections in which the original errors appeared. Exceptions are corrections of TV listings, which appear with the TV logs, and corrections for non-daily sections, such as Food and Travel. Those corrections are published twice, the day after the error was made and the next time the section in which the original error appeared is published.

In addition, editors have begun to listen to others within the organization, such as those in advertising, circulation and marketing. The relationship between the news staff and the revenue-generating departments historically has been strained because of the perceived need for separation between "objective" news and the subjectivity of advertising.

In recent years, however, because of the need to market the publication to remain competitive with other media, the newsroom and the other departments have become less distant from one another. News departments often are involved in writing and editing special advertising sections, such as back-to-school and home-improvement sections, and news executives sometimes participate in marketing promotions and surveys.

Ethics in the 21st century

Computer-based communications, whether in the form of text or graphics, embody a great deal of uncharted legal and ethical territory. But, because more and more journalists are using online information in their jobs, the ethics of such usage are in the process of being established.

As mentioned in Chapter 1, several thousand forms of traditional media worldwide have created online services. As consumers use these services to in turn create their own personalized news environments, some ethical questions come into focus:

▶**Question No. 1:** Because only about 30 percent of Americans own computers, is the market for online news sources a highly exclusive one? How do editors reconcile exclusive niche audiences with the press's traditional public service role of "comforting the afflicted and afflicting the comfortable"?

▶**Question No. 2:** Studies have indicated that the content of the media changes when it is commercialized. Will online news products be advertiser-driven to the same extent that printed news products are? What are the ethical implications if they are?

▶**Question No. 3:** If consumers choose *not* to receive information from a wide range of ideological sources online and instead narrow their news choices to information they agree with, what does that mean for the mass media's role as a forum for public opinion?

These are some of the broad questions journalists face today, and discussions are going on around the country about how traditional journalistic values might migrate into the new online environment and how such changes might affect the media's concepts about community leadership and the bottom line. But the emerging technologies present many day-to-day ethical questions as well, questions about reporting and editing and photography.

One of the most contentious debates involves the intrusion of "e-commerce" (advertising) on the editorial content of Web news sites. The debate takes many forms. For example, some question whether news sites should support the idea of "contextual online transactions," meaning should the news site juxtapose a staff-written review of the latest CD with an advertisement that allows users to order the CD with just one click of their mouse? To make the question even murkier, should the Web news site then earn a commission on each CD sold that way?

Steve Outing, who writes a column for Editor & Publisher Interactive, discussed the quandary in a recent online "point-counterpoint" with Eric Meyer of Newslink Associates and the University of Illinois journalism school. Meyer feared that such a practice could damage a news organization's credibility. He said online transactions connected to news sites were likely to be "the first uncertain step down a very slippery slope."

"It's not so much a question of whether a sales link tempts your critics to write favorable reviews, although it might," he wrote. "It's more a question of how a sales link influences which performances critics will review."

Outing argued that cyberspace publishing is a very different environment from traditional print media and that the same rules don't apply. "News Web sites should serve the consumer in the best way possible," he wrote. In this case, "the consumer is served with convenience; the retailer is served by having on the news site an effective marketing vehicle; and the news site is served by bringing in additional advertising dollars."

Other ethical questions surround the concept of e-commerce on Web news sites. In the struggle to be noticed online, advertisers have tried "interstitial" ads, which fade in and out on the screen; "popouts," which appear in a smaller window on the homepage; and "banners," which stream across the top of the Web page. But how far should these intrusions into the news space go? A column in the February 1999 issue of Brill's Content, a media-watchdog magazine, reported that advertisers and publishers were moving ads out of these usual online positions and going much deeper into editorial space.

Some publications were experimenting with banners that wrapped around the top of the page as well as streamed across the top of the page. Others featured "extramercials," advertisements that, with one click, actually obscure editorial content on the right-hand part of the page. The column noted that Hot Wired, a very colorful online publication, turned its homepage black and white to promote Hewlett-Packard's newest color printers. And USA Today's Web site featured an animated cartoon character (Homer Simpson) running out of an Intel Corp. ad and into the USA Today nameplate.

The digitization of photography has allowed one of the most common misuses of technology—the computer manipulation of photographs. It is true that editors have always been able to change a photograph, through cropping and sizing or through such darkroom techniques as dodging and burning. But today's technology allows an editor to manipulate any element in the photo in a matter of seconds and to change, in the process, its meaning and its substance. In other words, it is quite possible technologically to make the camera lie. Perhaps the most infamous example of computer photo manipulation is the O.J. Simpson arrest picture that appeared on the cover of Time magazine on June 27, 1994.

Time's "photo-illustration" cover of O.J. Simpson raised charges of racism and journalistic irresponsibility. Several magazines and newspapers used the same police photo from Simpson's arrest on murder charges, but Time used a computer to make Simpson appear blurred, darker skinned and more heavily bearded. Magazine representatives said they chose to manipulate the photo electronically to give it an interpretive twist that fit with the somber mood of the story. Former NAACP Director Benjamin Chavis Jr. said of the cover: "The way he's pictured, it's like he's some kind of animal." Dorothy Gilliam, then president of the National Association of Black Journalists, said the alteration made Simpson look more sinister and macabre. Time editors later said they didn't intend to offend anyone or imply Simpson's guilt and that their insensitivity was inexcusable.

As photojournalists continue to debate whether any manipulation of photos is ethical, editors have gone on record as disapproving of such techniques. The Associated Press is quite adamant in its policy of not allowing any photograph to be manipulated, as is the National Press Photographers Association, which states in its ethics policy: "As journalists we believe the guiding principle of our profession is accuracy. Therefore, we believe it is wrong to alter the contents of a photograph in any way that deceives the public."

In addition to deciding the ethics of photo manipulation, journalists must also grapple with traditional concerns about accuracy, balance and thoroughness, but more and more they must consider these values as they apply online. For example, good journalists agree that they should identify themselves when they plan to interview someone for a story. The same holds true for use of quotable information from online discussion groups, even though it is possible to view and retrieve information without such reporter identification.

Good journalists also agree that they must identify their sources in a story, but in an online world it is very easy for the sender of information to disguise himself or herself or to remain anonymous. Journalists, and particularly copy editors, must be vigilant in checking and double-checking the sources of online information. Two of the best examples of this kind of problem, a phenomenon Columbia

Journalism Review calls a "cyberhoax," came during the press coverage of the federal-building bombing in Oklahoma City in April 1995. In one, an inflammatory message appeared the day after the bombing on an Internet newsgroup viewed as a site used by militia groups. The posting, widely quoted in the U.S. press, later was discovered to have been a joke perpetrated by a journalism student. In the other incident, Dateline NBC and several reporters for the British media repeated a message that had appeared on America Online, purporting to be from Timothy McVeigh, a suspect in the bombing. The message described its sender as the "mad bomber," and urged readers to "take back the government…or die trying. Boom." The only problem was that the real Timothy McVeigh was in police custody when this message was sent.

A related ethical issue is one that involves the appropriation by traditional print publications of "cybergossip," distributed by such non-journalists as Matt Drudge. In addition to the Monica Lewinsky story, which Drudge reported in his online Drudge Report before it reached publication in the traditional media, he also became known for reporting rumors and gossip without verifying their accuracy. One example was a story about President Clinton's siring of a teen-age son of a black prostitute in Arkansas. The story had no validity, but it was picked up by the tabloid press and then as a legitimate news story by several mainstream newspapers.

Online Journalism Review Editor Robert Scheer took the media to task. "The rumor rapidly became a staple for rabid right-wing talk show hosts eager to blast Clinton. Suddenly the airwaves were filled with attacks on him as a 'deadbeat dad' who would not take responsibility for the child he had fathered." The false story "stained the president," Scheer wrote, "and this tawdry tale will be believed and spread by many who have not heard of the barely covered retractions or who just don't care what the facts are."

Needless to say, if journalists had used the same rigid techniques for determining the credibility or accuracy of information online as they usually use in the physical world, such hoaxes and fake quotations may not have survived into print or broadcast. The Virginian-Pilot in Norfolk, Va., has established newsroom policies for online issues, including source credibility. "In quoting from electronic communications," the policy says, "we will make certain the communication is genuine, as it is easy to fake Internet return addresses or log on as someone else. The Net is not controlled like a wire service; hoaxes can come from anywhere."

Online journalism promises to unveil a vast new landscape of ethical issues whose boundaries will be debated over time. For now, however, in the physical world at the turn of the century, discussions of journalistic ethics remain grounded in situations that unfold day by day in newsrooms across the country. Here are some examples:

▶**CNN and Time magazine** both apologized for and retracted a joint report that claimed the U.S. military used deadly nerve gas to kill American defectors during the Vietnam War. The two organizations are owned by Time-Warner. CNN staffers did the reporting for the TV account of "Operation Tailwind" and two of them also bylined an article for Time. Both CNN and Time said internal investigations showed the evidence could not support the story. Two CNN producers were fired, and a third resigned.

▶**The Cincinnati Enquirer** published a front-page apology to Chiquita Brands International Inc. for a series of stories questioning the company's business practices. The newspaper noted that its stories were untrue and based on stolen voice mail. The newspaper fired the lead reporter and agreed to pay more than $10 million to settle any claims that might arise from the series.

▶**Two Boston Globe columnists,** longtime staff member Mike Barnicle and Pulitzer-Prize finalist Patricia Smith, were forced to resign after editors learned they had fabricated people and quotations in their columns.

▶**Editors at The New Republic** apologized to readers after they learned that associate editor Stephen Glass had invented all or part of most of the articles he had written for the magazine.

It is not surprising that a 1989 survey by the American Society of Newspaper Editors Ethics Committee indicated that newspaper interns were ambivalent and somewhat skeptical about journalism ethics. One intern had this response:

> Ethics is something that cannot be effectively taught to individuals: that's like teaching morality. Literally, there are no right or wrong answers. Each individual finds a balance between his principles and the established code of the paper, which is, as often as not, an amorphous and ill-defined thing. Also, situations present varying challenges for different individuals. Frankly, being a plumber is a lot less burdensome.

Some students may lament the need to balance conflicting values when making ethical decisions and may yearn, as this intern does, for a less burdensome way to react to journalistic situations requiring an ethical response. Yet changing professions—becoming a plumber, for example—is not the solution.

Former public television correspondent Hodding Carter suggested that an "ethical vacuum" exists in the journalism practiced at the close of the 20th century. It is time for the media to fill that vacuum with a process that encourages careful consideration of today's increasingly sophisticated ethical concerns:

- Terrorism and the media

- The right to privacy

- Gruesome photographs

- Manipulated photographs

- Conceptual photographs

- Anonymous online sources

- Off-the-record information

- Political or advertiser pressure not to publish

- AIDS obituaries

- Deception and going undercover

- Quotations used out of context

- Disclosure of the juvenile crimes of adults in the public eye

Copy editors must be alert to all these potential ethical problems. They must question reporters about their conduct and call perceived ethical problems to the attention of the supervising editors. Copy editors need to be especially diligent in editing for accuracy, fairness and completeness and in making news judgments about which stories and photographs will be published.

The industry's codes of ethics and the policy statements drafted by individual publications can be used to help define the ethical situations faced by journalists every day. But only through development, teaching and use of ethical reasoning—based, of course, on subjective cultural values and coupled with an emotional component that often comes into play at the decisive moment—will tomorrow's journalists be prepared to grapple with modern ethical concerns.

The future of journalism   **By Cole C. Campbell**

THE future of journalism is in doubt because of profound technological, economic and social changes. That future will be secure when our work clearly answers two questions posed by a pair of New York University professors. Neil Postman, the educational theorist and social critic, asks: What problem does journalism solve? And Jay Rosen, the journalism theorist and media critic, asks: What are journalists for? Conventional, and incomplete, answers don't work anymore.

Individuals can search out tremendous amounts of data from original sources over the Internet, without need of journalistic intermediaries. News and information are free commodities in an era of multiple 24-hour news, talk and sports broadcasts. Advertisers can find less-expensive ways to build the audiences they need—and to surround their messages with information that builds credibility.

What value, then, do we journalists create for our readers and our communities?

Alongside the five W's and an H that describe the basic building blocks of a news story, we should put four I's and a C to describe the basic building blocks of journalism's value. That value comes from inquiry, integrity, interdependence, imagination and community.

▶**Inquiry:** Journalism is a discipline of asking questions that matter when they matter on behalf of the people to whom they matter. That requires a great eye for pattern and detail, to discern what's happening beneath the surface or behind public pronouncements. It requires the ability to switch one's frame of reference from expert calculation to childlike innocence to adultlike befuddlement. These questions can be put to a friendly tipster, a hostile subject or a database spreadsheet.

▶**Integrity:** Journalism is a discipline of wholeness and coherence, the *oneness* that is at the heart of integrity. Integrity means more than adhering to tough professional and ethical standards, although that's crucial. It also means—in the admonition of C.P. Scott, turn-of-the-century editor of the Manchester Guardian—seeing life and seeing it whole. In an era of fragmentation and atomization, the capacity to see life whole is essential to community life. In 1996 the Journalism Values Institute, a project of the American Society of Newspaper Editors, urged editors to expand the traditional canon of "balance" to incorporate "wholeness" and to ensure that newspapers capture not only the essence of the news but also the essence of the communities in which the news occurs.

▶**Interdependence:** Journalism is usually described as a discipline of independence, but that ignores essential relationships. Journalism does rely on internal professional standards, but it also depends on the vitality of public life and on the connection between citizens and the news. The best newsrooms manage three relationships—between the press and public life, between the press and citizens and between citizens and public life. We don't have to be dependent on any faction or give up independent judgment, but we do need to recognize the interdependence of our work and the citizens we serve.

▶**Imagination:** Journalism is an art—of compression, of storytelling, of asking what if. Journalism selects and compresses samples of what is happening to paint a fact-based picture of the world. (This is just a picture, not a mirror image.) Journalism tells stories that help people make sense of the world. And journalism can be an act of seeing possibilities—measuring the world against what it could be, measuring what we are as a society against what we aspire to become.

▶**Community:** Journalism is a discipline of community. It draws people together in real, sustained communities—not virtual, transient ones—by focusing on what binds and what divides people, by providing a common frame of reference for resolving conflicts and valuing differences. Community building is the culmination of inquiry about what matters, integrity in seeing life whole, interdependence between professional and citizen and public life and imagination in envisioning how life works—or could.

Failure to engage the community will doom us. In his 1996 book, *They Only Look Dead: Why Progressives Will Dominate the Next Political Era.* E.J. Dionne of The Washington Post writes

> Journalism is under such sharp attack now precisely because the public (and most journalists) suspect that it is not promoting a level of public debate that matches the seriousness of the choices the country confronts. ...The country is now engaged in one of the great arguments in its history, an argument in which many of the most basic questions—about definitions of morality, the role of government, the shape of the economy—are in play. If Americans in large numbers sit out this great debate and decide that politics has nothing to do with the problems at hand, and nothing to do with them, the whole political class—and perhaps *especially* journalists—will have failed.

Happily, elevating the debate is a problem we can solve, if we apply our journalistic skills and passions to the task. And fostering strong, healthy argument is something we can be for.

Cole C. Campbell

Cole C. Campbell is the editor of the St. Louis Post-Dispatch. A native Virginian, he received a bachelor's degree in English from the University of North Carolina at Chapel Hill, where he was editor of The Daily Tar Heel. He has been a reporter or editor at the Chapel Hill Newspaper, the News & Observer of Raleigh, N.C., and the Greensboro News & Record. He was editor of Tar Heel: The Magazine of North Carolina, and he has edited several books by fellow journalists.

He has taught journalism and writing courses at Guilford College and UNC-Greensboro and has participated in a number of workshops and panels at the American Press Institute, the Poynter Institute for Media Studies, the Southern Newspaper Publishers Association, the National Association of Minority Media Executives and the annual meetings of the Associated Press Managing Editors and the American Society of Newspaper Editors. He has been the chair of ASNE's Future of Newspapers Committee, a member of ASNE's Journalism Values Institute, a John S. Knight Fellow at Stanford University, a Pulitzer-Prize juror, a director of the Virginia Press Association and a member of the journalism advisory committee of Norfolk State University.

He borrows his journalistic credo from cartoonist Garry Trudeau: "The impertinent question is the glory of civilization. Doubt is what makes culture grow."

Suggestions for additional reading

American Journalism Review Web site, http://www.ajr.org.

American Society of Newspaper Editors Web site, http://www.asne.org.

Bagdikian, Ben H. *The Media Monopoly,* 5th ed. Boston: Beacon Press, 1987.

Bok, Sissela. *Lying: Moral Choices in Public and Private Life.* New York: Pantheon Books, 1978.

———. *Secrets: On the Ethics of Concealment and Revelation.* New York: Pantheon Books, 1982.

Christians, Clifford G., John P. Ferre and Mark Fackler. *Media Ethics: Cases and Moral Reasoning.* Boston: Allyn & Bacon, 1995.

Columbia Journalism Review Web site, http://www.cjr.org.

Goldstein, Thomas (ed.). *Killing the Messenger: 100 Years of Media Criticism.* New York: Columbia University Press, 1989.

———. *The News at Any Cost: How Journalists Compromise Their Ethics to Shape the News.* New York: Simon and Schuster, 1985.

Hulteng, John L. *The Messenger's Motives: Ethical Problems of the News Media,* 2nd ed. Englewood Cliffs, N.J.: Prentice-Hall, 1985.

Journalists and Readers: Bridging the Credibility Gap. Associated Press Managing Editors Credibility Committee Report. New York: Associated Press Managing Editors, 1985.

McCulloch, Frank. *Drawing the Line: How 31 Editors Solved Their Toughest Ethical Dilemmas.* Washington, D.C.: American Society of Newspaper Editors, 1984.

McKenna, George. *Media Voices: Debating Critical Issues in Mass Media.* Guilford, Conn.: Dushkin Publishing Group, 1982.

Meyer, Philip. *Ethical Journalism: A Guide for Students, Practitioners, and Consumers.* New York: Longman, 1987.

Newspaper Credibility: Building Reader Trust. Research Report. Washington, D.C.: American Society of Newspaper Editors, April 1985.

Online Journalism Review, University of Southern California, http://www.ojr.com.

Reddick, Randy, and Elliot King. *The Online Journalist: Using the Internet and Other Electronic Resources.* Fort Worth, Texas: Harcourt Brace College Publishers, 1995.

Rubin, Bernard (ed.). *When Information Comes: Grading the Media.* Lexington, Mass.: Lexington Books, 1985.

Schmuhl, Robert (ed.). *The Responsibilities of Journalism.* Notre Dame, Ind.: University of Notre Dame Press, 1984.

Schwartz, Marilyn, and the Task Force on Bias-Free Language of the Association of American University Presses. *Guidelines for Bias-Free Writing.* Bloomington: Indiana University Press, 1995.

Society of Professional Journalists Web site, http://www.spj.org.

Exercises

1. When the American Society of Newspaper Editors adopted its first code of ethics in the 1920s, William Allen White, editor of the Emporia (Kan.) Gazette, said the guidelines would not work. Read the following synopses of two real cases, then reread the ASNE Code of Ethics in Figure 7-2.

   Case A

   In 1981, Washington Post reporter Janet Cooke became known to all American journalists—not because she had just won the Pulitzer Prize but because she had fabricated her prize-winning story, as well as much of her own background.

   Early in April, the Pulitzer jury had awarded Cooke the prestigious prize for her feature story about "Jimmy," an 8-year-old boy who supposedly had been injected with heroin in Cooke's presence. Two days after Cooke received the award, the editors of The Washington Post returned it to Columbia University and the Pulitzer board.

   What had happened? Only hours after the Pulitzer Prizes were awarded, Vassar College and the Associated Press called The Washington Post about some discrepancies in Cooke's biography. Her biography said that she had graduated magna cum laude from Vassar, studied at the Sorbonne in Paris and earned a master's degree from the University of Toledo. Vassar and the University of Toledo claimed that Cooke had attended Vassar for one year, graduated without honors from the University of Toledo and had no master's degree. Moreover, the editors of the Post confirmed that Cooke was not fluent in French.

   Finally, the Post editors questioned Cooke about "Jimmy." Although she had written the story without using any last names, claiming they were confidential, and although editors allowed the story to be published, Cooke finally admitted that "Jimmy" did not truly exist. She said he was a composite of sources she had met while investigating heroin use in Washington, D.C. Cooke then resigned.

   Case B

   One day during the summer of 1980, a professional reporter attended an expenses-paid meeting sponsored by Westinghouse Electric Corp. In addition to food and transportation, Westinghouse provided guests with lodging and a $150 honorarium for listening to a speech advocating nuclear power.

   The reporter accepted the food, the travel, the lodging and the honorarium and returned to write a story for his newspaper.

   Does the ASNE Code of Ethics cover either or both of these cases? Explain your answer.

2. Read Exercise 1 at the end of Chapter 6. What ethical concerns are involved in this case? Write a brief statement either defending or criticizing the newsgathering tactics used by the reporter.

3. Use the three newsroom scenarios outlined on pp. 193 of this chapter as the starting point for a discussion about editors and ethics. Reason through each example, using the Potter box and your own values and moral standards. Then attempt to invoke one of the philosophical principles mentioned in the chapter (Kant, Mill or Aristotle) or name one of your own to help justify your ethical decision. Discuss your views in class.

4. Name five things you would do to help your hometown newspaper become more credible than it is. Share your ideas in class.

5. Reread the section in this chapter on situational ethics. Then try to find examples of stories in the newspaper for which the senior editors probably would have drafted a policy, such as listing the cause of death in obituaries or identifying juvenile crime suspects. Share your findings in class.

6. A magazine reveals that 25 years ago Stephen Goodman was released from prison after serving a 10-year term on a conviction of molesting children. During the past 25 years, Goodman has been an outstanding citizen in town and has been honored for his volunteer work with children. Goodman's family, friends and business associates were unaware of his past criminal conviction. What are the ethical implications of publishing this information?

7. Reread the section in this chapter on sensitivity and good taste. Then copy edit the following story, paying particular attention to stereotypical images:

Relatives of a Gypsy family with strong ties to Kansas City allegedly have stolen about one million dollars in at least 7 states over the last several years by defrauding dozens of fortune telling customers according to police, prosecuters, and lawyers.

At least 16 relatives of the Marks family, a klan of Gypsy fortunetellers that has for decades had roots in the Metropolitan area, have been found guilty or face charges in connextion with the alleged scams.

Officials are quick to add, however that not all people named Marks are gypsies, nor are all of the estimated 2 dozen Marks gypsies in the metropolitan area involved in fortunetelling fraud. Furthermore, only a small per centage of gypsies in the country are engaged in criminal activities officials said. Only 5 family members in this area have faced such criminal charges in recent years.

Police and prosecutors in several of the seven states where Marks family members have been charged have traded information, only to learn that the same persons allegedly had conducted similar skams in other locations.

Repeated attempts to contract Marks family members alleged to have been involved in criminal activities were unsucessful.

This year two Marks have been found guilty in Jackson County Circuit court of felony stealing charges, and another relative pleaded guilty in Jan. to a theft charge in Wyandote county.

Three family members, including one already serving a prison term, were indicted Friday by the Jackson County grande jury on charges of stealing over $150.00 by deceit. Det. William Cosgrove, of the Kansas City police department fraud unit, says that case involved alleged promises by fortunetellers to restore a local womans eyesite and to cure her of cancer.

Honest fortunetellers do exist, according to Terry Getsay, a national authority on gypsies who works as a intelligence analyst for the Illinois Dept. of Law Enforcement. "Most just provide a service, he said.

But fortunetelling also is the common denominator among those Marks relatives accused by prosecuters of playing the bujo, a centuries old confidence game that usually victimizes the elderly or those with emotional problems.

And even when the perpetrators are caught, the victims do not necesarily win.

"We've got two convictions (of fortunetellers in Jackson County), and those victims haven't got a dime back said Det. David Parker of the police fraud unit.

Mr. Getsay said the conviction and imprisonment of a gypsy fortuneteller is a rare occurrence. "The likelihood of restitution, probation or dismissal or reduction of the charges are much greater than imprisonment he said.

In the bujo, the fortunteller, after reading palms or Tarot cards, tells the client that the future holds evil. Slight of hand tricks, such as removing a clump of hair from a newly-broken egg, are used as "evidence" that a client is possessed by an evil spirit.

The fortuneteller then says she must have all the victim's money—the root of all evil—so it can be cleansed and the evil removed.

Some fortunetellers say the money will be used to buy special candles. Others say it will be burned or buried in a grave yard. Nearly always, however, the fortune teller promises to return the money, or even to double or triple the amount, once the evil has been exorcised.

Instead officials say, the victim frequently sees neither the money nor the fortune teller again. "This," Detective Cosgrove said, "is more than just palm reading.

8. Edit this story for the Centerville daily newspaper:

appointment

Mayor Dwight Smyth held a press conference yesterday afternoon at 3:30 P.M. at the City-county building in downtown Centerville. At the press conference the mayor made known to the assembled press, various city officials and interested public the identity of the newlyappointed Director of the Office of Economic Development, whom he selected from a list of three possibilities submitted to him by a search committee. The person selected by the mayor is Mrs. Mary Berryman, who has served in a similar capacity in the city of Riverside.

During the press conference the mayor said "Mrs. Berry, is a first rate organizer and planner and will do a first rate job for Centerville citizens in her new post. Her appointment culmenates a six month nationwide search and the search committee couldn't be happier with it's choice the major said. "We are indeed fortunete to have a person of Mrs. Berrys statute join our city staff Mayor Smyth told onlookers.

Mrs. Berryman is married to Reverend John Berryman, who is a minister of a Baptist church in Riverside. Reverend John Berryman said that his plans are uncertain now but that he hoped to relocate to Centerville now that his wife has gotten this new job. Reverend John Berryman has been pastor of the Second Baptist Church in Riverside for the past 5 years. Before that time he was pastor of a church in Lawrence. He graduate from Southwest Baptist Semenary in Ft. Worth, Tex. in 1975.

Mrs. Berryman was one of 15 applicants for the job in a nation wide search. She was one of three finalists whom was recommended by a search committee appointed by the City Council last July 1991. The search committee screened applicants, conducted interviews and forwarded 3 names to Mayor Smyth, who made the final selection.

As economic development director, Mrs. Mary Berryman will over see a staff composing two assistant directors and three clerical workers. The office is charged with bringing new businesses and industry to Centerville to help increase job opportunities and to broaden the cities' tax base. Mary, a youngish looking grandmother, wore a black dress and long gold earrings for today's ceremony. She used crutches during her introduction because she is recovering from a broken leg which she received last month.

She will move to Centerville from Riverside where she held the position of assistant economic development director for the past 2 years. She has over ten years of experience in municiple financial planning and economic development. She earned a masters degree in public administration in 1980. Mrs. John Berryman replaces Sam Spade in her new post. Spade left the office 6months ago after ten years on the job. He now has a similiar position in Podunk.

"Frankly, the office is in a financial mess and has been for the past ten years or so" Mayor Smyth said this morning during the announcement ceremony. "The city has spent a bundle on auditers but we still are unable to account for all the money that went through that office during Sam's tgenure, the mayor said. "Mary will be a careful and honest administrater" the mayor said.

Due to financial accounting problems in Centerville and several other cities in the state in recent years, legislation has been introduced in the state legislature which will require anual audits of all city funds in cities throughout the state.

Mrs. Berryman, an articulate black woman, answered questions from newsmen after she was introduced at the press conference. She inferred that she has all ready began efforts to attract a major manufacturer to Centerville. She said that farther meetings with the firm, that she declined to name, were scheduled for later this month. "I know that my predecessor was involved in some questionable financial dealings with city funds, but let me assure the citizens of Centerville that every penny will be accounted for while I'm in charge" Mrs. Berryman told newsmen. Berry said that as one of her first changes in the office, she planned to institute new computer software to facilitate bookeeping in the office.

Mrs. Berryman is a member of the National City Planners Association, the Women's Christian Temperence Union, and the National Organization of Women. City workers were disappointed that they did not get a free lunch yesterday. Original plans called for Mrs. Berryman to meet with city workers at a noon picnic in the park next to the CityCounty Bldg. but colder temperatures forced cancellation of the picnic. It will be rescheduled.

9. Conduct a search to find discussions of media ethics online. Try some of the Web sites of media organizations first, such as Online Journalism Review at http://www.ojr.com, the Poynter Institute at http://www.poynter.com, or the Society of Professional Journalists at http://www.spj.org. See if you can find others on your own. Share your results in class.

8

Typography

THE **personality of a newspaper** can usually be determined from a distance of five feet. It is expressed largely in the kinds of stories that are emphasized and in the quality of the writing. But with relatively few exceptions, story emphasis and writing style have the same flavor as the newspaper's design. A newspaper whose "black" or splashy design seems to shout at readers is likely to play up highly controversial or sensational stories and to be written saucily, raucously or both. A gray-looking paper is likely to demonstrate restraint in handling news and to feature quiet, sophisticated prose.

Look at Figure 8-1. The San Francisco Examiner shouts the news with a large banner headline and a large photograph. But it's business as usual for the immutable Wall Street Journal, one of the country's largest dailies. In the Journal's case, large, splashy headlines and graphics are not essential to maintain its dominant market position and million-plus circulation, whereas the Examiner is fighting for market share in its position as an afternoon newspaper. Most American newspapers fall somewhere between these two extremes.

Other publications, including magazines, Web sites and corporate publications, likewise reflect personality through typography. Consider, for example, type

Type sizes

Type widths

Type styles

Type weights

Type families

Legibility

Figure 8-1
Typography expresses the character of a newspaper. The San Francisco Examiner sometimes shouts the news, while The Wall Street Journal appears refined and sophisticated.

display in Wired magazine as compared with The Reader's Digest or even Sports Illustrated's more restrained approach to type.

The earliest known attempts to record thoughts visually—symbols depicting objects, called pictographs—date back 20,000 years. Succeeding pictographs were more abstract ideographs, cuneiforms and hieroglyphics, the latter perfected by the Egyptians around 2500 B.C. Ten centuries later, around 1500 B.C., the Phoenicians used the first formal alphabet, then made up only of consonants. The Greeks acquired the Phoenician alphabet about 1000 B.C. and refined it over the next six centuries into a 24-letter alphabet that included vowel sounds.

The origins of printing are difficult to trace, but it is known that by the 11th century, the Chinese were using movable type made of metal and clay. By the early 15th century, after papermaking, metalcasting and painting with oil (ink) had been developed, a German goldsmith named Johann Gutenberg saw the connections among these various crafts and developed a process for printing separate characters on a press with ink and paper. How he did it remains a mystery. By the end of the 15th century, presses were operating in all major European cities, publishing hundreds of thousands of books. Our common printed typefaces are simply imitations of early handwritten letters.

Today, teams of editors and artists design printed and electronic products, often using type created centuries ago. Many believe that design should reflect the elements of a product's personality.

Readers who pay attention to their publications find that the design can

- Attract their attention
- Grade the news for them, expressing the relative importance of items by headline size and placement
- Provide an orderly pattern for the currents of news flow

A large part of that design depends on typography, which combines with layout to create an integrated, cohesive and sometimes unusual graphic look.

Typography is the art of designing and arranging type to have desired effects on readers. All of us have ideas about typography, because some things look better to us than others. But it is the designer's job to assure that typography and design enable easier and faster reading. To do so, the designer—and the editors who perform page design and layout—must recognize the subtle ways in which type can be differentiated. Typefaces can differ in at least five ways: size, width, slant, weight and family.

Type sizes

Type has its own system of measurement. Feet and inches are the basic units of measurement for most of us, but for printers, the basic units of measurement are picas and points. A *pica* is equal to about ⅙ inch, and a *point* is equal to about ¹⁄₇₂ inch. Both 6 picas and 72 points, then, equal an inch. Within the type measurement system itself, the conversions are easy to make: 1 pica is equal to 12 points.

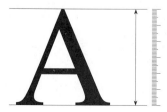

72 points = 6 picas = 1 inch

When we measure typefaces, we use points. When we measure larger elements, such as the width of columns or photos, we generally use picas.

Typefaces themselves used to be manufactured in standard sizes. A complete series of type would include at least the sizes shown in Figure 8-2. Today, however, phototypesetting and digital computer systems can produce any size of type simply by electronically manipulating the image.

Sizes smaller than 14 points are called text types or body types, while sizes of 14 points or larger are called display types. The text of a newspaper is set in body

Figure 8-2
The standard type sizes are still those used most often, although computer typesetting permits the use of non-standard sizes.

6 point abcdefghijklmnopqrstuvwxyz

8 point abcdefghijklmnopqrstuvwxyz

9 point abcdefghijklmnopqrstuvwxyz

10 point abcdefghijklmnopqrstuvwxyz

12 point abcdefghijklmnopqrstuvwxyz

14 point abcdefghijklmnopqrstuvwxyz

18 point abcdefghijklmnopqrstuvwxyz

24 point abcdefghijklmnopqrstuvwxyz

30 point abcdefghijklmnopqrstuvwxyz

36 point abcdefghijklmnopqrstuv

42 point abcdefghijklmnopqrs

48 point abcdefghijklmnop

60 point abcdefghijklmn

72 point abcdefghijkl

type—in fact, 70 percent of American newspapers use either 8-point or 9-point body type—and the headlines are set in display type. A 72-point headline is usually reserved for the most urgent news. Larger sizes exist but are rarely used.

Although in most modern newsrooms computers can set type in any point size desired, most editors continue to use the traditional type sizes, probably because they are easy to use under deadline pressure. Sometimes, however, copy editors may "squeeze" the type size and generate a 33- or 34- or 35-point headline instead of a 36-point headline to get the headline to fit. When type was set in lead, squeezing type was unheard of. In fact, many editors recall the days when backshop printers would yell out to the newsroom: "Type isn't made of rubber, you know!" The headline wouldn't fit unless it had been written with a high degree of exactitude.

On a typical news day, a 48-point or 60-point headline will serve to identify the main story on the front page. On the inside, 42-point headlines generally are large enough to identify the most important story on each page.

Type size can be a difficult concept to understand, but for our purposes, it is sufficient to define the size of type as the distance from the top of the ascender (the long upstroke over such letters as *b, d, h* and *l*) to the bottom of the descender (the long downstroke under such letters as *j, p, q* and *y*). Look at Figure 8-3. The type size of the word can be measured by first drawing a horizontal line across the top of the ascenders (*i, t, i, i* and *t*) and then a horizontal line across the bottom of the descender (*y*). Next, measure the distance between the two lines, using the point scale on a ruler or a pica pole. Your measurement should tell you that this word is set in 36-point type.

Figure 8-3
Two measures of type are commonly used: type size, from the tops of ascenders to the bottoms of descenders, and x-height, which does not include ascenders and descenders.

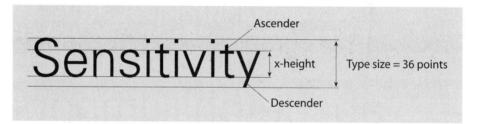

Another way to talk about type is in terms of the x-height of the letters. The *x-height* is simply the height of the lowercase letters without ascenders and descenders (see Figure 8-3). Even though not technically a means of measurement, the x-height is important because it helps determine the visual impact of the type. Typefaces of the same point size may appear unequal because of slight variations in the x-height. Look at the following examples of three different typefaces, all set in 10-point type, which appear to be different sizes because of slight variations in the x-height:

To determine the x-height of any typeface, simply use the point scale on your ruler or pica pole to measure the distance between the top and the bottom of any lowercase letter without ascenders or descenders.   (10-point Century Book)

To determine the x-height of any typeface, simply use the point scale on your ruler or pica pole to measure the distance between the top and the bottom of any lowercase letter without ascenders or descenders.   (10-point Times)

To determine the x-height of any typeface, simply use the point scale on your ruler or pica pole to measure the distance between the top and the bottom of any lowercase letter without ascenders or descenders.   (10-point Helvetica)

Type widths

Type is two-dimensional. In addition to its vertical size, editors also need to know its width. In the printing business, the width of a typeface, meaning the width of the lowercase alphabet, is referred to as its set width.

This is the lowercase alphabet in 12-point Times; its set width is 12 picas or 144 points

abcdefghijklmnopqrstuvwxyz

The set width of a condensed version of the 12-point Times lowercase alphabet is 10 picas or 120 points

abcdefghijklmnopqrstuvwxyz

In most typefaces, the width of a capital M is equal to the type size. In fact, typesetters often used to refer to the concept of an em, which is the square of the type size. The em, therefore, is a variable measure: An 18-point em is 18 points wide and 18 points high; it is bigger than a 14-point em, which is 14 points wide and 14 points high. In body type, "one em space" is a typical paragraph indention.

The em method of measuring type width is gradually being superseded by the more precise unit system. The reference point still is the capital M, but instead of being a variable measure, the M is divided into 18 units or some multiple of 18. The width of all other characters, and their letter spacing, is then defined as a certain number of these units. Lowercase letters such as i, j and l, for example, are usually 4 units wide.

If we take each character of the alphabet and squeeze it slightly, we reduce the set width of the alphabet; therefore it is slightly condensed. Both of the examples below are 18-point Helvetica type, but the bottom one is condensed:

Art is life reflected through vision.
(18-point Helvetica)

Art is life reflected through vision.
(18-point Helvetica condensed)

A complete inventory of display types at any publication includes some condensed and some extended typefaces, not only for contrast but also for situations in which the perfect word will not fit the available space. Publications with a predominantly horizontal design (see Chapter 11) use condensed typefaces sparingly and prefer faces of normal width. In a newspaper or other publication with a predominantly vertical design, however, condensed typefaces appear quite normal.

Body types apply the same rules. For example, more news can be packed into the newspaper by using condensed body type. But such use of type can make for a gray paper, which leads to difficulty in reading and tends to draw complaints from subscribers. To make a newspaper brighter, designers sometimes use the following techniques:

- Use a larger type size—9-point, for example, rather than 8-point.

- Use a normal, rather than a condensed, typeface.

- Use more paragraph indentions.

- Insert more space between paragraphs.

- Insert more space between lines.

This last technique, inserting more space between lines, is called ***leading*** (pronounced "ledding") or ***leading out***. The term comes from the practice of inserting strips of lead between lines of type in the days when type was cast from a molten lead alloy. Type that has no space between the lines is said to be ***set solid***— and sometimes the descenders of one line touch the ascenders of the line below it.

An 8-point type that has 1 point of leading is said to be set 8 on 9; an 8-point type that has 2 points of leading is said to be set 8 on 10, and so on. Here is an example of 8-point type set solid:

> The quantity and quality of informational graphics in newspapers increased dramatically in the late 1980s, largely because of the use of Macintosh computers and electronic graphics networks.

Here is an example of 8-point type set 8 on 9:

> The quantity and quality of informational graphics in newspapers increased dramatically in the late 1980s, largely because of the use of Macintosh computers and electronic graphics networks.

And here is an example of 8-point type set 8 on 10:

> The quantity and quality of informational graphics in newspapers increased dramatically in the late 1980s, largely because of the use of Macintosh computers and electronic graphics networks.

Leading—spacing between lines—usually makes type easier to read. On the other hand, studies indicate that too much leading may hinder readability, because the eye "gets lost" in switching from the end of one line to the beginning of the next line.

For the same reason, type that is set either too wide or too narrow is difficult to read. Research studies differ on the best line length, but a common approach is to use this formula:

$$O = lca \times 1.5$$

Optimum line length (O) is equal to the width of the lowercase alphabet (lca) multiplied by one and one-half.

So, for example, if the width of the lowercase alphabet is 112 points, the optimum line length would be 168 points (112×1.5), which equals 14 picas (168 divided by 12).

Type styles

Figure 8-4
The familiar Roman typefaces are characterized by serifs.

Typefaces can be classified in many ways, none of them precise. The classification system used most frequently in the field of graphic arts puts typefaces in seven main categories, also referred to as races of type: Roman, italic, sans serif, square serif, text, script and decorative.

▶**Roman typefaces** are familiar to us because most of what we read is set in Roman type. The chief characteristic is the ***serif***, a small cross stroke at the end of each main stroke of the letter, as shown in Figure 8-4.

Roman type gets its name from the similarity of its capital letters to the alphabetic characters chiseled by stonemasons on the public buildings of the Roman empire. In 1490, an imaginative Frenchman, Nicholas Jenson, combined these characters with a more ornate set of characters to create the complete uppercase and lowercase English alphabet we know today. (The terms *uppercase* and *lowercase* stem from the early typographers' habit of storing small letters in a case below that of the capital letters.) Jenson's typeface, known today as Cloister Old Style, is a classic example of old-style Roman type, known for its blunt serifs. Other examples of old-style Roman type are Garamond and Caslon.

Bodoni, a Roman typeface, has been one of the most popular headline typefaces in American newspapers. It was introduced in 1789 by Giambattista Bodoni, an Italian printer:

Art is life. (36-point Bodoni)

Times Roman and Century are Roman styles commonly used for body type. Times Roman was designed in 1931 by Stanley Morison for The Times of London:

Art is life. (36-point Times Roman)

Century was designed in 1894 by L.B. Benton and T.L. DeVine for Century magazine, a leading publication of its day:

Art is life. (36-point Century Book)

▶ **Sans serif type,** from the French sans, meaning "without," literally means "without serifs." In addition to the absence of serifs, sans serif typefaces—or gothic typefaces, as they sometimes are called—are recognizable by their uniformity of stroke. The following example reveals little or no variation in the widths of strokes used to create the characters:

Art is life. (36-point Futura)

In newspapers, sans serif typefaces play a significant role in headlines, captions and some informational material, such as stock market listings, sports scoreboards and television listings. Futura, Avant Garde and Univers are just a few of the many sans serif typefaces commonly used for headlines.

Art is life. (36-point Avant Garde)

Art is life. (36-point Univers)

Readers often have greater difficulty reading a sans serif typeface than a serif one, however, unless the sans serif typeface is either set large or leaded out. Most publications, therefore, have rejected sans serif type as their body type. The gothics do play important roles, however, in brochures, road signs, billboards, magazine advertisements and consumer product labels.

▶**Square serif typefaces** live up to their name. Their serifs are like small, rectangular slabs. Some typographers categorize these typefaces as Roman because they have serifs on them; others categorize them as decoratives. When treated as an independent group, they have been referred to as the Egyptians.

Examples of square serif, or Egyptian, typefaces include Glypha, Memphis and Lubalin Graph.

Art is life. (36-point Glypha)

Art is life. (36-point Memphis)

Art is life. (36 point Lubalin Graph)

▶**Italic typefaces,** characterized by slanted letters, were designed to save space:

Art is life. (36-point Italic Goudy Old Style)

Because italic type is difficult to read in large quantities, it is used sparingly in body type—and then only to emphasize words. Italic type is used in headlines, however, and sometimes as a special design element. Roman and sans serif typefaces all have italic variations.

▶**Text typefaces,** which sometimes are called Old English or blackletter typefaces, play only a nominal—albeit curious—role in newspapers. Many of this country's large newspapers—The New York Times, the Los Angeles Times, The Washington Post, the Portland Oregonian, and the San Francisco Chronicle, among others— use text typefaces in their nameplates, or flags—the name of the newspaper displayed on Page One. Despite this apparent allegiance to tradition, the use of text typefaces in this fashion is atypical, according to noted editor Harold Evans:

> The most hideous blackletter titles survive around the world from Victorian days because they are "traditional," but in fact the earliest titles, such as those of the first daily paper, The Daily Courant (1702), and the first evening paper, The Evening Post, and America's New England Courant (1721), were all in good bold Roman lowercase.

With all the breezy, modern sans serif typefaces available today, it is a wonder that the blackletters (the tight, bold types that originated in Germany) have managed to survive. A few famous ones are still in circulation, including Fette Fraktur and Linotext:

Art is life. (36-point Fette Fraktur)

Art is life. (36-point Linotext)

▶**Script typefaces** look like handwriting:

Art is life. (36-point Mistral)

Most of the time they should not be used in headlines or in the body of the paper. Occasionally, however, layout editors may use script typefaces on feature stories where such use is appropriate to the subject matter. Script typefaces are worth mentioning here only as an adjunct to a discussion of typography.

▶**Decorative typefaces** likewise play very little role in news typography but are developed to reflect trends in fashion and advertising. Parisian, for example, usually is associated with art deco and is currently enjoying a revival:

Art is life. (36-point Parisian)

Type weights

Most typefaces are designed and manufactured in lightface and boldface versions. A few also have medium, demibold and extrabold versions. Below are examples of the various weights of 24-point type:

Futura Light

Futura Medium

New Baskerville Bold

Palatino Demi Bold

Cooper Black

Helvetica Black

Futura Extrabold

Research studies on type legibility have indicated that, although boldfaces are more readable than lightfaces, because they contrast more with the background of the page, regular weights (medium) are preferred. The extrabolds are the least legible.

Type families

The individual members of type families share similar characteristics, yet they also vary in width, slant and weight. Some families have only a few members; others have quite a few. Here are some of the 30 members of the Helvetica family:

Helvetica Light

Helvetica Medium

Helvetica Medium Italic

Helvetica Medium Condensed

Helvetica Bold

Helvetica Bold Italic

Helvetica Bold Condensed

Helvetica Black

Publication designers generally try to limit the number of typefaces used to maintain a consistent appearance. For example, the body type might be Times Roman and the news headline font another serif typeface, such as Century Schoolbook. For captions, section labels and page headers, complementary fonts of a sans serif typeface such as Univers might be preferred.

Legibility

Sophistication about typography means nothing if legibility suffers. Even skillful, experienced designers occasionally engage in typographical experiments that force readers to work too hard to enjoy reading. On the whole, however, type experts guide design choices at newspapers and magazines to enhance legibility, thereby preventing eye strain and encouraging reading.

Ironically, advanced printing technology in some of its present applications threatens legibility. Computer software for desktop and Web publishing enables people with no knowledge about typography to call themselves editors or publishers, flooding mailboxes and the Internet with difficult-to-read materials. In an article titled "Why Type on the Web Is So Bad," Eric Eaton, senior designer at Wired Digital (http://staff.hotwired.com/) writes that typography is a difficult discipline that "has gone the way of the photograph—into the world of amateur shutterbugs who think being able to select a font from a pull-down menu makes them typesetters." The same idea applies to people who learn to manipulate desktop publishing programs and produce printed materials without knowing the principles of typography.

Professional publications—both print and online—engage professional graphic designers to make the dozens of decisions about type and other display elements that will define the overall look of a publication. After management personnel approve the new look, designers meticulously detail type specifications into a stylebook, which becomes a guide for consistently executing the design plan. So, although copy editors rarely play a major role in choosing families of type, and although the typography stylebook guides many routine decisions, editors still must make multiple typographical decisions every day that influence legibility.

Previous sections of this chapter discussing type size, width, slant and weight, include information about how type characteristics hinder or help ease of reading. Those legibility tips, plus a few others, are summarized here:

- Make type decisions according to purpose. Typography appropriate for a billboard, poster, business card, or wedding announcement won't work for body copy in a newspaper, magazine, newsletter or Web page.

- Use text type (smaller than 14 point) for body type, and use display type (14 point and larger) for headlines.

- Allow appropriate space between lines (leading) for type with a large x-height. Text type with a large x-height appears larger than the same size type with a smaller x-height and corresponding longer ascenders and descenders.

- Avoid body type set solid with no leading between the lines; conversely, too much space between lines hampers legibility.

- Reserve type variations, such as boldface, italics, condensed and expanded, for headlines or other emphasis. Do not use them for long passages or for an entire story. This admonition applies especially to Web sites because italic and condensed body typefaces are particularly difficult to read on a computer screen.

- Save reverse type (white letters on a black background) and type printed over grey or colored screens for special treatment, not for long blocks of copy.

- Use caution when superimposing type on a photograph or other image. Depending on the image, the type may be illegible and may obscure the image.

- Set type in appropriate widths to make it easy for eye movement to track from the end of one line to the beginning of the next line and to avoid excessive hyphenation. Type set too narrow leads to many hyphenated words at the ends of lines and makes reading more difficult. Use the $O = lca \times 1.5$ formula to determine the most legible line width for body type.

- Use a serif typeface for body type rather than sans serif typeface because research shows that the finishing strokes of serifs aid legibility.

- Avoid passages set in all capital letters. A combination of caps and lower-case letters (sentence style) enhances legibility.

- Save script, blackletter and decorative typefaces for emphasis, not body type.

Suggestions for additional reading

Baird, Russell N., Arthur T. Turnbull and Duncan McDonald. *The Graphics of Communication*, 5th ed. New York: Holt, Rinehart and Winston, 1987.

Bringhurst, Robert. *The Elements of Typographic Style*, 2nd ed. Vancouver: Hartley & Marks Publishers Inc., 1997.

Craig, James. *Designing with Type*. New York: Watson-Guptill, 1981.

Dair, Carl. *Design with Type*. Toronto: University of Toronto Press, 1982.

Design: The Journal of the Society of Newspaper Design, a publication of the Society of Newspaper Design, 11600 Sunrise Valley Drive, Reston, Va. 22091.

Eaton, Eric. "Why Type on the Web Is So Bad," *Wired Digital*. Online. http://www.hotwired.com/webmonkey/97/48/index3a.html?tw=graphics_fonts. Dec. 29, 1998.

Rehe, Rolf. *Typography and Design for Newspapers*. Carmel, Ind.: Design Research International, 1985.

Solomon, Martin. *The Art of Typography*. New York: Watson-Guptill, 1986.

Typographic Studies. TypoGRAPHIC. Online. http://typographic.rsub.com/index.cgi. Dec. 29, 1998.

Wilson, Adrian. *The Design of Books*. San Francisco: Chronicle Books, 1993.

Exercises

1. Identify each of the following samples of type according to its classification: Roman, sans serif, square serif, italic, text, script, or decorative.

Bookman   _____

Futura   _____

Lubalin Graph   _____

Times   _____

Zapf Chancery   _____

Palatino   _____

Helvetica   _____

2. Look at your campus or local newspaper, and identify the type size, style, weight and family for each of the following:

Largest headline on Page One   _____

Other headlines on Page One   _____

Nameplate   _____

Body copy on Page One   _____

Captions   _____

Section labels (logos)   _____

Bylines   _____

Agate type in the sports section _____

Does the paper use the same weight of type for all headlines on Page One? Does the paper use the same typeface and size for body copy throughout the paper (except for ads)?

3. As examples of how type reflects the personality of a publication, select either two magazines or two newsletters that use widely different typography. Identify the type size, style, weight and family for each publication for each of the following elements:

	Title of publication 1	*Title of publication 2*
Nameplate	_____	_____
Article titles in table of contents	_____	_____
Most frequently used body type	_____	_____
Cover story headline	_____	_____
Headline for another main story	_____	_____
Bylines	_____	_____
Photo captions	_____	_____
Uses reverse type in body type? (if yes, describe amount used)	_____	_____
Uses italics in body type? (if yes, describe amount used)	_____	_____
Uses boldface in body type? (if yes, describe amount used)	_____	_____

Based on your analysis of typographical treatment in each publication, briefly describe the personality of each.

4. Measure the following type samples. Express the measurements in points.

The flag hangs high above the Capitol.

The flag hangs high above the

The flag hangs high

The flag hangs

5. Measure the x-height (in points) for each sample:

18-point Bookman

18-point Helvetica

18-point Century Book

18-point Times

6. How much space (depth) is needed for each of the following headlines? Assume that each headline is set solid, meaning that there is no extra line spacing.

    a. 36 point, 2 lines: _____ inches or _____ picas

    b. 48 point, 1 line: _____ inches or _____ picas

    c. 48 point, 1 line with a 24-point underline: _____ inches or _____ picas

    d. 30 point, 3 lines: _____ inches or _____ picas

    e. 18 point, 3 lines: _____ inches or _____ picas

7. In each of the following pairs, which type is easier to read for body copy in a newspaper?

    a. Black type on white or reverse type (white type on black)?

    b. Serif or sans serif type?

    c. Text that is 9-point type leaded 1 point or 9-point type leaded 10 points?

    d. Caps and lowercase type or type in all caps?

    e. Roman type or text type?

8. Explain what is meant by "set width."

9. As layout editor for a company newsletter, you want to determine how wide to set a block of copy for best legibility. Explain how you would go about determining this.

Patience, diligence, painstaking attention to detail—these are the requirements.

—Mark Twain

Writing Headlines

I N today's busy world, newspaper readers are, to a large extent, headline skimmers. A joint project of the Poynter Institute for Media Studies and Gallup Eye-Trac research found that 56 percent of all headlines were processed by readers participating in the study. In comparison, the average participant in the study looked at only 25 percent of the stories.

Purposes of news headlines

Readers want information quickly, so the primary purpose of a news headline is to communicate quickly by accurately telling the most important idea in the story. If a headline is inviting and signals a story of interest, readers may pause to read the story. Thus, a second important role of headlines is to attract attention.

While communicating the main idea of the news story and doing it in a way to attract readers' attention, the headline writer must be careful to maintain the tone of the story. Just as you wouldn't wear a clown hat to a funeral, don't use an attention-grabbing headline that is inappropriate to the overall tone or mood of the story. Headlines are important indicators of a publication's general tone and overall approach to the news. Headlines written for a supermarket tabloid would be out of character in The New York Times or in most hometown newspapers.

Headlines are a key element in the design and layout of a news publication. The skillful layout editor decides the size and placement of headlines to help indicate the importance of the story and to make the page attractive. At many newspapers it is not uncommon for one person to edit copy, lay out pages and write headlines for one or more pages of the daily paper.

Perhaps no task involved in producing a publication is both as simple and as demanding as good headline writing. Anyone who can use the English language competently can learn, with practice, to write headlines. But headline writing is as much an art as a skill, and not everyone can compose news headlines that crackle or feature headlines that lure readers immediately into the mood of the story. Yet these talents are essential, for modern headlines are designed to

- Summarize the story

- Capture readers' attention

- Maintain the mood of the story

- Help set the overall tone of the publication

- Indicate the relative importance of the story

- Add to the attractiveness of the page

Characteristics of good headlines

When Benjamin Harris published the first newspaper in the colonies, Publick Occurrences Both Foreign and Domestic, in 1690, it contained no headlines. Nobody had thought of them yet. Besides, colonists who were literate were starved for news and needed no headlines as inducements to read every story in the newspaper. Today's proliferation of news media competing for readers' time and attention boosts the importance of headlines. Web sites rely heavily on well-written and informative headlines that induce readers to click their way deeper into the site.

"Never has the art of headline writing been so important" as on the Web, writes Mario Garcia, an internationally renowned designer of print and Web publications.* Garcia compares the role of headlines on the Web to the attention-grabbing headlines of competing tabloid newspapers in a bygone era—all barking to get noticed over the competition. Figure 9-1 illustrates a headline-dominated home page covering the House of Representatives vote to impeach President Clinton.

Headlines are written in skeletonized language. They use present tense to describe past action, and each headline must fit its allotted space. Each letter, punctuation mark and space in a headline is a unit or a portion of a unit. (Counting individual units of headlines is explained later in this chapter.)

Let's say you are writing a headline with a maximum count of 22.5 units to top a story saying that the New York Yankees won the pennant last night in the Eastern Division of the American League. You might frame the most important facts of the story in this skeleton sentence:

The Yankees won American League Eastern Division pennant

At 53.5 units, this effort is too long to fit the maximum count. It also violates the basic rule that headlines should not be written in the past tense. Present-tense headlines give the news immediacy, and present-tense verbs are often shorter than past-tense verbs. Nonessential words, especially articles (*a, an, the*), are usually

---

*Mario Garcia, *Redesigning Print for the Web,* Indianapolis: Hayden Books, 1997.

Figure 9-1
Headlines alone do tell the impeachment story on this segment of the home page of the Los Angeles Times Web site for Dec. 20, 1998. Each headline links to a story, which may in turn contain one or more links to other stories.

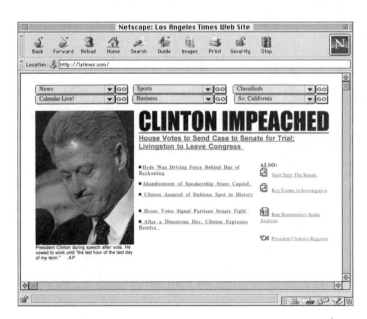

omitted to give the headline a sense of telegraphic speed and enable more ideas to be included in a limited space.

Let's try again:

Yankees win American League East Division pennant

The new headline is better because it eliminates the unnecessary article and uses present tense. But with 46 units, length is still a problem.

How about abbreviating American League? Headline writers in search of a shorter count must resist the urge to use unfamiliar abbreviations, but baseball fans won't have any problem understanding this abbreviation:

Yankees win AL East pennant

At 26 units, the new version is still a bit too long. *Yankees* could become *Yanks,* but we would save only two units on the count. How about *title* in place of *pennant?* That gives us

Yanks win AL East title

Because most papers allow headlines to be slightly shorter than the maximum, this 20.5-unit effort should suffice. But the headline writer willing to work a little longer could come up with a stronger verb and an exact count, 22.5 units:

Yanks clinch AL East title

Copy desk chiefs attending an American Press Institute editing seminar gave these descriptions of a good headline:

■ It is accurate in fact, tone, scope and focus, and it emphasizes the main themes of the story. It is balanced and fair and in good taste.

■ It is clear, succinct, grammatical, easy to read and easy to understand.

■ It has vitality and is strong, active, bright.

■ It catches readers' attention and entices them into the story.

■ It has freshness and immediacy.

■ By its size and shape, it accurately grades the news.

How to write headlines

A headline is written after the story has been carefully edited, a process that generally requires three readings of the story. During each of these readings, the copy editor makes mental notes about headline ideas.

Remember that, unlike the copy editor, the newspaper audience will read the headline before reading the story. A perfectly crafted headline that lacks meaning until after the story is read is unacceptable.

News heads

Well-edited publications try to conform to a number of guidelines.

▶**Be accurate.** This rule has no exceptions. No matter how interesting a headline may be, it is worth nothing unless it is accurate. Working against deadline pressure, even the best copy editor sometimes has to disregard one or more of the rules of headline writing—but never the rule regarding accuracy.

▶ **Understand the story thoroughly before writing the headline.** The copy editor who doesn't have a clear view of what the story says isn't likely to write a headline that communicates clearly and accurately.

▶ **Avoid "stuttering" by repeating the wording of the lead so that readers read the same words twice.** Nor should you steal the writer's punch line on feature stories written in suspended-interest form.

▶ **Focus on the most up-to-date information in a continuing story.** Don't put a first-day headline or lead on a second-day story.

First-day headline:

20 injured in tornado

Second-day headline:

'Sounded like a train,' tornado survivor says

▶ **Write headlines as specifically as possible within space limitations.** "Killer storm hits" is not as good as

Storm kills four

▶ **Use attribution in headlines that convey opinion and for direct quotations.** Otherwise, the news headline will read like an editorial-page headline. For example, "Budget unfair" is an opinion, which could be taken as the newspaper's unless attributed:

Budget 'unfair,' senator says

▶ **Avoid libelous statements.** (How to avoid libel is discussed in Chapter 6.) In many states, a libelous headline is grounds for a successful lawsuit, even if the story contains no libelous statements. The headline writer's problem is particularly acute because the headline does not afford space to include qualifying terms from a potentially libelous story.

▶ **Respect the rights of criminal defendants.** Don't convict an accused person in a headline. In our system of law, a suspect is considered innocent unless proved guilty. The burden of proof is on the prosecution, not the defendant. The headline "City manager steals from public treasury" could cause problems; a better alternative is

DA charges city manager with stealing public funds

On acquittal, the legal term is *not guilty* rather than *innocent*. However, many publications follow AP style and use *innocent* to guard against the word *not* being dropped inadvertently from *not guilty*.

▶ **Avoid headlines with double meanings.** Examples: "2 teen-agers indicted for drowning in lake," "FBI ordered to assist Atlanta in child slayings," "Church retains homosexual bar," "5 bullets hit bus on way to Louisville."

▶ **Don't repeat words in a headline.** Example: "Prosecutor charges city manager with embezzlement of city funds." Occasionally, repetition leads to a good headline. This example from the Lexington (Ky.) Herald-Leader is about an actor who turned his back on Hollywood to become a Benedictine monk:

Hollywood actor trades the footlights for the divine light

▶ **Tell what happened rather than what did not happen.**

Storm topples television tower

Storm rips roofs from homes

The headline "No one dies in storm" is less informative.

▶ **Use strong action verbs, preferably in the top line of a multiple-line headline.** Avoid *dead heads*, which merely label stories. For example, "Council session" tells readers very little; a better alternative is

Council fires city manager

This rule applies to news headlines but not necessarily to feature or news-feature headlines, which often use magazine-style titles. Many newspaper editors are flexible about requiring every news headline to have a verb if the final result is an exceptionally good headline.

Do not use forms of the verb *to be* when a strong verb will fit the meaning and the space. They detract from the vigor of a headline. When used, *to be* verbs—*is* and *are*—are often implied rather than stated. But not always, as in this feature headline from The New York Times on a story about quantum physics:

Where Uncertainty Is King and Paradox Shares Throne

Or this news headline, also from the Times:

Under Press Curb, Bad News Is No News

The *to be* verb must not be omitted if it is the principal verb in a clause, unless the clause begins the headline. Generally, a *to be* verb is needed after the verbs *say, deny, assert, warn, allege, maintain, affirm* and *contend,* which would normally be followed by an object. The headline "Mayor says policy fair" sounds awkward, and it is grammatically incorrect. *Policy fair* is a separate clause here, not a direct object of *says.* The word *policy* is used as a subject of the clause *policy is fair.* Assuming that the story isn't about the mayor's ability to enunciate words, the subject of the second clause needs an expressed verb:

Mayor says policy is fair

If the order of the clauses is reversed, then the *to be* verb can be implied without confusing readers:

Policy unfair, mayor says

▶ **Provide a subject for every headline.** Otherwise, the publication becomes sprinkled with commands, like this gem: "Throw child in river." Where attribution is essential to avoid editorializing in a headline, copy editors sometimes yield to the temptation to begin a headline with a verb of attribution without any subject: "Says taxes must increase." Resist such temptation.

▶ **Use the present tense to indicate both present and past action; use future tense for future action.** Instead of writing "Jones defeated Smith," write

Jones defeats Smith

▶ **Use the active voice, rather than the passive voice.** The active voice gives the headline greater impact. Instead of "Walkout staged by nurses," for example, write

Nurses stage walkout

▶**Keep thought units together on the same line in multiple-line headlines.** That is, don't separate parts of a verb, proper nouns that go together, a preposition from its object, or a modifier from the word it modifies. Observe where the lines break in the following examples:

**Teachers seek
pay increase**

**Teachers call
for pay hike**

**New tax revenue
to improve streets**

▶**Omit the articles *a*, *an*, and *the*, as a general rule.** This saves space and speeds the pace of a headline. Sometimes, however, an article is essential to understanding. The meaning of "King takes little liquor" is different from the meaning of "King takes a little liquor." Sometimes articles are needed for flow and phrasing of a headline, as in this example from The New York Times:

Game Trophies: What's Good for a Goose Is Bad for a Moose

▶**Avoid confusing abbreviations and acronyms in headlines.** Except for abbreviations commonly used in writing for a public audience, abbreviations should not appear in headlines. For example, this headline uses abbreviation correctly:

Navratilova gets win No. 100

This headline misuses abbreviation in three places: "Floods close Calif., Nev. mtn. passes." *California, Nevada* and *mountain* should all be spelled out, as they are in ordinary writing.

Some acronyms—words formed from the initial letters of a name, such as NASA for National Aeronautics and Space Administration—and combinations of initials have become readily understood vocabulary in the United States. *NATO, SWAT* and *AIDS* are acronyms that most American readers immediately recognize and understand, as are the abbreviations *U.S., GM, IBM, CIA* and *FBI.* These familiar terms should be used to condense headlines. Many more acronyms and combinations of initials are not familiar to readers, however, and should not be used in headlines.

A practical method for deciding whether to use a particular abbreviation or acronym in a headline is to make a short list of those that are familiar to readers and common in ordinary public writing. Then, when you question whether you should use an abbreviation or acronym, check your list; if the term is not on it, you may be wise to spell it out or rephrase the headline rather than abbreviate it or reduce it to initials.

▶**Punctuate headlines correctly.** In most instances, headlines are punctuated like sentences but without a period at the end. Headline punctuation is discussed later in this chapter.

▶**Use the available headline space to communicate specific facts rather than pad the headline merely to fill space.** For example, in the headline, the phrase, "Stocks finish ahead, after weak start," *after weak start* provides additional information, whereas *in trading today* would have filled the space with the obvious instead of adding a thought. Headline padding is distracting, is usually obvious and weakens an otherwise good headline.

▶**Check the headline carefully before returning it to the copy desk chief for approval.** Check the facts against the story, recount the lines, and ensure that clarity of meaning and appropriateness of tone have been maintained. One good method to use in checking for ambiguity or obscurity is to put the headline back into skeletonized sentence form to see if it is easily understandable.

Feature headlines

Many feature headlines, like feature stories, are considered "dessert." A copy editor has the same license in composing feature headlines that a reporter has in writing feature stories. In fact, a headline should strike the same tone as the story. A Lexington (Ky.) Herald-Leader copy editor properly topped a feature story about a convention for match cover collectors in this way:

It's probably not a good idea to smoke around these people

Literary devices such as rhyme, alliteration and puns can be particularly effective in feature headlines, as long as they reflect the tone of the story. A serious headline tops a feature about a serious topic, while a breezy or even funny headline is appropriate for a story written in that spirit. One sure way to anger a feature writer who uses a surprise ending is to give away the punch line in the headline.

Online headlines

Web page headlines and e-mail subject headers often lack the contextual cues—photographs, headline decks, accompanying article and placement on a page—that add meaning to headlines in printed publications. In many instances, writers and editors for online media control neither the formatting of their headlines on computer screens nor the content appearing simultaneously on those screens. Online readers may view headlines as: a long list of search engines hits, bookmarks for a Web browser, a list of incoming mail messages or multiple homepage links to stories.

If a brief summary of the article accompanies the headline, it competes with other headlines and summaries in the small space of a computer window. Research shows that people dislike reading large amounts of text online and tend to scan headlines and ignore the summaries. Online readers don't have time to click on each headline and wait for each story to load from its home server and appear on the computer screen. Unlike print media, with all stories and headlines readily available for immediate reading, skimming or skipping, each mouse click to retrieve a single story becomes a considerable time investment for online readers. The headline alone triggers the decision to invest in retrieval and reading time for a particular article.

Headline writing guidelines described previously in this chapter—with accuracy leading the list—also apply to online headlines. An online environment suggests these additional guidelines:

- Concentrate on key information for the first word of a headline, both to facilitate reader scanning and to gain better positioning in alphabetized lists. Definitely avoid articles (*a, an, the*) as the first word in an online headline.

- Communicate clearly the central idea of the article rather than use teaser headlines. This means avoid puns or other cryptic heads that readers are likely to ignore rather than take time to download.

■ Avoid words that lead readers to mistake news or feature content for unwanted advertising messages. This is especially important for subject headings on e-mail, where readers are increasingly annoyed by unsolicited commercial messages, known as spam, and are almost certain to delete rather than read such messages. The compilation of headlines in Figure 9-2 illustrates the headline-writing guidelines explained thus far in this chapter.

Figure 9-2
These headlines were featured on the American Copy Editors Society Web site. For more examples of good headline writing, see the ACES site at http://www.copydesk.org.

Examples of good headlines

Six-shooter//6.0 6.0 6.0 6.0 6.0 6.0 6.0 5.9 6.0 / Kwan just misses perfection on a piece about the skater's record-making score (Dan Brown, San Jose Mercury News).

I Sue You, You Sue Me on a story about lawsuits against Barney imitators and others selling the costume without permission (Chuck Ervin, San Jose Mercury News).

Smoggy air apparent? on a piece about how Houston is closing the gap on Los Angeles as the nation's smog capital (Laura Hayes, The Houston Chronicle).

Overa-Cheever wins Indy on a story about Eddie Cheever winning the Indianapolis 500 [Marc Johnson of The Fort Wayne (Ind.) News-Sentinel].

CASINO: No dice on a piece about the failure of a casino gambling proposal (Margaret Lord, The Baltimore Sun).

Tennessee board sharpening clause over big-cat sanctuary for a story about legislation to regulate a privately owned sanctuary for tigers (Cliff Pinckard, The Akron Beacon Journal).

Mets reward Lance a lot on a piece about the major league baseball team signing outfielder Lance Johnson to a contract worth $10 million [Craig Schmidt, The Asbury Park (New Jersey) Press].

He takes history and makes it stick on a story about a man who puts state history onto refrigerator magnets (Robin Smith, the Times Herald, Norristown, Pa.).

Whole lotta Bacon goin' on for a profile of actor Kevin Bacon (Doug Wagner, the Rocky Mountain News).

A desire named streetcar was a subhead on a story about an artist who paints scenes of bygone Detroit. The piece included a section about the great demand for his paintings of trolley cars in motion (Marty Kohn, the Detroit Free Press).

Washington Schlepped Here for a story about Revolutionary War sites around New York (Tim Sacco of the New York Post).

Headline punctuation

A headline is generally punctuated like a sentence without the ending period.

▶**Commas** may be used to replace the word *and*, as in these examples:

Wind topples tower, rips roofs from homes

President selects Smith, Jones as envoys

▶**Semicolons** are used in headlines, as in sentences, to separate independent clauses:

Wind topples tower; rain floods city streets

A semicolon is needed in this example because the headline contains two separate clauses, each with its own subject and predicate verb.

▶**Periods** are used in headlines for some abbreviations. They are not used to designate the end of a headline.

▶**Ampersands** should not be used in headlines except when they are a customary part of a title or phrase, such as *AT&T.*

▶**Hyphens** should not be used at the end of a line in a headline, because they interfere with the line-by-line approach that readers use for reading headlines. If you end up with an end-of-line hyphen—

Post goes to write-
in candidate, Jones

—rewrite it:

Write-in candidate
wins mayor's race

▶**Exclamation marks** are almost never needed in a headline. However, in its zeal to emphasize the unusualness of two major league no-hitters in a single day, an Ohio newspaper used seven exclamation marks:

O my! 2 no-hitters!!!!!!!

It was a rare feat. One exclamation mark in a headline is normally one too many.

▶**Question marks** are rarely effective, because a news headline should answer questions rather than ask them. Exceptions are those few stories that pose questions without answering them or the occasional headline that not only asks a question but immediately answers it, as in this example from The New York Times:

Fake Cheese? No Whey!

▶**Quotation marks** in headlines should be single quotation marks, rather than double quotation marks, to save space:

Senate leader calls tax plan 'a windfall for big business'

▶**Colons and dashes** may be used in headlines to indicate attribution. A verb of attribution, such as *says,* is preferred. But where space does not allow a word, a colon or dash may take its place:

Sen. Jones: budget 'unfair'

Budget 'unfair'—Sen. Jones

Use a colon after the name of the person and *before* the opinion. If the opinion comes first, use a dash.

Headline capitalization

In an earlier era, newspapers and magazines commonly set headlines all in capital letters. But legibility research has demonstrated that type set all in capitals is more difficult to read than type set in capitals and lowercase letters, so most publications have abandoned the all-caps headline style.

Try reading this paragraph:

> DOWNSTYLE AND UPSTYLE HEADLINE CAPITALIZATION HAS SEVERAL ADVANTAGES OVER USING ONLY CAPITAL LETTERS. MORE CHARAC-TERS FIT LEGIBLY IN EACH LINE OF A HEADLINE IN DOWNSTYLE THAN UPSTYLE, AND DOWNSTYLE REQUIRES FEWER KEYBOARD FUNCTIONS FOR TYPISTS. MOST IMPORTENT, RESEARCHERS DISCOVERED DURING THE '50S THAT USING ALL CAPITAL LETTERS SLOWS READING.

All-cap type is just as hard to read in headlines as it is in body type. In the paragraph you just read, for example, you may have put so much effort into making out words that you didn't spot the typographical error (*importent*) purposefully included in the paragraph.

Some newspapers, such as The New York Times and Washington Post, capitalize the first word of each line and all other principal words. This practice is called "false capitalization" or *upstyle.* Researchers have discovered that upstyle also slows reading. Try reading this paragraph in upstyle:

> Downstyle Headline Capitalization Has Several Advantages Over Upstyle. More Characters Fit Legibly in Each Line of a Headline in Downstyle, and Downstyle Requires Fewer Keyboard Functions for Typesetters. Most Important, Researchers Discovered During the '50s That Starting Each Word With a Capital Letter Slows Reading.

The same reading difficulty you experienced as you read this paragraph affects readers of headlines as well.

Most U.S. newspapers now use *downstyle* headlines, meaning that sentence-style capitalization is used—the first word of the headline and proper nouns. All other words are set in lowercase letters:

Stocks finish ahead after weak start

Headline counting

Earlier in this chapter we referred to the difficulty of writing a good headline within limited space. Now it's time to face the problem squarely by learning how to count the units—letters, punctuation marks and spaces—that make up a headline.

Until recent years, copy editors wrote their headlines on paper, often on half-size sheets of typing paper, and counted each unit themselves. A single headline might be counted many times as words were changed repeatedly in an effort to compose a well-written headline that fit the allotted space.

Although computers can be programmed to "head fit," students should know how to count headlines without the aid of a computer because not all newspapers, magazines and public relations firms have computers with headline-fitting programs. A young journalist shouldn't risk being rejected for an internship or job for not knowing how to manually count headlines.

Counting manually

Various styles of type vary slightly in width, but the unit value of each letter, punctuation mark and space in a headline can be estimated as follows:

Lowercase letters = 1 unit (except *l, i, f, t* = 1/2 unit; *m* and *w* = 1 1/2 units)

Uppercase letters = 1 1/2 units (except *M* and *W* = 2 units; *I* = 1 unit)

Numbers and symbols = 1 unit (except the numeral *1* = 1/2 unit)

Punctuation marks = 1/2 unit (except a dash and a question mark = 1 unit)

Space between words = 1/2 unit

At a typical newspaper, the process of headline writing begins when the copy editor is given a story to edit. Usually a headline size and style have already been assigned to the story to conform to the page layout. But sometimes the copy is marked *HTK*, meaning "headline to come," so the copy editor can work on the story while the layout is being completed.

Headline size and style are usually specified in code. For example, the headline designation 1-30-3 BB means that the editor wants a headline one column wide, in 30-point type, with three lines. *BB* refers to the family of type, in this case Bodoni Bold. (Type styles and sizes are discussed in Chapter 8.) Because 72-point type is an inch tall, each line of a 30-point headline is slightly less than half an inch tall.

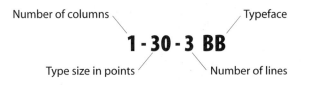

After receiving the headline assignment, the copy editor consults a headline schedule like the one in Figure 9-3 to determine the maximum number of units in a 1-30-3 headline. The schedule shows that a maximum of 11 units of 30-point

Figure 9-3
A headline schedule is used
to determine how many
units can fit in the space
allotted for a headline. The
entries in the body of the
table are the maximum
numbers of units for a given
type size and column width.
The absence of exact multi-
ples in some columns is due
to a rounding error.

Typeface: **Bodoni Bold (BB)**
Bodoni Bold Italic (BBI)

Type size in points	Number of columns wide					
	1	2	3	4	5	6
14	22	45				
18	18	35	52			
24	13	26.5	40	53		
30	11	21	33	47	55	
36	9	18	27	35	44	53
48	7	13.5	20	27	34	41
60	5	11	17	21.5	27	33
72	4.5	9	13	18	22	26

Bodoni Bold type will fit on each line when it is set one column wide. The same size of type set two columns wide will accommodate 21 units.

After a few weeks on the copy desk, editors have most of the headline schedule for their publication memorized. The unit counts listed in the headline schedule are the maximum number that will fit for each type size and column width. Most publications allow headlines that are as much as two units short of the maximum count.

Copy editors who count headlines manually work out their own techniques for counting units. One system uses pencil marks above the line for each whole unit and marks below the line for each half unit. Figure 9-4 shows how to count a headline that will fit the 1-30-3 BB assignment. With practice, you should be able to count quickly without using little marks above and below the line.

Counting with computer software

Computers simplify the job of headline counting. A copy editor working at a computer screen can strike one or more keys to instruct the computer to count a headline. Commands vary slightly according to the computer system and layout software, but all are relatively easy to learn.

With one widely used computer system, the copy editor hits one key to instruct the computer to enter the "head fit" mode. Then the editor inserts a code for the typeface and size, hits the Execute key, moves the cursor to the top of the story and begins composing the headline. A line at the top of the screen provides a running count of the width as each unit is typed. All guesswork is removed from the process, because the computer has been programmed with the precise width of each letter, number and punctuation mark for all available typefaces and sizes.

With another popular computer system, a highlighted bar at the top of the story shows exactly how much space the editor has for the headline. Any letter typed beyond that highlighted space exceeds the maximum.

Headline writers in the computer era receive another break in fitting headlines, because computers are not bound by the standard point sizes of display

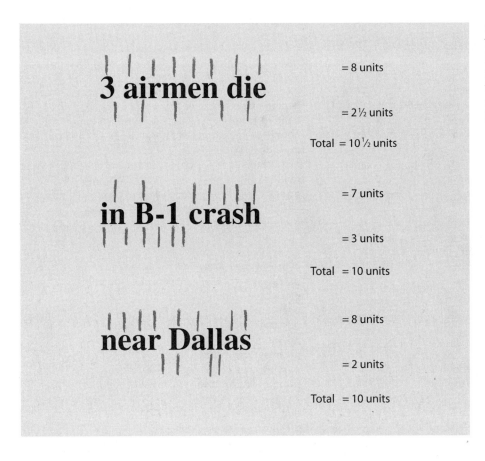

type: 14, 18, 24, 30, 36, 42, 48, 60, 72, 84. Let's say that the copy editor has written an excellent headline for a 2-36-2 BB assignment, but one line of the headline counts 18.5 units. As you can see from Figure 9-3, 18 is the maximum number of units for each line of a 2-36-2 headline. The editor might achieve the desired width by instructing the computer to set the type at 35 points or even 34 points, just a little smaller than 36 points. Although purists object to deviating from standard point sizes in headlines, this slight variation usually goes unnoticed.

Until recently, copy editors were instructed that the maximum headline count was absolute, because "you can't squeeze type." Today, however, type can be "squeezed" slightly through a technique known as *kerning*. Computers can be programmed for *positive kerning*, which means fitting letters together more closely, or *negative kerning*, moving letters farther apart. But many editors frown on kerning because squeezed and stretched type has an unnatural look.

Space limitation is one of the greatest difficulties facing the headline writer. The restrictive unit counts indicated by the headline schedule can so intimidate new copy editors that they feel defeated before they begin. The real difficulty may be a reluctance to discard old ideas and try new ones.

Hanging onto a headline idea that is not working is not symptomatic of new copy editors alone. Many experienced editors become so attached to the first line of a headline that they are reluctant to give it up even when they are unable to find a second line to go with it. Editors should see the headline as a whole rather than as a group of separate lines.

Able headline writers keep a good thesaurus close at hand and have many synonyms filed away in their brain. Their headline vocabulary includes many short words, as in Figure 9-5.

Figure 9-5
A vocabulary of short synonyms is a great aid to headline writers.

accident: crash, wreck, collide
accuse, charge: cite
acknowledge: admit, confess
acquire: get
advocate: urge, push, spur
agreement: accord, pledge, pact, harmony, compact
allocate: give, allot, issue, award
alteration: revise, fix, change
answer: reply
appointment: post, job
apprehend: catch, arrest, seize, trap, capture
approve: accept, back, confirm, laud
argument: debate
arrange: set, plan, shape, slate
arrest: seize, hold, net
assemble: meet, gather, rally, unite
attempt: try
beginning: start, opening, initial
bewilderment: puzzle, confusion, mystery
celebrate: mark, stage, perform, fete
celebration: fete, event, party
choose: name, elect, pick
climax: peak
command: lead, rule, direct, reign, sway
commander: leader, guide, chief, ruler
committee, commission: body, panel, board
compete: vie
confess: admit
conspiracy: plan, plot, scheme
construct: build, erect, rise
contract: pact
convene: meet
criticize: score
criticize strongly: blast, flay
damage: hurt, impair, raze, scar, wreck, harm
danger: risk, peril, threat
decision: rule, order, writ, decree
decline, decrease: dip, fall
defeat: loss, fall
defraud: steal, dupe, fleece, rob, swindle, trick, raid
demonstrate: show, display, exhibit, test, try, melee, rebellion, revolt, riot, tumult, turmoil, uprising, uproar, discord, din
destroy: raze
diminish: trim, reduce, lop, cut
discrimination: bias, prejudice
earthquake: quake, jolt, shock, temblor, tremor
encourage: spark, help, aid
examine: scan, study
expose, reveal: bare
former: ex
impede, halt: balk
increase: hike, rise, add, gain, up, add
inform: tell

investigate: probe, study
leader: guide, chief, head, expert, ruler
limit, restrain: curb, relax, save, soften, temper
meeting: session, parley, assembly
murder: kill, slay
nominate: slate, pick, choose, name
nullify: void
opposition: battle, clash, challenge, combat, differ, divide, lash, quarrel, rap, rebuff, upbraid
organization: board, body, band, club, firm, group, unit
organize: join, form, unite, tie, link, merge
overcome: win, beat
perceive: see, understand, envision, foretell
pledge: vow, agree, oath
position: job, post
postpone: delay, defer, put off, shelve
prevent: bar, ban, curb, stop
promise: vow, pledge, agree
pursuit: chase, hunt, seek, track, follow, trail
puzzle: awe, confuse, stun, mystery, surprise, nonplus, perplex
quarrel: tiff, clash, argue
question: quiz, ask, inquire
realignment: revise, alter, change, shake up
reconcile: settle, peace, patch, pacify, heal
relieve: allay, cure, ease, end, free, help
request: ask, beg, bid, exhort, implore, plead, urge, seek, plea
resign: quit
restrain: stop, avert, check, curb, curtail, deter, foil, halt, hinder, impede, limit, quell, repress, slacken, slow, stall, stem, tie up, pause
reveal: tell
revise: alter, change, shift, vary, switch, transfer, modify
ridicule: chide, deride, insult, jeer, mock, taunt, tease, twit
salute: greet, hail
schedule: slate, set, plan, arrange
separation: rift, break, split
settlement: accord, deal, pact, truce, bargain
silent: mum, mute
steal: rob, loot, take
suggestion: plan, idea, offer, design
suspend: stop, end
thwart: foil, stop, limit
transfer: shift, alter, adjust
violence: battle, struggle, fray, fracas, furor, brawl, chaos, clamor, clash, combat
wrangle: argue, debate
wreck: raze
zealous: ardent, fervent, avid

Placement of headlines

Typically a headline is placed above the story, as in this example:

Japanese company to build auto plant in Tennessee

A headline should never appear below the story, but it may be placed to the side. A *side head* is almost always placed to the left of the story, although in extremely rare circumstances a side head to the right can be effective. A side head is particularly useful for filling a wide, shallow space at the top of an inside page, like this:

**Japanese company
to build auto plant
in Tennessee**

Generally, a headline should cover all columns of a story. That is, if the layout calls for the story to be wrapped across more than one column, then the headline should extend across the top of all the columns. *Raw wraps*, also called *Dutch turns*, are columns of type without a headline above them. Raw wraps should not be used routinely, but they can help give good display to a graphic or other artwork. They also prevent the problem of side-by-side headlines, which are called *tombstones*. The following example shows raw wraps at the tops of columns 2, 3, 4 and 5.

**Crash diets
don't work**

The placement of headlines within a page layout is explained in greater detail in Chapter 11.

Styles of headlines

The main element of a newspaper headline is known as the *top*. A secondary heading under the top is known as a *deck* or *bank*. The top of a headline should contain the main highlights of the story. The decks, if used, should give more information about the story rather than repeat in different words what is already said in the top. Although both the top and the decks should follow the usual headline-writing rules and should be able to stand alone, the decks usually depend on the top for full meaning.

When newspapers were printed on flat-bed presses, mechanical restrictions limited headlines to one column wide. Lead strips, placed between each column to help hold the metal type in place as the page was put together, prevented headline type from extending beyond a single column. In addition, although newspaper pages historically were somewhat wider than today's page, they were divided into eight or nine columns, meaning that headline writers had even less space per column to work with than today's copy editors. These restrictions led to multiple-deck headlines that, for a major story, might run most of the length of a page. This 16-deck headline, with each line centered and each deck ended by a period, was typical of newspaper headlines during the Civil War:

THE WAR.

Highly Important News from Baltimore.

The Massachusetts Volunteers
Opposed in Their Passage
Through the City.

Bloody Fight Between the Soldiers and the Mob.

Two Soldiers and Seven Citizens Killed.

The Volunteers Succeed in
Forcing Their Way Through.

TOTAL DESTRUCTION OF THE ARSENAL
AT HARPERS FERRY BY THE FEDERAL TROOPS.

Seizure of Northern Vessels in Virginia.

Delaware Assumes the Position
of Armed Neutrality.

IMPORTANT FROM WASHINGTON.

PROCLAMATION OF THE PRESIDENT.

BLOCKADE OF THE SOUTHERN PORTS.

Departure of the Rhode Island,
Massachusetts and New York Troops for Washington.

The Seventh Regiment,
Nearly One Thousand Strong,
En Route for the Capital.

Immense Turnout of Ladies
and Citizens to See Them Off.

Pathetic Leave Takings
at the Railroad Depot.

By the time the readers got through all those decks, they found little new information in the body of the story. The New York Times topped its story about the assassination of President Abraham Lincoln with the words "AWFUL EVENT," followed by seven decks.

The Civil War headline features lines centered within one column and a mixture of upstyle and all-capital decks. Today, top headlines alone with at most one or two decks, all set flush to the left of columns, most commonly appear in newspapers, magazines and corporate publications. Although flush left headline alignment dominates, Figure 9-6 illustrates some other styles.

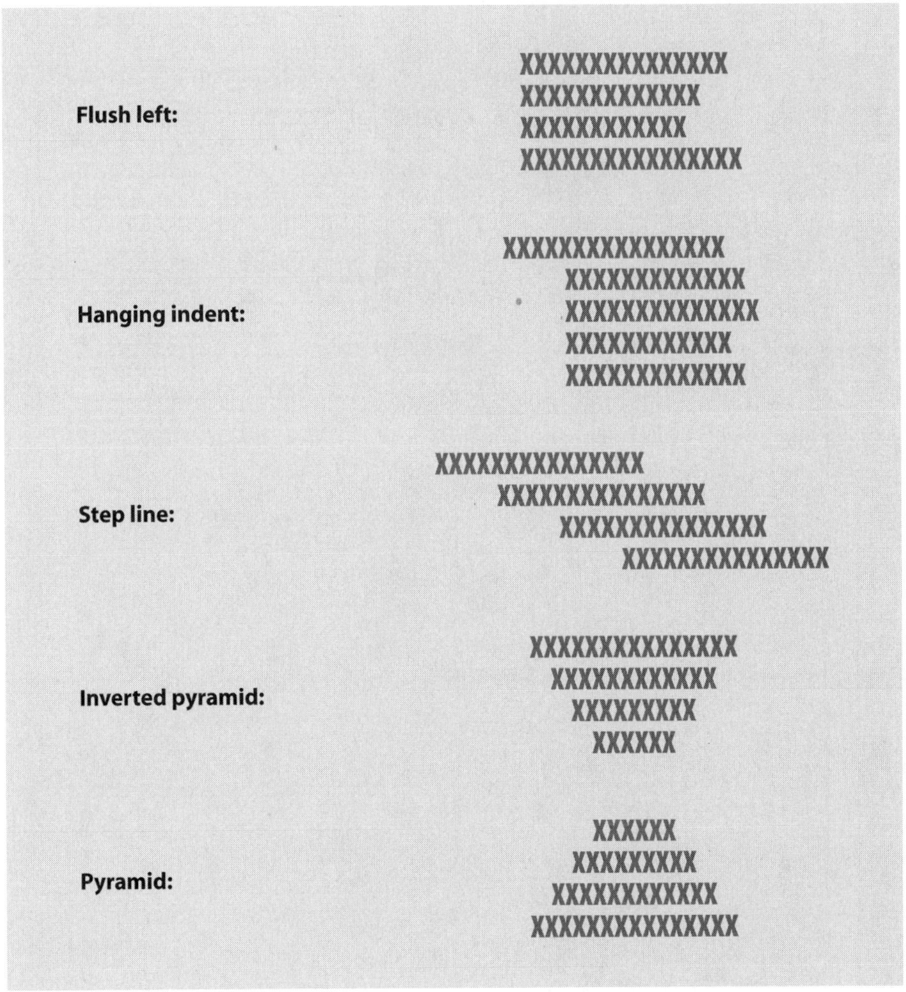

Flush left:

XXXXXXXXXXXXXX
XXXXXXXXXXXX
XXXXXXXXXXX
XXXXXXXXXXXXXX

Hanging indent:

XXXXXXXXXXXXXX
XXXXXXXXXXXX
XXXXXXXXXXXXX
XXXXXXXXXXX
XXXXXXXXXXX

Step line:

XXXXXXXXXXXX
XXXXXXXXXXXXX
XXXXXXXXXXXXX
XXXXXXXXXXXXX

Inverted pyramid:

XXXXXXXXXXXX
XXXXXXXXXX
XXXXXXXX
XXXXX

Pyramid:

XXXXX
XXXXXXX
XXXXXXXXXX
XXXXXXXXXXXX

Figure 9-6
The style of headline alignment used by modern publications varies considerably, although flush-left style is used most frequently.

Modern typesetting and printing technology accommodate a wide variety of headline sizes, typefaces and widths. *Banner* headlines, sometimes called *screamers* or *streamers*, can run the entire width of the page. A *skyline banner* is a headline that runs the width of the front page and is placed above the nameplate. The skyline banner, also referred to as a *promo* or a *teaser*, is used to promote or call attention to an important story on an inside page of the paper.

Research shows that readers today want more information quickly in easily digested chunks. Editors have responded with shorter stories, more graphics and more headlines—especially headlines in styles that allow readers to grab more information at a glance.

A *readout* headline, also called a *dropout*, is often used in combination with a banner headline to draw the reader into the body of the story (see Figure 9-7).

Figure 9-7
A readout headline is one device used to create greater reader interest in a story and more variety in the look of a page.

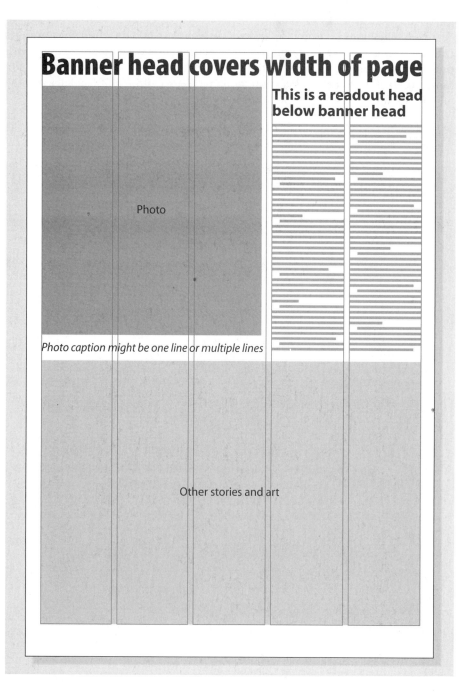

Banner head covers width of page

This is a readout head below banner head

Photo

Photo caption might be one line or multiple lines

Other stories and art

The readout headline should be written to stand independently of the main headline and should add to information given in the main headline. The example in Figure 9-7 shows the readout beneath the end of the main headline, but the readout can also be placed in the first column, under the first words of the banner.

Decks set as *underlines* and *overlines* are sometimes used in combination with a multicolumn main headline and are set in type about half the size of the main headline. An underline would look like this:

Main head is flush left, larger type
Underline is in smaller type, usually centered

An overline would reverse the positions of the two lines, with the smaller type above the larger type. Each headline should be a complete thought unit, with the underline or overline amplifying on the main headline.

A *kicker*, also called an *eyebrow*, is another headline style. The kicker is sometimes just a label or phrase rather than a clause, with a subject and verb. The main headline should not depend on the kicker for its meaning; that is, the kicker should not read into the main headline. Instead, the kicker should depend on the main headline for its meaning. In addition, the kicker should be set in type no larger than half the size of the main headline and in a different type weight. Because one purpose of the kicker is to introduce white space into the layout, the kicker should extend no more than two-thirds the width of the main headline, usually less, and the main headline should be indented by the same number of points as the size in which it is set. Many publications underline kickers. Here is an example of a headline with a kicker from the Los Angeles Times:

Patchwork Laws
Government
Financing:
Call It Chaos

A *hammer*, also called a *reverse kicker* or *barker*, reverses the ratio of the kicker to the headline's main element, using type twice as large as the main element of the headline. The hammer is set either flush left or centered above the main headline. The main element of a hammer headline should be two lines long and indented the same number of points as the type size of the hammer. Two lines of main headline are needed to create enough optical weight to draw the reader's eye. The indentation forms an area of white space beneath the hammer to balance the space to the right of the main headline. Here is an example:

Plane crash
43 people drown
in Gulf of Mexico

Used less often than the kicker or hammer are three other styles of headlines that add variety to newspaper or magazine layouts. The *tripod* headline has a single line of large type at the left and two lines of smaller type at the right. This headline from the St. Petersburg Times is a typical tripod:

Ticket Wars: Now you can see first-run films for less—at some theaters

Here is an example of a *wicket* headline:

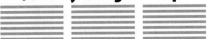

The *slash* headline is like the wicket and tripod headline in type sizes and arrangement, but a six- to nine-point rule is set at a 45-degree angle between the two parts of the headline. The top edge of the left module should be as high as the top of the slash and the bottom edge of the right module as low as the bottom end of the slash. Here is an example:

For maximum effectiveness the large type in a tripod, wicket or slash headline should be at least twice the size of the smaller type. The break between the two modules composing such a headline should occur in the middle of a column of body type. If the break is at the space between columns, readers might mistake the bimodular headline for two separate headlines. The easiest way to make sure that the break between modules will come midcolumn—and it is easy indeed with computerized "head fitting"—is to keep the subsidiary element in the headline as short as one-and-a-half columns or even half a column wide.

Two other types of headlines—the *subhead* and the *jump headline*—are named for their purpose rather than for their appearance. Many newspapers and magazines use subheads to break up large gray areas of copy and make pages look more inviting for readers. Although subheads run in the body of the story rather than above it, they are usually written by copy editors.

Subheads may be centered or flush left, in the same size as the body type or slightly larger, in boldface or italic. Subheads function as little headlines for the paragraphs immediately below them. Except for being only one line long, subheads are written just like headlines, but they are often without verbs. This example of a subhead comes from a long story in The New York Times on environmental damage caused by an oil spill off the coast of Alaska:

> The enormous toll on wildlife in the Sound, catalogued in an 18-page summary of 58 scientific studies, also includes losses of killer whales, extensive reproductive defects in salmon and herring fry, and widespread and lingering damage to sea grasses and other plants in tidal zones along 1,200 miles of the western boundary of the Sound and down the coast in the Gulf of Alaska, which were coated by oil for months.

> **Better Left Alone**
> Government scientists also said today that efforts to clean hundreds of miles of the Sound's shorelines with pressurized and heated sea water caused more damage to shellfish, sea grasses and other organisms in the tidal zones than if the shorelines had been left alone.

Newspaper feature pages use other spacing and typographical devices to relieve the tedium of reading paragraph after paragraph of body type. Sometimes large capital letters begin occasional paragraphs, allowing extra white space between the end of the previous paragraph and the one with the *initial letter*. For example:

> The enormous toll on wildlife in the Sound, catalogued in an 18-page summary of 58 scientific studies, also includes losses of killer whales, extensive reproductive defects in salmon and herring fry, and widespread and lingering damage to sea grasses and other plants in tidal zones along 1,200 miles of the western boundary of the Sound and down the coast in the Gulf of Alaska, which were coated by oil for months.
>
> Government scientists also said today that efforts to clean hundreds of miles of the Sound's shorelines with pressurized and heated sea water caused more damage to shellfish, sea grasses and other organisms in the tidal zones than if the shorelines had been left alone.

Some publications simply insert 12 or 18 points of white space between occasional paragraphs or insert *dingbats,* such as dots or small symbols related to the story's content or the nature of the publication. Some publications use boldface *lead-ins,* meaning that the first two or three words of occasional paragraphs—every fifth or sixth paragraph, for example—are set in boldface, either capitals and lowercase or all caps. Here is an example of the use of boldface lead-ins:

> The enormous toll on wildlife in the Sound, catalogued in an 18-page summary of 58 scientific studies, also includes losses of killer whales, extensive reproductive defects in salmon and herring fry, and widespread and lingering damage to sea grasses and other plants in tidal zones along 1,200 miles of the western boundary of the Sound and down the coast in the Gulf of Alaska, which were coated by oil for months.
>
> **GOVERNMENT SCIENTISTS** also said today that efforts to clean hundreds of miles of the Sound's shorelines with pressurized and heated sea water caused more damage to shellfish, sea grasses and other organisms in the tidal zones than if the shorelines had been left alone.

Another popular method of breaking long passages of type is to use a *breakout quotation,* or *pullout quotation,* within a story. This is an interesting or important passage in the story, often a direct quotation, that is repeated in larger type and set in a box or sideless box within the story. A very long story, particularly one that jumps to another page, may have more than one breakout quotation. This treatment relieves the grayness of the page and provides another point of entry to lure readers into the story. Figure 9-8 is an example of a breakout quotation.

Figure 9-8
A breakout quotation, also called a pullout quotation, relieves the grayness of the page and provides another point of entry to lure readers into the story.

Headline at top of story

"Pull-out quote goes in this area. Type is larger than body type."
Source name

Jump heads are used to identify a story that is being continued from a previous page. Readers often complain about having to turn to another page to read the rest of the story, and they find it particularly irritating to have to search for the continuation of the story on the jump page. How a newspaper or magazine treats its "continued" lines and its jump headlines is part of the publication's overall design and should be consistent from page to page and issue to issue so readers become familiar with the style.

Some newspapers write a separate display headline, often multicolumn, for the part of the story that is jumped. A line placed at the top of the first column of body type under the headline informs the reader that the story is "continued from Page 1." Other editors dislike this style because they think it confuses the reader and needlessly uses valuable space. These editors prefer to use a one-word headline, often set in 24-, 30-, 36- or 42-point type, that repeats the main word of the top headline or is the key word of the story. That word is followed by the "continued from Page 1" line. For example:

Jones
(continued from Page 1)

Headline writing is an art form

By Peter Bhatia

PLEASE ponder the following four headlines. Just think about them a little. Do they work for you? Do you want to read the story? Do they make you smile? Then, let's talk . . .

Sample 1: **All the Basques in one exit**

Sample 2: **Life's jest a goal of merry**

Sample 3: **50 ways to love your liver**

Sample 4: **Simpson takes a stab with a pen**

Headline writing is difficult work. It is an art form within the larger art form of journalism. It is an art form that doesn't receive enough attention in newsrooms today. The reasons for that are complex, relating to the necessary emphasis on writing and reporting, the key to any successful newspaper effort. After all, if readers don't read it, why have we bothered? Technology is a factor, too. In an era when how well editors can run a computer is sometimes as important as what they make the computer produce, it is only natural that fine, specific specialties such as headline writing are becoming less and less important in many newsrooms.

At the risk of sounding like an old fogy, most of us who help run newsrooms these days remember an era when this wasn't so. Heck, we even remember when caption writing was a specialty . . . but that's another lost art. I cut my headline-writing teeth (note to students: keep clichés like cutting teeth out of headlines) at the San Francisco Examiner in the late '70s, when that paper ran 84-point, page-width banner headlines on two editions a day that were sold in the afternoon, primarily to commuters. Trying to catch the essence of a complicated lead news story and writing the banner (called "The Line," as in: What's The Line for the third edition?) is indeed a form of art. You had four words to sum up the breaking news of the day, knowing that the sales of the paper that day would in some part be dependent on how good—or bad—that headline was.

Circulation directors lived and died for the day's line. If they were too obnoxious, they were threatened with "New fighting in Mideast" or "Consumer prices inch up." Of course, there were incredible news days when the banner was simply: REAGAN ROMPS … or even REAGAN SHOT. A reminder that simple is best on a huge story.

But in this contemporary era of new technology, it is very important to not lose sight of the great impact headlines have in our papers. They are our billboard to the news. Write a great head, there's a better chance of getting people to read the story. Right a lousy or inappropriate headline, the opposite occurs. It is really that simple. The headline writer needs to stretch, needs to take risks, needs to push the envelope to make sure the headline is as good and convincing as it can be and sells the story as well as it can. All of that, of course, without overstepping the appropriate bounds of taste and what the market will bear.

And that is an important aspect to remember: We live in a more sensitive world, so accuracy is more important than ever in writing headlines. Now this may seem obvious. And I suppose it is. But be warned: Readers notice more than ever when a headline is slightly off center on its meaning. Sure, a lot of the complainers have an agenda. But that doesn't lessen the headline writer's role. In a political debate, even if the writer chooses to declare one candidate as having the upper hand, the headline writer must seek a higher level of balance. Why? Because the nuance a news story can have can't be contained in the few words you have to write the headline. This chapter explains this well. And it can't be emphasized too much: The No. 1 rule in headline writing is accuracy, accuracy, accuracy … and, of course, you have to do it in five or six words 20 times or more a day if you're working on a copy desk rim. It isn't easy.

But back to those headlines for a minute. These are all real headlines, culled from the pages of different newspapers. A word about each and what they represent:

Sample 1: **All the Basques in one exit**

The story from the New York Daily News: the running of the bulls in Pamplona, Spain. A wonderful—actually brilliant—play on "all your eggs in one basket." My favorite kind of head. And appropriately done on a story that doesn't necessarily call for a serious point of view.

Sample 2: **Life's jest a goal of merry**

The story from the Asbury Park Press: a clown convention. Another brilliant play, on "Life is just a bowl of cherries." If you can train your mind to move words around like these headline writers have, you will be in great demand.

Sample 3: **50 ways to love your liver**

The story from The Oregonian: a food feature (which was fortunately not a health story). Taking off on a song title ("50 Ways to Leave Your Lover"). Again, very nice.

Sample 4: **Simpson takes a stab with a pen**

The story: O.J.'s book that came out during his trial. The verdict here: Guilty of poor taste. Forget for a second whether he was guilty or innocent; there were people stabbed to death in this case. This head may be funny, but someone should have saved the writer from doing this.

Why these four headlines? Again, to stress the creativity that headline writing calls for. Much of headline writing requires a straightforward approach. There are many, many stories where a play on words, a pun or other frivolity is totally unwarranted (see O.J. above). But when you set out to write a headline I urge you to keep this goal in mind every time: *Always, always write the best headline you can.* Bend the rules, break the rules if you must. Always, always stretch to convey the meaning of the story in as powerful a way as you can. And don't be satisfied with what you come up with the first time. Run it through your brain again to make sure you haven't missed a nuance or another way to phrase it that might be even a little bit better.

Take this non-traditional but wonderful headline from a story about aerobics classes in prison, from the Wall Street Journal:

**These guys must already know
all about doing long stretches**

And remember to use active verbs and descriptive words. We have a wonderfully rich language. Use it to your advantage. Don't have a boat hitting a bridge; have it bopping a bridge. I cite that just because it is a headline I remember writing way back when. Don't have Tonya Harding *leaving* her ex-husband; have her *dumping* her ex-husband. Well, that may not be the best example, but I had to get Tonya in here somewhere.

And please, I beg you, avoid clichés. Avoid them like the plague. Avoid them as if there is no tomorrow. Really. That's the long and short of it. No matter how things ebb and flow, or which way the wind is blowing. If you avoid them, it will be a whole new ballgame. The only times clichés are allowed in heads, it seems to me, is when you're making fun of clichés. And you can take that to the bank.

If you do all of that and heed the excellent lessons in this chapter, you can write marvelous headlines such as these:

Head for the heels, Imelda Marcos is coming to town
(Pittsburgh Press)

If you take Amish from famished you get fed
(Toledo Blade)

Hospital workers told to drag their butts outside
(A no-smoking story from Tampa Tribune)

And can avoid ones such as this:

Chargers may lose Butts for the rest of the year
(Butts in this case was running back Marion Butts … although they did lose him for the rest of the season.)

Peter Bhatia

Peter Bhatia is executive editor of the Portland Oregonian. He came to the paper in November 1993 and has since helped lead its conversion to a team-based newsroom structure.

Previously, he was executive editor of The Fresno Bee, managing editor of The Sacramento Bee, editor of the York (Pa.) Dispatch and Sunday News, managing editor of the Dallas Times Herald, deputy managing editor of the San Francisco Examiner and a reporter and editor at The Spokesman-Review in Spokane, Wash.

Bhatia serves on the board of directors of the American Society of Newspaper Editors and was program chair for its 1999 convention in San Francisco. He served two terms on the board of the Associated Press Managing Editors organization and served four times as a Pulitzer-Prize juror. He has been an editor on three Pulitzer-winning projects. He is a native of Pullman, Wash., and a graduate of Stanford University. His wife, Elizabeth Dahl, is a journalist. They have two children, Megan and Jay.

Suggestions for additional reading

Bernstein, Theodore M. *Watch Your Language.* New York: Atheneum, 1976.

Garst, Robert F., and Theodore M. Bernstein. *Headlines and Deadlines,* 3rd ed. New York: Columbia University Press, 1961.

"Heads Up! A collection of good heads from around the country." American Copy Editors Society. Online. Available: http://www.copydesk.org. Jan. 10, 1999.

"The Lower Case," a regular department in Columbia Journalism Review, published bimonthly by the Columbia University Graduate School of Journalism.

Walsh, Bill. *The Slot.* Online. Available: http://www.theslot.com/. Jan. 10, 1999.

Exercises

1. Read at least one issue of the Columbia Journalism Review, especially the inside back cover, which features "The Lower Case," a collection of awkward headlines cited by the editors. Then skim the headlines in several newspapers and bring to class the best candidates for a place in "The Lower Case."

2. For each of the following words, list at least three synonyms that would take less space:

   a. `falsehood`

   b. `organization`

   c. `contributor`

3. Shorten each of the following phrases:

   a. `during the time`

   b. `on the order of`

   c. `at that time`

   d. `due to the fact`

   e. `a softly blowing wind`

   f. `attain victory`

4. The two headlines below have "bad breaks," or awkward line splits. Rewrite each one to keep verb phrases together on one line and to keep modifiers and the words they modify on the same line. Don't worry about the count, but try to keep all lines about the same length.

   a. **Provost will
   resign today**

   b. **Russia may
   ratify new
   treaty today**

5. Rewrite these headlines to remove unproven accusations:

   a. **Child murderer goes on trial**

   b. **Cops nab 40 hoods in gambling raid**

6. Rewrite this headline to correct unattributed opinion:

**Regents hit students
with stiff tuition**

The Board of Regents today set tuition for next year at $2,000, an increase of 12 percent more than the current level.

7. Correct the punctuation in these headlines:

a. **Mayor opposes tax cut;
prepares new budget.**

b. **"President is doing a good job",
head of veterans group says.**

c. **"President doing good job":
Vets chairman**

d. **Tennessee beats Kentucky;
claims SEC championship**

e. **State assembly votes no on death
penalty bill, and ends session**

8. Show correct capitalization for downstyle headlines:

a. **President Signs Trade Treaty With Japan**

b. **Educators Consider Ways to Combat Illiteracy**

9. Refer to the headline-writing rules discussed in this chapter. Then, without considering the count, explain why each of the following headlines is poor:

a. **School board plans to
study admission policy**

b. **Fair manager tells plans for fair**

c. **Beat grandmother, three children**

d. **Kidnap victim trys to identify captors**

e. **Ashdown, Smith spar in
second campaign debate**

f. **Inmate escaped from prison farm**

g. **Council passes sales
tax despite protest**

10. Use the standard headline-counting method explained in this chapter to give the count for this headline:

**Amityville horror real,
psychic detectives say**

11. Refer to the headline schedule in Figure 9-3 to give the maximum number of units for each line of these headline assignments. Remember, the first number refers to the number of columns; the second number is the point size of the type; the third number is the number of lines in the headline.

    a. 2-48-2 _____

    b. 1-24-3 _____

    c. 5-60-1 _____

    d. 4-36-2 _____

12. Use the standard headline-counting method explained in this chapter to give the count for this headline:

**Governor summons
special session**

Does the headline above fit properly for a 2-48-2 headline assignment? If not, change it so each line will be within the maximum count and no shorter than two units less than the maximum count.

13. Here are four news stories that need headlines. You will find a headline assignment at the top of each story. Refer to the headline schedule in Figure 9-3. Practice writing your heads on scrap paper; then transcribe the completed version to the appropriate place at the top of each story.

    a. 2-30-2:

A 62-year-old man, blinded in a traumatic accident nine years ago, regained his sight after he was struck by lightning near his home, his wife and doctor said yesterday.

Doctors confirmed that Edwin E. Robinson, a former truck driver, could see for the first time since he became blind as the result of a spectacular highway accident nine years ago.

"It (his sight) isn't completely restored," Robinson's wife, Doris, said. "But he can see straight in front of him, which he hasn't been able to do in nine years.

"You read about things like this, but you can't really believe them," she said.

Robinson was knocked to the ground by lightning Wednesday when he took shelter under a tree during an afternoon thunderstorm. After 20 minutes, he managed to climb to his feet, said Mrs. Robinson, who found him in his bedroom later that afternoon.

"I can see you! I can see you! I can see the house! I can read!" she quoted him as saying. She also said he was able to hear perfectly well without his hearing aid.

Dr. William F. Taylor examined Robinson yesterday and confirmed that he had regained both sight and hearing. Calling it "one for the books," Dr. Taylor said the rubber-soled shoes Robinson was wearing when he was struck by the lightning may have saved his life.

Robinson's ophthalmologist, Dr. Albert Moulton, of Portland, Ore., attributed the dramatic event to trauma.

"It was traumatic when he lost his sight, so maybe his sight was restored by this trauma. Anything is possible," Dr. Moulton said.

Mrs. Robinson said she was being deluged with calls from friends and well-wishers who heard about her husband's recovery.

b. 3-24-1:

KUWAIT—Five Muslim fundamentalists offended by a "Hagar the Horrible" cartoon burst into the offices of an English-language newspaper Saturday and chased an editor out of the building at gunpoint.

The five were captured, one by a worker at the daily Arab Times and the others by police after a car chase, an Interior Ministry statement said. No one was injured.

The U.S. comic strip, about a boorish but lovable Viking and his eccentric family, showed Hagar on a hill saying: "I pray and pray, but you never answer me."

A voice from the clouds answers: "Sorry if you don't get through right away, keep trying. These days everyone wants to talk to me."

Many Muslims saw the cartoon as sacrilegious. A magazine published by a group of fundamentalist Sunni Muslims said the comic strip was "mocking God and communication between humans and their God."

The Al-Mujtama magazine accused the newspaper's non-Muslim employees of poking fun at Kuwait's laws and religion.

The newspaper ran an apology Thursday, 11 days after the cartoon appeared. It said the "inclusion of the cartoon was inappropriate but unintentional and done without malice."

"They took the mistake and turned it into a conspiracy," said the paper's American managing editor, Tadeusz Karwecki. "Everyone makes mistakes, but you don't go out and shoot people for them."

c. 2-24-3:

Jacques Bailly, a 14-year-old eighth-grade student from Denver, yesterday won the National Spelling Bee by correctly spelling "elucubrate."

Jacques got his chance when Paige Pipkin, a 12-year-old seventh grader from El Paso, Texas, missed on "glitch." She spelled it "glitsch."

After Jacques properly spelled "glitch," he breezed through "elucubrate" before pronouncer Richard Baker could provide the definition.

Jacques is no stranger to elucubration—laborious work, especially at night or by candlelight.

"Well, you read a lot and you work a lot," he said, explaining his secret of success.

Jacques and Paige were the top of 112 finalists who came to Washington for the 53rd annual competition sponsored by Scripps Howard Newspapers.

Jacques spelled "auburn," "finesse," "maladroit," "nimiety," "juratory," "davit," "abecedarian," "frijoles," "blatherskite," "wassail" and "halcyon" to reach the final face-off.

Jacques won $1,000 and a loving cup. Paige won $500.

d. 4-48-1 with 4-30-1 underline:

WASHINGTON—More than two-thirds of Americans believe television contributes to violence, erodes family values and fosters a distrust of government, according to a new poll released Saturday.

The public also is troubled by increasingly graphic portrayals of sex during prime time, said the poll, which will appear in the U.S. News & World Report issue on newsstands Monday.

Nearly 80 percent of Hollywood executives questioned by mail in a separate survey agreed there was a link between TV violence and violence in real life, but they were not nearly as concerned about TV's role in other social problems.

Fifty-three percent of the executives said TV contributed to distrust of government, and 46 percent thought it contributed to the decline of family values. Thirty-four percent believe TV played some role in America's divorce rate.

One thousand adults were interviewed for the poll, which had a margin of error of plus or minus 3 percent. U.S. News said 570 of the 6,500 Hollywood executives who received the mail surveys responded to them. "It is not a scientific survey, but the total number of responses was significant and suggests that many Hollywood leaders are concerned about trends in the television business," the magazine said.

Eighty-four percent of the general public said they were concerned about the relationship of extramarital sex on TV and real-life problems. In contrast, 43 percent of the Hollywood executives said they were concerned.

Seventy-five percent of the public said they were concerned about the portrayal of passionate encounters and heavy kissing on TV, compared to 28 percent of Hollywood leaders.

When asked about the solutions they would favor, 95 percent of both groups agreed that parental supervision was the most important step, the magazine said.

"Strong majorities also supported the installation of a V-chip on TV sets to allow parents to block out shows to which they object," the magazine said. "Eighty-three percent of the public backed the V-chip, and 62 percent of the Hollywood elite did."

To examine the kinds of messages the public receives over TV, the magazine looked at a week's worth of prime-time programs on ABC, CBS, NBC and the Fox networks in mid-March.

Of the 58 shows monitored, almost half contained sexual acts or references to sex, U.S. News said.

"Sexual innuendo and scatological humor are rampant even during the 8 p.m.-to-9 p.m. slot that used to be reserved for family-friendly programming," the magazine said.

14. The following headlines appeared in various newspapers in the United States. Can you find fault with any of them? Identify any problems in conceptual terms.

    a.   **Gorillas vow to kill Khomeini**

    b.   **School chief hears offer in men's room**

    c.   **Volcano killed by suffocation**

    d.   **Police brutality postponed**

    e.   **Court orders church to produce woman**

    f.   **British aide says all inmates to gain now that fast over**

    g.   **State provides motorists with winter conditions**

    h.   **Excess of vitamins harmful, expensive specialist warns**

    i.   **Airport commission to consider holding hearing on runway**

    j.   **Shuttle passes test; a worker is killed**

    k.   **Museums utilizing TV to attack visitors**

    l.   **Defendant's speech ends in long sentence**

    m.   **Jury is still out on composting toilets**

Readers depend on their newspapers to not only provide interesting pictures, but to tell them what is happening, to explain all parts of a picture that might puzzle them and to make certain they have a clear understanding of what the photo is portraying.

—*Jenk Jones Jr., Tulsa (Okla.) Tribune*

Editing Pictures and Infographics

THE term *visual journalist* has assumed increased importance for both print and online publications at the dawn of the 21st century. The concept of repackaging the news to attract new readers and to regain former subscribers has sparked a flurry of redesign projects. Generally, redesigns, like Web pages, call for shorter stories and increased use of visual elements to help produce "reader-friendly" products. Journalists skillful at communicating information quickly and clearly have gained enhanced status in newsrooms.

Better visuals through teamwork

Marty Petty, of the Hartford Courant, speaking at an American Press Institute seminar, said the visual journalist of the future will be a hybrid reporter-editor-artist:

> The artists producing news graphics must also strengthen their journalistic skills. Newspapers will shift responsibility for the basic one-column and two-column chart, graph or map to the layout desks, copy editors and maybe reporters and origination editors. We will rely on them to have advanced computer skills, solid reporting and research skills and analytical skills as well as possibly a specialization in illustration. . . .
>
> The graphics editor, art director and photo editor will play much more active roles in planning the news sections, news packages and special sections. Technology will make the execution of their traditional tasks simple and fast, and increase the number of graphics on our pages. Again, solid journalistic skills will be a first priority for them as well as a complete understanding of the production process. They will need to know how to build data for expanded news packages and graphics.

Typically, copy editors at newspapers, magazines or public relations firms exercise little or no influence during the initial planning for visual elements to accompany a story or story package. The traditional process calls for staff or free-lance photographers to produce photographs to accompany a story and deliver hard copy or digital images to a photo editor or assigning editor. That editor, sometimes in consultation with the photographer, selects individual photographs for publication. At this point, the copy editor first becomes involved in the process, cropping and scaling the pictures to fit page layouts and then writing cutlines or editing captions written by the photographers. The traditional process for informational graphics and other visual elements is similar.

As noted earlier in this book, management strategy today increasingly emphasizes a team approach that involves workers at every stage of product development, whether the final products are automobiles, printed materials or Web sites. Now, instead of the old Life magazine procedure in which photographers had absolutely no control over their pictures after shooting them, photographers today often work closely with reporters, writers, editors and page designers throughout the process: generating story ideas, planning the most effective methods for gathering information and combining text and visuals to package information clearly and concisely.

Selecting pictures

Rob Heller, a design consultant and photography teacher, suggests that photographers give special attention to these elements, and the same advice applies to copy editors when selecting pictures for publication:

▶**Point of view.** Always look for a more interesting angle from which to take the photograph. High or low angles can present the world in a unique way.

▶**Subject contrast.** Make sure that the subject stands out from the background. Dark against light or light against dark allows the viewer to distinguish the important parts of the photograph.

▶**Framing.** Examine all parts of the frame very carefully as you look through the viewfinder. This is the time to look for distracting elements such as a telephone pole coming out of a subject's head.

▶**Lighting.** The lighting should enhance the photograph, not detract from it. Stay away from flat, frontal lighting. Look for more interesting light from the side or back of the subject.

▶**Camera-to-subject distance.** An overall or long shot establishes the location of an event. A medium shot describes the action. A close-up examines the details of a situation. Shoot all three to give coverage as complete as possible.

▶**Decisive moments.** Make sure to always tell the story of an event or news situation. Try to capture the decisive moment, the instant when all the above elements come together to form a powerful photograph.

The procedures for showing photographs to editors vary from publication to publication. Some photographers make *contact prints*, proofs of the negatives that are the same size as the negatives themselves. Although small, they are easily inspected with a *linen tester*, a small 8- or 10-power magnifying glass. Editors work from contact prints to select the photographs to be printed. The prints are usually enlarged to 8 inches by 10 inches, although some economy-minded publications use 5-inch-by-7-inch prints. At other publications, the photographer may skip the contact prints and make 8 × 10 or 5 × 7 prints of the best photographs. Increasingly, digital photography is replacing film and photographic prints on paper. In a digital environment, editors display multiple small pictures on their computer screens, select those to be published and then electronically crop and size them.

The primary goals of photojournalism are used by editors and photographers in making picture selections:

- To communicate effectively, as either stand-alone art or accompaniment to a story

- To attract readers' attention and provide a point of entry to the page

- To enhance the overall appearance of the page

Space is a valuable commodity, so editors must choose wisely in allocating that space. Will a photograph best accomplish the goals within limited space, or should an informational graphic be used? Or perhaps a sidebar to accompany the main story?

Criteria that make a story newsworthy also apply to picture selection:

▶**Impact.** Pictures that illustrate events and situations with an impact on many people are more likely to be published than pictures with limited scope.

▶**Unusualness.** Shots of an unusual happening or pictures taken from unusual angles or that use different approaches to routine events win favor with editors.

▶**Prominence.** Readers like to see photographs of famous and infamous people.

▶**Action.** Modern cameras, with fast shutter speeds and high-speed film, allow photographers to freeze action. Editors may be compelled to use an occasional "grip and grin" or lineup photo, especially in small-town papers, but such trite pictures are largely a relic.

▶**Proximity.** People want to see pictures of their friends and neighbors, of people in their own community. Other factors being equal, editors give the nod to local photographs over wire photos.

▶**Conflict.** Just as conflict makes an event or situation worth writing about, it also adds to the value of photographs. But editors must guard against selecting a conflict-filled photo that distorts an event. It would be poor news judgment, for example, to publish a photo of a minor fight that was an isolated incident at an otherwise peaceful event.

▶**Timeliness.** In judging the timeliness of photographic coverage, editors must consider whether readers are still interested in something that happened last week or even just this morning. Television also influences newspaper photo selection, because editors seek to publish pictures different from those seen on television.

▶**Technical quality.** A blurry, out-of-focus print rarely attracts a second look from photo editors—unless its news value vastly outweighs its poor quality. Pictures of the first moon landing and the assassination of President John F. Kennedy are among the rare examples of news value overcoming poor technical quality.

Preparing photographs for publication

Once the responsible editor has selected photos and other illustrations, the art must be cropped, sized and scaled for the production department. In addition, photographs sometimes need to be retouched.

Cropping

If working with hard copy rather than digital images, everyone who handles photographs and other artwork should do so with care. Fingerprints and smudge marks may show up when the art is published, so keep it clean. Never cut a picture to eliminate unwanted parts. Instead, use a wax or soft-lead pencil to mark, with both horizontal and vertical lines, the part of the photograph that should be reproduced. These *crop marks,* as they are called, can be erased and changed if necessary.

Never write on the face of a photograph. Place crop marks in the margins of the photo, and write instructions to the production department on the back of the picture or on an instruction tag attached to the picture. To write on the back of a picture, use a grease pencil or soft-lead pencil. A ball point pen or hard-lead pencil may crack the glossy face of the photograph or show through.

To crop a picture is to decide how much or what part of a print should be published. Editors crop to eliminate busy backgrounds, people who are superfluous to the photo's theme and other elements that distract from the picture's center of interest.

Begin cropping by covering up parts of the photo that contain no information or irrelevant information. What remains will have greater impact if reproduced at an adequate size.

To help decide how the picture should be cropped, editors often frame the picture with a rectangle formed between extended thumbs and forefingers, with strips of paper or with "cropping angles" designed for this purpose.

Keep in mind the following guidelines when cropping photographs:

- Avoid cropping pictures in fancy or irregular shapes unless there is an unusual and compelling reason for doing so.

- For head shots, most editors prefer to leave some space on the side that the subject faces. At a few newspapers and magazines, however, all head shots—also called mug shots—are cropped extremely tightly, so that ears and sometimes the top of the subject's head are trimmed.

- For an action picture—for example, a racing boat or a runner—leave space in front of the thrust of the action.

- Body parts can be cropped, but avoid amputating at joints such as ankles, knees, wrists or elbows.

- Remain sensitive to the mood or atmosphere captured in the photograph. Avoid tight cropping if background elements help tell the story.

- Consider that extreme enlargements will reduce picture quality. If the layout calls for a large photo, avoid cropping and enlarging just a small portion of the original. Select a different picture for that particular layout.

Figure 10-1 shows how to place crop marks and how cropping affects the image's impact.

Scaling

After a photo is cropped for its greatest impact, the next step is to scale it to fit the desired page layout. Other terms for scaling are *proportioning* and *sizing*. Few publications print photographs or draw artwork "to size," meaning the exact size that they will appear in the finished publication. Deadline considerations preclude a return to the darkroom to print photographs to size after page layouts are

Original photo with crop marks

Figure 10-1
Crop marks are placed in the margins of the photograph, along both the horizontal and the vertical dimensions. Cropping a photograph gives it greater impact.

Anxious moments during championship game

Cropped photo as it appears in print

completed; in fact, layouts for the latest news and sports pages often are finished only minutes before press time. Thus, publications that still work with film and hard-copy prints rather than digital images generally use 8×10 or 5×7 glossy prints and scale them for enlargement or reduction (called the *reproduction* size).

Proportion is the key concept in enlarging or reducing photographs. A vertical picture cannot fit a horizontal space on the layout, unless, of course, the picture can be cropped to make it horizontal. In an ideal world, the person who does the page layout has a variety of excellent photographs to select from and, knowing that the desired shape is available, can design an attractive page.

But this isn't an ideal world. Often the layout editor has no choice about the shape of the photograph and must plan the layout accordingly. The layout editor can choose, however, to enlarge or reduce the photo.

Editors can figure the enlargement or reduction size while maintaining proportionality in one of four ways:

- Compute it with a mathematical formula

- Use a mechanical scaling device, such as a proportioning wheel or slide ruler

- Apply the diagonal-line method

- Work from digital images with computer software like Adobe Photoshop, PageMaker or QuarkXPress

   A ruler, preferably one calibrated in picas, is needed for the first three methods.

Regardless of the method used, remember to work with the dimensions of the photograph or other artwork *as cropped*. If part of an 8×10 photo has been cropped, then the part of the picture that has been eliminated is not used in figuring the new size. After cropping, when we speak of the ***original*** or ***present*** size, we mean the cropped size, the size within the crop marks.

▶**Formula method.** The formula method is simple and requires no special tools other than a ruler. The three known dimensions (the width and depth of the original photo and one of the dimensions of the reproduction size) are plugged into this formula:

$$\frac{\text{Reproduction width}}{\text{Original width (as cropped)}} = \frac{\text{Reproduction depth}}{\text{Original depth (as cropped)}}$$

This formula can be applied to any unit of measurement: inches, picas, feet, and so on.

In addition to the reproduction dimensions, the production department must know the percentage of reduction or enlargement. This figure should be written on the back of the picture or on an instruction tag attached to the photo. To determine the percentage of reduction or enlargement use this formula:

$$\frac{\text{Reproduction width (or depth)}}{\text{Original width (or depth), as cropped}}$$

When computing the percentage, mentally check to be sure that the percentage is "going in the right direction." If the published art is to be smaller than the original art, the percentage should be less than 100 percent. If the original is to be enlarged in the published version, the percentage should be more than 100 percent.

Percentage errors occur if the formula is turned upside down. Comparing depth and width instead of the same dimensions (depth with depth or width with width) will also produce an incorrect percentage of reproduction. Measuring in picas rather than inches eliminates calculating with fractions. Although the figures for dimensions in picas will be larger than when calculating in inches, multiplying and dividing whole numbers is easier than working with fractions with different denominators. It is permissible to round off dimensions to the nearest one-half pica.

People who are inexperienced at scaling photographs sometimes become confused when their task is reversed and they start with the reproduction size. This reversal occurs when the layout is completed before the art is scaled. Assuming that the layout editor did not lay out a horizontal space for a vertical picture that can't be suitably cropped, this assignment should pose no difficulty.

The first step is to determine one of the artwork's original dimensions. Measure the dimension that is least flexible (the dimension that cannot be cropped or that can be cropped the least). Now you have three of the dimensions: reproduction width, reproduction depth, and either original depth or original width.

Plug these known dimensions into the formula. The fourth dimension can be figured readily. Once you have the fourth dimension, do not forget to crop the original photograph accordingly.

▶**Proportioning wheel.** A scaling device such as a proportioning wheel uses the same principle as the formula method. But the proportioning wheel is more commonly used, because it eliminates the need to multiply and divide. Several companies produce proportioning wheels, most with directions for their use printed on the wheel itself.

The wheel consists of two circular pieces of cardboard or plastic, one slightly smaller than the other. The pieces are attached in the center so they can revolve. Calibrations, which can represent any unit of measurement, are printed on the rim of each circle. In addition, a cutout area near the center of the wheel indicates the percentage of original size.

To operate the wheel, an editor first crops the artwork and measures the dimensions within the crop marks. Then the known reproduction dimension, usually the width, is located on the outer circle of the wheel and lined up with its counterpart dimension of the original photo, as cropped, on the inner circle. In that alignment, the two measurements of the other dimension, usually the depth, align—original dimension on the inner circle, reproduction dimension on the outer circle. An arrow in the window of the wheel points to the percentage of reduction or enlargement. (See Figures 10-2 and 10-3.)

Figure 10-2
This illustration explains how to use a proportioning wheel and a mathematical formula to compute the reproduction size and percentage of a photograph.

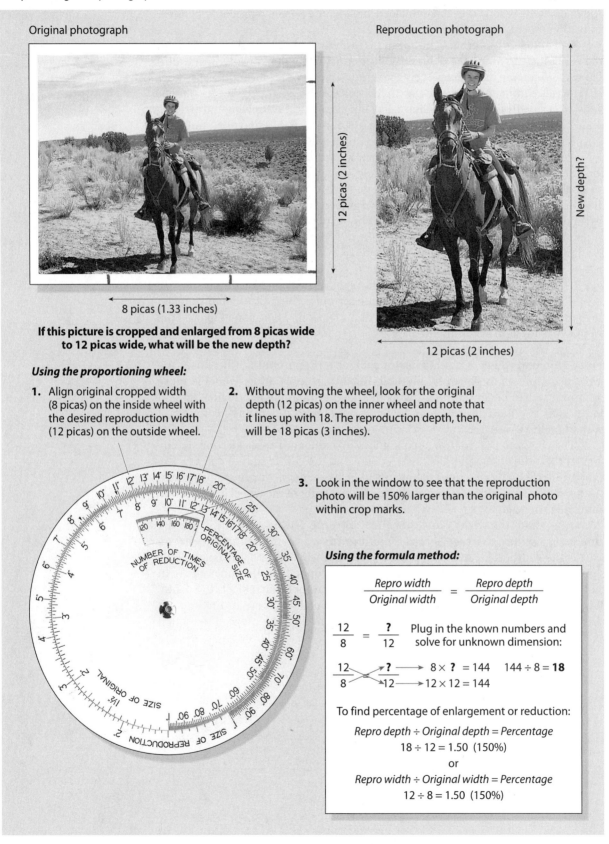

Original photograph

Reproduction photograph

12 picas (2 inches)

New depth?

8 picas (1.33 inches)

12 picas (2 inches)

If this picture is cropped and enlarged from 8 picas wide to 12 picas wide, what will be the new depth?

Using the proportioning wheel:

1. Align original cropped width (8 picas) on the inside wheel with the desired reproduction width (12 picas) on the outside wheel.

2. Without moving the wheel, look for the original depth (12 picas) on the inner wheel and note that it lines up with 18. The reproduction depth, then, will be 18 picas (3 inches).

3. Look in the window to see that the reproduction photo will be 150% larger than the original photo within crop marks.

Using the formula method:

$$\frac{Repro\ width}{Original\ width} = \frac{Repro\ depth}{Original\ depth}$$

$$\frac{12}{8} = \frac{?}{12}$$ Plug in the known numbers and solve for unknown dimension:

$$\frac{12}{8} \begin{array}{c} ? \\ 12 \end{array}$$ $8 \times ? = 144$ $144 \div 8 = \mathbf{18}$
$12 \times 12 = 144$

To find percentage of enlargement or reduction:

Repro depth ÷ Original depth = Percentage
$18 \div 12 = 1.50$ (150%)
or
Repro width ÷ Original width = Percentage
$12 \div 8 = 1.50$ (150%)

Figure 10-3
This editor is using a proportioning wheel to size a photograph for publication. (Photograph by Tom Farrington, San Diego State University/ courtesy of the San Diego Union-Tribune)

▶**Diagonal-line method.** The diagonal-line method is yet another way to scale photographs. Place a sheet of clear plastic or a sheet of onion-skin paper over the photograph. Place the overlay with its edge aligned with the vertical crop marks on the left side of the photograph. Draw a diagonal line from the top left of the cropped photo to the bottom right, again at the crop mark. The vertical and horizontal dimensions of any right angle intersecting on the diagonal will be in proportion to the original photograph.

Some editors prefer this method because it allows them to keep the art in view throughout the process. However, the other two methods are more popular and less cumbersome. If you decide to use the diagonal-line method, it is worth investing in a commercial plastic overlay instead of using onion-skin paper. The commercial overlays have inches or picas marked along both the vertical and horizontal axes and come with a diagonal piece or a string attached at the upper left corner that can be rotated to the proper position. For newspaper use, some of the commercial overlays are ruled in column widths.

Digital images

Proportioning wheels and diagonal-line scaling devices may soon become as obsolete as Linotype machines, once used to set type. Cameras that use film, darkroom chemicals and light-sensitive paper may also be relegated to museums, replaced by digital cameras and electronic darkrooms and picture desks. Digital cameras capable of producing maximum quality printing are still too expensive for many news and public relations organizations, but scanners have become widespread.

Scanning photographs or other art is relatively simple. Using a scanner linked to a computer, open the scanner and place the image on the glass bed. To view the image on computer, activate the image editing software program that accompanies the scanner. The image should appear on the computer screen, ready for you to crop and size.

Click on the "scan" icon, and the scanner lights up and electronically converts the hard copy image into pixels (picture elements). The more pixels a scanner can capture, the greater the image quality, referred to as *resolution*, or *pixels per inch*, referred to as *ppi.*

When the scan is complete, the software program will prompt you to name and save the electronic file to a disk or computer hard drive. Common file formats are *TIFF* (Tagged Image File Format), *EPS* (Encapsulated PostScript), *GIF* (Graphics Interchange Format) and *JPEG* or *JPG* (Joint Photographic Experts Group). Typically, the next step involves importing the image to a page layout, using pagination software such as QuarkXPress or PageMaker. Pagination software allows still more changes to image sizes and shapes.

The dog photo below was electronically scanned, cropped and enlarged.

Original scan

Scan cropped and reproduced at 100% (original size)

50% of original size

200% of original size

If you enlarge or reduce artwork without keeping it in proportion, your image will be dimensionally distorted.

Editing informational graphics

Those ubiquitous charts, graphs, diagrams and maps on printed materials and Web sites are called *informational graphics.* They serve at least two important purposes: to convey information in a visual, easy-to-understand form and to add color and variety to a page. Graphics skills, like copy editing expertise, are in high demand throughout the publishing industry today because of the increased value placed on good informational graphics—also called infographics.

Several factors account for the graphics explosion in all media, particularly newspapers:

▶ **Need to attract larger audiences.** Advertising and circulation revenues are based on audience size, so print and broadcast media, as well as a print-broadcast hybrid medium like the Internet, compete with each other and with expanded leisure-time activities for public attention.

▶ **Changes in reading habits.** People are busier than ever. They have become "scanners," moving through a newspaper or magazine rather quickly, glancing at headlines and art, stopping less frequently than in the past to read articles or look at advertising. Layout editors and designers strive for eye-catching elements, called *points of entry* to get readers to "enter" a page.

▶ **New technology.** What high-speed cameras and film and offset printing were to photojournalism in the 1960s, developments in color reproduction, computers, computer software and laser printers were to graphics in the 1980s. Relatively inexpensive scanners, digital cameras, more complex imaging software and the growth of the Internet in the 1990s further broadened the appeal of dazzling graphics, even adding movement to the mix. Satellite technology and computers linked by phone modems permit fast transmission of computer graphics from news services to individual publications. Desktop publishing is the norm for newsletters and brochures created by public relations firms, and small newspapers without in-house artists can brighten their pages with computer graphics created by non-artist staff members.

▶ **Example of USA Today.** USA Today entered the market in 1982 with extensive color and graphics, a formula layout and uncommonly short news stories. The newspaper did not win universal critical acclaim, but it did attract attention. Other newspapers copied its graphics techniques, especially the color weather map.

Advice for graphic artists

The process of creating an infographic varies, of course, from publication to publication and from artist to artist. Graphic artist Martin Gehring emphasizes the importance of early and ongoing communication among reporters, editors and artists on each assignment that has graphic potential. If the artist is involved at the time the reporter begins working on the story, graphic possibilities are less likely to be overlooked, and the artist will have more time to produce high-quality graphic art.

Speaking to students in an editing class at the University of Tennessee, Gehring explained a 12-step process artists can use to help themselves think visually and produce infographics:

1. *Listen.* Talk with the reporter and editors working on the story. Listen carefully and take notes. Try to understand as much as possible about the story at the time the reporter begins working on it.

2. *Question.* Ask the reporter and editors for their ideas about the kind of art that might accompany the story. Brainstorm with them. What tone should the graphic use? How many pieces of art are needed? What is the deadline? What is the working title for the infographic?

3. *Believe.* Believe that you can produce work to accompany this particular story better than anyone else can.

4. *Gather information.* Reporters and editors should supply you with information as well as printed material available from interview sources. Reporters should remember to ask their sources for such materials, including maps, diagrams, reports and statistics. Even though the reporter may not plan to use these materials in the story, they can be immensely valuable to you. Also get a copy of the reporter's early drafts of the story. In addition to getting information from the reporter, you will often have to conduct research at a library. Reference librarians at the newspaper library or at a public or university library can be among the artist's best friends.

5. *Think.* After you have the necessary information, you must mull it over and decide how much of the information to present and the most effective way of presenting it to readers. What will communicate best—a bar chart, pie chart, fever chart, table, diagram, map, illustration, photograph or photo illustration?

6. *Write.* Using the working title and ideas gathered during earlier stages in this process, create two lists: a concept list and an emotion list.

7. *Draw.* Create many thumbnail sketches from your concept list. Don't hold back at this stage. Be daring.

8. *Judge.* Sit back, look at your sketches, and decide which one is most appropriate to illustrate the story. Draw a rough sketch of that particular thumbnail to the approximate size that it will be published.

9. *Justify.* Think of all the reasons you can to justify why you used the concept that you chose. Be prepared to present these arguments to your colleagues and your boss.

10. *Show.* Show all of your thumbnail sketches to your colleagues in the art department. Get feedback from these experts. Then select no more than three of the sketches to show the art editor and other editors involved in producing the story. More than three sketches tend to confuse the issue.

11. *Get approval.* Get feedback and make improvements. Finally, get your boss's approval.

12. *Finalize.* Create the final camera-ready art. Then take a break.

Role of the copy editor

The artist may be ready for a break, but the art doesn't go to the production department until the copy editor checks it. Ideally, copy editors are involved in the early stages of creating a graphic, to check the accuracy of information that the artist uses. After the artist delivers the camera-ready art, the copy editor again is called into service to check every aspect of the graphic.

Copy editors should edit informational graphics with the same care they give to stories: Make sure the numbers add up; check the labeling on maps to be sure that cities, states or entire countries haven't been misplaced; look at typefaces to ensure consistent size and style for parallel items. Finally, if the graphic is not drawn to its reproduction size, it will need to be scaled.

Lulu Rodriguez, a researcher at Iowa State University, conducted a content analysis of small newspapers in Iowa and observed the following as the most common mistakes:

■ Violations of chart-making conventions

■ Misrepresentation of data using percentages

■ Non-comparability of data

■ Inappropriateness of charts

■ Overdressed graphs

■ Conflicting information in related text and graphics

First, copy editors should check to see that the graphic contains these five essentials, as shown in Figure 10-4:

■ Headline

■ Explainer

■ Data or body

■ Source of the data

■ Credit line for artist or others

Headline
Easy-to-read label for the graphic

Body
Data, perhaps a drawing or cut-away, or a map; verbal information transformed into visuals

Source
Line that identifies the origin of the information

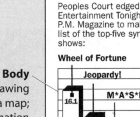
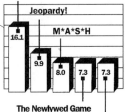

The verdict on syndicated TV

Peoples Court edged Entertainment Tonight and P.M. Magazine to make the list of the top-five syndicated shows:

Wheel of Fortune

Jeopardy!

M*A*S*H

16.1

9.9

8.0

7.3

7.3

The Newlywed Game

Peoples Court

One ratings point represents 859,000 TV households.

Source: Electronic Media, Sept. 15; A.C. Nielsen Co.

GEORGE RORICK/ The Detroit News

Explainer
Short paragraph that explains not only what the graphic is about but why the information is important to the reader; does not restate the obvious facts provided in the visuals but expands on the information or puts it into perspective

Credit
Artists, and very often the researchers or the reporters, who produced the graphic

Figure 10-4
An infographic has five essential elements: headline, body, source, explainer and credit.

Infographics should be able to stand alone, understandable to people who do not read the accompanying story. Guard against overly complex graphics that may confuse readers.

Be sure that the infographic format matches the data. Charts relate numbers to facts, but not all charts effectively illustrate all types of numerical data.

▶**Pie charts** are circles segmented to show the parts composing a whole. Various colors or shadings of gray for each pie slice indicate the portion of the whole allocated to each of its parts. Percentages and labels can be printed on each slice, or a separate legend may be used. A caution: A circle with a large number of slices indicated by subtle shading differences will be difficult to decipher. In that situation, use a different type of infographic.

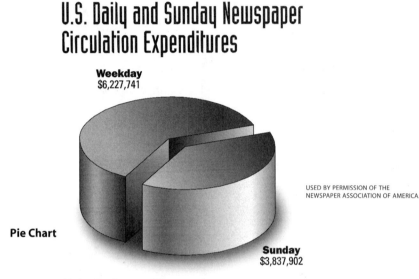

U.S. Daily and Sunday Newspaper Circulation Expenditures

Weekday
$6,227,741

USED BY PERMISSION OF THE
NEWSPAPER ASSOCIATION OF AMERICA.

Pie Chart

Sunday
$3,837,902

NAA Facts About Newspapers 1998

▶**Line charts,** also called fever charts, illustrate how amounts change over time. Time is marked on the horizontal (X) axis, and amounts are shown on the vertical (Y) axis. A caution: The Y axis should begin at zero in most line charts to avoid distortion.

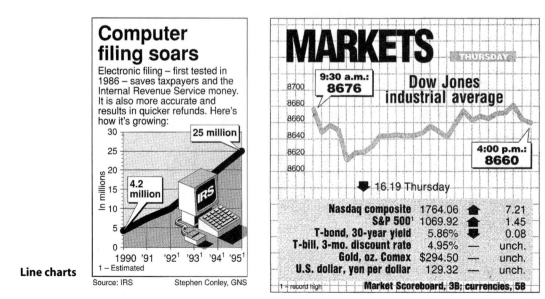

Line charts

Computer filing soars

Electronic filing – first tested in 1986 – saves taxpayers and the Internal Revenue Service money. It is also more accurate and results in quicker refunds. Here's how it's growing:

25 million

4.2 million

In millions

30
25
20
15
10
5
0

1990 '91 '92[1] '93[1] '94[1] '95[1]
1 – Estimated

Source: IRS   Stephen Conley, GNS

MARKETS

THURSDAY

9:30 a.m.:
8676

Dow Jones industrial average

8700
8680
8660
8640
8620
8600

4:00 p.m.:
8660

▼ 16.19 Thursday

Nasdaq composite	1764.06	▲	7.21
S&P 500[1]	1069.92	▲	1.45
T-bond, 30-year yield	5.86%	▼	0.08
T-bill, 3-mo. discount rate	4.95%	—	unch.
Gold, oz. Comex	$294.50	—	unch.
U.S. dollar, yen per dollar	129.32	—	unch.

1 – record high   **Market Scoreboard, 3B; currencies, 5B**

© USA TODAY. REPRINTED WITH PERMISSION.

▶**Bar or column charts** compare sizes of items. The bars may run either horizontally (bars) or vertically (columns) with the varying lengths of bars indicating how categories compare with each other. It is easier to depict numbers less than zero in a bar or column chart than in a line graph. A caution: As with line charts, the scale for a bar chart should be zero-based. If space considerations require a break in the scale, the chart should show the break distinctively to alert readers so that the overall appearance will not be visually deceptive.

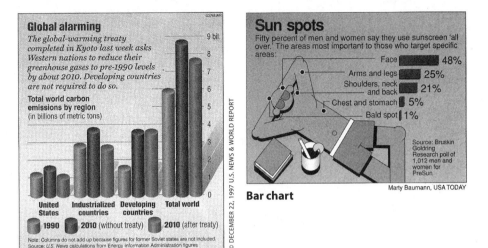

Column chart

Bar chart

As in the previous line and bar charts, other graphic elements such as drawings or symbols may further illustrate a chart, but they should not clutter or distract from the data.

In addition to using the correct format for the data to be illustrated, copy editors need to examine the typefaces for consistency in size and style. Attention should be given to the use of white space within and around the graphic. In the following example, the headline and body type are too small, especially in comparison with the type size of the source line.

Yet another weakness of this graphic is its inappropriate use of a pie chart comprising too many slices so that variations in shading are hard to distinguish and the legend is too complicated. The percentage stated in the body copy is also incorrect.

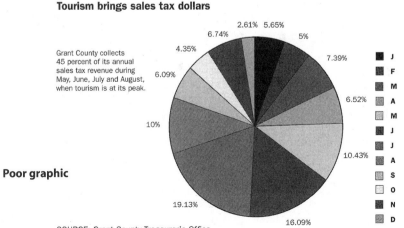

Poor graphic

A line chart, rather than a pie chart, better shows change over time. The same tourism data that was confusing in the previous pie chart is easy to understand in the following line chart. Readers can see immediately which months generated the greatest percentage of tourist dollars.

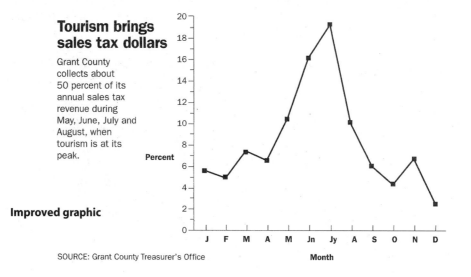

Tourism brings sales tax dollars

Grant County collects about 50 percent of its annual sales tax revenue during May, June, July and August, when tourism is at its peak.

Improved graphic

SOURCE: Grant County Treasurer's Office

The headline and body type sizes are increased, and the copy is correct. Although improved, this infographic is still missing one of the essential elements— a credit line for the artist.

▶**Tables and lists** provide another way of visually depicting facts and figures for fast, easy reading. Newspapers publish many tables and lists every day for sports scores and statistics, stock market quotations and even recipes. Public relations

'Titanic' eludes 'Marshals'

Titanic remained atop the box office for the 12th consecutive week with $17.6 million. This brings the film's total to $449.2 million. *U.S. Marshals* opened in second place with $16.9 million. The top 10:

		Box office (millions) Wkd.	Total	Avg. per screen	Pct. change	Weeks out
1	Titanic	$17.6	$449.2	$5,674	-10%	12
2	U.S. Marshals	$16.9	new	$5,987		
3	The Wedding Singer	$6.2	$57.1	$2,194	-29%	4
4	Twilight	$5.9	new	$4,342		
5	Hush	$5.7	new	$2,921		
6	The Big Lebowski	$5.5	new	$4,585		
7	Good Will Hunting	$5.2	$103.4	$2,525	-22%	14
8	As Good as It Gets	$3.2	$117.2	$1,801	-21%	11
9	Dark City	$2.8	$10.2	$1,618	-49%	2
10	The Borrowers	$2.1	$17.3	$1,312	-27%	4

Source: Exhibitor Relations Co. Inc.

Tables

Thursday's box scores

HEAT 97, CAVS 74

Cleveland	min	fg m-a	ft m-a	rb o-t	a	pf	tp
Henderson	28	2-5	1-2	1-5	0	2	5
Kemp	31	4-14	0-0	3-5	0	1	8
Ilgauskas	23	5-8	1-2	3-6	0	2	11
Person	28	2-8	4-4	0-3	1	1	10
Knight	18	2-5	2-2	0-2	4	0	6
Sura	8	0-3	0-0	1-3	2	0	0
Anderson	34	6-16	2-2	1-3	3	0	16
Potapenko	26	4-9	0-2	2-5	2	5	8
Thomas	19	1-6	0-0	1-1	0	1	3
Brooks	15	2-4	1-2	0-3	0	0	6
Scott	10	0-1	1-2	0-3	0	1	1
TOTALS	240	28-79	12-18	12-39	12	13	74

Percentages: FG-.354, FT-.667. 3-point goals: 6-13, .462 (Person 2-3, Sura 0-1, Anderson 2-4, Thomas 1-4, Brooks 1-1). **Team rebounds:** 9. **Blocked shots:** 4 (Ilgauskas 2, Henderson, Scott). **Turnovers:** 16 (Anderson 3, Henderson 3, Knight 3, Potapenko 2, Thomas 2, Ilgauskas, Person, Sura). **Steals:** 5 (Anderson 2, Person, Scott, Thomas).

Miami	min	fg m-a	ft m-a	rb o-t	a	pf	tp
Majerle	26	5-8	0-0	0-5	3	0	11
Brown	30	4-8	4-6	2-11	2	2	12
Mourning	21	4-10	5-6	3-8	1	4	13
Lenard	21	4-9	0-0	1-1	2	0	9
Hardaway	27	4-14	0-0	0-2	6	1	10
Barry	23	3-5	2-2	0-3	3	3	9
Strickland	22	6-8	1-2	1-3	3	3	13
Causwell	27	2-7	0-2	4-12	0	2	4
Murdock	23	2-8	0-0	0-3	6	3	4
Conlon	12	2-4	0-0	0-2	0	2	4
Walters	8	3-3	0-0	0-1	1	0	7
TOTALS	240	39-84	12-18	11-49	28	18	97

Percentages: FG-.464, FT-.667. 3-point goals: 7-16, .438 (Majerle 1-3, Lenard 1-2, Hardaway 2-6, Barry 2-3, Murdock 0-1, Walters 1-1). **Team rebounds:** 11. **Blocked shots:** 12 (Mourning 4, Causwell 4, Brown 2, Barry, Strickland). **Turnovers:** 12 (Barry 3, Hardaway 2, Mourning 2, Causwell, Conlon, Majerle, Strickland). **Steals:** 8 (Barry 2, Hardaway 2, Brown, Lenard, Majerle, Murdock).

Cleveland	17	15	13	29	—	74
Miami	30	23	18	26	—	97

Flagrant fouls: Cleveland 1 (Ilgauskas, 3:56 2nd). **A:** 15,063. **T:** 2:00. **Officials:** Dan Crawford, McCutchen, Michel.

Wednesday's late boxes

JAZZ 110, KINGS 95

Sacramento	min	fg m-a	ft m-a	rb o-t	a	pf	tp
Williamson	29	8-14	5-6	0-1	1	2	21
Owens	25	3-7	1-2	0-2	2	3	7
Thorpe	24	3-4	0-0	2-2	3	4	6
Richmond	32	6-16	8-9	0-1	2	1	21
Johnson	25	2-4	0-0	1-1	2	4	4
Funderburke	23	6-11	2-4	2-3	1	1	14
Hendrickson	19	3-3	0-0	2-4	3	4	6
Polynice	18	0-2	0-0	0-4	3	3	0
Dehere	23	1-7	0-0	1-2	2	1	3
Robinson	12	4-7	0-0	1-4	1	2	9
Abdl-Wahad	4	1-3	2-2	0-0	0	1	4
Stewart	6	0-1	0-0	0-5	3	0	0
TOTALS	240	37-79	18-23	9-29	23	26	95

Percentages: FG-.468, FT-.783. 3-point goals: 3-10, .300 (Williamson 0-1, Richmond 1-5, Dehere 1-3, Robinson 1-1). **Team rebounds:** 7. **Blocked shots:** 4 (Johnson 2, Stewart 2). **Turnovers:** 8 (Dehere 2, Richmond 2, Williamson, Funderburke, Owens, Robinson). **Steals:** 4 (Owens 2, Robinson, Abdul-Wahad).

Utah	min	fg m-a	ft m-a	rb o-t	a	pf	tp
Keefe	32	4-4	1-3	1-7	4	3	9
Malone	29	11-15	3-6	2-9	9	3	25
Foster	16	1-1	0-0	1-2	1	1	2
Anderson	31	6-8	1-2	0-1	2	3	14
Stockton	23	3-7	2-2	0-2	8	3	16
Eisley	29	2-10	3-3	0-5	5	2	7
Carr	27	1-5	0-0	1-3	0	3	2
Russell	25	5-6	4-4	1-5	2	3	17
Morris	22	3-9	6-6	0-1	0	1	13
Vaughn	6	2-4	1-2	0-1	0	1	5
Hornacek		DNP (sore right knee)					
TOTALS	240	41-69	21-28	6-35	31	24	110

Percentages: FG-.594, FT-.750. 3-point goals: 7-13, .538 (Anderson 1-1, Stockton 2-3, Eisley 0-3, Russell 3-3, Morris 1-3). **Team rebounds:** 11. **Blocked shots:** 7 (Keefe 2, Carr 2, Anderson, Malone, Morris). **Turnovers:** 13 (Malone 4, Anderson 2, Carr 2, Keefe 2, Foster, Stockton, Vaughn). **Steals:** 4 (Anderson, Eisley, Keefe, Malone).

Sacramento	21	24	24	26	—	95
Utah	28	25	33	24	—	110

Technical fouls: Sacramento 1 (Owens, 3:00 3rd). **A:** 19,911. **T:** 1:59. **Officials:** Clark, Fehr, Jones.

NBA LEADERS

Through Wednesday

SCORING

Player, Team	G	FG	FT	Pts	Avg.
Jordan, Chi.	62	658	435	1770	28.5
O'Neal, LA-L.	39	417	223	1057	27.1
Malone, Utah	61	578	451	1608	26.4
Richmond, Sac.	64	508	386	1519	23.7
Robinson, Mil.	56	534	215	1308	23.4
Rice, Cha.	62	484	346	1413	22.8
Webber, Was.	53	499	141	1192	22.5
Robinson, S.A.	56	435	373	1244	22.2
Walker, Bos.	62	533	248	1376	22.2
Abdur-Rahim, Van.	60	471	379	1331	22.2
Finley, Dal.	62	496	248	1313	21.2
Hill, Det.	61	467	349	1285	21.1
Rider, Por.	53	402	184	1091	20.6

REBOUNDING

Player, Team	G	Off	Def	Tot	Avg.
Rodman, Chi.	60	317	580	897	15.0
Williams, N.J.	60	408	411	819	13.7
Barkley, Hou.	57	212	467	679	11.9
Duncan, S.A.	62	203	534	737	11.9
Mutombo, Atl.	61	206	485	691	11.3
Hill, Mil.	52	200	372	572	11.0

SATURDAY'S GAMES

Minnesota at Seattle, 3:30
Washington at Charlotte, 7:30
New York at Cleveland, 7:30
New Jersey at Dallas, 8:30
Sacramento at Houston, 8:30
Chicago at San Antonio, 8:30
Philadelphia at Milwaukee, 9
Portland at Denver, 9

SUNDAY'S GAMES

Miami at Orlando, noon
Utah at Detroit, noon
L.A. Lakers at Vancouver, 3
Boston at Atlanta, 3
Indiana at New York, 7:30
Dallas at Phoenix, 8
Toronto at Golden State, 8
L.A. Clippers at Portland, 10

agencies use them for such items as financial statements in corporate annual reports. Rules or alternate shading are typically used to separate lines of type in a table, especially if the type is set across multiple columns.

▶**Maps** help readers understand the *where* of the story—where it will be warm or cool today; where the accident happened; where the president is traveling. Maps showing weather patterns across the United States are a daily staple of U.S. newspapers. Also common are locator maps used to pinpoint specific geographical areas where an event took place. Locator maps typically combine two graphics: one map to detail the specific area where the action took place—like a neighborhood—and another to relate that location to the overall area—like the city or state containing the neighborhood. (See the San Antonio, Texas, map locator below.)

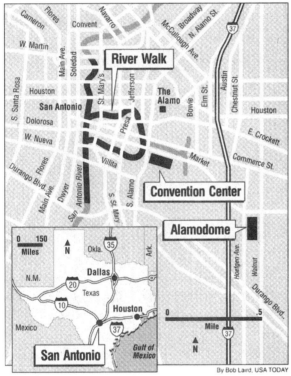

By Bob Laird, USA TODAY

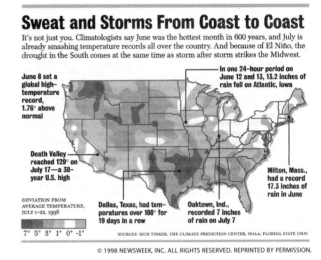

Sweat and Storms From Coast to Coast

It's not just you. Climatologists say June was the hottest month in 600 years, and July is already smashing temperature records all over the country. And because of El Niño, the drought in the South comes at the same time as storm after storm strikes the Midwest.

June 8 set a global high-temperature record, 1.76° above normal

In one 24-hour period on June 12 and 13, 13.2 inches of rain fell on Atlantic, Iowa

Death Valley reached 129° on July 17—a 38-year U.S. high

Milton, Mass., had a record 17.3 inches of rain in June

DEVIATION FROM AVERAGE TEMPERATURE, JULY 1–22, 1998

7° 5° 3° 1° 0° -1°

Dallas, Texas, had temperatures over 100° for 19 days in a row

Oaktown, Ind., recorded 7 inches of rain on July 7

SOURCES: RICH TINKER, THE CLIMATE PREDICTION CENTER, NOAA; FLORIDA STATE UNIV.

Maps

▶**Diagrams** are drawings that help readers understand *what* something is, *how* it works or the sequence of events. Unlike simple charts that copy editors or others without art training can produce with computer tools, diagrams are best left to the talents of skilled artists. Diagrams often require careful study on the part of readers, but, if well executed, they can communicate more information faster than paragraph after paragraph of narrative.

A complex diagram may include dozens of type clusters in addition to a headline and body type. In addition to spelling and grammar accuracy, copy editors need to check type for font and size consistency and study every detail of a diagram to ensure that labels—often in balloon format—are clear and concise.

Anatomy of an Injury

The vertebrae protect the spinal cord, which links the brain to nerves that branch out through the body.

Cervical vertebrae

6th and 7th vertebrae
The site of Sang Lan's injury. Because nerve fibers don't repair themselves, this type of fracture can cause paralysis.

Thoracic vertebrae

Lumbar vertebrae

Diagrams

Mound builders' puzzling legacy

A thousand years before the arrival of Christopher Columbus, the Hopewell – a nation of mound builders – developed a sophisticated culture centered in Ohio but extending west into Iowa, north to Wisconsin and south to St. Louis.

Map area

Ind. | Ohio | Pa.
Mound City | Columbus
Cincinnati | Chillicothe | Marietta
Hopewell Mound | W. Va.
Ky. | Charleston

Mound: ▲

Ind. | Ohio | Pa.
Ky. | Va.

Anatomy of a typical Hopewell mound

- Capped with gravel and pebbles
- Five alternating layers of sand and earth
- A low earth mound
- Ashes, cremated human remains and fragments of artifacts: pottery, copper tools and spearpoints
- Clay platform lined with an inch-deep layer of sand or fine gravel

Size comparison

The largest of the mounds, the Hopewell Mound, was 33 feet tall, 500 feet long and 180 feet wide

The Hopewell Mound

Football field (330 feet long and 159 feet wide)

Source: National Park Service, U.S. Dept. of Interior   Stephen Conley, Gannett News Service

Neonatal intensive care

Here's a look at the care typically given babies in a hospital's neonatal intensive care unit.

1 Infant's first stop
Ohio bed
- An open radiant warming bed
- Heat lamps mounted latterally above infant
- Allows health care team easy access to the infant until he or she is stabilized.

2 Infant's first trip
Transport isolette

3 Infant's first home
Regular isolette
The infant reaches the neonatal intensive care unit and is placed in an isolette and monitored according to the doctor's orders.

Informational graphics sometimes contain multiple visual techniques as illustrated in these prize-winning pages.

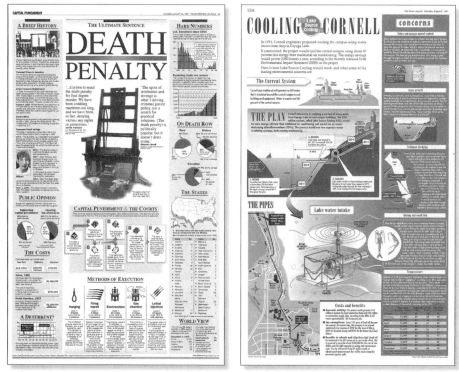

DEAN DIMARZO, POUGHKEEPSIE (N.Y.) JOURNAL   PAULINA REID, THE ITHACA (N.Y.) JOURNAL

Editing captions

The key to fusing words and pictures is to write *to*, not merely *about*, a picture or series of pictures. Many editors write most successfully to a picture by imagining that it is the lead of the story and that the caption, or cutline, is a continuation that explains and amplifies the lead. It is essential, however, that the editor first distinguish the obvious from the obscure.

Responding to an Associated Press Managing Editors survey, one editor wrote

> Photo captions are some of the most important text we write every day. Standards of clarity, good writing, accuracy and completeness are—if anything—higher than for body text. Desk chiefs should give the highest priority to writing photo captions.

Another editor made this observation about the importance of captions:

> The picture captures a moment, but few pictures stand alone and almost all pictures are enhanced by basic information that will help the viewer/reader audience understand the particular moment caught by the image.

In an APME report, compiled by Jenk Jones Jr. of the Tulsa (Okla.) Tribune, editors said that these are the goals in producing well-written captions:

▶**Explain fully.** Few individual pictures exist without the framework of an event. Freezing a particular moment in time freezes only that moment. It tells nothing of the moments and events that preceded that image—or what followed. Only the photographer can place that picture in perspective by providing the necessary background information. In doing so, the photographer becomes more than a photographer; he or she becomes a photojournalist. A good caption includes the outcomes of events such as sporting contests and elections.

▶**Avoid ambiguity.** Explain unusual objects; don't leave the reader wondering. Explain any ambiguities. For example, is the pope laughing or crying? Usually captions should identify anyone whose face is clearly recognizable and who appears to be part of the main action.

▶**Avoid duplication.** One of the most frequent sins of captions is stressing something the picture already has made obvious to the reader; even worse is to state something in the caption that the picture shows is obviously not true. When a picture accompanies a story, it is also foolish to spend much space in the caption duplicating information in the story. Avoid duplicating the headline on the accompanying story.

▶**Be accurate.** Have the photograph in front of you when writing the caption; don't guess or write from memory. You cannot make sure you have everyone identified if you are not looking at the picture. Count the number of names in the caption and make sure that number corresponds with the number of people; look at the crop marks to ensure that those identified in the caption have not been cropped out of the photo.

▶**Make it interesting.** Tell it with punch, with sound descriptive words. The same standards used for writing stories should be used in writing captions. Don't ramble, and use the active voice. The key details should come near the beginning of the caption. Make captions short, but do not write them like telegrams. Eliminate such references as *is shown, is pictured* and *pictured above.*

▶**Pay attention to verb tense.** Generally, a caption for an action picture starts with a sentence in the present tense. This practice is in keeping with the idea of fusing words and picture. The photographer has captured a moment in time, and the words that enhance the moment should be in the present tense to heighten the effect. However, sentences that are more indirectly related to the picture—references, for example, to the subject's actions at another time—are usually written in the past tense. A cardinal rule is that verb tense should never be changed within a sentence. Editors and reporters should distinguish between action pictures and posed pictures. Action is in the present; posed is from the past.

▶**Avoid editorializing.** "Club-swinging police officer" may cast a shadow on the officer, but "eyes blazing defiance, the protester" may shift prejudice in the opposite direction. Let the reader make value judgments from the look of the clubs and the eyes. Don't describe a picture as *beautiful, dramatic* or *grisly* or use any of the other colorful adjectives. Let the viewer decide. Don't use facial expression to try to interpret what the photographic subject was feeling or thinking.

▶**Avoid libel.** People can be libeled in a photo caption just as in text and headline copy.

▶**Achieve a compatible tone between photo and caption.** It is just as jarring to read a tragic story and see a smiling face in an accompanying photo as it is to read a caption that is out of tone with the photo. Don't try to be light and bright in the caption unless the photo warrants. Again, look at the photo while writing the caption.

▶**Be honest with readers.** Point out anything unusual about the way the picture was made, particularly if perspective has been altered, magnification is extreme, a wide-angle lens was used, or the photo was taken under unusual lighting conditions. If file pictures are used and the time lag is relevant, let readers know.

Picture stories

Good picture stories are like picture essays: Both must be planned. Great picture stories require a theme or central idea before the photographer starts work. Certainly happy accidents can result from haphazard shooting, but experience teaches that a good picture story is developed rather than stumbled upon.

A good picture story is usually created by

- Choosing a dominant picture
- Avoiding the cluttered look that results from crowding too many pictures into the available space
- Facing pictures toward the related text
- Avoiding "rivers of gray" caused by captions meeting irregularly near the same level
- Using a caption with each picture and a headline overall
- Arranging similar captions to have the same width, type and number of lines
- Focusing simultaneously on a subject or personality as well as a theme or mood

Writing to a picture story differs from writing to a single picture. The writer must focus on both individual pictures and continuity from photograph to photograph. Continuity can be achieved with a central block of copy that relates to all the pictures and echoes the spirit of the pictures as a group.

Ruthlessly hold captions to a maximum length. Readers like to leap from picture to picture, so each caption should be short. Captions can be related to pictures by proximity, keyed letters or numbers, or arrows—preferably by proximity and contiguity. Don't put a caption too far from the photo. The reader's eye moves from photo to caption and back to photo, perhaps several times.

It is advisable to include a headline for a photo layout of two or more pictures on the same subject to tie the package together.

Caption styles

In addition to giving careful attention to the content of photo captions, editors are concerned about the style of presentation. Captions are an important element of the publication's overall design, and editors should maintain graphic consistency. (This idea is discussed in Chapter 11.) The photo caption style for any publication— newspaper, magazine or brochure—should include the following components:

▶ **Type size and style.** Publications generally set captions in a typeface that contrasts with the typeface in the body so that captions stand out. For example, captions may be set in a sans serif typeface (such as Helvetica or Gothic), in boldface or in a slightly larger type size, such as 10- or 11-point type alongside nine-point body type. (Type is discussed in greater detail in Chapter 8.)

Some publications introduce captions with a brief *lead-in*, also called a *tagline* or *legend*. The lead-in typically is set in boldface or in capital letters (see Figure 10-5). The first several words of the caption can become the lead-in.

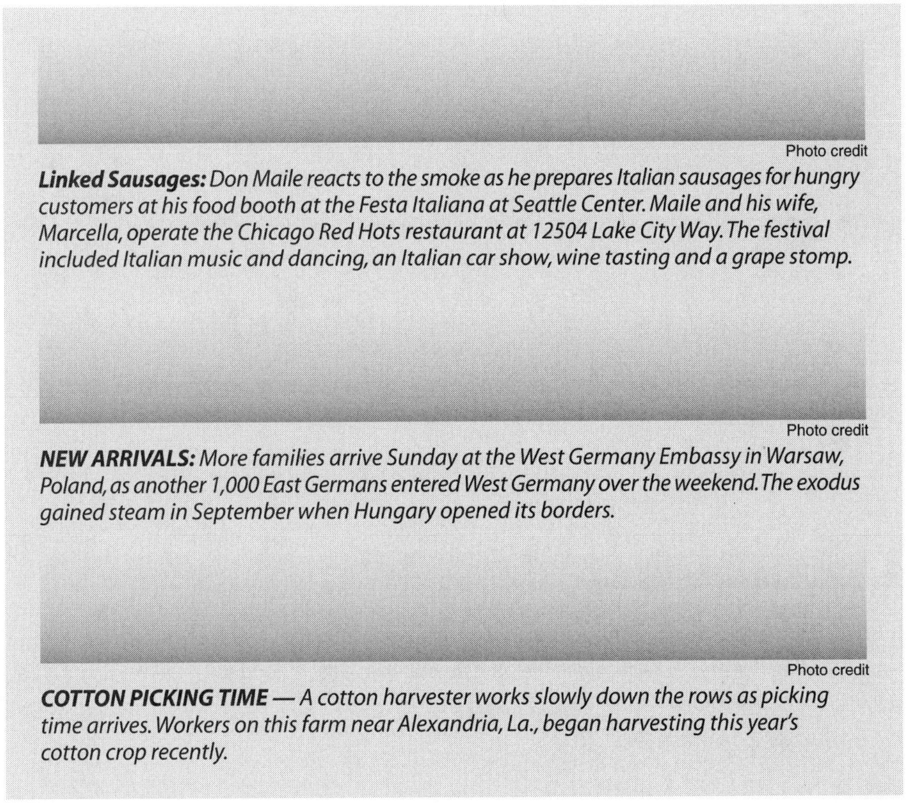

Figure 10-5
Captions often begin with a lead-in. Notice the variations in the capitalization, type style and punctuation of these lead-ins.

Photo credit

Linked Sausages: Don Maile reacts to the smoke as he prepares Italian sausages for hungry customers at his food booth at the Festa Italiana at Seattle Center. Maile and his wife, Marcella, operate the Chicago Red Hots restaurant at 12504 Lake City Way. The festival included Italian music and dancing, an Italian car show, wine tasting and a grape stomp.

Photo credit

NEW ARRIVALS: More families arrive Sunday at the West Germany Embassy in Warsaw, Poland, as another 1,000 East Germans entered West Germany over the weekend. The exodus gained steam in September when Hungary opened its borders.

Photo credit

COTTON PICKING TIME — A cotton harvester works slowly down the rows as picking time arrives. Workers on this farm near Alexandria, La., began harvesting this year's cotton crop recently.

▶**Width of type block.** The captions that go under one- and two-column photos usually are set the width of the photo. Some publications set captions one or two picas less than the width of the picture on each side so that the resulting white space helps captions stand out.

For photos wider than two columns, captions with only one or two lines of type can run the full width of the photo without hindering readability. When two lines are used, the second line of type should fill most of the space, avoiding a *widow*, a line of type containing only a word or two so that the line is mostly white space (see Figure 10-6). If the second line cannot be filled without obvious padding, the caption should be edited to one line.

Under photos wider than three columns, captions longer than one or two lines should be set in two columns (see Figure 10-7).

Figure 10-6
The top caption has a one-word widow, which should be avoided. The lower two captions reflect more careful editing. Lines run the width of the caption, and no widow carries over to the bottom line.

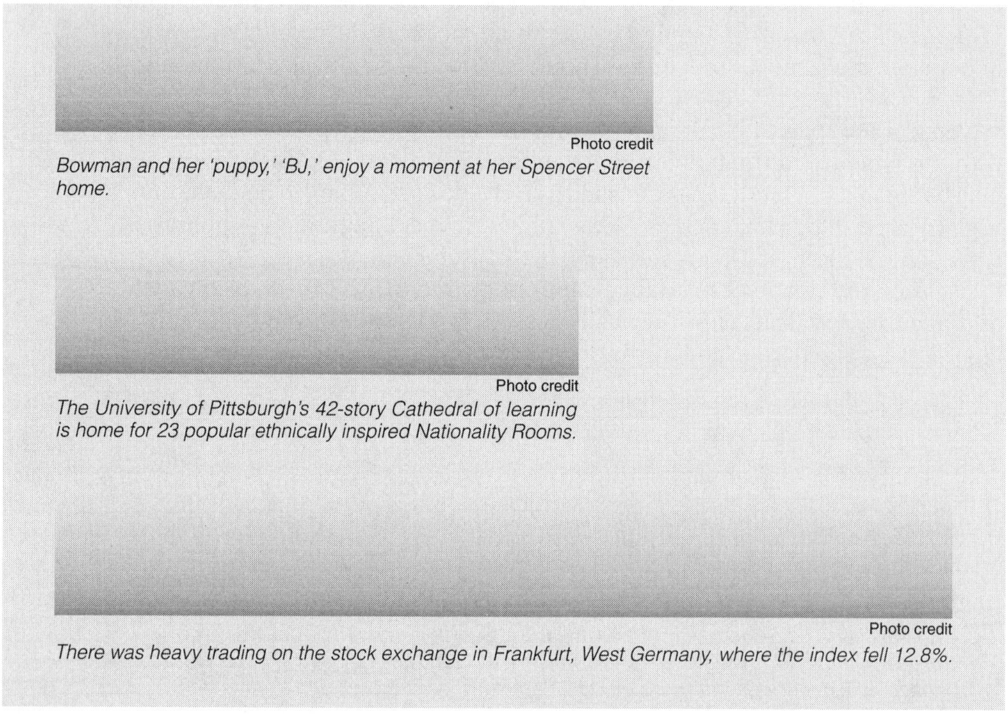

Photo credit
Bowman and her 'puppy,' 'BJ,' enjoy a moment at her Spencer Street home.

Photo credit
The University of Pittsburgh's 42-story Cathedral of learning is home for 23 popular ethnically inspired Nationality Rooms.

Photo credit
There was heavy trading on the stock exchange in Frankfurt, West Germany, where the index fell 12.8%.

Figure 10-7
Multiple lines under a photo three columns or wider should be set in two columns rather than running the width of the photo. Note in this example the unequal number of lines in each column. An even number of lines is preferable.

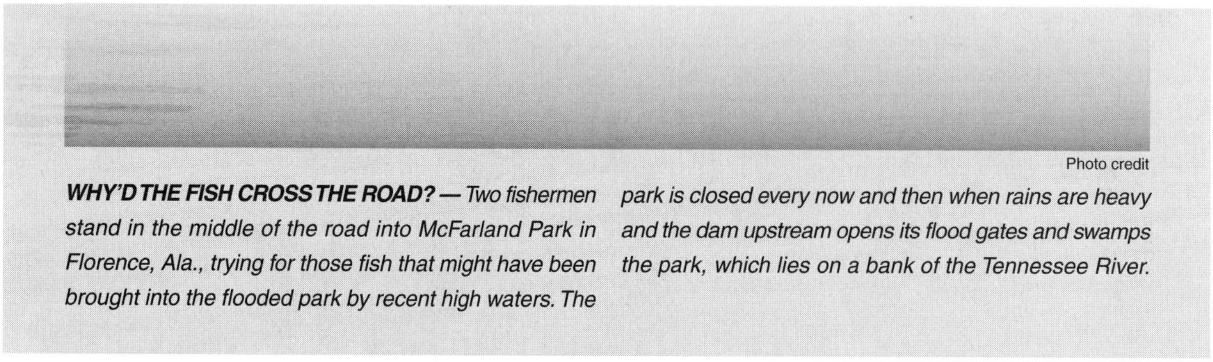

Photo credit

WHY'D THE FISH CROSS THE ROAD? — Two fishermen stand in the middle of the road into McFarland Park in Florence, Ala., trying for those fish that might have been brought into the flooded park by recent high waters. The park is closed every now and then when rains are heavy and the dam upstream opens its flood gates and swamps the park, which lies on a bank of the Tennessee River.

▶**Placement in relation to photo.** Standard placement for a caption is directly under the photograph, but captions may be placed to the side of photo. Captions rarely are set above photographs except where one caption accompanies two or more related photos.

▶**Overlines.** An *overline* is a word, phrase or clause set in headline type, placed above a photo or between a photo and its caption (see Figure 10-8). Some publications consistently use overlines, also referred to as "catch lines" or "taglines," for standalone photos that do not accompany a story. Overlines are effective devices to attract readers' attention, add information about the photo and allow open space into the layout.

▶**Credit lines.** The source of the photo, usually the name of a photographer or news service, should always be indicated. The photo credit line may come at the end of the caption, set off by parentheses. More commonly, it is set in type smaller than the caption type and placed under the lower right corner of the photograph.

Figure 10-8
Overlines to captions can be treated in various ways. Note the type styles and sizes and the placement of these examples.

Photo credit

An eye for art
Chicago students look over a sculpture called "Song of Spring," which is part of the East Side Sculpture Walk on the banks of the Chicago River east of Michigan Avenue.

Radiant City

TURN ON THE LIGHTS — Many downtown Chattanooga buildings, such as American National, had all their lights on Thursday night to allow local photographers a chance to participate in the "Chattanooga at Twilight" photography contest. A booklet of the entries will be compiled by Creative Yard Concepts and the Chattanooga Area Convention and Visitors Bureau. Also participating in the project is Downtown Alliance. (Photo credit)

Photo credit

CUB'S JEROME WALTON LEAPS INTO IVY
Spearing Long Drive By Giants' Robby Thompson

Photo credit

A gathering of legends
London was the site of a gathering of three of boxing's greats Tuesday when Joe Frazier, left, George Foreman, center, and Mohammad Ali appeared in a ring at the London Areana. The three former champions were promoting the release of "Champions Forever," a videotaped tribute to their careers.

Photo credit

Airport protest in Japan
Leftist students and workers on Sunday protest the expansion of the Tokyo International Airport.

Graphics require good reporting   **By Lynne Perri**

TO develop a visual strategy for most stories, start with what you know—good journalism: then decide what you want to show in a graphic. Whether the display is with photographs, graphics or a combination of both, use the same guidelines as if you were writing a story: accuracy, clarity and simplicity.

Good visuals illuminate a story and create a partnership with the prose that invites the reader to linger a little longer. Good visuals also allow reporters to write stories differently, sometimes by reducing the need for number-intense paragraphs or complex descriptions of how something works.

First steps

The best graphics start the way the best stories do—with good reporting.

Over-report statistics. Ask for 10, 20 or 30 years worth of data rather than only the three years' worth distributed at a press conference. The additional numbers might add depth to the story or result in a better graphic.

Look for surprises. If poll results aren't new or surprising, they probably won't work as graphics. Sketch out ideas first. If the results show that the content is worth the space, re-do the sketches.

Aim for depth. Try to move beyond pie charts. This is more difficult, but the results are more rewarding for the creator and the reader.

Write, edit and rewrite. Rework art and text so that the two don't repeat the same information or message. Tight writing and editing do not mean fragmenting sentences.

Find visual resources. Copies of maps, sketches made at a scene, handout art or videos can be useful. Some sources can draw (ask them); others can provide copies of schematics, blueprints or diagrams.

Other tips

- Stay within the same family of typefaces, point sizes and the newspaper's color palette to provide consistency.

- Share visual style guides with all departments. That helps those not closely working with graphics and photo staffs to understand the philosophy behind the packaging and the guidelines to make it happen.

Lynne Perri

Lynne Perri is a recruiter for the Gannett Company, Inc., and a visiting lecturer at Northwestern University.

She worked as a reporter from 1976 to 1979 in Marion, Ind., and Clearwater, Fla. She then moved to assistant features editor at The Tallahassee (Fla.) Democrat until 1981.

From there she went to the Tampa (Fla.) Tribune for five years, working stints as entertainment editor, assistant features editor, graphics and photography director. From 1987 to 1996, she was deputy managing editor for graphics and photo at USA Today.

Suggestions for additional reading

Black, Roger and Sean Elder. *Web Sites that Work.* Indianapolis: Adobe Press/ Macmillan Computer Publishing, 1997.

Brady, Philip. *Using Type Right: 121 No-nonsense rules for working with type.* Chicago: NTC Publishing Group, 1995.

Calishain, Tara and Jill Nystrom. *Official Netscape Guide to Internet Research: For Windows & Macintosh,* 2nd ed. International Thomson Publishing, 1998.

Design: The Journal of the Society of Newspaper Design, a publication of the Society of Newspaper Design, P.O. Box 17290, Dulles International Airport, Washington, D.C. 20041.

Finberg, Howard I., and Bruce D. Itule. *Visual Editing: A Graphic Guide for Journalists.* Belmont, Calif.: Wadsworth, 1990.

Garcia, Mario. *Redesigning Print for the Web.* Indianapolis: Hayden Books, 1998.

Garcia, Mario, and Don Fry. *Color in American Newspapers.* St. Petersburg, Fla.: Poynter Institute for Media Studies, 1986.

Gassan, Arnold. *Exploring Black and White Photography.* Dubuque, Iowa: Wm. C. Brown, 1989.

Holmes, Nigel. *Designer's Guide to Creating Charts and Diagrams.* New York: Watson-Guptill Publications, 1984.

Holtzschue, Linda and Edward Noriega. *Design Fundamentals for the Digital Age.* New York: Van Nostrand Reinhold, 1997.

McDougall, Angus and Veita Jo Hampton. *Picture Editing & Layout: A Guide to Better Visual Communication.* Durham, N. Car.: National Press Photographers Association, 1990.

Pocket Pal: A Graphic Arts Production Handbook. 17th ed. New York: International Paper, 1997.

Tufte, Edward R. *The Visual Display of Quantitative Information.* Cheshire, Conn.: Graphics Press, 1983.

Williams, Robin. *The Non-Designer's Design Book.* Berkeley, Calif.: Peachpit Press, 1994.

Exercises

1. Refer to the photo below:

a. Size this picture to be reproduced four columns wide for a newspaper that uses columns 12 picas (2 inches) wide with 1 pica (⅙ inch) of white space between columns. Show crop marks, even if you decide not to crop anything out of the photo. Indicate the size of the original as cropped, the size of the photo as it will be published and the percentage of reproduction.

b. Write a caption with an overline to accompany this standalone photo. Here is information for the caption:

Who: estimated 300 marchers, sponsored by ProChoice of your state

What: parade by pro-choice group, with anti-abortion adherents watching from along parade route

Where: around state Capitol building in your state

When: yesterday at noon

Why: pro-choice and anti-abortion proponents seeking to persuade state legislators to pass legislation supporting their respective points of view; state legislature expected to vote this session on legislation concerning abortion

Photo credit: Miles Carey, Knoxville (Tenn.) News-Sentinel

2. Refer to the following photo:

a. Crop this photo to run one column (12 picas or 2 inches) wide. Show your crop marks, the size of the original as cropped, the reproduction size and the percentage of reproduction.

b. Write a caption that can be used in a layout combining this photo and the photo in Exercise 1 (see the information in Exercise 1).

Who: Molly Yard, former president of the National Organization for Women

What: rally of pro-choice supporters

Where: on steps of state Capitol building in your state capital

When: yesterday at noon, immediately after pro-choice parade

Why: (see information in Exercise 1)

Other: size of crowd at rally, which included supporters of both pro-choice and anti-abortion positions and curious onlookers, estimated by Capitol security officers at 3,000

Photo credit: Miles Carey, Knoxville (Tenn.) News-Sentinel

3. Refer to the following photo:

a. Crop and proportion this photo to fill a space four columns (51 picas or 8½ inches) wide by 28 picas (4⅔ inches) deep. You may crop one or more of the young dancers from the photo if necessary. Show crop marks, the size of the original as cropped, the reproduction size and the percentage of reproduction.

b. Write a caption for the picture. Unfortunately, the list of names of the children has been misplaced, and it is close to deadline time, so you will have to write the caption without naming the children.

Who: five girls waiting their turn to audition

What: audition for "The Nutcracker"; 28 girls auditioned

Where: at Monroe Auditorium

When: auditions last night; "The Nutcracker" to be presented at the Monroe Auditorium December 1 through December 6

Photo credit: Miles Carey, Knoxville (Tenn.) News-Sentinel

4. Refer to the following photo:

   a. Without cropping anything, size the photo so it can be reproduced two columns (25 picas) wide. Specify the depth and the percentage of reproduction.

   b. Crop and size the photo so the piece of sculpture alone will be published in a space two columns wide by 46 picas deep. Don't forget to mark the margins for cropping. Specify the size of the original, as cropped, and the percentage of reproduction.

5. Refer to the following photo:

a. Size this photo to run three columns (38 picas or 6⅓ inches) wide. Specify the reproduction size of the original, as cropped, and the percentage of reproduction.

b. Write a caption from the following information. Use an all-capital, boldface lead-in.

Who: John Smith (No. 41 in white uniform) from Central High, Bryan Langford (dark uniform) from Halls High School

What: Smith's touchdown run during fourth quarter; 30 seconds left to play

Where: Central High Stadium

When: last night

Other: Central High had ball on Halls' 45-yard line; Smith took hand-off from quarterback, went around right end and scored; Bryan Langford had hold of Smith's jersey as Smith turned corner, but Langford lost his grip; no other Halls defender could catch Smith; this was winning score; Central won 14–7

Photo credit: Miles Carey, Knoxville (Tenn.) News-Sentinel

6. The public relations department of an insurance company is preparing a brochure to promote life insurance sales. A selling point will be the cost of raising a child from birth to age 17. Decide which type of informational graphic is most appropriate for this information and use the following figures to create a graphic.

   A middle-income family raising a child born in 1995 can expect to spend $7,610 on the child in 1995; $8,020 in 1996; $8,450 in 1997; $9,140 in 1998; $9,640 in 1999; $10,160 in 2000; $10,790 in 2001; $11,370 in 2002; $11,990 in 2003; $12,620 in 2004; $13,300 in 2005; $14,020 in 2006; $16,130 in 2007; $17,000 in 2008; $17,920 in 2009; $19,170 in 2010; $20,210 in 2011; $21,300 in 2012 when the child is 17 years old and ready for college. These figures come from the U.S. Department of Agriculture, Center for Nutrition Policy and Promotion and assume an average annual inflation rate of 5.4 percent.

7. A newspaper reporter has included the information below in a story. Decide which type of graphic is most appropriate for the information in each paragraph and use the figures to create two graphics.

   a. According to a survey at the local shopping mall yesterday, a 7-year-old child here in Centerville receives an average of $2 a week from his parents as an allowance. A typical 8-year-old gets $2.50 a week allowance. By the time the child is 10, he or she typically receives $3.50. On average, an 11-year-old will get $4.25 for a weekly allowance; at age 12 that increases to $4.50; $5 by age 13, $10 at age 15 and $15 at age 16. Parents surveyed also said they often shell out considerably more per week in exchange for routine household chores.

   b. What do children spend their allowances on? Our survey indicates that this varies from age to age, but here is the breakdown for the average 16-year-old respondent: 20 percent on food; 15 percent on tapes and CDs; 23 percent on clothes; 10 percent on gifts, including church contributions; 6 percent savings toward a specific purchase; 1 percent on school supplies; 25 percent on tickets for movies, concerts, athletic or special events.

8. Create an informational graphic for a month-to-month comparison of the number of home runs Mark McGwire hit during the 1998 season.

   Here are the figures:

   In March he hit 1 home run; 10 in April; 16 in May; 10 in June; 8 in July; 10 in August; 15 in September for a total of 70 home runs.

Good order is the foundation of all good things.

—Edmund Burke

Design and Layout

T HE **main purpose of publication design** is to communicate, to help move readers easily and efficiently through the page. Editors who design and lay out pages are responsible for telling readers which stories are most important and for helping readers find the stories they want to read.

In addition to having a knowledge of news values, copy editing and typography, the layout editor must understand some of the principles of design, the basic structures or forms of layout, and the language of design.

Design principles

All designers call on the basic principles of design to help them create. Beginning layout editors should follow these principles until they become experienced. The standard design principles are balance, contrast, proportion and unity.

Balance

Many early designers believed that page balance was achieved by matching identical elements (copy, headlines, photos, borders, colors) on the page. This *formal balance* had only one requirement: The right half of the page (at the time, four columns on an eight-column page) had to be matched on the left side with the same elements (see Figure 11-1). Not only did editors have to match the lower right corner with the lower left corner exactly, they also had to match headline weights across the page. For example, a two-column, 24-point, two-line headline in columns seven and eight called for exactly the same size of headline in columns one and two. A one-column, 36-point, three-line headline in column six called for the same size of headline in column three. Even the headlines and photographs at the bottom of the page were balanced symmetrically.

Formal balance, however, tended to sweep the news into a form with no consideration for its importance. In other words, the news of the day didn't seem to matter as much as design—form dictated content. Because formal balance required that the page be divided down the middle, the resulting balance was from side to side. And because headline schedules universally required that important stories be billed with large headlines and placed high on the page, top-to-bottom balance was not feasible. Big, bold headlines and large photos dominated the top

Figure 11-1
The Los Angeles Times of 1980 used formal balance, so that elements on the right side of the page were balanced by similar elements on the left. (Reprinted by permission)

of the page, and the bottom trailed off into grayness, like a news story written in inverted pyramid style.

Balance is not achieved by merely matching identical elements on the page. Other factors, such as the apparent weights of the elements on the page, come into play. *Informal,* or asymmetrical, balance can be achieved with little specialized knowledge.

To balance the right against the left and the top against the bottom (remember that formal balance only matches the right against the left), beginning layout editors should section the page into four *modules* or quadrants, splitting the page down the middle vertically and then horizontally across the fold (see Figure 11-2). Each module should contain some graphic mass or weight—a headline, a photograph, a piece of artwork, white space—to help balance the page, but the weighted elements can extend beyond the boundaries of the modules.

Experienced layout editors make little effort to attain line-by-line balance. Neither must the page remain in quadrants; an arrangement of several rectangular modules may flow from the basic page division.

The sequence of the design also becomes important in achieving balance. The layout editor should attempt to place the major display element—whether it is a photograph, a story or both—just to the left of the *optical center* of the page (a point just above the measured center). Such placement serves as a focal point for balancing the rest of the page (see Figure 11-3).

Edmund Arnold, author of several books on newspaper design, has written about the way readers visualize and use a piece of printed information. He notes that the first place a reader looks—called the *primary optical area,* or POA—is the upper left corner of the page (see Figure 11-4). The lower right corner—called the *terminal area,* or TA—also has strong visual attraction, because readers know they have finished when they reach that area. The two remaining corners of the page, upper right and lower left, are called *fallow corners.* They require special design attention, because the reader's eye doesn't travel there automatically.

Arnold suggests that the basic movement of the eye follows a diagonal line from upper left to lower right, in a pattern that resembles a *Z*. The reader stops along the way, lured by "optical magnets," such as photographs and headlines. The designers of USA Today, for example, determined that the lower left fallow corner would be anchored by an info-graphic (see Chapter 10) and that the terminal area, which USA Today editors called the "hot corner,"

Figure 11-2
The layout editor should consider left-to-right, diagonal and top-to-bottom balance.

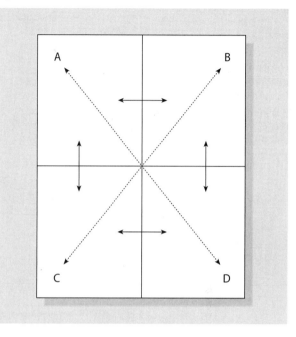

Figure 11-3
This page is laid out in modules. The major visual element—the dominant element—is placed just to the left of the optical center of the page.

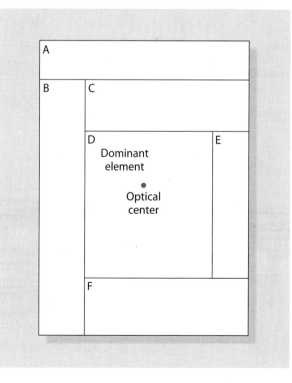

Figure 11-4
The reader's eye progresses diagonally through the page from the primary optical area (POA) in the upper left corner to the terminal area (TA) in the lower right corner. The remaining two quadrants on the page are fallow corners. A strong design will attract the reader's eye to the fallow corners so that it follows a Z pattern across the page.

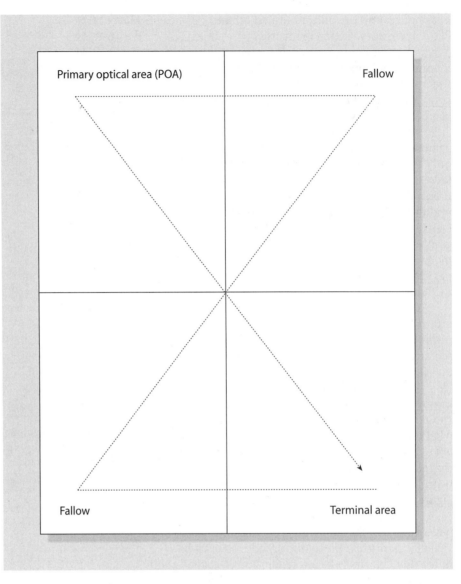

always would contain a bright, interesting story to grab the reader's attention (see Figure 11-5).

Noted designer Mario Garcia makes a case for a somewhat different concept, one he calls the *center of visual impact* (CVI). He suggests that the two points on the page traditionally associated with the point of entry (the primary optical area) and the point of exit (the terminal area) need not be located in the corners of the page. He suggests that the CVI, which should attract the reader's visual attention at a glance, may be located anywhere on the page. The CVI then becomes the reader's point of entry into the page (see Figure 11-6).

Garcia recommends using only one CVI on a page, because including other strong elements weakens the total effect. Photographs, typography and packaging all can be used as dominant elements on the page, leading the reader's eye to the point of greatest visual interest.

Figure 11-5
The "hot corner" story about the TB threat ensures that the reader's eye will progress to that entry point on the page; the story is screened in a color box and placed in the terminal area. Notice that the dominant element near the center of the page—the graphic and story on "Tweeners," people stuck between generations—is another guaranteed entry point. (Copyright 1996, USA Today. Reprinted with permission)

Figure 11-6
The center of visual impact on Page One of The Denver Post is the photo package on cold weather. Notice the eye-pleasing modular layout. (Reprinted courtesy of The Denver Post)

Contrast

A broadsheet or tabloid newspaper page, a magazine page, a newsletter page or even a part of a page, such as an advertisement, should have a focal point or center of visual interest surrounded by smaller, contrasting elements. The point of focus reveals the publication's priorities and shows readers what the editor believes is important. The layout editor may emphasize a particular element—a story or a photograph—simply by making it larger than any other element. This concept of contrast, similar to Garcia's center of visual impact, is called the ***dominant element***. On a standard, open (no ads) page, a dominant horizontal element should extend across more than half the page.

In addition, printed materials increasingly rely on color to bring contrast to a page. The use of a color border around a photograph or a color screen behind a story can spotlight the element for the reader.

The layout editor also may use contrasting typefaces and shapes to focus and balance a page. Many modern publications use lightface dropheads, also called ***underlines***, and breakout quotations to contrast with boldface main headlines. Designers often choose sans serif type for captions, standing headlines and drop-in logos to accent the serif type used in body type and headlines.

Layout editors also use contrasting shapes to lend visual interest to a page. Items placed horizontally contrast with those placed vertically—for example, a thin, horizontal story contrasts with a strong vertical photograph. The use of differing shapes of elements adds visual impact to the layout. The key is simply to remember to work in modules.

Proportion

The ratio between elements on a page is called ***proportion***. Artists have discovered that the most aesthetically pleasing ratio is 3 to 5. Whenever possible, the shapes of elements should be rectangular, similar to a 3×5 notecard. In design, rectangles are more pleasing to the eye than squares.

Not all elements on the page have to follow this proportion rule, of course. But if many elements do, the one unusual shape will become the focal point.

Unity

To achieve unity, a publication carries its design themes throughout all pages as well as within individual layouts. In a unified publication, all elements of the design are related. The section headings, headlines, captions and column logos are stylistically consistent, and the sections and columns appear in the same place in each issue.

Unity also refers to the idea that individual stories or related elements packaged together can have greater visual impact if they are designed in a modular fashion. That is, laying out stories or packages of related elements as if they were bounded by an imaginary rectangle helps create a sense of unity and cohesion for the reader. Most contemporary newspapers and magazines use a modular format, and layout editors who imagine each element of the page as a module—whether it is a long, vertical photograph or a rectangular, horizontal copy block—are able to create simple, uncluttered designs that aid in readability.

Figure 11-7
Roger Fidler's checklist can help layout editors evaluate their own work. (Reprinted from Newspaper Design Notebook, Vol. 2, No. 1, by permission of Roger Fidler)

A checklist for functionally integrated design

Functionally integrated layouts are not created with magic words or rigid rules. They require organized and creative thinking developed through experience. And even with experience, not everyone has the visual sensitivity and judgment to become a good layout editor.

The following checklist is by no means all-inclusive. It is merely a tool for assessing layouts and should not be regarded as a newspaper design dogma.

If you can answer yes to all questions designated with an open box and no to all those designated with a filled box, the page layout is probably well-designed.

Organization

- Are readers guided smoothly and naturally through the page?
- Do all elements have a reason for being?
- Are all intended relationships between elements readily apparent?
- Are packages clearly defined?
- Does the design call attention to itself instead of the content?
- Does the page appear cluttered?
- Do any type or art elements appear to be floating on the page?
- Do any elements appear lost?
- Are any editorial elements easily confused with advertising?

Readability

- Are the starting points for all stories easily determined?
- Do any elements interrupt reading or cause confusion?
- Are any legs of type perceptually truncated by art or sell lines (i.e., quotes, liftouts, etc.)?
- Is the line width of any text too narrow or too wide for easy reading?
- If text is set to follow the shape of adjacent art, is the story difficult to read?

- Do any headlines or sell lines compete with headlines or sell lines in adjacent columns?

Accuracy and clarity

- Does the layout accurately communicate the relative importance of the stories contained on the page?
- Do the art elements accurately convey the tone and message of the stories?
- Are logos consistent and differentiated from headlines?
- Are the devices used in a layout appropriate for the content of the page?

Proportioning and sizing

- Are all elements sized relative to their importance?
- Are the shapes and sizes of elements appropriate for the content of the elements?
- Do the shapes of elements add contrast and interest?
- Does the page have a dominant element or package of elements?
- Does the shape of an element appear contrived or forced?
- Do any logos or headlines seem out of proportion with the size of the story or column?
- Are several elements similar in proportion and size?

Efficiency and consistency

- Do all areas of white space appear as if they were planned? (When it appears as if something fell off the page, the white space is not functional.)
- Is spacing between elements controlled and consistent?
- Are areas of white space balanced on the page?
- Is all type, especially agate material, set at the most efficient measure for the information contained?
- Is the size of column gutters constant?
- Does the number of elements or devices used in a package seem excessive?

Most publications, including Web sites, have very detailed stylebooks that attempt to ensure such consistency in design. Without these stylebooks, clutter and chaos result, and the reader can be left confused. Most modern design, beautiful in its simplicity, puts a premium on unity because a unified approach communicates the message more effectively to readers.

Several years ago, noted newspaper designer Roger Fidler published the checklist for unified design shown in Figure 11-7. It is a good tool to help assess layout.

Design elements

Modern editors combine at least six basic elements to lay out pages:

- Type for body copy

- Display type (headlines)

- Borders or rules

- Open space

- Art, which includes photographs, illustrations and informational graphics, such as maps, graphs and charts

- Color, as a design element

Editors for Web sites add video and sound to this mix of layout elements.

Body type

Most body copy is set in 8- or 9-point type with 1 point of leading, or space, between lines. Most newspaper pages today are set in a six-column format, forced by the standardization of advertising units in the 1980s. Most columns are set on a 12- to 14-pica measure, allowing optimum readability.

Most newspapers continue to *justify* their body type, meaning that the copy is set both flush left and flush right. A few newspapers and magazines, however, set their body copy ***ragged right***, meaning that the copy lines up evenly on the left but has irregular space at the end of the lines on the right. Some newspapers use the ragged-right format when setting editorials.

When laying out a page, particularly in a horizontal format, editors often place body copy in several adjacent columns. Such columns of type are called *legs*. A story that is laid out over four columns, for example, has four legs of type.

Display type

Some of newspapering's most colorful jargon is related to headlines. As noted in Chapter 9, headlines serve two major functions: They summarize the news for busy readers, and they grade the relative newsworthiness of each story. As a typographic device, headlines introduce large areas of black and white to give the page visual interest.

Headlines usually range from 14-point type to 72-point type, although some newspapers magnify headline type even larger when an extraordinary story occurs (see Figure 11-8).

As we saw in Chapter 9, layout editors designate headlines according to size and space. A 2-36-3 headline, for example, is a two-column, 36-point, three-line headline.

Typically, the most noticeable display type on Page One is the ***nameplate***, or ***flag***, which tells the name of the publication and usually the date, the price and the city of publication. Some nameplates also include *ears*, information set on either side of the name itself, such as the weather, a daily quotation or a small index.

A *banner* is a headline that extends horizontally across all the columns of the page. Usually the banner is the lead headline, and it is set larger than all the other headlines on the page. Many newspapers reserve the use of banners for highly significant stories and use smaller lead headlines, extending perhaps across only three columns, on a day-to-day basis. Other forms of banners are known as ***streamers*** or ***ribbons***. These headlines usually are smaller than Page One banners and are frequently used on inside pages.

Figure 11-8

The Battle Creek (Mich.) Enquirer was among the estimated 30 percent of U.S. daily newspapers that published an extra edition on Oct. 3, 1995, when a California jury found former football player O.J. Simpson not guilty of murdering his ex-wife and her friend. Notice the extra-large (more than 200-point) headline and the large dominant photo. (Reprinted courtesy of the Battle Creek Enquirer)

A *deck* is a smaller headline just under the main headline that gives the reader more information about the story. Early U.S. newspapers often used one-column decks that numbered scores of lines and extended halfway down the page.

A *kicker* is a small headline above the main headline, used most often by layout editors when white space is desired. The kicker is set half the point size of the main headline (an 18-point kicker above a 36-point headline, for example). Often it is flush left over an indented main headline, and it may be underlined. Kickers generally extend no more than a third of the width of the main headline.

A *jumphead* appears above a story as it continues from one page to another. The jumphead usually is smaller than the main headline and may contain typographic devices known as *dingbats*—ornamentation such as dashes, stars, *ballot boxes* (small squares) or *bullets* (circles or dots). Jumpheads usually repeat a key word or phrase from the main headline to help guide readers to the continuing story. Careful copy editors also make sure that the story's *jumpline* (last line of type before the jump, referring readers to the correct page number) contains the same key word or phrase as the jumphead.

Upstyle headlines are those in which the first letter of all the words except prepositions is capitalized; *downstyle* headlines are those in which only the first word and proper nouns are capitalized. Most modern newspapers use a downstyle format. Some traditional newspapers, however, such as The New York Times, retain upstyle headlines.

Examples of these headlines and many others are displayed in Chapter 9.

Borders

Publications use a variety of borders to separate one page element from another. Most advertisements are boxed, some with ornamental borders; some stories are also boxed, but usually with simple, plain lines called *rules*. Because the rules are placed along the edge of the column, elements within the box—body type and art—must be narrower.

Rules and borders are often produced by applying tape manufactured with lines in varying widths and styles; they can also be produced on a computer. Most commonly used in editorial pasteup are 1-point and 2-point rules, but many publications are designed to use heavy 6-point or even 12-point rules.

Rules are used to box stories and to border photographs and other artwork or to underline kickers. They are also used as design elements in standing headlines, page headers (such as Sports) and column logos, and as cutoffs to separate unrelated elements.

Open space

The use of *open space,* sometimes called white space, helps achieve unity of design. Well-designed publications use consistent amounts of open space between columns of type, between photographs and their captions, above and below headlines, between the flag and the rest of the page, between the headline and the byline, and between the byline and the first paragraph of the story.

Open space can also be used to relieve large quantities of gray type. The use of liberal amounts of open space on pages that tend to be type-heavy, such as editorial pages, is a good design technique.

Open space should be thought of as a frame around the page. Layout editors should try to push it to the perimeter of the page, never letting open space become trapped on the interior of the page. Trapped open space is particularly unattractive on photo-page layouts.

Some newspapers use more open space between elements in certain sections than in others. Liberal use of open space in the arts and entertainment sections, for example, provides them with a personality distinct from that of the news sections.

Art

For most layout editors, art is the starting point for laying out a page. In some cases, the shape of the art actually determines the layout.

Most art requires reduction or enlargement before it is published (see Chapter 10), and the layout editor determines the size.

Simple black-and-white illustrations (sometimes called line art) need only be the correct reproduction size before they can be pasted onto the page. Black-and-white photographs, however, require one additional step before they can be printed on a press; they need to be *screened*, or converted into halftones by breaking the continuous image into dots. Other names for a halftone are *PMT* (photo-mechanical transfer), *velox* or *screened print*. They all mean a photo print whose image is in a dot pattern rather than in continuous tones.

Color illustrations or photographs require several other, more complex, production steps before they are ready for printing.

The art of layout is to know not only how to size and crop but also how to judge the value of photos and illustrations on a page. In most circumstances, the art is the dominant element on a page; as a result, its quality and use require special attention.

Color

Editors are increasingly using color in photographs and in artwork to add meaning to the content of the newspaper. Color is quickly and easily processed by the brain, and a person's response to color is both learned and inherited. The response depends on such factors as age, gender, intelligence, education, temperature, climate, socioeconomic background and regional attitudes.

Basically, color consists of various wavelengths of light. A ray of sunlight reflected through a prism is diverted into visible bands of color. Red is the least diverted, violet the most diverted. Red has the longest waves, violet the shortest. This phenomenon, known as the color spectrum, was first recorded by Sir Isaac Newton in the early 18th century.

The main purpose of using color as a design element is to draw attention to the content. Most studies indicate that color is better than black and white for grabbing readers' attention. However, black-and-white images are better for a response requiring more thought.

Most of the time, color is available either as *spot color* (an extra shade of ink used along with black) or as full color, which is a combination of four color inks: cyan (blue), magenta (red), yellow and black. Full color is also called *process color*.

Full-color halftones are being used more often, as the technology for quickly processing color film has become available. High-speed *scanners*—machines that make high-quality color separations—have revolutionized the way color photos are handled and have become affordable for most newspapers.

For new designers and layout editors, the best rule to follow when adding color to a page is not to use too much. Resist the temptation to splash color everywhere. Instead, color should be used as an accent that connects related elements and enhances the meaning of the content.

Robert Bohle, in his book *Publication Design for Editors,* suggests that spot color be used sparingly. He recommends a few of the ways to do so:

▶ **Use color as a content connector, or as a "people mover."** To do so, use color as a background for an entire spread, thus tying everything into a neat package, or use it to link similar items, such as small boxes in an informational graphic, so that the reader can see the layout as a whole and not just as a bunch of parts.

▶ **Use color to color "things," not background.** Color the elements on the page, such as certain type, illustrations and graphics. Screening the background of a box of type is a weak use of color.

▶ **Use color as a background for color photographs.** Sometimes a complementary color can be used to help a photograph pop out from the page. The key is contrast. Selecting a dominant color from the photograph is a weak choice because of the lack of contrast. A light gray is a good choice; the colors look brighter compared to the gray.

As in all good design, the key to using color is to keep it simple. More is not necessarily better.

Forms of layout

Vertical layout, most notably displayed in The New York Times and The Wall Street Journal, is characterized by columns of type that run vertically down the page. Vertical newspapers tend to publish few headlines or photographs more than two columns wide. Most headlines are a single column wide, and stories often run the full length of the column. A striking vertical effect was achieved by early newspapers using eight- or nine-column formats. Today's standard six-column formats mean wider columns, but a vertical look is still possible (see Figure 11-9).

Newspapers that use a vertical layout generally have a high story count on the front page. They are relatively easy to produce, both in the newsroom and in the composing room.

Horizontal layout is characterized by columns of type that flow across the page. Wide photographs—sometimes spread across the full six columns—contribute to this effect, and the many multicolumn headlines form wide blocks that give the pages their horizontal appearance. These large photos and headlines attract the reader's attention and add contrast to the page (see Figure 11-10).

Today's modern layouts often are not readily identifiable as either vertical or horizontal. However, almost all are modular. Many layout editors use both vertical and horizontal forms to create balance, focus and contrast on the page (see Figure 11-11).

Figure 11-9

The Shorthorn, campus paper at the University of Texas at Arlington, won second place for Page One design in the 1995 Associated Collegiate Press/Adobe Designs of the Year competition. This vertical page uses modular layout and an attractive centerpiece package on campus cats to attract busy readers. (Reprinted courtesy of the Shorthorn)

Figure 11-10
The Bainbridge Island (Wash.) Review is laid out on a horizontal format, with one large photo and one story on its tabloid Page One. The color promo graphics above the nameplate also provide a point of entry to the page. (Reprinted courtesy of the Bainbridge Island Review)

CHORALE
Bainbridge Chorale raises its collective voice for a concert.
Kitsap Week

BACK TO WESCO
Spartan baseball boys will resume league play Thursday.
Page A17

ANOTHER AWARD
Bainbridge author Dave Guterson gets more kudos for his first novel, "Snow Falling on Cedars."
Page A13

MIDWEEK EDITION
Bainbridge Island
Review

VOLUME 96, NO. 17   WEDNESDAY, APRIL 12, 1995 • 75¢

Arrest an equestrian

Staff photo by Terry Poe

Bainbridge Police Officer Erik Sulonen rounds up a stray pony on Tolo Road Monday afternoon. The horse, Bucky, was reported wandering the streets, and after a search, was found munching idly in the backyard of a nearby home. Not one to be easily coaxed, it took the lure of a bundle of grass to corral the animal in a nearby pasture. "He wouldn't do anything with 'giddy-up' or 'yah!'" Sulonen said. "But he did respond to 'go.'" Reserve Officer Bob Ashbrook (right) and Officer Lori Felix assisted with the round-up.

Bleakney tried for position in Oregon

By Jim Christie
Staff writer

Bainbridge School Superintendent Bill Bleakney nearly had a job offer with a school district in Oregon.

In November, Bleakney quietly applied for a superintendent opening with the North Clackamas School District, a suburban district southeast of Portland.

Bleakney was one of three finalists, but was not accepted for the position.

The post is now open again, however, after the number-one finalist backed out.

"We're back to the drawing board," said Larry Anderson, the North Clackamas district's director of personnel services. "We've reopened the position, and we're operating under the premise that we're starting at scratch."

Bleakney told the Review Monday that he has no current plans to reapply. Oregon, though, figures prominently in his ideal short-term plans.

"I was asked if they wanted me to keep my name in the hat, and I said no," Bleakney said. "This was just a very good position that game along."

A move to Oregon would bring Bleakney and his wife closer to where their parents live, one major consideration in applying for the North Clackamas opening.

The other consideration, he said, was advice given by a professional "mentor," who suggested Bleakney get his name "known" in Oregon if he wants to be considered for work there after he retires from teaching in Washington.

"This is my 29th year in the business and at some point in time I may choose to retire," said Bleakney. "I was pleased to be considered, but my plans call for me to get my 30 [years]."

Assuming the management of the North Clackamas district would have been a substantial change from Bainbridge Island, where total enrollment in the district is about 3,200 students.

The North Clackamas district serves just under 14,000 students, takes in three high schools, four junior high schools and 17 elementary schools and a vocational "occupational skills center."

"By Washington standards, that's mid-sized," said Anderson. "By Oregon standards, it's the fifth-largest [district] in the state."

Bleakney has been superintendent of the Bainbridge Island School District since 1989. His contract was extended last fall, to run through 1997.

"I have a very good job here; I don't feel a need to leave," Bleakney said. "To be perfectly honest, I'd be looking to take the next step in the next few years."

School Board President Vicki Clayton said she was "flattered" Bleakney had been considered for the Oregon position.

INSIDE

Letters	A9	Calendar	A22
Opinion	A6	Movies	A22
Obituaries	A14		
Sports	A17		

Printed with recycled paper and environmentally friendly soybean oil-based ink.

"The only newspaper in the world that cares about Bainbridge Island"

Figure 11-11

The Sagamore at Indiana University-Purdue University at Indianapolis won first place for Page One design in the 1995 Associated Collegiate Press/Adobe Designs of the Year competition. This page combines both horizontal and vertical elements, as well as color photos and graphics to attract reader attention. (Reprinted courtesy of The IUPUI Sagamore)

Newspaper layout

Laying out a page is known as *dummying*. The dummy, as a mock-up of a page is called, is used as a map by pasteup personnel for placement of stories, headlines, photographs and captions. The dummy is completed by layout editors in the newsroom and sent to the composing room, where compositors view the map as an exact guide for the placement of page elements. Figure 11-12 is a list of terms used in layout and printing.

Figure 11-12
Layout editors and pasteup artists use these terms as they lay out a newspaper's pages. After the editor sends a page dummy (a kind of map or blueprint) to the production department, the "backshop" staff trims and pastes up type, headlines and other page elements onto a flat. The editor then receives a full-page proof and makes any final changes. The page will be photographed and the resulting negative used to make a plate, which is then mounted on an offset printing press. (Photographs by Tom Farrington, San Diego State University/courtesy of the San Diego Union-Tribune)

Agate line: Standard of measurement for the depth of advertisements; roughly, 14 to the inch.

Bleed: Extending the printed image to the trim edge of the page; used more often in magazines than in newspapers.

Crop marks: Indication to eliminate unwanted areas in a photograph or other piece of art.

Double truck: Two pages at the center of a section designed as a single unit.

Dummy: Diagram outlining the layout of a page, as it will appear in its printed form; blueprint for pasteup.

Flat: Layout sheets, also called grid sheets, onto which the publication's copy and artwork are pasted. For offset printing, a photograph is taken of the finished flat, and the negative is used to make a printing plate, which is then placed on the press for printing.

Folio: Page number, date and name of publication on each page.

Galley: Shallow tray used to hold metal type; almost non-existent in today's modern production facilities.

Gutter: Margin between facing pages or between columns on the page.

Legs: Columns of type placed adjacent to each other.

Logo: Specially designed signature in an advertisement or design element used consistently with certain features, such as editorial columns.

Moiré (pronounced *muare-ay*): Undesirable pattern caused by incorrect screen angles when overprinting halftones.

Register: To fit two or more printing images on the same paper in exact alignment. A color photograph is said to be in registration if all the color layers are aligned and the resulting picture has clarity.

Tombstone: Bumping headlines of the same size, so that one headline reads into the other; to be avoided.

Widow: A line of type with only one or two words appearing at the end of a paragraph, usually at the top of a column of type; to be avoided.

As more newspapers and magazines invest in pagination technology, dummies will become relics. Pagination is a system of electronic dummying, which allows the editor to lay out the page on the computer and print it in its final version, bypassing the pasteup functions of the composing room altogether.

Most newspapers are printed in one of two forms: broadsheet or tabloid. The vast majority of daily newspapers in the United States publish broadsheet pages, usually about 13 inches wide by 21 inches deep. These pages often are laid out in a six-column format, especially on inside pages where the advertising department

Figure 11-13
Nancy Christensen of the University of Nebraska won second place in the 1998 Associated Collegiate Press/ Adobe Designs of the Year competition for her Page One designs. This sports-feature page from the Daily Nebraskan shows Christensen's versatility in working with the news-paper's tabloid format. Many collegiate newspapers are tabloids, usually laid out on either a four-column or a five-column format. This page runs text over three regular-set columns and uses a headline and smaller photo at left in a somewhat wider measure. (Reprinted courtesy of the Daily Nebraskan)

sells standard advertising units (SAUs) to fit in a six-column format. Each column is about 12 picas, or two inches, wide, with a pica of gutter space between columns. Many broadsheet newspapers use a variety of layout formats on Page One and section fronts, however, adopting a more creative approach for these cover pages. Much of the college press publishes tabloid pages, usually about 11 inches wide by 14 inches deep. These pages are usually laid out on either a four-column or a five-column format.

A good dummy is proportional in size to the actual printed page. For a broadsheet page, for example, a proportionate dummy page would be 6.5 inches wide by 10.5 inches deep, roughly half the actual size of the page. Or, the dummy could be 8.5 inches wide by 13.5 inches deep, roughly 65 percent of the actual size. The point is that the layout dummy sheet should be proportional to the printed page (see Figure 11-14).

The first and most important rule of dummying the page is to keep the dummy neat and legible. The more precise and detailed the dummy, the better the chances of precise and accurate pasteup.

Figure 11-14
The broadsheet dummy (a) is scaled to a regular newspaper page, which is generally 13 inches wide by 21 inches deep. This dummy sheet is for a six-column page and has inches marked along the left and right borders, columns marked across the top, and pica column widths across the bottom. The tabloid dummy (b) is scaled to a tabloid page, which is usually about 11 inches wide by 14 inches deep. This dummy sheet is for a five-column page and has inches marked along the left border.

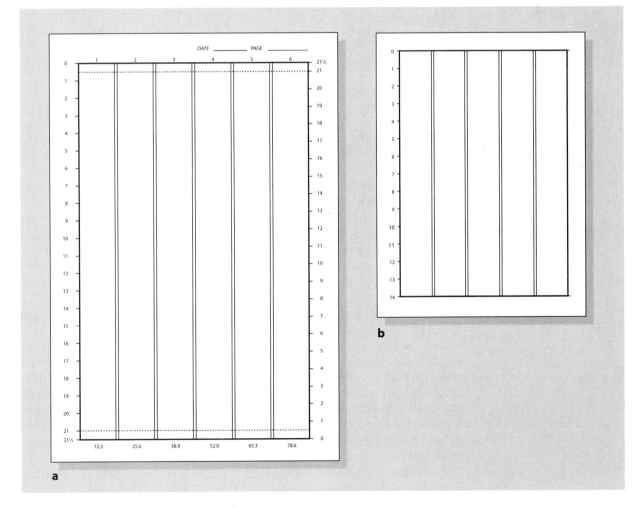

Basic guidelines

Sometimes, beginning editors peer at the blank dummy sheet resting on the desk in front of them—the dummy sheet that eventually will become their first page layout—and freeze, wondering how to begin. Following are some suggestions that may help.

▶ **Choose the Stories.** Before dummying begins, the layout editor must assess the day's news. At small newspapers, news judgments may be made by the editor who also does the layout. At mid-sized and large newspapers, however, the judgments about what stories are placed on which pages are made by news editors in consultation with other department editors at meetings called story conferences or news meetings. Section editors (sports, business, local news, wire news, lifestyle, and so on) at morning newspapers usually bring the budgets, or summaries of each section's stories for that day, to the late-afternoon news meeting. Editors of evening newspapers have the same kind of meeting, but often very early in the morning, because the newspaper "goes to bed," or gets put on the press, at mid-day. Regardless of the time of day, the editors bring all the major stories together and begin the process of assessing what stories, photos and art will be published in the next edition.

Most newspapers rely on the traditional news values discussed in Chapter 1 when judging the significance of stories:

- Timeliness

- Proximity

- Prominence

- Unusualness

- Conflict

- Human Interest

- Significance

Judgments vary about which stories are significant, of course, depending both on the newspaper's philosophy and mission and on the individual editor's (or publisher's) interests or biases. Some newspapers emphasize local news; others emphasize national or international news. Some (especially morning papers) might put a premium on timeliness and consider last night's city council meeting important enough for Page One. Others (especially evening papers) might emphasize another news value, such as unusualness, and play up a story about a bizarre occurrence.

In addition to the traditional news values, editors also make judgments about what to publish based on a very pragmatic consideration—space. For each day of the week, and for each section of the paper, space for news is generally determined by the amount of advertising sold. Some publishers allow editors to allot a minimum number of columns of space each day. Others base the entire daily "newshole" on the amount of advertising sold and determine a news/advertising ratio. Often, publishers determine that 40 percent of the day's space will be devoted to news and 60 percent will be devoted to advertising. The more space advertisers buy, therefore, the more columns of newshole can be allotted to the various sections (news, sports, features, business, etc.).

The news services help local editors make news judgments by providing summaries of the major wire stories of the day. Often the news budgets, or news digests, lead with the stories considered most important by the news-service editors. The Associated Press also transmits a separate list of stories that AP recommends editors consider for Page One. For example, from an AP News Digest, the AP recommended the following stories for use on Page One:

> STATE OF THE UNION: President Clinton sought to ease American economic anxieties Tuesday night in an upbeat State of the Union address designed to trace the themes of his upcoming re-election campaign. With tempers rubbed raw by the budget fight, Republicans readied an alternative vision. AM-State of Union. By White House Correspondent Terence Hunt. Eds: Speech begins 9 p.m. EST; prospects for advance text uncertain.

> THE UNION SPEAKS: By the numbers, there is little argument that the state of the union is reasonably good. Yet Joan Henson is worried. No, frightened. "As a country I think we are very insecure and we need somebody to rally us," the retired teacher says. Given the chance to stand in President Clinton's place Tuesday night, everyday Americans would paint a conflicted picture of a country with too much political bickering and too little economic security, a place where something important but often intangible, a shared sense of values, seems to have gone awry. AM-The Union Speaks. By Political Writer John King.

> BUDGET SHOWDOWN: House Republicans rallied on Tuesday behind a plan to avert a new federal shutdown this weekend. But Senate Majority Leader Bob Dole reacted coolly to a proposal by House leaders to tack a tax cut to the measure. AM-Budget Showdown. By Alan Fram.

> DISABLED TRANSPLANT: A woman with Down's syndrome who was initially refused a heart-lung transplant because doctors didn't think she was smart enough to handle the aftereffects underwent the desperately needed operation Tuesday. AM-Disabled-Transplant. By Richard Cole.

> IRATE CHEFS: Some of France's top chefs are suffering a major case of heartburn. The 1996 GaultMillau food guide is out, and it boasts a new, tougher rating system designed to weed out what it calls overpriced mediocrity. Some long-established restaurants have been taken down a few notches. In the 1995 guide, 30 restaurants earned the top rating of 19 points and four toques—the tall white hats chefs wear. But this year, only 12 made the grade. Why the cutbacks? "There was toque inflation," the editor says. AM-Irate Chefs. By Marilyn August.

In addition, the major news and supplemental wire services transmit a list of stories that the next day's newspapers will use on Page One. For example, The Washington Post told newspapers subscribing to its news service that it would publish these stories in these positions on Page One the day following the State of the Union address:

> Top of page:
> Cols 1-6: President Clinton gives his State of the Union address, with art (UNION-POST; upcoming).

> At the fold:
> Cols 1-3: Most at-risk children in D.C. are often treated like criminals, report says.

```
Cols 4-6: Va. housing authority votes to deny affordable-housing
loans to unmarried and gay couples, with art.

Below the fold:
Cols 1-5: A 72-year-old Serb woman Tuesday releases a 52-year-
old Muslim woman she held hostage in the basement of her house
for three years because Muslims had imprisoned her own daughter
(BALKANS; moved).
Col 6: Washington Opera company proposes new home downtown, with
art.

Bottom of page:
Col 1: A blue ribbon panel says the government should stop
subsidizing foreign-trained doctors because of impending doctor
glut (DOCTORS; moved).
Cols 2-5: Keys to stories inside, with art.
```

Such lists and budgets are used to determine the content and play of stories and are among the reasons newspapers often publish the same stories in the same relative positions on any given day.

▶**Dummy the standing items.** After decisions have been made about what stories to use on the page, the layout editor is ready to begin dummying. The first step is to dummy all the standing items, those elements that appear every day. For Page One, standing items include the nameplate (or flag), the index, promotional boxes (sometimes called refer boxes), the weather and so on. Usually, the nameplate appears at the top of the page, just under promotional boxes, if they are used. The index and weather often appear at the bottom of the page.

▶**Choose and position the dominant element.** Next the layout editor selects and dummies the dominant visual element for the page. Often the dominant element is a piece of art—a photograph, illustration or infographic, such as a map. Sometimes the dominant element is a combination of several related elements, such as a story, a sidebar and a photograph all packaged in one modular unit. The page's dominant element is not necessarily the most significant or important story of the day; it simply is the most visually attractive and represents a point of entry for the reader's eye.

Placement of the dominant visual element automatically creates positions for the other elements on the page. The lead story, if it is not the dominant element, can be dummied above or adjacent to the dominant element. Secondary stories and packages can be placed below the dominant element. Special care should be taken, however, to make certain that the bottom of the page also contains interesting visual elements.

Actual markings on the dummy include these:

- The areas allocated for all pieces of art—photographs, illustrations and infographics—are marked with a large *X* to distinguish them from stories.

- Stories that will be boxed are drawn as boxes on the dummy and are labeled with the story slug and the word *box*. Usually the size of the border rule to be used is noted as well (1-point, 2-point, etc.).

- Stories that will jump to an inside page are indicated by writing on the dummy the word *jump* and the page number to which the story will be continued.

- A small *x* usually signals the start of the story; a number sign (#) signals the end. Both symbols are circled on the dummy.

One of the most difficult problems facing layout beginners is choosing headline sizes. Traditionally, headlines at the top of the page are larger than those at the bottom. Horizontal formats have changed that tradition, however, and today the length of the headline often is more of a determinant of size than placement on the page is. Another factor is the design philosophy of the publication. Some newspapers are designed to use smaller headlines than other newspapers.

Here are some general rules for choosing headline sizes:

- **One-column headlines.** Usually one-column heads range between 18- and 36-point type. The larger type size is generally used at the top of the page. A larger headline requires greater writing skill than a smaller one, because of its short count (see Chapter 9). Most one-column headlines run two or three lines, although some contemporary newspapers allow five or six lines.

- **Two-column headlines.** Generally two-column heads range between 24- and 42-point type; larger sizes appear near the top of the page. Most two-column headlines run two lines, although some newspapers allow three lines on larger-sized headlines, such as those used on lead stories.

- **Three-column headlines.** Generally three-column heads range between 36- and 48-point type. Most three-column headlines run two lines, although some newspapers allow one line with a kicker.

- **Four-column headlines.** Generally four-column heads range between 36- and 60-point type, depending on placement on the page. Most four-column headlines are one line.

- **Five- and six-column headlines.** These large heads range between 48- and 72-point type, depending on placement on the page. Some newspapers allow 36-point headlines on five- and six-column stories at the bottom of the page. Most five- and six-column headlines run one line.

Headline sizes and the number of lines are clearly marked on the dummy, as is the headline slug (first two words).

Good layout editors are careful to mark any special instructions on the dummy sheet. Such instructions might designate colors, screens, "refers" to related stories, special typesetting instructions or art sizes and the like. As a final check, the layout editor makes sure the dummy reflects the following dos and don'ts:

- Think about balance, contrast, proportion and unity as you dummy the page.

- Remember to work in modular units.

- Avoid tombstones (bumping headlines) unless your newspaper's design allows them.

- Avoid raw wraps (when a story wraps into an adjacent column without a covering headline).

- Avoid juxtaposing similar elements; don't dummy unrelated photographs next to each other, for example.

- On inside pages, avoid placing art adjacent to advertising.

- Avoid "paneling," allowing the gutter between columns to run the full length of the page.

Dummying Page One

Beginning layout editors can learn to dummy Page One by following the step-by-step procedures below, using Figure 11-15, Page One of the Lariat at Saddleback College in Mission Viejo, Calif., and its paper dummy.

▶ **1.** The first order of business when dummying a page is to make proper news judgments about the content; the form of the page will follow. In this case, the Lariat's layout editor, probably in consultation with other senior editors on the staff, has decided to use these stories: *Aid,* lead story about legislation to cut student financial aid; *China,* off-lead story localizing the Conference on Women

Figure 11-15

The Lariat at Saddleback College in Mission Viejo, Calif., won second place for Page One design for two-year schools in the 1995 Associated Collegiate Press/Adobe Designs of the Year competition. Notice that the dummy for this Page One is neat and legible and that all elements are marked for easy identification. The Lariat is paginated on QuarkXPress, but editors are encouraged to create paper dummies as well. (Reprinted courtesy of the Saddleback College Lariat)

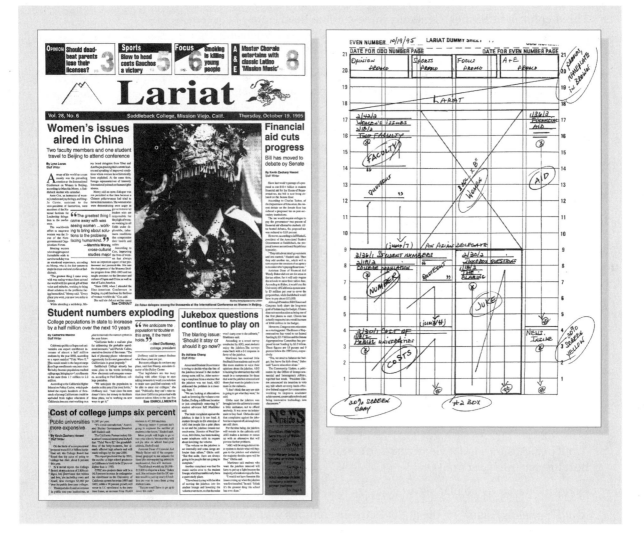

in Beijing, with photo; *Enrollment,* about projected increases in student populations; *Jukebox,* about the fate of a jukebox on campus; and *Costs,* about the spiraling price of college tuition.

▶ **2.** The first six-column horizontal line on the dummy shows how deep the nameplate (or flag) is: about 2.0 inches from the bottom of the promo boxes at the top of the page. The size of the nameplate is constant from day to day. Note that the promo boxes take up about 1.5 inches of vertical space.

▶ **3.** Immediately under the nameplate, about 3.5 inches from the top of the printed page, are two headlines separated by a photograph. The lead headline is an unusual one-column head, set in 36-point type and three lines deep. It is slugged on the dummy with the first two words of the headline, "Financial aid." The off-lead headline is two columns, 42-point type and two lines deep, with a subhead in 18-point type, also two lines deep. The main headline is slugged "Women's issues," and the subhead is slugged "Two faculty." Note that lines are designated on the dummy for each line of the headline; three lines are drawn and centered above the *Aid* story, and four lines (two for the main headline and two for the subhead) are drawn and centered above the *China* story. Also note that the slugs of the stories, which may be different from the headline slugs, are written on the dummy.

▶ **4.** Between the *Aid* and *China* stories is a photograph. Photographs and artwork are designated by an *X.* Each piece of art requires the marking of its size, a slug and the first couple of words of the cutline. The *Women* photo is three columns wide by 8 inches deep and is marked 3 col × 8" on the dummy. The cutline begins, "An Asian delegate."

▶ **5.** The vertical lines drawn down the center of the columns show where the body copy is to be placed. Some layout editors mark a small *x* (circled) at the beginning of each story to help compositors paste up quickly. If a story extends across several columns, diagonal lines should be drawn to connect the legs of type. The vertical lines end in an arrow. An end mark (# circled) is also required if the story ends on the page. If the story jumps to another page, that fact should also be marked on the dummy ("jump to 7" on the *China* story, for example).

▶ **6.** Borders or other unusual typographical treatments are marked in the margins of the dummy. Note the markings for colorizing the promos and nameplate in brown, for using a 20 percent gray screen behind the *Costs* story, for using a No. 2 rule to box the *Jukebox* story, and for using a 20 percent yellow screen behind the index (*News Inside*).

▶ **7.** Type or artwork requiring special treatment should also be noted on the dummy. Both the *China* and *Enrollment* stories, for example, will be displayed with a **quoteout**, a particularly poignant quotation pulled from the story and set in larger type to be used as a graphic device. Quoteouts for both stories are marked on the dummy.

▶ **8.** The dummy is now ready to send to the composing room for pasteup. If the dummy is neat and accurate, the page will be pasted up just as the layout editor envisioned.

Dummying inside pages

Laying out pages inside the newspaper is at once easier and more difficult than laying out Page One or section covers. Although most of the same rules apply—such as maintaining modularity in design—inside-page layout differs because inside pages contain advertisements.

Usually, layout editors for daily newspapers receive the inside-page dummies from the "product makeup" person in the advertising department the day before publication. The product makeup person dummies ads on pages based on a variety of factors, including their size (only one five-column-by-17-inch ad will fit on a page, for example), their content (tire ads usually go in Sports, movie ads usually go in Entertainment), their use of color (only a few color positions are available), and their competition (competitors are not usually placed adjacent to each other).

Most modern newspapers and magazines are laid out using one of two advertising configurations: pyramid construction or modular construction (see Figure 11-16). In a pyramid format, ads are stacked either to the left or to the right on the page. News content touches each of the ads, as desired by the advertising department. In a modular format, ads are "squared off" across the bottom of the page. Some ads may be stacked atop others to accomplish this modular design.

Most editors like to work with a modular ad format because it is easier to design and it often improves the look of a newspaper or magazine. But for editors who must lay out stories and art around ads in a pyramid format, attractive design is still possible. Professor Daryl R. Moen, in his book *Newspaper Layout and Design*, suggests that editors can create modular units with the non-advertising space on

Figure 11-16
In this pyramid ad layout, ads are dummied to the right up the page. In the modular layout, ads are squared off across the bottom of the page, giving editors greater flexibility in dummying stories and pictures.

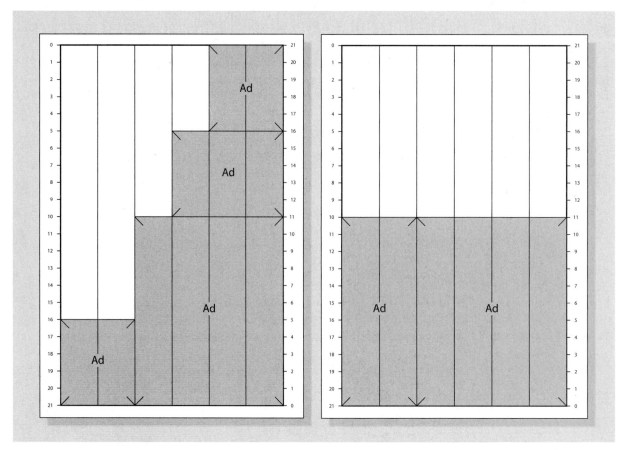

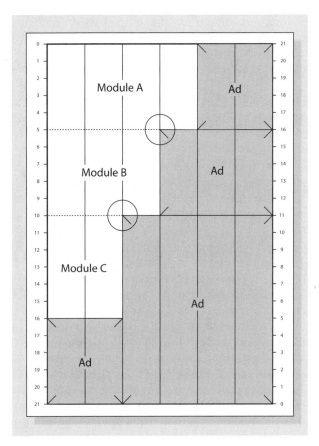

Figure 11-17
Designing modular units for editorial content is a matter of drawing imaginary dotted lines from the corners of the ads to the edge of the page. The letters designate the modular units created; each module may be divided into more modules.

a page by working off the corners of the ads. By that he means that editors may draw imaginary dotted lines from the corners of the ads to the margins of the page to create modular layout units (see Figure 11-17). Such modules may then be used for editorial copy and artwork.

Pagination

Newspaper industry analysts predicted 25 years ago that pagination, the electronic dummying of pages, would sweep through newsrooms in the 1980s and 1990s and that most U.S. newspapers would be fully paginated by the turn of the century. For a variety of reasons, neither has happened.

David M. Cole, a newspaper consultant based in San Francisco who publishes a monthly newsletter and a Web site http://www.colegroup,com about news technology, said that in 1996, less than 10 percent of all U.S. newspapers were entirely paginated—meaning they produced all their pages on the computer whole, with text, rules, photographs, graphics and advertising in place. He suggested that moving newsrooms from a composing-room model, where printers pasted the pages onto "flats," which then became "plates" that went on the press for printing, to a pagination model was more difficult than anyone had anticipated. Cole also suggested that the technology was inefficient and the suppliers knew little about editorial text and deadlines.

Because of the huge initial costs of the equipment and the desire to wait until the best system is developed, newspaper executives have used caution in committing to pagination.

Pagination involves two very different processes: page planning, the electronic equivalent of dummying, and page assembling, the electronic equivalent of pasteup.

Full pagination means that editors can put together entire pages—including copy, ads, photos and graphics—on a computer terminal. Manipulating this vast amount of computer data requires sophisticated technology. The resulting material is then printed as a complete page, bypassing the pasteup function formerly served by compositors. Then the page is photographed, producing a negative from which a printing plate is made. Some systems use laser platemakers or direct-to-film output, eliminating the manual steps of both page pasteup and negative/plate production.

Publications using pagination systems have onscreen layout grids corresponding to the paper dummies formerly used to design pages (see Figure 11-18). Editors may electronically position, move or remove from a page such elements as stories, captions, headlines, photographs and graphics. Type for stories is electronically wrapped from column to column, and the editor may watch this phenomenon on the video screen.

Editors who responded to a technology survey, co-sponsored by the American Society of Newspaper Editors and the Society of Newspaper Design in 1996, indicated that no perfect model to integrate pagination into a newsroom's production process exists. What works for an editor in Maine might not work for an editor in Colorado.

Although publishers and owners invest in pagination because it can result in substantial labor savings, many editors believe that at least one downside to pagination is that editing suffers as copy editors devote a disproportionate amount of their time to layout. "What do you lose?" asked Vikki Porter, then editor of the Olympian in Washington State. "Stories that aren't read or are read only once. You lose overall thinking. Pagination has hurt our ability to edit."

At the same time, editors believe that pagination helps put ultimate control of the content of the newspaper in the hands of newsroom personnel, resulting in the improvement of overall quality.

Figure 11-18
A designer uses a computer to plan a page layout. Pagination, the process of using a computer to place elements on a page, is expected to become more widespread in newsrooms in the new millennium, eliminating the pasteup stage of print production. (Photograph by Tom Farrington, San Diego State University/courtesy of the San Diego Union-Tribune)

Magazine layout

The basic principles of design—balance, contrast, proportion and unity—as well as the six design elements described in this chapter apply to both newspapers and magazines. Likewise, newspaper and magazine editors follow similar guidelines to dummy pages.

Formats

Magazine formats, meaning the shape, size and style of the publication, vary more than the typical broadsheet or tabloid format of newspapers. During their careers, magazine editors might lay out small, pocket-sized magazines (Reader's Digest, TV Guide), 8 1/2 inch by 11 inch pages (Time, Newsweek) or even large-format pages 10 1/2 by 13 inches (Life magazine). Printing press mechanical limitations influence publishers' format decisions. In addition, magazine editors must consider standard paper stock sizes to avoid waste when multiple pages are placed together on one large sheet of paper to go through the printing press.

A magazine's primary purpose also plays a major role in format choices because content, ranging from primarily text, primarily art or an equal mix of the two, flows from purpose. If the purpose is to convey information—whether television listings or scholarly research results—then text, not photographs, will dominate pages, making the additional paper and postage costs of a large-format publication unwarranted. If, on the other hand, photography best suits the purpose of the magazine, then the larger the page, the more impact good photographs and drawings will have.

A magazine's subject matter also helps set its style or tone, another aspect of its format. Serious subject matter needs a more conservative approach to layout and design than less serious subjects. Most magazines today, unlike Life and Look magazines of two generations ago, serve special-interest audiences, not broad cross-sections of the population. This niche approach enables magazines to attract advertising targeted at special audiences. By the same token, special-interest audiences vary widely in their enjoyment or appreciation of wild, splashy graphic designs as contrasted with low-key, traditional design elements. Magazine editors, like successful newspaper editors, must know their audiences and tailor layout and design accordingly.

Basic guidelines for magazine layout

After identifying the subject matter, target audience and purpose and taking into account available printing facilities, graphic designers create an overall format for a magazine. With the magazine's basic design and "look" in place, editors and designers, working in tandem, plan page layouts to display content most effectively and imaginatively.

▶ **Use a layout grid.** A grid is a layout sheet with page margins drawn to show the printed area of the page, plus vertical and horizontal lines dividing the printing area into multiple rectangles, referred to as modules. The grid shows columns, like a typical newspaper layout sheet, plus horizontal lines. In fact, some newspapers use layout sheets with both vertical and horizontal lines. For magazines, double-page grids rather than single pages are the norm. Here are three samples of magazine grids: a two-column, a three-column, and one with two equal columns plus a narrower column on the outer side of each page.

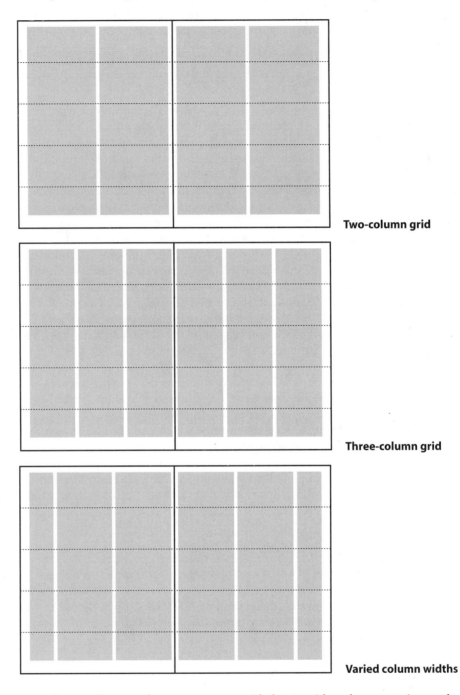

Two-column grid

Three-column grid

Varied column widths

    Some editors prefer to use paper grid sheets, either the same size as their magazine pages or a miniature, proportional size. Others use layout and graphic design software to create computer templates.

    Grids help layout editors align elements with each other to maintain a unified, orderly look to pages throughout the magazine. This does not mean that every page or double-page spread looks exactly alike, which would be boring, but adherence to a basic grid from spread to spread gives readers a foundation. Readers want variety, but they also want enough consistency to recognize that all spreads are part of the same magazine.

▶**Use consistent and progressive margins.** As with newspapers, the open space surrounding the page acts as a frame for the elements on that page. Margins should be the same throughout the magazine, and no type should extend beyond the margins.

Most magazines use progressive margins, meaning that the smallest width is the gutter margin, the side where facing pages come together. Margin widths increase progressively around the page, counterclockwise for left-hand pages and clockwise for right-hand pages. This places the widest margin at the bottom of pages, in keeping with the principle that a page's optical center is slightly higher than its geometric center. The gutter margin is typically half as wide as the bottom margin. If gutter margins are too wide, the alley of open space between two facing pages visually separates instead of unifying the spread. Here is a double-page layout sheet with progressive margins.

Progressive margins

Some magazine designers insist that at least one layout element—art, display or body type—touch every margin on each double-page spread. Certainly this should be the practice on most spreads to maintain margin consistency through the magazine.

For special effect, editors occasionally allow photographs to extend beyond margins and *bleed* off the edge of the paper, giving the art greater impact. Depending on its content and composition, the photo can give the illusion of extending indefinitely instead of stopping at the edge of the page. Too, bleeding beyond margins provides several picas more space for editors to work with. Two cautions about bleeds:

■ Never bleed type because letters can be cut away when printed pages go through the folding and trimming process.

■ Either bleed artwork off the edge of the page or stop at the established margin; bleeds aren't a halfway proposition.

▶**Work in double-page spreads.** Magazine layout editors must work in double-page spreads because readers see facing pages when they open a magazine. If advertising occupies part of the spread or if a one-page article is on the left-hand page and a new article begins on the right, the layout editor must design for best effect. Some techniques:

■ Use a two-column layout for one page and a three-column for the other.

■ Don't let photographs or other art compete for attention. Art for a new article starting on the right can be placed later in the article on the next spread.

■ Box one page or use a tint block to set the articles apart.

■ Use different display type on each page.

Ideally, the layout editor works with two facing pages for the start of a new article. To link the two pages into one unit, design elements must cross the gutter without disappearing into it. Never let type fall into the gutter. Keep body type within the margins and make sure that the gutter space falls between words if display type crosses from one page to the other. If you bleed photographs across the gutter, make sure that faces, or the center of action, in the photograph aren't lost.

If the two facing pages are not a ***natural spread***, alignment problems can result, causing two sides of a photograph or a continuing border to look slightly out of kilter. By the same token, layout editors should take advantage of natural spreads where photos or rules can cross the gutter with alignment assured.

To understand the concept of natural spreads requires a little knowledge about magazine printing and binding and the ***imposition*** of pages on a printing press. Magazine pages are grouped together (imposed) and printed on both sides of large sheets of paper (press sheets). Each side of the sheet is called a ***printing flat***. After the sheets are printed, they are folded and trimmed, producing a 4-page, 8-page, 16-page or 32-page ***signature***. A natural spread is a pair of facing pages within a printing signature that falls on the same side of the printing flat.

Imposition varies from printer to printer, based on several factors, including how sheets are turned over and gripped on the press after one side has been printed ("work-and-turn" or "work-and-tumble" methods). Magazine editors should ask their printer for a printer's dummy, which shows placement of pages on the press sheet and how that sheet will be folded and trimmed so that pages will be in the proper order.

Editors seeking to get the most color into their magazines for the least cost need to know which pages fall on the same side of a printing flat. As explained earlier in this chapter, a page must go through the printing press four times for process (full) color. If all process color within one printing signature is placed on pages imposed on the same side of the printing flat, printing costs are less than if color photos are placed on both sides of the flat.

The number of pages determines the number of printing signatures needed for a magazine, which in turn influences how magazine pages are bound for delivery. The large size of broadside newspaper pages makes binding unnecessary, but magazine pages must be stapled or glued to keep them from falling apart.

Two types of magazine binding are ***saddle-stitched*** and ***perfect***. For saddle stitching, signatures of folded and trimmed pages fit into each other on a V-shaped saddle, and stitches, usually wire staples, go into the back and fold at the center spread. Newsweek and Sports Illustrated are examples of saddle-stitched bindings. In a 64-page saddle-stitched magazine printed in two 32-page signatures, for example, page 1 and page 64 will be imposed on the printing press in the same signature and on the same side of the flat.

Saddle stitching is insufficient to hold together thick magazines, which require perfect binding. The number of pages at which a magazine outgrows saddle stitching depends largely on the paper stock it uses. In perfect binding, signatures are stacked on top of each other and glued together within a four-page cover (front, back, inside front and inside back pages). For example, a 128-page perfect-bound magazine printed in four 32-page signatures would have pages 1 and 32 in the first signature, pages 33 and 64 in the second signature, pages 65 and 96 in the third, and page 97 and 128 in the fourth signature. All four signatures would be glued inside a four-page cover signature.

Binding can influence layout to some extent (i.e., Playboy's centerfold treatment when the magazine became too thick to be saddle stitched and had to switch to perfect binding). It also influences color placement and color costs because of the different ways signatures go together for the two binding styles.

▶ **Start with a dominant center of interest.** Once the layout editor establishes a grid pattern, the first decision about page content is to select an element to give the double-page spread a center of visual impact. A large, dramatic photo, strong informational graphic or perhaps a typographical special effect like an oversized initial letter or tint block immediately attracts readers' attention and provides a starting point for looking at the spread. Without such a dominant center, layout elements compete for readers' attention and make the spread seem confusing and disorderly. (See Figure 11-19.)

Figure 11-19
These double-page spreads from The Razorback at the University of Arkansas feature strong photographs as the center of visual impact. Creative use of headline type, large caption lead-ins and ragged right copy blocks also add visual interest.

Figure 11-20
The headline is the dominant center of interest in this spread from the Columbia Journalism Review. In the original, the word *lust* was printed in red. The photograph on the right page aligns with the top of the subhead, and the small photo in the lower left corner aligns with the byline. Under the byline, the first paragraph of the story exactly fills the space to touch the bottom margin, illustrating careful copyfitting.

▶ **Align elements with the grid pattern.** Once the dominant element is in place, other artwork, display type, body type or borders are placed in alignment with each other on the layout grid. Alignment can be vertical, horizontal or both, as shown in Figure 11-20. Dominant and secondary elements can be placed in relation to each other to achieve perfect balance or informal balance.

Careful alignment demands absolute accuracy in copyfitting and photo cropping and sizing. Layout shouldn't dictate content of copy blocks, but creative editing can often trim a line or two to bring a copy block into perfect alignment with another page element. Editors must copyfit more precisely for magazine layouts than for newspaper pages.

▶ **Plan open space.** News magazines, academic journals and many other magazines whose primary purpose is to impart information fill most of the space on each page, much like typical newspaper pages. Other magazines go for an open, airy look with ample amounts of open space on facing pages. Editors must plan the effective use of open space carefully. The amount of space between design elements—called internal margins—should be a consistent width, often one pica. Larger blocks of open space should be placed to the outer edges of double-page spreads, never trapped doughnut-fashion in the center, giving the visual effect of elements pushed apart rather than unified.

▶ **Control eye direction.** The dominant center of the spread alerts readers to the starting point, but from there the layout editor must place elements to create visual motion to guide readers' eyes in the intended direction. English speakers are accustomed to reading from left to right, so a logical starting point for headlines and body copy is the upper left of a double-page spread. The dominate center of interest may be elsewhere on the spread, but a secondarily strong element, such as a graphic or large headline, must draw attention to the upper left. Alternately, the dominant visual center may occupy the upper left spot, with display type immediately below or to the right.

Other elements that influence the direction of eye movement are borders and rules or photographs depicting action or faces. The action within a picture or the eyes of photo subjects should face into the double-page spread, not off the page toward the right, which visually invites readers to turn the page.

▶**Work for contrast.** Variety in sizes, shapes and textures gives page spreads life and makes them more visually exciting. Art should be rectangular—rarely, if ever, any hearts, star shapes or weird cutouts—but the size and shape of the rectangles should vary. Difference in widths of borders and rules and percentages for screens or tint blocks can also create contrast.

While using contrast for best effect, editors want to reflect a sense of harmony in the overall look of the magazine. This can be achieved with some standardization on each spread—perhaps the body type or something as simple as the folio lines—but the subject matter and tone of each article should guide its layout and design. An article predicting future technological developments, for example, would dictate different type and layout treatment than one depicting pioneer life in the 1800s. Once the mood is set on the opening spread for an article, it should remain consistent on subsequent pages of that article. Figure 11-21 from two university yearbooks illustrates effective use of open space and contrast.

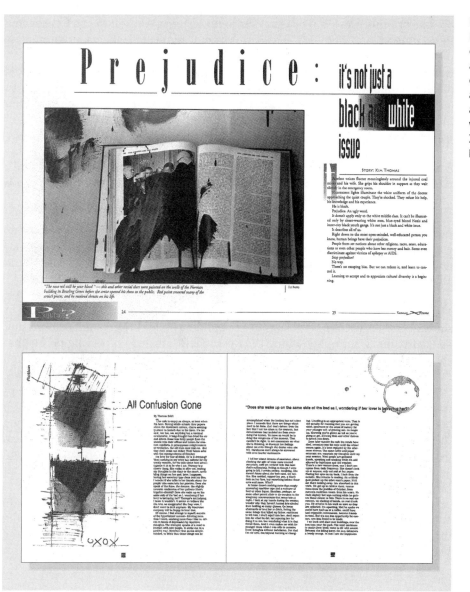

Figure 11-21
Each spread illustrates effective use of open space and contrast. The top example is from the Legacy at Louisiana State University, and the example below it was published in Talisman Xposure at Western Kentucky University.

Web layout and design

Professionals who design pages for both traditional print media and the Web note that most rules of classic design apply on the Web. Designing for the Web simply opens up a whole new range of possibilities; at the same time, Web technology imposes its own set of design limitations. Editors must understand the technical limitations of their medium and work within them.

Two limitations of present Web technology influencing designers are bandwidth constraints and lack of total control over how pages will appear on computer screens. Limited bandwidth adds to the time it takes pages to appear on computer screens, discouraging designers from taking advantage of such exciting Web features as animated graphics, and video and sound clips. Once loaded to individual computer screens, pages vary in appearance according to the brand and version of Web browser used and readers' personalized default font selections. Too, the quality of the user's monitor influences how pages appear. Whereas designers control type and color selection for printed pages, the same level of control is not possible with current Web technology.

Just as their counterparts at newspapers, magazines and newsletters don't operate printing presses or analyze computer systems, Web editors aren't expected to become wizards at HTML, JavaScript or cascading style sheets, or at creating mouseover tricks, snapping buttons, crackling menus, popping windows or whatever Web innovation emerges next. Staff members or contract personnel hired for their computer skills perform those tasks, and develop templates for writers and editors to insert copy and images to build Web pages. Experts in the computer intricacies of creating and maintaining Web sites are referred to as **webmeisters** or **webmasters**.

Still, editors should know enough about the fundamentals of good Web site design and page layout so that they, rather than computer technicians, dictate a Web site's overall appearance, usability and content. Effective communication is the site's primary goal, not to show off the multimedia potential of the Web.

Content, not technical gimmicky, is key to the Web. Recall the five Web site purposes described in Chapter 5—personal, advocacy, informational, marketing and news. Good ideas for content executed in good writing and editing will enhance any site, regardless of its purpose. The Web's full complement of visual and sound effects, on the other hand, is not uniformly appropriate for all types of Web sites.

It is relatively easy to create Web sites today, either by learning HyperText Markup Language (HTML) or with the aid of readily available Web authoring software. At this writing, serious Web site builders prefer the greater flexibility and creativity they achieve by writing their own HTML instead of relying on off-the-shelf software. With diligence and patience, anyone without extremely sophisticated computer knowledge can incorporate the Web's sophisticated multimedia features.

Books exist to lead newcomers through the process, but usually the most up-to-date information about the ever-changing Internet world resides on the Web itself. Online references for HTML tags and Web building information are among the resources listed in Chapter 5 of this textbook. Internet search engines, also described in Chapter 5, can uncover even more online help. One particularly helpful site is C/NET Builder.com, which describes itself as "the site for site builders," at http://www.builder.com/Authoring/Basics.

The purpose of this section of this textbook is to teach editors how to evaluate sites and communicate with Web designers and computer technicians so that the informational purposes of sites receive top priority and aren't overwhelmed by the bells and whistles of Web technology.

Mapping a Web site

Editors find paper and pencil dummies useful in determining the overall look of individual Web pages, much as newspaper and magazine page designers use dummies or layout sheets. However, Web designers must give additional consideration to planning an entire Web site and determining how individual Web pages work within that site. This is not to underestimate the attention editors give to ordering newspaper and magazine pages, but designers for traditional print media generally can assume that readers see the cover or front page of the publication and that readers know what publication they are reading. Web surfers, on the other hand, can enter a page from anywhere in the virtual world, not necessarily through the front door. People often arrive at a site by using search engines, URLs they receive from friends and colleagues and links from other pages. Editors and Web designers must structure their site carefully so that users know exactly where they are within it, what else the site contains and how to get to selected pages quickly. In Web terminology, planning the site's individual sections and pages is referred to as mapping, architecting or storyboarding the site.

Hierarchical arrangements work well for Web sites. A *hierarchy* is a tree-like structure that begins with a single point, or node, which describes the most general aspect of a topic. This node, often referred to as the root, is then divided into branches that contain increasingly specific information. For example, a Web site about basketball might include branches for professional, college, high school and youth leagues. Offshoots for each playing level could be separate segments of the site for men's and women's teams with secondary branches for each individual professional team, each NCAA division, subdivided further by conferences, followed by each college team, and so on. This tree structure could comprise literally thousands of individual pages. Web designers recommend building deep sites with short pages because testing shows that users tend to prefer short pages with clear navigational tools.

Helping readers navigate a site

Like its namesake spider web, a site on the World Wide Web is a complex structure of intricately woven threadlike filaments. Editors and site designers must work together to craft navigational devices that help readers move through the site efficiently, avoiding entanglements in the spider web of pages.

The front door or first page of a Web site is called the *home page*. A home page, at a minimum, should show the name of the site, identification of its sponsor, a list of major subject categories it covers and navigational tools for moving from page to page within the site. In his book *Redesigning Print for the Web*, Mario Garcia, a print media and Web site designer, refers to subject categories as "baskets." A news site's home page might have four or five well-defined baskets—news, business, sports, community—identified on the home page, with sub-baskets of content on inside pages. Home page designs should not be overly complex or busy; otherwise, site visitors can't get a quick read of what's available.

The opening page of the Chicago Tribune Internet Edition, shown in Figure 11-22, uses a minimalist design that lists the seven sections on the site and uses a series of "splash screens" that rotate automatically until users decide exactly where they want to go on the site. Buttons at the top of the screen enable readers to view their electronic newspaper in "traditional" design or a "text-only" version. Readers also have the choice of further customizing their news content with PointCast, a free Internet service that broadcasts news to personal computers at intervals specified by individual users. Other navigational tools on the opening screen offer help tips about the site, a search engine and a site map.

Figure 11-22
The Internet Edition of the Chicago Tribune uses a series of splash screens that function as a three-dimensional front page. The link at the lower left of the opening screen will take readers to Digital City Chicago and Digital City Community sites, also owned by the Chicago Tribune Corp.

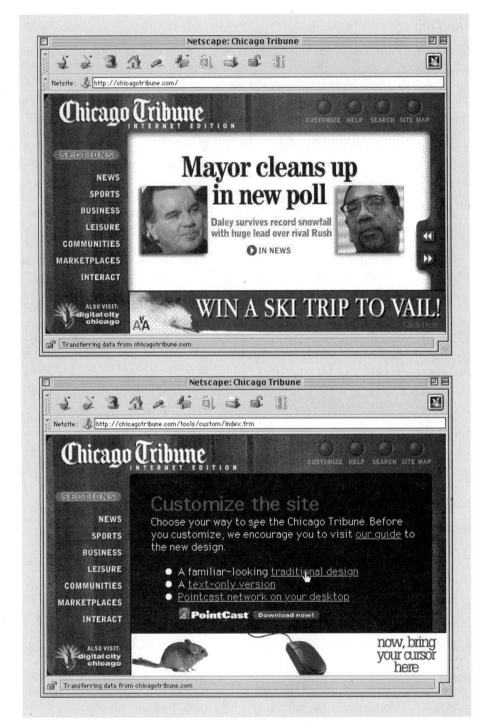

Buttons, icons, labels, headlines, words within sentences and toolbars at the top, bottom or along the side of a page serve as typical navigational tools. Roger Black, an award-winning print and Web designer who has worked for The New York Times and Rolling Stone magazine, argues that icons make better hypertext links than simple texts because they are more intuitive, but not all designers agree. Also, images take longer to load. In fact, users may turn off their browser's image capabilities to save download time. For that reason, editors should insist that images be accompanied in HTML scripts by *ALT tags*—text that identifies content and provides a link for users to select if they aren't viewing images. The alternate

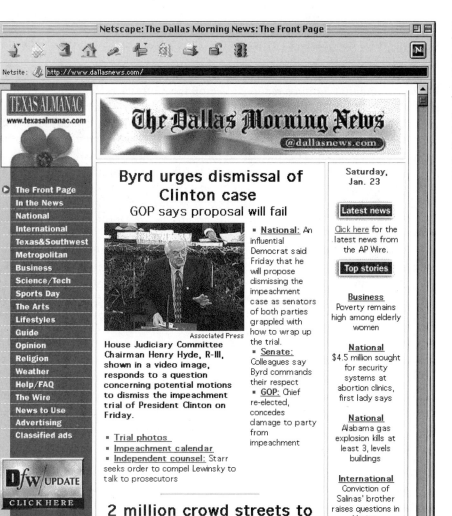

Figure 11-23
This is the first of four screens in "the front page" section of The Dallas Morning News Web site. The four screens feature a photograph, a caption, a headline and links to stories for each of several categories listed in the index at the upper left.

text and accompanying images will not appear simultaneously on the screen, so they aren't redundant.

Whether in the form of images or text, all pages need pointers or highlighted labels so that users always know where they are within a site and what they can expect if they click to a different page within the site. As shown in Figure 11-23, a pointer in The Dallas Morning News index panel along the upper left of the screen shows that "the front page" is now loaded.

Present Web bandwidth constraints increase the importance of designing sites so that pages load to the user's computer as quickly as possible. For that reason page logos, if used, should be simple but distinctive. Web sites and individual Web pages should be uncluttered so that users don't have to waste time loading or deciphering content. Experts recommend stripping from sites all doodads that add nothing to the information or navigation.

In consideration of variations in browsers, Web editors should avoid reference to particular browsers because it is impossible to know which browsers individual readers are using. For the same reason, editors shouldn't instruct users to "select a number" from a list. Just link a key word or number because not all browsers accommodate number selection. Web users will understand how their particular browser works to connect to a link, so it isn't necessary to tell them to "click here" or "select this link."

Editors should check for logic and ease of navigation within a single page, especially one that requires readers to scroll through several screens. A table-of-contents type listing at the top or side of the document with each item linked to its place within the document will enable readers to jump to specific portions. Consider whether the end of each section of the document needs a link to take readers back to the table of contents at the top of the page.

Links can be an integral part of screen displays to emphasize text and make it easier for readers to skim. Like boldfaced words in a copy block, however, links can be overdone so that they disrupt the flow of reading. Choose links so they support sentence and concept structure, and try to match the link text that users click on with the title of the resulting page.

Test links frequently, especially links to sites owned by others. Web pages and even entire sites are transient. A great list of links to lead readers to additional information about a subject covered on a company's site is useless if the linked pages no longer exist. If people hit dead ends, they get frustrated and doubt the accuracy of information contained on the referring site, figuring if the links aren't reliable, neither is the other information.

Editing pages within a site

Editors handling layout and design for Web sites—whether the sponsor is a news organization, a company, an association or a non-profit organization—should follow the design principles discussed earlier in this chapter. Once editors ensure that the site's hierarchical structure and navigational tools are sound, they can turn their attention to the layout and design of individual pages within the site. Items to consider are discussed in this section.

▶ **Tables.** Bandwidth constraints, browser variations and computer screen resolution problems were described earlier in this chapter. Other Web technology limitations for editors are the inability to control spacing (leading) between lines of type and difficulty in placing elements precisely on pages. Tables come in handy for addressing the latter problem.

HTML tags can be inserted to create tables to break text or images into columns, much like columns in printed publications. Web editors must take into account, however, that newspaper-style columns running the entire length of a page won't work for placing long articles on Web pages. Such an arrangement would force readers to scroll back and forth, perhaps for several screens, from the bottom of a column to the top of the next column. Typically, editors and webmeisters use tables to design multicolumn pages. A common layout features a narrow column containing a table of contents and navigational tools on the left side of the page with the remaining page width divided into two or more columns. In a three-column page, the widest column containing an article and headline is often centered between two narrower columns as in the Society of Professional Journalists Web site shown in Figure 11-24. The Public Relations Society of America home page consists entirely of navigational buttons.

▶ **Frames.** The Web technique of framing divides a page into two or more mini-pages, each separately scrollable. Although some attractive, effective sites employ this Web technique, frames are in disfavor with designers and users because they exacerbate the load-speed problem and cause headaches if users try to save the page electronically or print it. The Nando Times home page, shown in Figure 11-25, uses two frames but gives users a "no frames" option.

Figure 11-24
The Electronic Journalist site (a), sponsored by the Society of Professional Journalists, shows a center column flanked by two narrower columns, one for navigational labels and the other for news about the organization. The Public Relations Society of America home page (b) features two columns of oversized navigational buttons and a narrower column on the left with links to its student counterpart and other public relations groups. Reproduced here in black and white, the sites used color effectively.

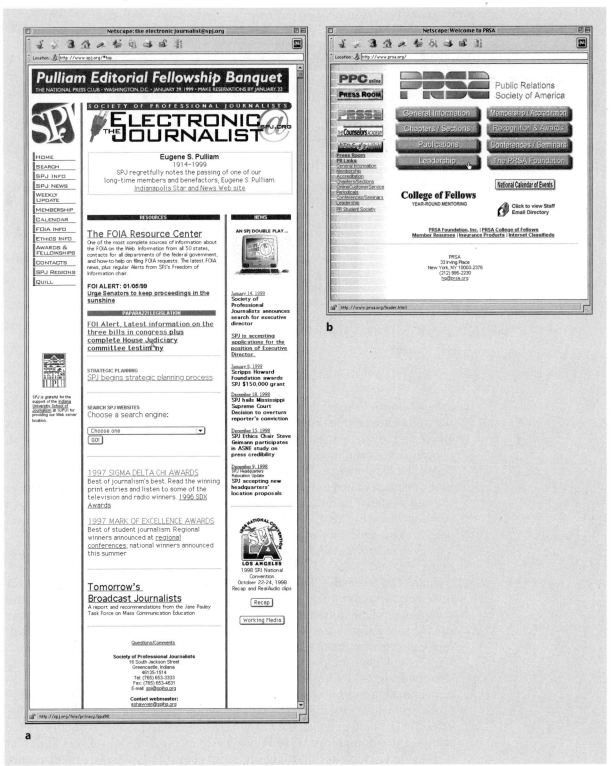

Figure 11-25
The Nando Times (a), a Web site published in Raleigh, N. C., by the McClatchy Co., uses two scrollable frames, one containing an index and another for top stories of the day. At the bottom of the page, a Yellow Pages advertisement (not shown here) allows users to search for telephone numbers. Readers may elect to use a "no frames" version (b). That version includes one story on the home page, along with the index. The telephone search feature appears in the middle of the page in this version.

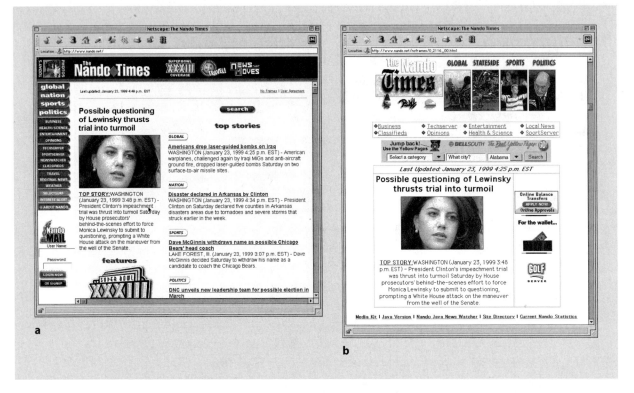

a

b

▶**Page Length.** To scroll or not to scroll? Research of users in the earliest years of the Web indicated that only 10 percent scrolled beyond the information that was visible on the screen when a page appeared. Thus, designers worked to place all critical content and navigation options on the top part of the page and to avoid pages that filled more than one screen. More recent studies show, however, that users are more willing to scroll now for interesting content than they were earlier because it is faster to scroll to subsequent computer screens than it is to wait for a new page to load. This may change in the future if increased bandwidth permits pages to load significantly faster.

Still, editors and designers should take advantage of the non-linear features of the Web and devise ways to break long stories into multiple angles, each with a separate page. Readers can decide for themselves whether to follow all links or to select particular ones. This will automatically result in short stories and minimize scrolling. To facilitate printing or saving to personal computers, editors can instruct webmeisters to provide a separate page combining all segments of multiple-page documents.

In mid-1998, for example, Boston.com, a pioneer in today's ubiquitous city sites, redesigned its home page, moving away from a compact design with navigational buttons that steered visitors to the extensive content of the Boston Globe and its Web partners. The redesigned opening page is lengthy, requiring extensive scrolling to see all the headlines and story summaries with links to full stories and photographs. (See Figure 11-26). This same trend was apparent worldwide as Web sites, particularly those sponsored by news organizations, reverted to a more traditional newspaper look with greater emphasis on news or

Figure 11-26
The home page for Boston.com, a city site sponsored by The Boston Globe, switched from a compact design to one with more content and requiring scrolling. The screens are combined here.

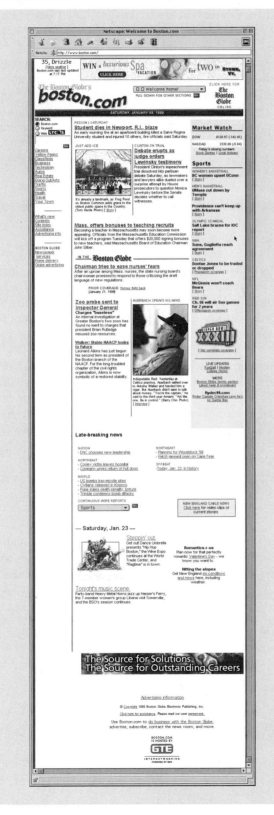

other textual content. The trend may be another reaction to the slowness of loading Web pages to desktops, a situation that future technology may overcome.

▶ **Page backgrounds.** Anything that can be produced as a digital image can be incorporated into a page background, referred to as "wallpaper" for the page. The key rule is to avoid backgrounds that interfere with legibility. Generally, avoid patterns or photographs as backgrounds because they increase download time and decrease legibility of type. White backgrounds enhance legibility over the gray used by default in many browsers.

▶ **Color.** If you use background colors other than white, be careful about text color. Black type on a dark blue background, for example, is difficult to read and vice versa. Text set in light hues isn't as easy to read as brighter hues. Black and red are the most legible colors with a white or appropriately colored background.

Avoid the temptation to use too many colors on a page, causing the page to lack unity and giving it an overly busy appearance. Color works well to emphasize items on a page, as well as provide readers a sense of their place on the Web. Color can also improve the perceived resolution of images.

Editors should insist the default colors for hypertext links be maintained because readers expect these to be blue, changing to purple or red after a link has been visited. This color scheme is among the few navigational aids that are standard in most Web browsers. A site inconsistent with universal practice may confuse readers and cause them to get lost within the site or leave without exploring it fully. The blue-purple pattern allows readers to retrace their steps if they wish or prevents their selecting links that have already been followed. It also alerts users to what new territory remains to be explored within the site.

▶ **Graphics.** A good rule is to minimize the use of graphics files, and to use ALT tags so pages make sense with graphics switched off. Likewise, use Java scripts and constantly running animations sparingly except perhaps for personal Web pages. Friends and family may not resent waiting minutes for an animation or sound or video clip to load, but busy users in search of specific information or news don't want to be bothered.

The same idea applies to blinking words or images. Human physiology has us wired to treat motion as a "blink" feature. People notice change or motion more readily than color or size. Blinking text on a page will draw a reader's eye away from all other text or image content.

Some Web designers recommend never using a graphic where HTML text will do, cautioning editors that designers sometimes design more for their own pleasure than for their users. They'll put text labels within graphics as a way to ensure that users see a particular font. (Remember that text can be controlled by users' browser settings, whereas an image will appear as the designer intended. Unless, of course, the user has images turned off to save loading time.) Don't label icons. They are a graphic way of conveying meaning, so if a label is necessary, the icon isn't doing its job.

Designers shouldn't ignore the multimedia features of the Web. Obviously, sound and video can convey additional information about a news event, a feature story or advertising. The best plan is to incorporate these features, but make them optional for Web users. Don't force users to listen to excerpts from a speech or a song, much less a sales pitch. Include enough information about the accompanying sound or video clip to let users decide whether to select them and wait for them to load. Let users know also if special plug-ins are required to hear or see the clip. If they are, make it easy for users to download the programs.

▶ **Page titles.** The ideal length is 64 characters or less to accommodate screen width, search engines and index services, some of which truncate longer titles. Every page should have a title or headline that indicates the content of the page.

▶ **Orphaned pages**. Because readers can enter a page from anywhere in cyberspace, editors should include a logo or text to identify the site and the place of this page within the hierarchy of the Web site. Blind-alley pages confuse users, so avoid them. Every page should have a link to the site's home page and navigational devices to give readers a sense of where to go next within the site.

▶ **Sign it**. Even personal Web sites should include identifying information about the author because it helps users judge the credibility of material found on the site. A separate link can take users to another page with information about the sponsoring company or individual, or names and titles can be included somewhere on the page. Clickable e-mail addresses will encourage feedback, which commercial sponsors generally desire.

▶ **Date it**. Remember, content is king on the Web, but up-to-date content is the most royal of all. News sites must be perceived as timely, and all Web pages should include information to tell users how current the information is.

▶ **Accessibility**. Depending on the intended audience for the site, editors should be alert to special requirements of some Web users. For example, color-blind people can't distinguish red from green, so design pages where distinguishing between these two colors won't matter. People with other visual impairments may use machines to read Web pages aloud, so avoid spot art or navigational images unrecognized by such machines.

The only layout guide you'll ever need   By J. Ford Huffman

THE person sitting next to you in class spots the folded newspaper you have stuck into your stack of books. She asks if she can see your paper. Or maybe he asks if he can look at your paper. *See? Look?* Readers do that—look—before they leap into reading. Why? A newspaper is a visual medium. Readers look at 25 percent of the text in newspapers, says The Poynter Institute's "Eyes on the News" study, and they read about half of that.

As a designer, it's your job to entice readers into reading more than just 12 percent of the text you put in your newspaper. Here's what layout people need to keep in mind in order to get more people to take a look at your visual medium:

Don't be lost in space. Whether you dummy on a proportionately correct dummy or on a computer screen, the empty space is a blank canvas, a place to create a poster. Doing a page is an opportunity to combine your talent, the paper's architecture and the news content. The result ought to be a typographically correct work of art.

The grid should be ironclad. Make certain the reader will be able to establish a foundation. No matter the number of columns on your grid, no matter how much open space (some call it "white" space) you integrate, no matter your individual layout: Follow the grid. If you align your vertical and horizontal elements by following the established, invisible grid, you will provide a structure.

Every page needs a dominant element. The dominant element can be type or art or space. Your dominant element, or *lede,* can be anywhere you want it to be. The "primary optical area," as some call it, is not fixed.

Every element on the page needs a dominant part. If your page's dominant element is a package of three photos, one of those pictures needs to be bigger than the other two. This size hierarchy helps organize reading.

Design is organization, not decoration. When you are starting to add things to your page, stop. The time to integrate elements on a page is during the initial layout.

Type is type. Do not "add" color or shadows or outlines or screens or condensation or expansion. Maintain some integrity. (Sure, you can have fun with type on the Mac, but keep it on the Mac.) By maintaining a consistent typeface, you help create character for your newspaper.

Opposites attract. Contrast the bold with the light, the big with the small, the horizontal with the vertical, the roman with the italic, the open space with the filled. Contrast is the key to balance and harmony.

Content is what matters. The best designs stem from the best content. The best layout conveys the tone and theme of the story in a presentation. If you're doing the page and haven't seen the story, ask for it. If you're on deadline and the story's not available, ask the reporter or editor to tell you what the story is all about. Then, ask them what the headline is.

Headlines are titles. Headlines are the first sentence of the story. Headlines sell and tell our stories. They ought to intrigue and inform simultaneously. Write the headline. Then figure out what point size to make it. Let the layout fit the content of the headline if possible.

Establish a working headline. In developing a short- or long-term enterprise effort, establish a working headline early—at the story's assignment or initial discussion. If the editor, writer-reporter, artist, photographer and designer know the headline—the title, the theme—the reader will likely figure it out, too. If you establish the working headline, you can come up with the concept for the art. Then, you can decide on the style and form of the art (whether it's a photo, a drawing, a graphic, etc.).

Simplify. The best-designed pages are the ones that call your attention to the content. Take color selection, for example. Designer Roger Black says red, black and white are perfect colors on the printed page and have been for several hundred years. You can't beat 'em for impact.

Bad color is worse than no color. Fuzzy or grainy color photos may have "pretty good" reproduction on your antiquated press and cheap newsprint, and you may be proud of it. But if you're not doing realistic color, the photo and your paper lose journalistic integrity.

Revisit your color theory books. Know how a hue's value (its lightness and darkness) and intensity (its brightness) can work for you. Know why a little dab o' yellow will do ya.

Find a color palette that works for your newspaper and for your page. Know the environment your paper is in. Can reader-familiar colors be used in the paper to make the paper seem even more "local"?

Avoid the message and the image of comic book, Sunday comics colors: Bright green "land" on bright blue "water" on a map locating a tragic event can be misleading. Bright, primary colors belong in the funny pages. When in doubt, go with earthtones and neutrals. Gray and black and white are colors, too.

Crop your photos. If there's a fluorescent light in the ceiling that's part of your interior shot, you can be sure—unless the story is about fluorescent lights—the light doesn't need to be there.

J. Ford Huffman

J. Ford Huffman's first published work was a pencil drawing of an Ohio River barge in Jack & Jill children's magazine sometime in the 1950s.

A quarter-century later, he again hit a national audience—when he was on the design committee that developed the prototype editions of USA Today.

But his awareness of the challenges of visual communication and of the integrity of typography was first stimulated by watching his father hand-letter signs at the family's grocery store in Paden City, W. Va. Then he developed his own lettering style—on posters for school dances at Paden City High and on the nameplate for the mimeographed school paper.

Currently, Huffman is managing editor for features, graphics and photography at Gannett News Service in Arlington, Va., where he's been since 1986 except for his invited visits to at least 35 Gannett newsrooms. He has led discussions for groups such as the American Press Institute, the Southern Newspaper Publishers Association, the National Writers Workshop, and the Freedom Forum—in Warsaw, Poland, and Budapest, Hungary.

In college, he majored in art, English education and drama before landing in West Virginia University's School of Journalism. After graduating magna cum laude, he did layout while on the copy desk at the Wheeling (W. Va.) News-Register. He refined his layout skills as the features editor—the job included art directing—at the Times-Union in Rochester, N.Y. In the early '80s he helped create a new look for the Times-Union, and later he redesigned—with graphics editor Randy Stano—the Democrat and Chronicle in Rochester.

A resident of Washington, D.C., he studies at the Art League School in Alexandria, Va., and has designed sets for the Oglebay Institute (W. Va.) Towngate Theater. He is president of the Washington, D.C. Front Runners; and a member of the American Society of Newspaper Editors, the Society of Newspaper Design, and the National Lesbian and Gay Journalists Association. He did graduate work at the University of Maryland College of Journalism.

Edit your photos. Don't ask the reader to take out the stuff you left in.

Clip and save a file of your favorite pages. Then borrow those ideas.

You gotta have a gimmick only if you're in burlesque. If you are laying out a story about a basketball player, the reader ought to be able to recognize the subject. If you decide that adding a little drawing of a basketball will help say "basketball," go get a drink of water.

Buy yourself a treat. At a newsstand, in magazines, images on TV, computer screens, theater sets, gallery exhibit space. Look around you. Art is everywhere.

Make sure your readers are in your paper, visually. Make sure the subjects of your photos and illustrations mirror your potential readership. If all of the people in your pictures and drawings look like you, you haven't been outside your newsroom enough.

Make every attempt not to perpetuate a stereotype or portray a specific person as the norm for a group of people. In a food-page shot, make certain you're not showing only "mom" in the kitchen (a premise that would be, at best, inaccurate). In a crowd shot, try to represent the crowd—not the most picturesque.

Don't duplicate images, words or phrases. If there are numbers in your graphic, do not put all the numbers in the story, too. The reader will become frustrated, having read the graphic first. Information ought to be *in* the graphic or map. If you need to add a cutline below a graphic, it wasn't done right.

Encourage "word" editors to take art courses. Encourage art editors to take language courses.

Bad display—a poor layout, ugly or unclear art—can ruin a good story. Why? Nobody will be able to find the story and then read it. Conversely, a good display can attract the reader to even the most dull or poorly written, poorly reported story—until about halfway through the second graf (when the dull writing becomes obvious).

A newspaper is a visual medium. Readers need to be compelled to look. To see. Then, if you did your job right, they will be compelled to read.

Suggestions for additional reading

Bohle, Robert H. *From News to Newsprint: Producing a Student Newspaper.* Englewood Cliffs, N.J.: Prentice-Hall, 1984.

———. *Publications Design for Editors.* Englewood Cliffs, N.J.: Prentice-Hall, 1990.

Campbell, Alastair. *The Graphic Designer's Handbook.* Philadelphia: Running Press Book Publishers, 1983.

Editors of the Harvard Post. *How to Produce a Small Newspaper: A Guide for Independent Journalists,* 2nd ed. Harvard and Boston: The Harvard Common Press, 1987.

Garcia, Mario R. *Contemporary Newspaper Design: A Structural Approach,* 2nd ed. Englewood Cliffs, N.J.: Prentice-Hall, 1987.

Garcia, Mario. *Redesigning Print for the Web.* Indianapolis: Hayden Books, 1997.

Guide to Quality Newspaper Reproduction. New York and Washington, D.C.: American Newspaper Publishers Association and National Advertising Bureau, 1986.

Harrower, Tim. *The Newspaper Designer's Handbook,* 4th ed. New York: McGraw-Hill College, 1997.

Lichty, Tom. *Design Principles for Desktop Publishers,* 2nd ed. Belmont, Calif: Wadsworth Publishing Co., 1994.

Moen, Daryl. *Newspaper Layout and Design: A Team Approach,* 3rd ed. Ames, Iowa: The Iowa State University Press, 1995.

Morrison, Sean. *A Guide to Type Design.* Englewood Cliffs, N.J.: Prentice-Hall, 1986.

The Next Newspapers. Future of Newspapers Report. Washington, D.C.: American Society of Newspaper Editors, 1988.

Pocket Pal: A Graphic Arts Production Handbook, 17th ed. New York: International Paper, 1997.

Exercises

1. Pin up on the wall three different newspaper front pages. Judging from the display type and layouts, guess from five feet away which of the papers feature highly controversial stories. Then read the three front pages and report on your findings at the next class meeting.

2. Compare the layout of Page One of The New York Times to the layout of the first page of the Times' business section. What differences do you notice, and why do you suppose such differences exist?

3. Review Page One of three daily newspapers for one week. Choose the Page One that, in your view, is the best-designed front page. Write a one-page explanation of why you think so, using as criteria what you have learned in this chapter about layout and design and what you have discussed in class. Include with your explanation a tearsheet of the page you have chosen. Then copy the layout of the page on the dummy sheet provided.

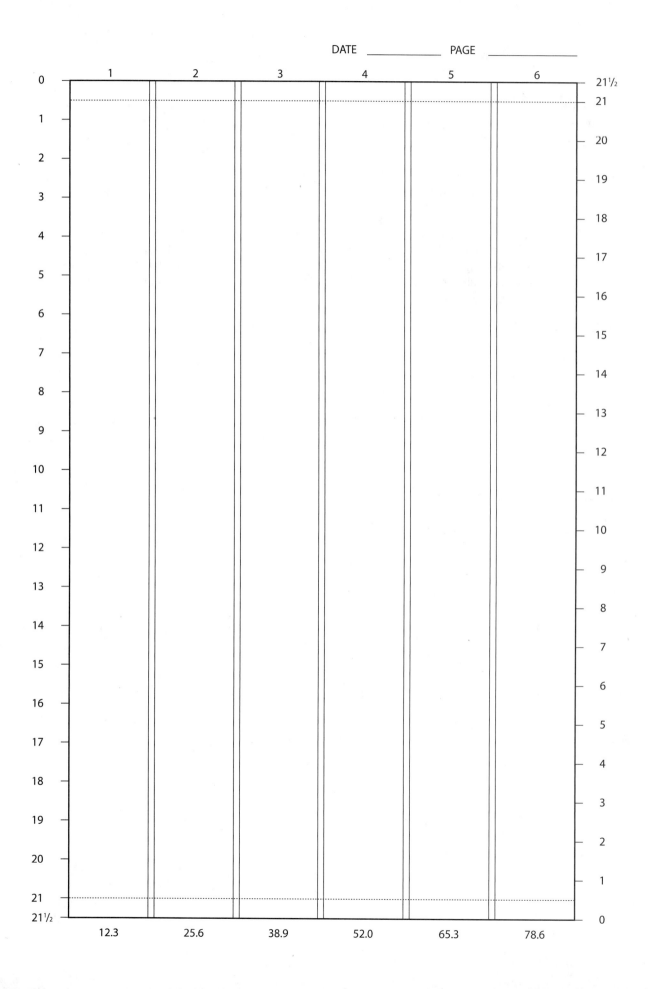

4. You are the news editor of the Daily News. Your newspaper has a six-column format, and the nameplate is six columns across and 2 inches deep. The headline type runs from 14 points to 72 points.

You have 10 stories and six pictures available for Page One (see table below). You cannot place all of them on Page One, so use your editorial judgment to select the most important stories while providing variety on the page. Keep in mind that you can jump stories. A 30-inch story, for example, need not be finished on Page One. How much of the story will appear on the front page is up to you.

A dummy sheet is provided on the following page.

Story slug	Col. inches	Description
Ahearn	21	Local story. Karen Ahearn, president of the local university, announces her resignation after losing a bitter fight to get a better budget.
Streakers	15	Wire story. Roundup showing a nationwide revival of the streaker craze.
Demos	30	Wire story. Ben McClinton wins the party's nomination for the presidency at the Democratic National Convention.
Demo clash	18	Wire story. Demonstrators and police clash outside the Democratic convention hall in Miami.
Hurricane	12	Local story. The U.S. Weather Bureau warns that Hurricane Adam may come close enough to do damage.
Mayor	10	Local story. Mayor Joyce Durham holds a press conference and says she supports salary increases for firefighters.
China—space	20	Wire story. China announces that it has put its first spaceship into orbit.
Ransome	25	Local story. William Ransome, local author and recent winner of the Pulitzer Prize, is interviewed by the Daily News.
Burglary	8	Wire story. Burglars break into the Museum of Modern Art in New York and steal a valuable Picasso.
Diet	15	Wire story. Physician in Atlanta, Ga., devises a new diet. The dieter eats nothing and drinks a gallon of sarsaparilla every day.

Picture slug	Size	Description
McClinton	2 col. x 5"	Wire photo. Presidential nominee speaking to convention delegates.
Ransome	1 col. x 3"	Local photo. Mug shot of the interviewed author.
Clash	3 col. x 5"	Wire photo. Action shot of the fight at the Democratic convention.
Streakers	4 col. x 4"	Wire photo. Streakers disrupt a viola recital; one of the incidents mentioned in the roundup story.
Ahearn	1 col. x 3"	Local photo. Mug shot of the university president.
Kids	4 col. x 7"	Local photo. Three boys, each 4 years old, try to boost a large dog into a bathtub; good stand-alone feature picture.

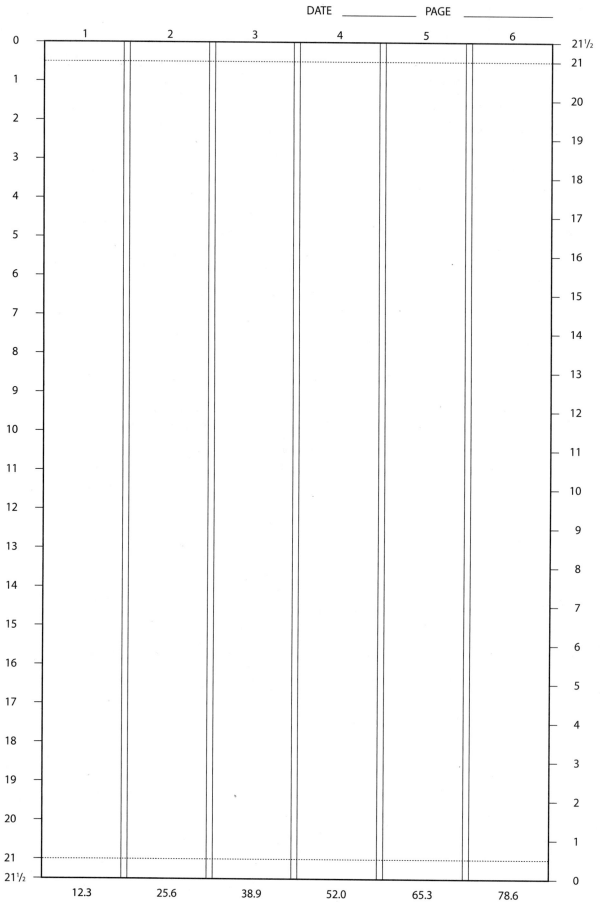

5. Use the copy and pictures left over from your Page One layout in Exercise 4 to fill the news holes on the two inside pages below and on the next page. Use a modular format.

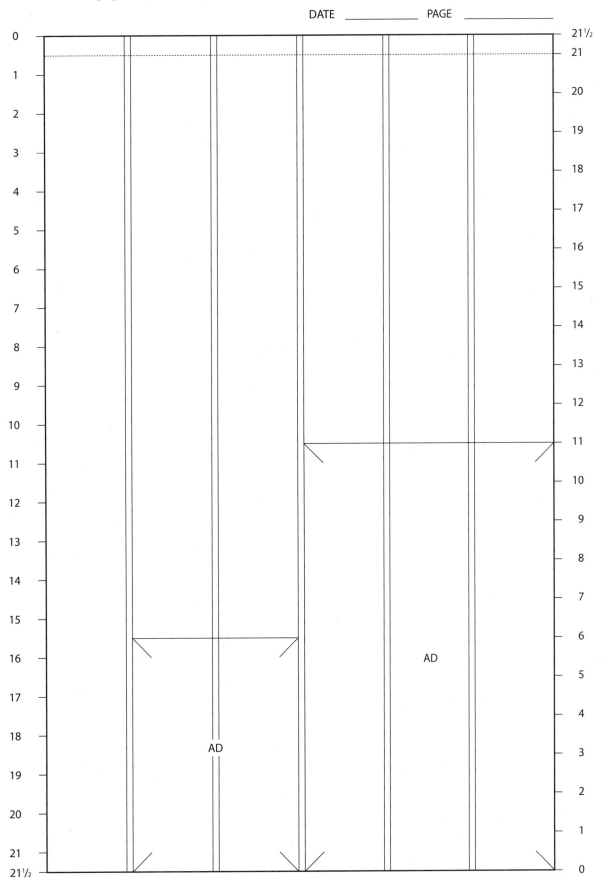

DATE _____ PAGE _____

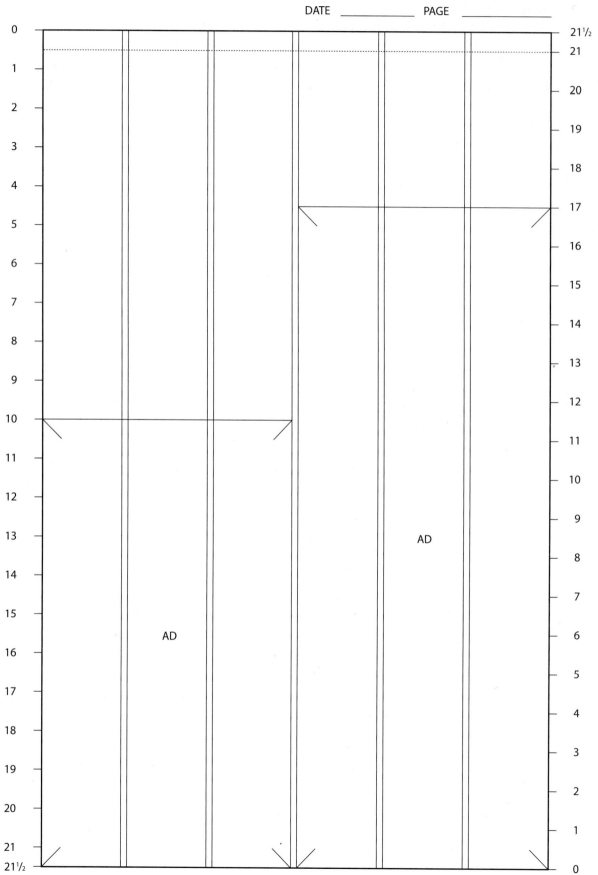

6. Using the dummy sheet on the following page, prepare a front page for tomorrow's Trumpet, Philadelphia's lively new newspaper. Select no more than six of the most important or interesting stories and illustrations for display on Page A-1. The stories and art are listed below. Design the page, making certain that you identify all elements on the dummy with the appropriate slug. That includes stories, headlines, art and cutlines. Reread the information in this chapter to determine the appropriate headline size.

Keep in mind that you can jump stories to an inside page. You may make the art any size you choose, and you may assume that you have mugshots to illustrate any of the stories, in addition to the art that accompanies some of the stories. If you dummy a mugshot, however, you must dummy it in one of only two sizes: ½ column by 1½ inches (this is called a half-column mug), or 1 column by 3 inches.

National/international

Story slug	Col. inches	Description
Crash	15	The pilots of a corporate jet and a small plane that collided in New Jersey knew they were near each other minutes before the crash.
Budget	30	Congressional leaders prepared an escape hatch to prevent an unprecedented financial default by the government. **With art.**
Justice	21	In Raton, N.M., a group has formed to deal with terrorists. They call themselves Bounty on Terrorist Inc., and they're for real.
Rapist	5	In New York City, a prosecutor turned in her own brother as a serial rape suspect after seeing his face on a wanted poster.
Death	15	The House has amended a crime bill that would allow condemned state and federal convicts to escape the death penalty if they can show a pattern of racial bias.
Japan	20	Tsutomu Hata is expected to be named Japan's prime minister after a government dispute over economic issues is settled. **With art.**

State/Local

Story slug	Col. inches	Description
Garbage	15	Philadelphia garbage could fill a Christmas list that would bring tears to any shopper's eyes.
Weather	12	Area to receive a dose of winter after a brief fling with spring. **With art.**
Port	15	A consultant has found that two port sites in Philadelphia meet the requirements for handling new, super-fast ships.
Provost	25	Judith Rodin, the new president of the University of Pennsylvania, has chosen a San Diego professor for her second in command. **With art.**
Sclerosis	30	As a result of AIDS research, scientists at Thomas Jefferson University Hospital have found what could be a treatment for multiple sclerosis.
Chase	8	The Philadelphia police commissioner has banned high-speed traffic chases by city police officers because of injuries and lawsuits.

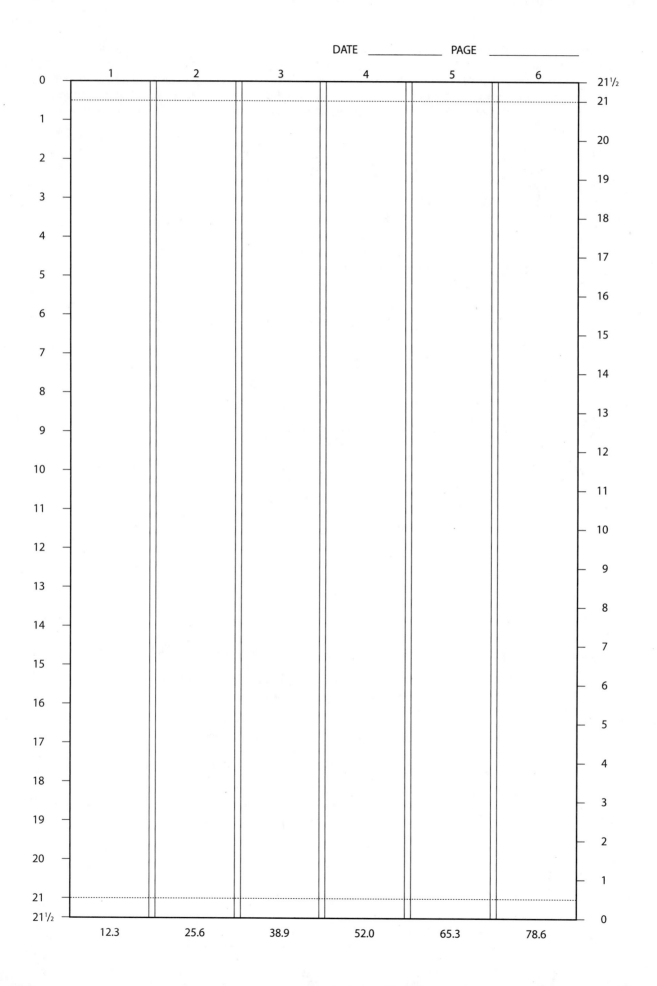

	1	2	3	4	5	6	
0							21½
							21
1							20
2							19
3							18
4							17
5							16
6							15
7							14
8							13
9							12
10							11
11							10
12							9
13							8
14							7
15							6
16							5
17							4
18							3
19							2
20							1
21							0
21½	12.3	25.6	38.9	52.0	65.3	78.6	

7. Use the copy and pictures left over from your Page One layout in Exercise 6 to fill in the news holes on the two inside pages below and on the next page. Use a modular format.

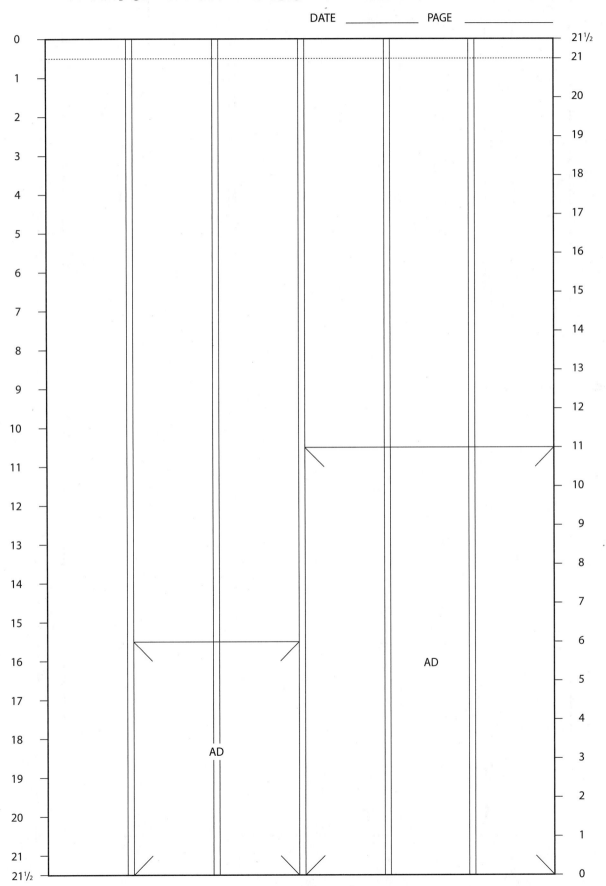

DATE _____ PAGE _____

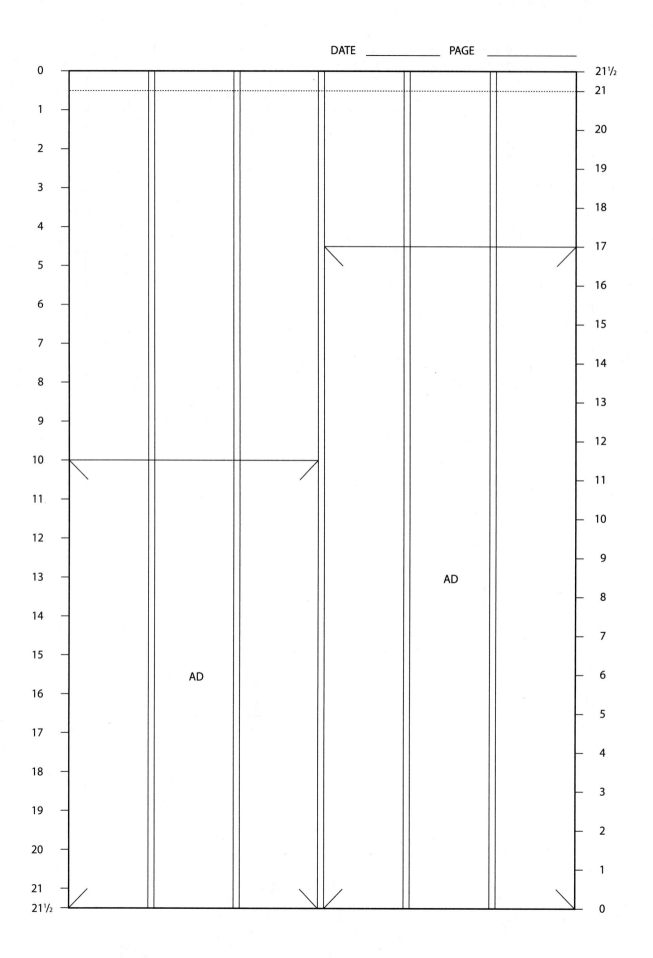

8. Now, try dummying a tabloid page. The elements include:

- The newspaper's nameplate (The Trumpet), which is 4 columns wide by 2 inches deep.

- A standing feature of campus briefs, which is boxed in the far-left column each week and runs down the whole page.

- A lead story about a campus drug bust, about 12 inches long, but trimmable. The story is accompanied by a strong, vertical photo of the police leading suspects away.

- A second story about a hike in tuition costs, about 12 inches long, but trimmable. The story is accompanied by a mugshot of the school president.

- A very short, humorous story about a dog and a Frisbee, about 5 inches long, with no art.

Use the tabloid dummy on the following page.

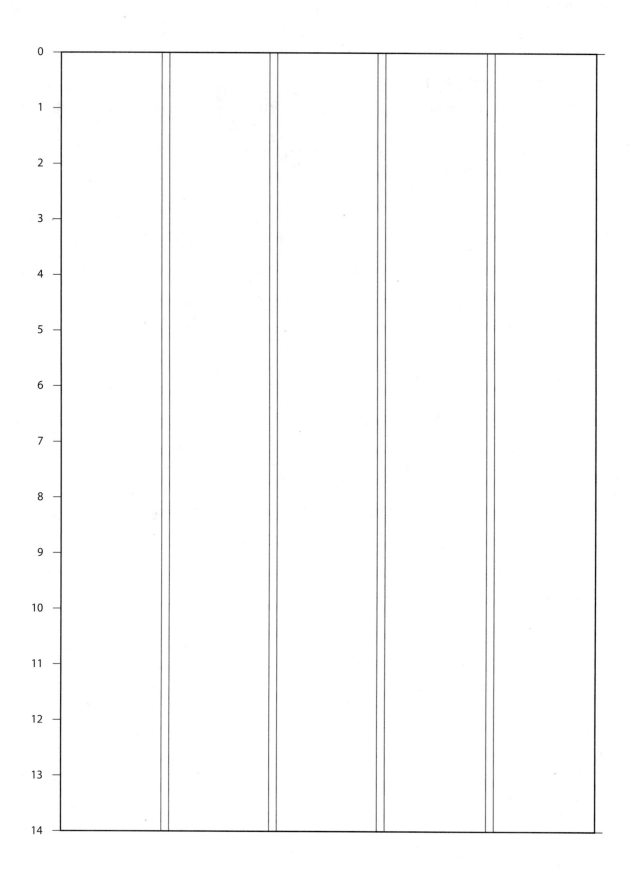

9. Peewee baseball newspaper layout. Lay out a photo page for a community newspaper. Select from these six photos and write captions for those you use. In addition to the photos and captions, you have a story that is 8 column inches long for the page.

Caption information: This is a summer peewee baseball league. The Rocky Hill Rangers are playing the Bearden Bobcats. In this league, adults serve as pitchers and try to pitch so that every batter has a good chance of hitting the ball. Both boys and girls play on the teams. In this particular game, the Rocky Hill Rangers beat the Bearden Bobcats by a score of 12 to 8.

Photo #1: Parents of the players cheering on the sidelines.

Photo #2: Joel Cantrell is returning to his second-base position. He has just hit a home run that put his team, the Rocky Hill Rangers, ahead by one run. This is the last time at bat for the opposing team.

Photo #3: Sammy Sowell bats for the Bearden Bobcats during the final inning. The Rocky Hill catcher is Jimmy Sweet. The pitcher is James Sweet, Sr., Jimmy's father.

Photo #4: Sarah Leaverton standing in centerfield.

Photo #5: Tiffany Smyth is on first base during the third inning of the game. She has just hit a ground ball and beaten the shortstop's throw to first base.

Photo #6: This is the Rocky Hill Rangers' coach, Mr. Robert Sowell. He is standing at first base while his team bats.

All photos were taken by Rob Heller

Photo 1

Photo 4

Photo 2

Photo 5

Photo 6

Photo 3

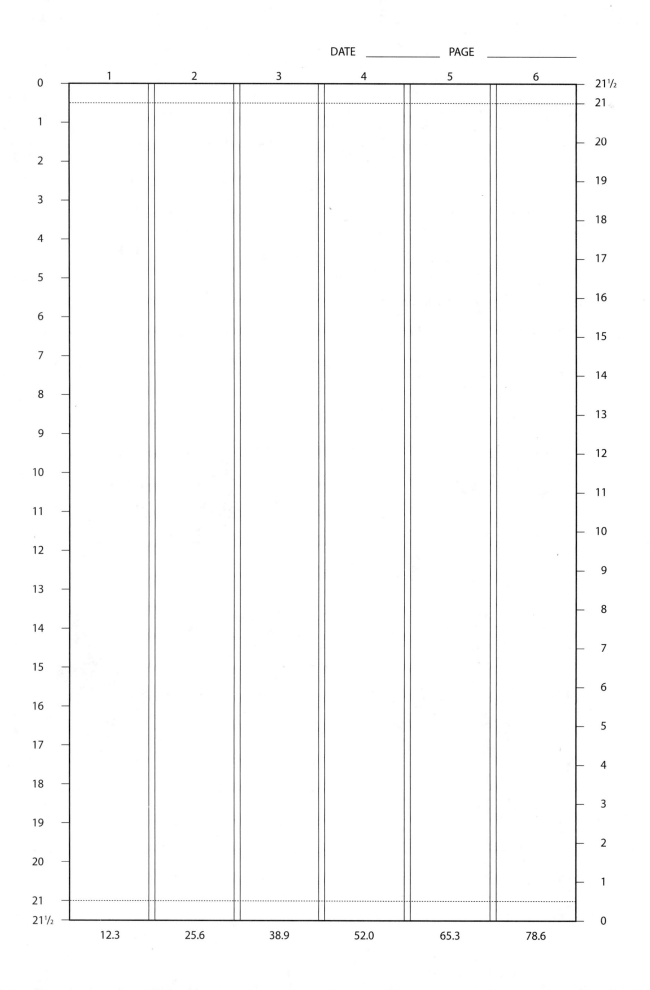

10. **Peewee baseball magazine layout.** Use the same pictures, caption information and copy length to lay out a double-page spread for a magazine published by the city recreation department. The printed page is 6½ × 9 inches. Use the grid sheet furnished here or one that your instructor provides. The story is 8 column inches long when set in a column 12 picas wide. The grid sheet is divided into 3 columns, each 12 picas wide with a 1½-pica (1 pica, 6 points) gutter. Or you may use a 2-column format with each column 18.9 (18 picas, 9 points) wide with a 1½-pica gutter.

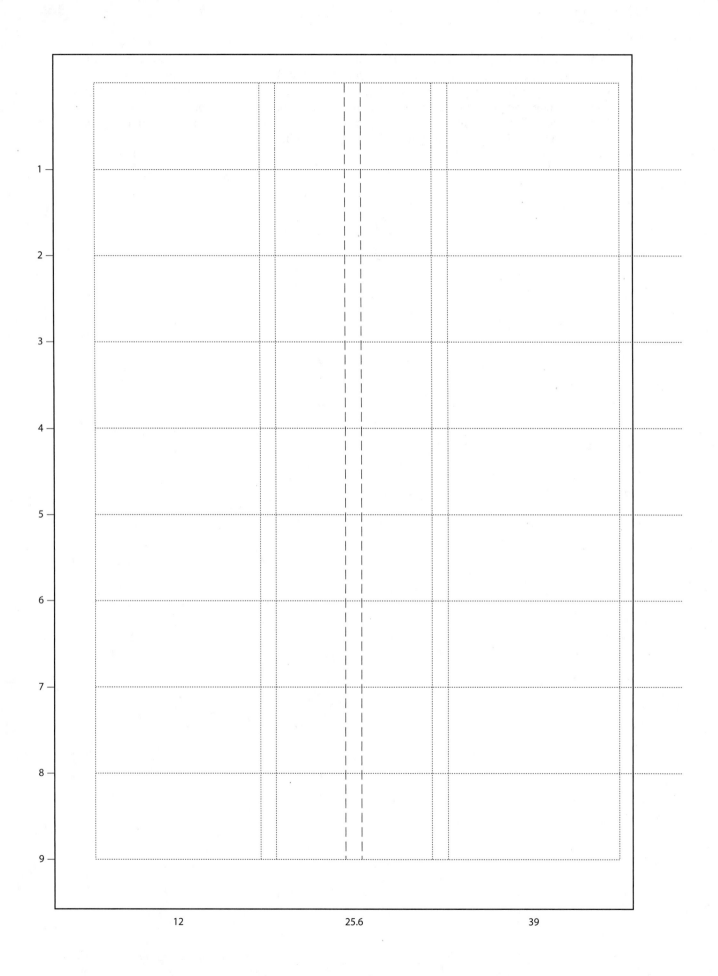

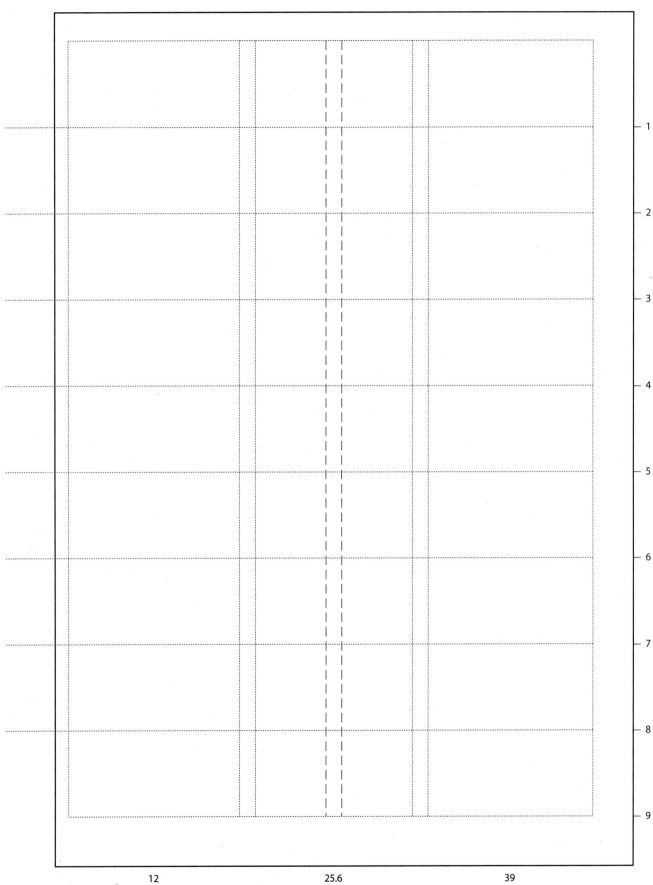

11. **Outlaw Historical Endurance Ride.** This package is about an endurance ride in which equestrians race over rugged terrain for five days, covering 250 miles. Such races are strictly supervised by veterinarians. This particular race—the Outlaw Historical Endurance Ride—is in Utah and is described as the "Ultimate Endurance Adventure."

    The story for this package was written by a woman who rode her horse Salazar in the race. It is written in first person like a diary with a day-by-day description of the experience.

    Using the same elements for each, lay out *both* a newspaper page and three magazine pages (6½ × 9 printed format with this package beginning on a double-page spread and continuing on a third page).

    Material to select from for this package:

    ■ Four photographs shown on next page

    ■ A map of Utah, showing the route of the 250-mile ride

    ■ Story 30 column inches long when set in 12-pica width (you must use the story in both the newspaper layout and the magazine layouts)

    ■ Sidebar story (can be a separate story or you may use this information to create an informational graphic for your package). Here is the information for the sidebar or graphic:

    How do you pack for a 12-hour day on a horse in the wilderness when the day may be in the '80s or may bring snow? Most riders pack carefully and with the worst-case scenario in mind.

    Water: 4 water bottles: two on the saddle and two in the wither bags that hang on either side of the horse's shoulders.

    Rider food and supplies: In the right wither bag are homemade trail mix with raisins, M&Ms and peanuts, sesame sticks, homemade beef jerky, a small camera, a Powerbar, Advil.

    Horse food and supplies: In the left wither bag are grain, carrots, electrolytes and a hoof pick.

    Essentials: In a mini-waist pack are personal hygiene items, knife, map, lip balm, sunscreen, emergency space blanket, waterproof matches, mini-flashlight.

    Extra items for rider and horse: A "rump run" under the saddle that can be unrolled to keep the horse's hindquarters from cramping in the cold, a Gore-Tex jacket for the rider, a sponge tied to the saddle to use if horse overheats.

    Rider clothes: Polartec fleece tights and T-shirt, flannel shirt, jacket, gloves, helmet, boots good for both riding and walking.

    Horse tack: Custom-made endurance model, breast collar to help keep saddle in place and provide space to tie items to, a hackamore that allows horse to eat and drink more freely than a bit.

Caption information:

Photo #1: A "hoodoo" or pinnacle formed by centuries of erosion at Bryce Canyon, Utah. The word comes from "voodoo."

Photo #2: A rider from Washington grabs her horse's tail for help up a steep ascent.

Photo #3: Wynne Brown and Salazar at a veterinary check point.

Photo #4: Wynne Brown, Knoxville, Tenn., and her horse, Salazar, pose for a picture at the finish line.

Story written by Wynne Brown

Photographs by Wynne Brown and Hedley Bond

Photo 1

Photo 2

Photo 3

Photo 4

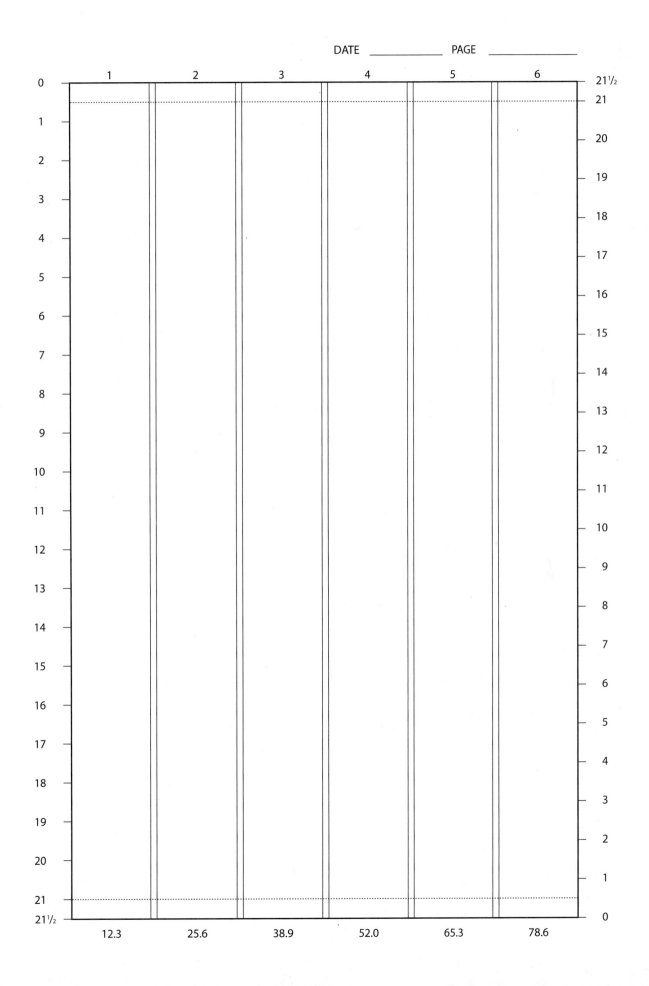

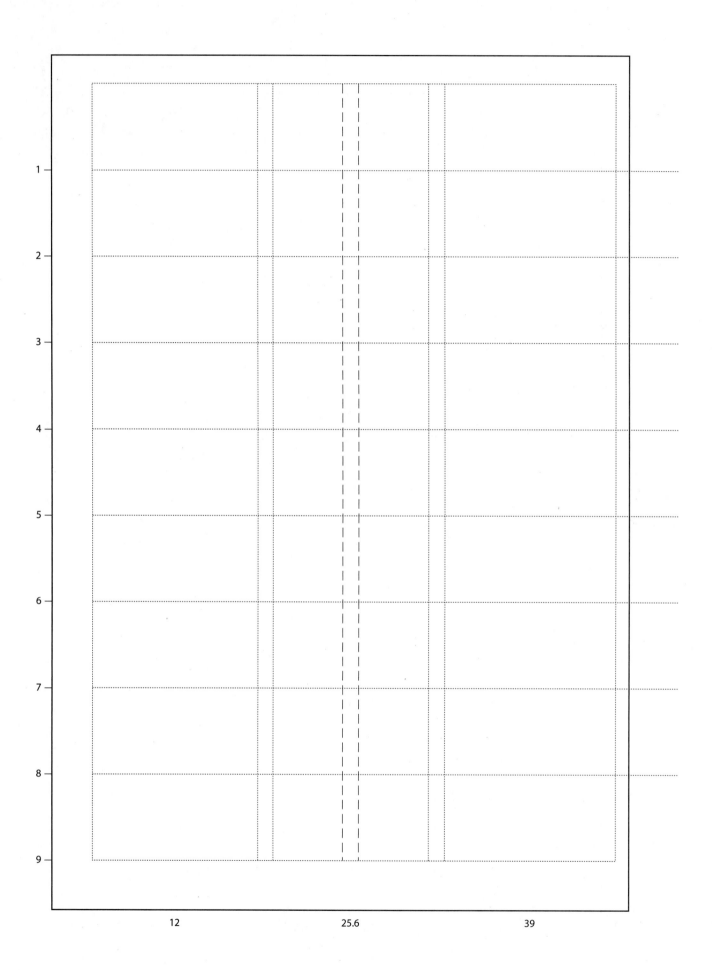

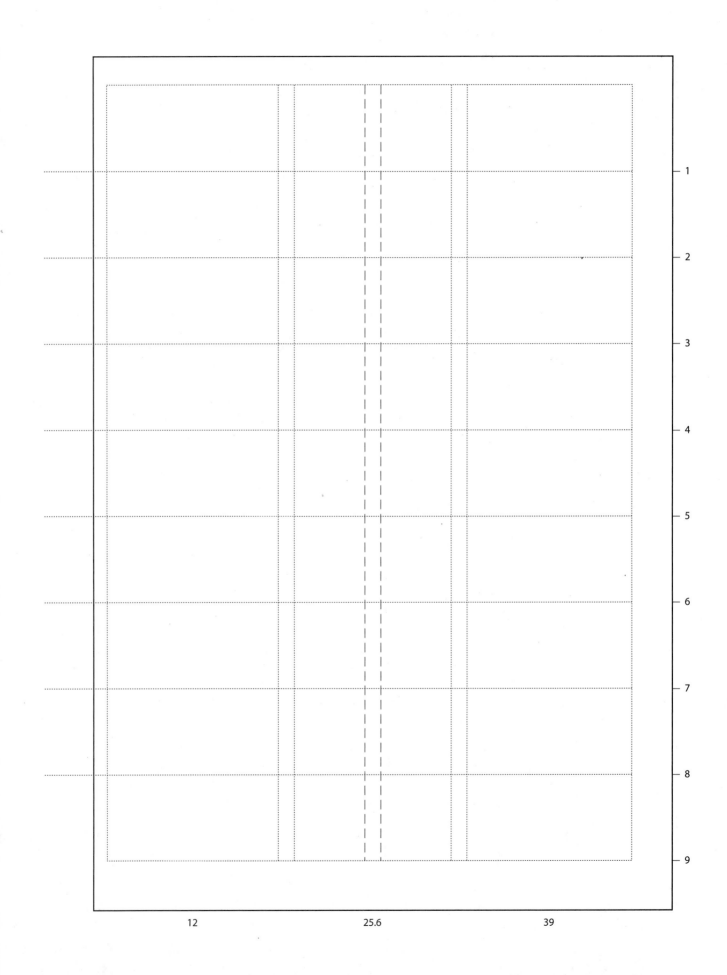

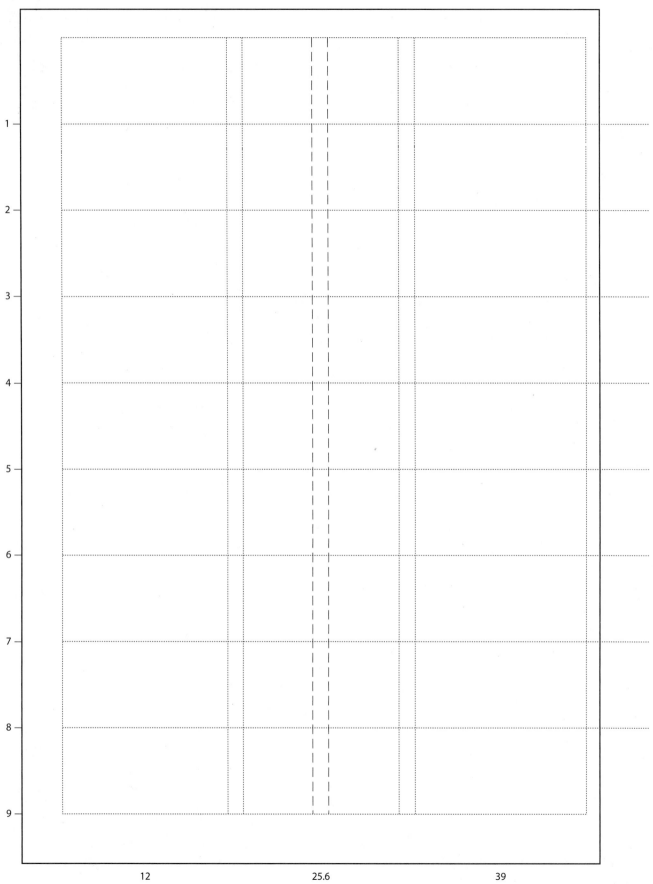

Although the writer always gets the credit for the story, the truth is that
nearly every article is a collaboration between writer and editor.

—*Jann Wenner, founder, Rolling Stone*

Creating Fliers, Brochures and Newsletters

By Rebekah Bromley, a former public relations practitioner and now a faculty member at The University of Tennessee, Chattanooga

THE **professional ranks** of public relations and marketing are filled with public relations specialists and former print and broadcast journalists. Each day, the professionals create fliers, brochures or other specialty print items for their companies and organizations. The secret to producing specialty print materials comes from understanding the unique characteristics of each medium. After that, the materials require the same well-written and well-edited copy needed for newspapers and magazines. Basic design principles also apply across media. This chapter will discuss the purposes, content, layout and design of fliers, brochures and newsletters.

The flier

The brochure

The newsletter

Challenges of corporate communications

The flier

Each day, several times a day, tennis coaches remind players to keep their eyes on the ball. Coaches repeat this instruction because it is a key for hitting a tennis ball successfully. For flier designers and writers, a key coaching tip is to keep the design and writing simple because, above all else, a flier requires simplicity of purpose, message and design (see Figure 12-1).

Yet it is difficult to reconcile this message of simplicity with the variety of uses, designs, distribution methods and even names associated with fliers. It is not uncommon for fliers to be called handbills, leaflets, circulars, broadsides and fact sheets. This versatile item has been used to tout the advantages of political candidates, announce subscription discounts, motivate acts of civil disobedience and promote awareness of yard sales, holiday socials and fund-raising events.

You have probably received text-filled fliers in the mail, seen hand-lettered fliers posted on bulletin boards and telephone poles or had coupon leaflets slipped under your door or car windshield wiper. On occasion you may have seen fliers as large as movie posters and as small as postcards.

Fliers are designed to be posted as a single sheet. As such, fliers must be concise and visually appealing to attract and hold the attention of targeted audiences. Although fliers may persuade and serve educational purposes, they are designed to inform and, by doing so, create awareness. Most importantly, fliers present one message in a timely fashion and have a short shelf-life. Typically, fliers are distributed and posted seven to 10 days before an event and should be removed the day after the event.

375

Figure 12-1
These student-produced fliers are informative, concise and visually appealing. Each presents one timely message—a new play schedule for a student-run radio station, voting information for SGA elections. For visual appeal, example (a) used WUVT's call sign. The SGA logo was selected for example (b).

Purpose of a flier

Properly executed fliers inform a targeted audience of one thing and one thing only. Fliers are visually attractive "written sound bites," timely one-shot messages, designed to inform a specific audience about a single event, activity or issue. Although the flier may be so well done that its readers are motivated or persuaded to take a specific action, a flier primarily provides specific information in a timely fashion. For example, a flier might inform company workers that health department personnel will administer free flu shots to employees in the company's cafeteria next Thursday between 11 a.m. and 1 p.m. Because of the convenience of the location, time and no cost, employees may be persuaded to get flu shots. The primary purpose of the flier, however, is to inform employees of the opportunity to obtain flu shots. In contrast, an advertisement in the company newsletter might dramatize the personal benefits of preventive health actions in an attempt to persuade employees to get a flu shot.

Multiple-message, text heavy fliers may communicate effectively as direct mail pieces, but posted fliers have additional design constraints. For example, a posted flier, typically no larger than this textbook page and surrounded by numerous same-sized messages, must compete for the attention of an audience in motion. The average size of the posted flier, its location and the potential audience's speed of travel require posted messages to be simple and to the point if the message is to be remembered. Think of posted fliers as small highway billboards when designing and constructing them.

Recall a memorable billboard. Was it filled with adjectives describing multiple benefits of a specific beverage, or did it simply say, "Drink 'Brand XXX' Cola"? Did the billboard show 10 people, or even four people, drinking the beverage, or did it show one person drinking the cola?

A memorable outdoor ad will lack visual and written clutter because the advertiser remembered the design constraints of the medium. A short direct message will be dramatized by clean, simple art that is visible among other distractions and read quickly by motorists.

Now, think smaller. Recall memorable fliers you have seen posted about town. Did the fliers have a single message? Most likely they did. The fliers were memorable because the editorial content focused on a single idea that was enhanced by a simple design.

Writing headlines

Writing a good headline for a flier is as difficult as producing a good head for a news story. Many of the basic rules of newspaper headline writing outlined in this textbook apply to fliers as well. A flier headline needs to

- Capture readers' attention

- Use future tense for future action

- Omit the articles *a, an,* and *the*

- Use the active voice

Flier editors too often rely on punctuation, such as an exclamation mark, question mark or ellipsis, to add excitement and interest to an otherwise ordinary headline. The best way to avoid this trap is to banish the use of these overused punctuation marks from your headline tool kit.

Two additional pitfalls await the beginning flier headline writer: a headline that is nothing more than a label and a headline that sounds good but doesn't fit the message. Examples of label heads include "Holiday Social," "Membership Renewal" and "Awards Banquet." In these examples, the headline accurately conveys the topic of the flier but does little to attract attention or enhance the flier copy.

In an exercise designed to encourage new flier editors to avoid labels and develop creative headlines, students were asked to rewrite the "Holiday Social" head for a flier announcing a Christmas party in Blacksburg, Va. Knowing that many people fall prey to holiday depression, the most creative editor exhorted the local audience to "Beat Those Bleaksburg Blues." With some thought and originality, the editor was able to replace a dull label with an attention-grabbing headline.

Another student fell victim to the sounds-good-but-doesn't-fit syndrome, coming up with "Get Toasty," to replace the "Holiday Social" head. "Get Toasty" projected the warm, comfortable feeling the editor wanted to convey about the social. However, the new headline also implied that alcoholic beverages would be served. (Students often refer to excessive drinking as "getting toasted.") Although the headline might have worked for an open-bar social sponsored by thermal underwear manufacturers, it was inappropriate for the particular event, which was sponsored by an academic department that neither provided alcoholic beverages at student socials nor supported underage drinking.

Writing text copy

Too often, flier developers see a piece of notebook-sized paper and feel compelled to fill the space, much like a typical newspaper page. Although the five W's have served journalists well in their construction of news leads, the typical posted flier

Figure 12-2
To attract the attention of an audience in motion, these text-heavy fliers require significant editing.

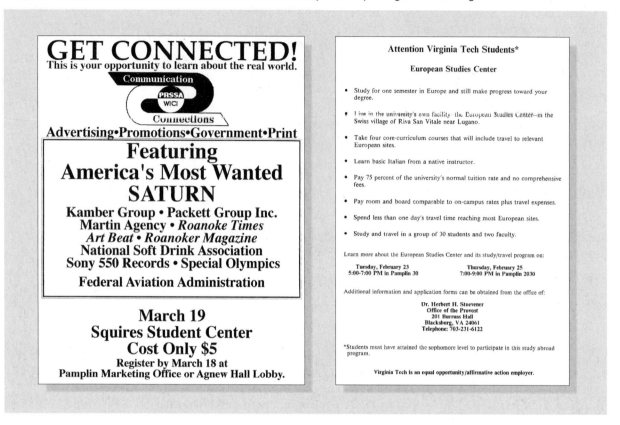

manages at best only three or four of the five W's. The what, when, where and sometimes who are the essential elements of flier copy. Anything else is extraneous.

Because of limitations imposed by space, competition and a distracted, moving audience, little elaboration of "what, when and where" is possible. For example, a flier announcing a food collection drive sponsored by the local animal shelter may contain information about the time, date and collection center locations: "Food donations for Smalltown Animal Center will be collected all day Tuesday, May 15, at most area grocery stores." The text of the posted flier should not explain why the food donations are required, list specific addresses of all collection centers, or explain how, when and for what reason donations will be used. A mailed or hand-distributed flier can, of course, contain additional text, but, even then, less is more (see Figure 12-2).

The best outdoor boards contain no more than seven to 10 words. Because a pedestrian has an average foot speed much less than an automobile's 55 mph, fliers don't have to meet such a stringent copy requirement. However, writers and editors should attempt to keep all text under 20-25 words for posted fliers.

To make copy concise, editors should review it several times, perhaps eliminating entire sentences. On the second pass, editors may further pare remaining sentences to four or five words by eliminating unnecessary adjectives, adverbs, phrases and clauses. With a third review of the copy, editors may add words that were previously eliminated but are now absolutely necessary to convey the information. The final edits of the copy are then made to correct any text inaccuracies or errors of style, grammar and taste.

Although this editing process is a tried-and-true approach to obtaining accurate, clear and concise copy, flier editors and designers must be able to simplify the process by first selecting the minimum information that must be *included* rather than attempting to find and eliminate what can be *excluded*. In the following example, copy for a flier, designed for posting on employee bulletin boards, had been written to remind organization members to turn in reservations for an upcoming member-guest luncheon. The editor, with the single purpose of the flier in mind, read the copy and highlighted only the essential information:

The **Society of Professional Journalists** will host a **member-guest luncheon Friday,** Sept. 16, at the Smalltown Restaurant on 303 S. Main St. to kick off the 18th annual membership drive. **Reservations** should be given **to** the membership chair, **Jo Ann Smith,** at **Extension 1234** no later than **3 p.m. Wednesday.** The price of the luncheon for individual members will be $15. Members will be billed at the end of the month. There will be no extra charge for one invited guest. Members who invite more than one guest should give Jo Ann $10 for each additional guest.

In one quick read, the editor was able to reduce more than 90 words to less than 25 words that gave the essential information: "Reservations for Friday's Society of Professional Journalists member-guest luncheon due to Jo Ann Smith, Ext. 1234, by 3 p.m. Wednesday."

This requirement of conciseness frequently leads writers and editors to group short text blocks under headings of What, When, Where and Who. Using the text from the previous example, the grouping would appear as follows:

What: Reservations for the Society of Professional Journalists member-guest luncheon

When: Wednesday, Sept. 14

Who: Jo Ann Smith, membership chair, Ext. 1234

Although this is a sure-fire method of reducing elaboration and explanation, the technique is overused, and resulting fliers may be overlooked by the audience. The successful editor accepts the challenge of presenting basic information in a straightforward manner, letting the headline and flier design attract audience attention in a more original manner. For example:

SPJ—RSVP—ASAP

Reservations for Friday's Society of Professional Journalists' member-guest luncheon due by 3 p.m. Wednesday, Sept. 14, to Jo Ann Smith, Ext. 1234.

CNPL

Call Now, Pay Later

Design and layout

Keeping text presentations simple and unadorned also works best for flier designers. However, computer software packages such as Adobe PageMaker, Adobe Illustrator and QuarkXPress provide editors with tempting art enhancements and unique layout capabilities. Beginning designers should avoid the temptation to use too many of the software enhancements in any one flier.

The best designers surround flier text with a generous amount of controlled open space (see Figure 12-3). As discussed in Chapter 11, white space should be thought of as a frame around the page. Layout editors should try to push it to the

Figure 12-3
Although not perfectly designed, these student-produced fliers allowed for a generous use of open space to surround the text and attract audience attention. The screened box in example (a) provided a backdrop for a line drawing of a handshake, not shown. The open space surrounding the dollar signs in the "free money" flier is a bit excessive but is easily corrected.

perimeter of the page, never letting white space become trapped on the interior of the page.

Lines and borders, used to draw the eye to textual material or frame the message, are often unnecessary when text blocks are carefully shaped and bordered by planned white space. Tints and screens, which add visual variety to text-only material, may be excessive for a small flier already supporting a dominant piece of art (see Figure 12-4).

The creative use of type sizes and fonts can enhance a flier, although readability should be the governing factor in type selection and size. As a general rule, display type should be no smaller than 14 points and script fonts that mimic handwriting should be used infrequently. Type may be boldface, underlined, shadowed, reversed or italicized to emphasize an important piece of information or add visual interest to the flier. However, using several type enhancements in a single flier appears contrived, is visually unattractive and should be avoided.

As with newspaper design, one visual element should be dominant. Any single element—a headline, text block or art—may visually control the flier while other elements take a supporting role (see Figure 12-5).

Flier layouts come in two broad categories: vertical and horizontal. Typically, fliers appear in a vertical format with a headline at the top, followed next by art and then body copy. When viewed as a whole, the broad outline of the flier is often in the shape of an inverted pyramid. The headline at the top is used to attract attention and identify the flier topic; the art is used to reinforce the message of the head, and the body copy following the art provides the necessary

Figure 12-4
Graphic enhancements can add visual appeal to a flier, but excessive use of computer-assisted graphics, exhibited in example (a), can be distracting to the audience. In example (b), the background screen and the outline of the telephone number have been removed.

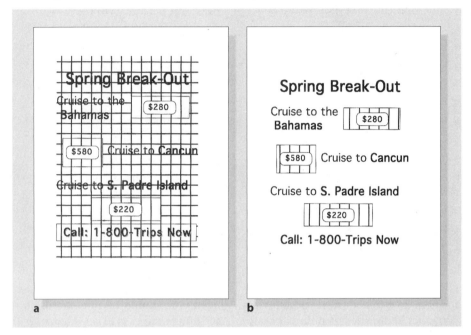

Figure 12-5
The combined text and art in example (a), the headline in example (b) and the art in example (c) demonstrate how different elements became the visual focus for these three student-produced fliers.

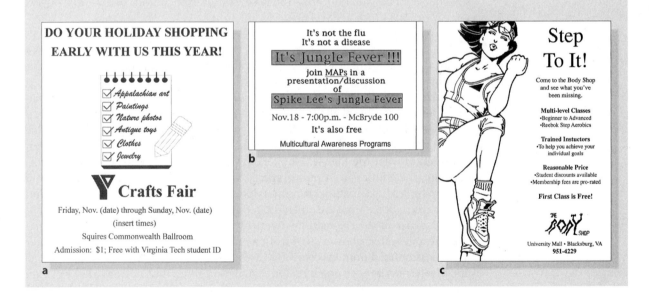

details. This format is commonly used because it works and is visually appealing. However, it is not the only format available to flier designers. For example, an extremely appealing photograph or illustration may be placed at the top of the flier, with the headline following. In horizontal formats, appealing layouts may be achieved by extending the headline across the entire width of the paper and having the text block positioned at the right side of the page and the art on the left, just under the headline.

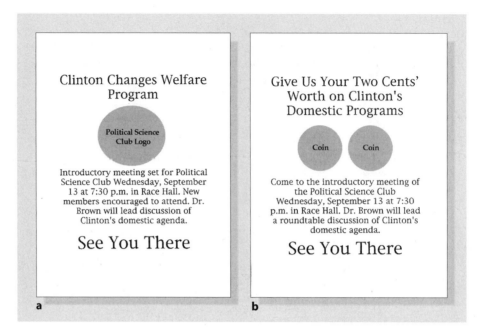

Although one element of the flier—art, text or body copy—may be the visual focus in a vertical or horizontal format, all elements should be integrated. Body copy should provide headline elaboration, not a different message (see Figure 12-6). Art should support the copy and headline. An example of a poorly integrated headline and body copy might feature the headline "Find Your Dream at the APEX Bazaar" but then list ordinary sale items such as yard tools and games in the body copy. The flier loses its potential impact by attracting the wrong audience—dream searchers, not bargain hunters—and falsely raises expectations of potential buyers.

Production considerations

Today, the final, camera-ready layout for fliers is often produced in-house rather than by a commercial typesetting and printing firm. This approach is referred to as ***desktop publishing***. That is, the design or look of the flier and the flier layout—the ordered assembly of all flier elements—is easily accomplished with a computer software package such as PageMaker or QuarkXPress. The computer software has virtually eliminated the dummying process, in which the designer creates a mockup or sketch of what the flier will look like when completed. With the aid of layout software, the editor can import graphics, photos, illustrations or cartoons with a few keystrokes. Text existing in another document may also be copied and imported into a layout, or text may be created directly on the layout page.

Because of their versatility, relatively low production costs and short-term use, fliers are often photocopied from a master copy produced on a laser printer. Masters produced from laser printers are adequate, but evidence of ragged edges and bleeds may be seen on larger fonts. In developing a master from a laser printer, remember:

- Toner quality may vary and you may want to ask your computer lab manager to either install a new cartridge before printing or to remove and shake the existing cartridge to distribute the toner more evenly.

- Toner cartridges can be expensive, so it is cheaper to photocopy numerous copies of a flier than it is to print multiple copies with the laser printer.

- Most laser printers restrict printing to within one-quarter inch of the paper's edge. If your master will not be printed by a phototypesetter, your flier design will have to accommodate this mechanical limitation.

- Some laser printers limit paper size to letter and legal sizes.

- Photographs lacking sharp contrast or large black areas, such as reverses, will gray when reproduced. Narrow rules and borders, line art, illustrations, minimal reverses, and high-contrast photos reproduce best.

- Keep the printer from jamming by using paper of text weight (20- to 24-pound) that is fine-grained.

The brochure

Brochures do not take a single form (see Figure 12-7). Brochures—a catchall category for a variety of publications including booklets, pamphlets, bulletins and tracts—are print items valued for their versatility and adaptability.

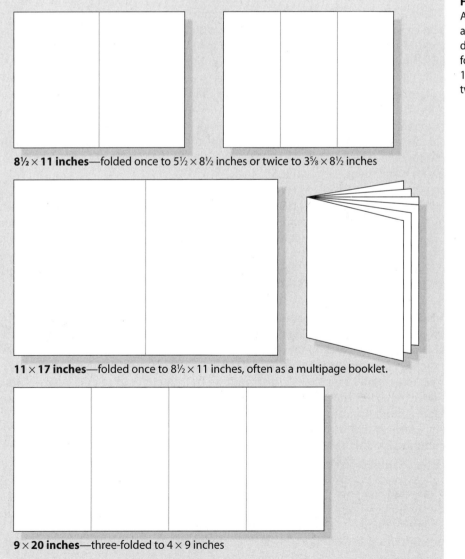

8½ × 11 inches—folded once to 5½ × 8½ inches or twice to 3⅝ × 8½ inches

11 × 17 inches—folded once to 8½ × 11 inches, often as a multipage booklet.

9 × 20 inches—three-folded to 4 × 9 inches

Figure 12-7
A variety of formats are available to the brochure designer. The most common format is the 8 ½-inch by 11-inch horizontal sheet with two folds.

In part, size and construction make brochures difficult to pigeonhole. Although brochures are smaller than books, they can take the form of the information-laden, multiple-paged items, bound with side-stitching or staples, called booklets. As an example, the nation's largest electrical utility has used booklets to provide builders with sufficient information to construct energy-efficient homes. In their smallest form, brochures, or pamphlets, may be produced from a single sheet of legal- or letter-sized paper with two, three or four folds. A publication is often called a leaflet when it has a single fold.

Characteristics of a brochure

For our discussion, a print item may be categorized as a brochure when it has a relatively short shelf-life, serves as a standalone publication, features a single topic, reflects the culture of the producing organization and targets a specific audience.

▶**Shelf-life.** A brochure has a shelf-life of more than a year but no greater than five years. Although the information contained in brochures may become dated in less than a year as the result of unexpected changes, most brochures require some degree of longevity to be cost effective.

Brochures that have not been revised in more than five years most likely contain dated information. As a rule, brochures more than two years old should be reviewed quarterly with an eye toward revision. Quarterly review exceptions may include brochures similar to those produced by the National Park Service or museums that provide historical or basic public use information.

▶**Standalone nature.** Although brochures may be developed as one of a series of publications on a single topic, each brochure must stand alone. Unlike, for example, a monthly magazine for dog owners, which may present a two- or three-part series on the care, training and breeding of miniature Schnauzers, a brochure cannot be produced under the assumption that audience members will return for future installments.

▶**Single topic.** Brochures may come in all shapes and sizes and serve many purposes, but they are similar to fliers in that only one topic or issue is addressed in a single publication. Unlike fliers, brochures can have comprehensive messages. As examples, brochures from a newspaper may give advertisers detailed subscriber demographics by zone, tell readers how news is printed or provide reporters with a reference guide for avoiding libel.

▶**Reflection of organization.** Brochures should reflect the image and culture of the sponsoring organization. For example, a brochure explaining the printing process of The New York Times should have a different look and writing style than a similar brochure created by USA Today. In design and content, The New York Times' brochure should mirror the organization's traditional writing and design styles. Conversely, USA Today should ensure that its brochure reflects the organization's more contemporary approach.

In establishing a strong corporate image, a successful organization or company strives for image consistency with each business transaction and customer contact. A brochure in the hands of a reader is a customer contact.

▶**Targeted audience.** Effective brochures are targeted to a specific audience such as new home buyers, potential newspaper subscribers or valued customers, not to a mass audience. Although a utility company may produce 100,000 copies of a brochure to persuade homeowners of the need to add attic insulation to older homes, the brochures should not be targeted to customers living in new residences or apartments and mobile homes.

A brochure written, edited and designed for a poorly defined or general audience runs the risk of losing message focus. The mass audience does not exist for brochure editors. Even brochures that provide basic park regulations for the millions of visitors to the Great Smoky Mountains National Park should target specific categories of visitors—hikers, tent campers or day visitors—not all visitors.

Purpose of a brochure

Brochures may be used by automobile dealers as persuasive product sales pieces, by politicians to explain positions on complex social issues or by newspapers to give clients detailed information about newspaper advertising and subscription rates.

Unlike fliers, which are primarily used to inform quickly, brochures may be designed to inform, to educate or to alter attitudes and behavior. The federal government produces a variety of brochures to inform and educate citizens about its activities or concerns. From a federal directory of publications listing thousands of published items, consumers may obtain brochures about such topics as fire prevention, voter registration, automobile safety and organic gardening. Organizations regularly use brochures to inform members about essential characteristics of the organization or issues affecting it. For example, a brochure from the Society of Professional Journalists may provide members with the organization's code of ethics, while nonprofit organizations may produce brochures to increase awareness or alter attitudes about issues such as handgun ownership, recycling, abortion and literacy.

Message construction

Brochure message construction requires precise planning. As with travel, unless you know where you are going, you won't know what to pack, the best route, how much money you will need or even when you've arrived at your destination.

Before producing the first draft, you should know the desired communication outcome. Should readers be encouraged to purchase a specific product or make product comparisons based on your organization's standards? Should financial contributors be persuaded to make a donation or have a positive attitude about your organization? Producing a brochure simply to write about an organization's founders, awards or award-winners and philanthropic programs is insufficient justification for production.

When you know the outcome desired from a specific audience, you must learn all you can about that audience. What does your potential audience like and dislike? What do they value and believe? You need to get inside the heads of readers. Knowing the audience's age, income and education level is not enough. You need to know, for example, what messages will encourage occasional young newspaper readers to become subscribers. Are they more likely to respond to messages about content options or about the innovative display of content?

With audience's wants and concerns in mind, you can produce a first draft. Editors can then hone the copy so that the text reinforces what readers want. The editor also sculpts the copy so as to reduce audience constraints in arriving at the desired communication outcome. This task is not as difficult as it first appears. For example, suppose a university wants to produce a brochure that will increase freshman enrollment of out-of-state students by targeting parents of high school seniors. With this in mind, an editor would significantly reduce copy about the beautiful campus and extracurricular activities and emphasize the safety and value-for-dollar messages.

Before the final copy is produced for internal review, the text should be edited for errors in taste and sensitivity, grammar, style and spelling. The commonly adopted newspaper rules governing taste and sensitivity, provided in an earlier chapter, are an appropriate reference for brochure editors, as are the grammar, usage and style pitfalls discussed in this textbook.

Because a brochure is a standalone specialty print item reflecting the organization's image, a brochure editor has two additional editing responsibilities:

- The brochure must attract and hold the audience's attention on its own. Consequently, brochure headlines should sparkle, and copy should have a logical, smooth flow.

- The brochure must be accurate and truthful. Because the content of this specialty publication is controlled by the producing organization, not an objective third party, the burden of accuracy and truthfulness increases, not decreases. A poorly crafted brochure will probably not ruin or severely tarnish the reputation of an organization, but the wise editor assumes that it could.

The difference between an average brochure and a good brochure is in the details. Brochure editors should keep in mind:

- Copy should be easy to understand, the writing style informal. Use of the pronouns *you, our* and *we* projects informality and aids reader identification with the organization.

- Examples should be provided for clarity.

- Long narrative paragraphs can be daunting to the reader. Lists are best presented in bullet form.

- Copy should feature short sentences and paragraphs written in the active voice.

- Copy should encourage and facilitate readers to take action. At a minimum, include a phone number and an address so that readers may request additional information.

- Replace abstract thoughts, ambiguities and vague references with factual information, complete explanations and specific identifications.

- Avoid frequent references to the name of the sponsoring organization. Such appearances seem unduly self-serving to readers. However, the brochure sponsor and the brochure publication date should be identified.

- Exclude information that may become dated in less than one year. As a general rule, a listing of officers or managers should be avoided because personnel changes are common.

Design and layout

Design and layout decisions are made when an editor has the first draft of the brochure in hand, not before. Writers should not be asked to provide copy for a predetermined format. In brochure design, form follows function. That is, the message and distribution method should dictate design. For example, a brochure to be inserted in billing statements must be sized to fit inside the billing envelope.

Writers often suggest photographs and illustrations in drafts of brochure copy. Editors should also be alert to the potential of graphs, tables and charts for presenting statistical information in a concise and visually appealing format.

Figure 12-8
Using type, such as raised or dropped letters (a), as a graphic element can give textual material a point of interest, provide readers with a starting point or resting place, attract attention or provide relief for a body of gray text. A drop shadow (b) is easy to create with page layout or graphics software.

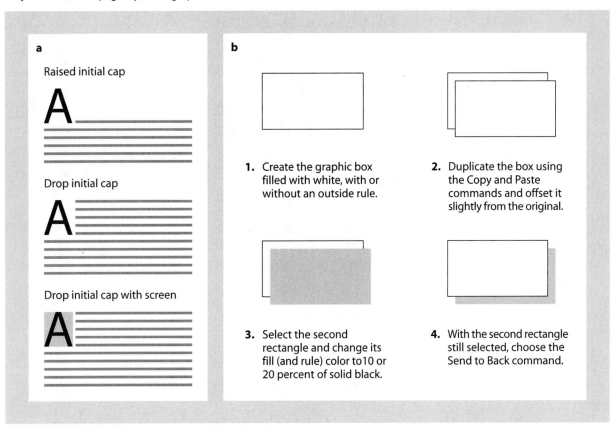

a

Raised initial cap

Drop initial cap

Drop initial cap with screen

b

1. Create the graphic box filled with white, with or without an outside rule.

2. Duplicate the box using the Copy and Paste commands and offset it slightly from the original.

3. Select the second rectangle and change its fill (and rule) color to10 or 20 percent of solid black.

4. With the second rectangle still selected, choose the Send to Back command.

It is also the editor's job to use design elements and plan layouts so as to emphasize primary copy points and information blocks. Rules, borders, screens and art draw readers into text you wish to feature. If you lack art to break up large blocks of gray text, you may find screens, drop caps, box shadows or subheads useful (see Figure 12-8).

Readability may be enhanced by design, specifically your choice of type and type sizes. Choose type fonts and sizes wisely. For example, text type smaller than 12 points, and in some faces a size less than 14 points, should not be used in a brochure targeted to senior citizens. As a general rule, text type smaller than 10 points or larger than 14 points greatly reduces readability and should be avoided for brochure copy.

Because brochures are standalone print items, cover design is particularly crucial. Just as newspaper front pages are designed to attract attention and promote rack sales, brochure covers must grab readers' attention. It is the cover that sells the brochure. Good brochure covers feature a strong visual element (see Figure 12-9). Even inexpensively produced brochures can feature line art, clip art, an illustration or a black-and-white photograph. Rarely are words alone asked to sell the brochure, although it is always better to use text alone if good art is not available. Generally, art created specifically for a brochure is superior to clip art.

Interestingly, many editors will not resist the urge to use photographs produced by a non-professional. They should. When faced with the choice of using poor art or no art, go without art or use type as the graphic element.

Figure 12-9
Most brochure cover designs have art to help attract readers. However, a cover
with a strong headline or graphic display of text may also be appealing.

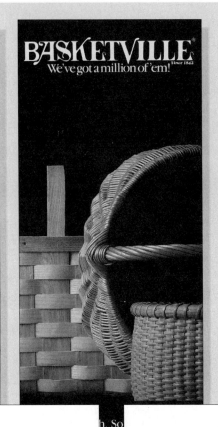

Stop throwing away money on rent and own your student's home away from home.

Pheasant Run Townhouses
LaBrie & Associates
(703) 552-5556
or
800-690-4495

BASKETVILLE®
We've got a million of 'em! *Since 1842*

Newspaper Reporter ● Radio Sta
Executive ● Marketing Specialist
● **Virginia Tech** ● Editor ● Media M
Customer Service Representative
Technical Writer ● Public Relations
Agency Account Executive ● Sp
Coordinator ● **Virginia Tech**
Communications Manager ● Graph
● Legislative Assistant ● Fund Ra
Manager ● Hospital Public Relatio
● **Virginia Tech** ● Magazine W
Salesperson ● Community Affai
Tourism Bureau Director ● Virg
College Student Affairs Staff Memb
Virginia Tech ● Environmental Writ
Magazine Editor ● Television Direc
● Chamber of Commerce Staff Mem
Tech ● Newspaper Editor ● Radio
Trade Association Communications
● Law Student ● **Virginia Tech**
Communications Specialist ● Spor
Analyst ● Copyeditor ● Graduate S
Political Campaign Manager ● Cor
Coordinator ● **Virginia Tech** ● Adve
Account Executive ● Conflict Reso
Negotiator ● Weather Forecaster
● Radio News Director ● Television
Anchor ● **Virginia Tech** ● Governm
Teacher ● Na

COMMUNICATION STUDIES

Help Fund Our Future Home

ΑΨ
2001

Date Rape

Reduce the
Chance of it
Happening
to You

Figure 12-10
A variety of interior layout options are available for a two-fold, three-panel brochure designed on an 8 ¹/₂-inch by 11-inch page.

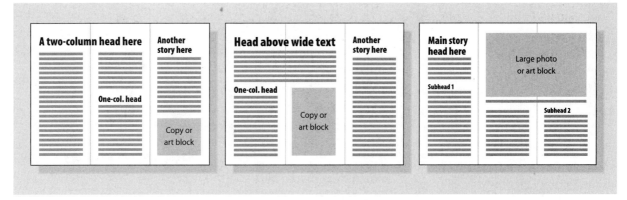

Although it is impossible to provide examples of all interior layout options available, some commonly used formats are shown in Figure 12-10. As a general rule, interior design should enhance the copy, provide for a logical ordering of material and smoothly direct the reader through the information. Key points or messages should hold the primary locations. For example, from habit a reader's eye will go first to the left panel of a three-panel brochure. This critical space should not be wasted on background material such as the origins of the organization.

Although desktop publishing programs have virtually eliminated the need for experienced editors to draw a dummy for a brochure, beginners should prepare a paper-and-pencil mockup, experimenting with design elements before trying to execute the final layout on a computer. Without a dummy to guide them, inexperienced brochure editors may spend many frustrating hours electronically manipulating design elements through trial and error.

The basic layout guidelines given in Chapter 11 for newspaper and magazine pages also apply for brochures. Following are some other useful design and layout tips for brochure editors.

▷ **Colored ink and paper** can enhance a brochure's visual appeal. For example, a warm, creamy beige or a stately blue-gray paper would be appropriate for a Founder's Day brochure. Spot color—an extra shade of ink in addition to black—may be used for headlines or borders.

▷ **The pain of copyfitting**—accurately measuring the amount of space typeset copy will occupy—has been significantly reduced by software packages. With a few keystrokes, column widths can be altered, fonts and type sizes changed, and art resized. However, the ease of manipulation tempts editors to "eyeball" or "guesstimate" placement of graphics and text. For polished, professional-looking brochures, editors should always use grids.

▷ **Body copy** will have an informal style and reader appeal if text is set flush left and ragged right. As with newspapers, the usual narrow column widths of a brochure invite the use of short paragraphs or text blocks and discourage the use of automatic hyphenation and justified text.

▷ **Headlines** should cover all columns of a story. A copy block that wraps to two columns should have a headline that goes across both columns. Columns of text without a headline, called a raw wrap, should be considered an exception, not a rule. In general, raw wraps are visually unappealing, particularly in the interior of

Figure 12-11
With the raw wrap (a), it is difficult for the reader to determine whether the first story ends in the second column or the third. Raw wraps may be used to showcase art (b) and may be screened (c) to provide unity.

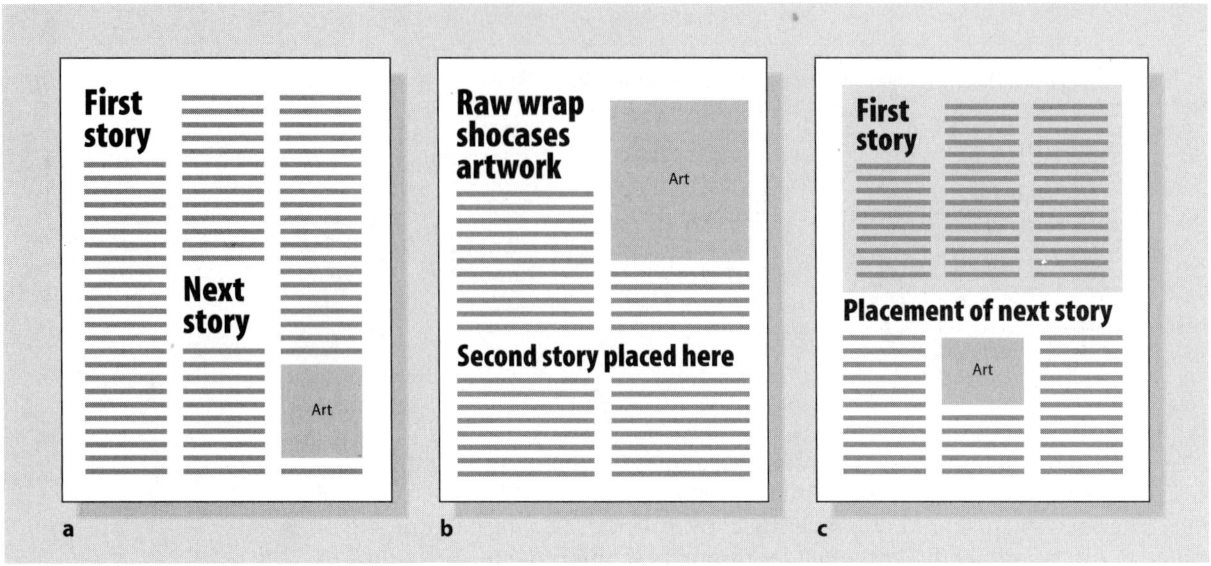

a small brochure, and may confuse readers. However, raw wraps are sometimes used effectively to showcase artwork, avoid side-by-side headlines or fill broad shallow spaces at the top of an interior page. Screens and boxes can often provide unity for copy blocks with raw wraps (see Figure 12-11).

▶**Gutters—the open space between columns—**should generally be twice the width of the outside margins of two-, three- or four-fold brochures produced from a letter- or legal-sized sheet of paper. For example, if the left and right outside margins of a brochure are 3 picas, the gutters should be 6 picas. Without this adjustment the cover panel and foldover panel will appear off center.

▶**A single strong photograph to accompany a copy block** is usually a better choice than multiple photographs, because of the relatively small size of most brochures (see Figure 12-12).

▶**All photographs and photo spreads should have brief captions.** The captions, sometimes called cutlines, describe the photographs. For a head shot, only the name of the person is needed. Caption type sizes should be smaller than the body copy, and a contrasting typeface, such as bold or italic, is recommended.

▶**As with fliers, simple is best.** Software programs provide many easy-to-use design and layout options. Resist the urge to try too many in a single brochure.

Production considerations

Within a large bureaucratic organization, developing a comprehensive brochure from concept to distribution of finished copies takes an average of 60 to 85 working days, or three to four and a half months. The schedule may be shorter if organizational approval is either quick or not required, if the brochure is simple, if brochure work continues through the approval processes, if art is readily available,

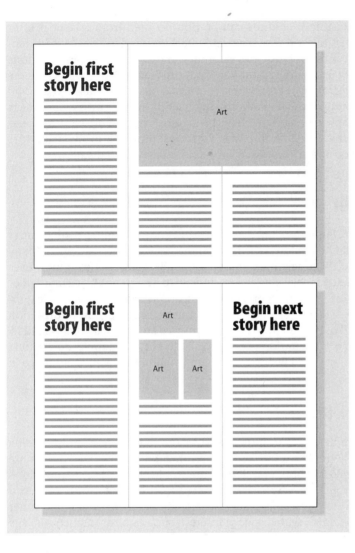

Figure 12-12
Using one large photograph can be more attractive and appealing than several smaller photographs, particularly for the interior panels of a small brochure.

and if printing and distribution are easily accomplished. Assuming that one week is five working days, the typical schedule would be as follows:

1 week—Preliminary research

1 week—Concept planning and development; preliminary budget and production schedule developed

1 week—Concept, schedule and budget approval

1 week—Subject and audience research

1-2 weeks—Writing and editing

1 week—First draft approval

1-3 weeks—Preliminary design and layout; art selection or production; revised draft for final approval

1 week—Final copy approval; preliminary design and layout approval

1 week—Development of camera-ready pages

1 week—Final approval of brochure

1-2 weeks—Camera-ready pages at printers (before press run, ask for a press proof and approve)

1-2 weeks—Distribution of final copies

Perfectly serviceable brochures can be photocopied from a laser printer master. However, after investing the time and effort required in the typical three- to four-month process of brochure development, most firms and organizations choose to spend a few extra dollars per page to reproduce camera-ready masters from a phototypesetter or page compositor. The master can then be used to develop plates for offset printing of the final copies. In offset printing, a press reproduces brochure pages from plate images that have been transferred, or offset, to a rubber blanket or cylinder that puts ink to paper. Offset printing will produce sharper images than photocopying and allow for four-color and oversized pages.

The newsletter

Frustrated by the U.S. Supreme Court's inability to define obscenity, Justice Potter Stewart once said that he couldn't define it, but he knew it when he saw it. Many communication specialists feel the same way about newsletters. The multiple uses and formats of newsletters make newsletters difficult to describe. When a magazine-quality publication for stockholders, created and produced by communication experts, and a letter-sized piece of paper that carries organization information written, designed and published by a clerical employee are both called newsletters, it is no wonder a precise definition is difficult to construct. Literally, newsletters are periodic publications designed to deliver information to a special audience in a timely manner.

Purpose of a newsletter

Most newsletters are designed to inform and to create a sense of unity among readers. Some newsletters emphasize factual information, whereas others are primarily opinion pieces. Many newsletters are published for an organization's members or a company's employees, whereas others are published and distributed for profit to subscribers, such as stock market investors. Still other newsletters serve audiences with a special interest, such as bird watchers, college alumni or journalists.

Newsletters published by a particular organization or business may be distributed horizontally within the company (to all of a newspaper's reporters, for example) or vertically (to all newspaper employees from the owner to the carriers). Many have a small, letter-sized format constructed from an 11-inch by 17-inch sheet of paper folded in half to create four pages. Some are tabloid-size publications that use a vertical format and have a layout like that of tabloid newspapers (see Figure 12-13).

Content decisions

As with the development of brochure content, the selection of information and writing of stories for a newsletter come after its purpose, message plan and audience have been determined. Will the newsletter be sent to company employees, to clients or both? Will the newsletter provide information in a straightforward manner, or will entertaining and persuasive devices be used?

These decisions, made up front, determine not only how stories and messages will be constructed, edited and packaged but also how many of what type stories will be used. For example, an informational newsletter designed to improve the quality of writing for all reporters in a newspaper chain may dedicate 20 percent of the content to showcase the group's best stories and 30 percent to writing tips. In contrast, if the primary purpose of the newsletter were to build a sense of community among reporters, personality features and personal achievement stories would dominate the copy.

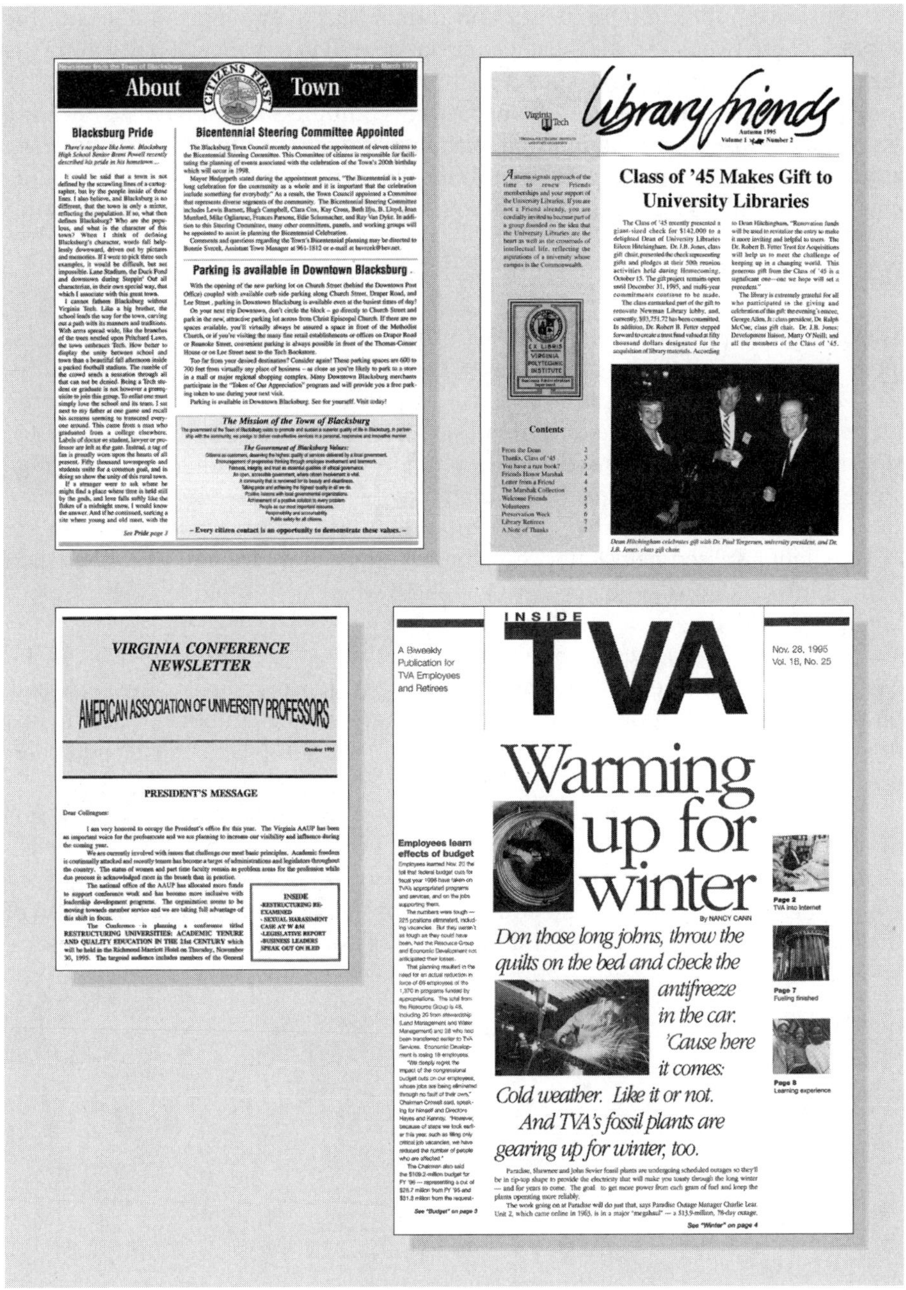

Figure 12-13
Newsletters come in all shapes and sizes. The format reflects the newsletter's purpose, distribution method and frequency, organizational culture and resources and audience.

As a general rule, newsletter editors, like newspaper editors, decide what regular features will be included in each issue. For example, will the newsletter carry letters, editorials, marriage and birth announcements, opinion columns and news briefs? These decisions, which affect not only the content but also the design and layout, depend on the audience and purpose of the newsletter. It is hard to imagine, for example, that a constituent newsletter sent to university alumni would exclude a "Where are they now?" column that reports on graduates' activities.

Creating a newsletter also requires coming up with a name, one of the most challenging tasks facing an editor. Too often, this critical decision is forfeited to a committee within the company or organization or, worse still, becomes the object of an employee name-the-newsletter contest. The name should be carefully chosen by communication specialists who know the newsletter's intended purpose, audience, content and style. The name, which will appear on the front page of every issue, is also key in gaining reader attention and identification.

Because publishing frequency and format play a large part in determining content, these two decisions must also be made well in advance of publishing the first issue. Available funding, staff resources, audience interest, readers' need for timely information and newsletter purpose are combined and weighed in deciding the publishing frequency and format. Although it might be nice to send university graduates a monthly update on organization activities, for example, the mailing and production costs would be prohibitive for most four-year public institutions.

Design and layout

The basic principles of newspaper design, discussed in Chapter 11, apply to newsletter design as well. There are, however, some special newsletter considerations.

All four design principles—balance, proportion, contrast and unity—should be applied with a specific audience in mind. For example, a newsletter for stockholders of a conservative company might have a traditional formal design while a newsletter for Internet users might have a more contemporary look.

Newsletter format also determines how design elements are applied. A large, tabloid-sized newsletter can support larger graphics and headlines than a standard-sized four-page newsletter, created when an 11-inch by 17-inch piece of paper is folded.

Some beginning designers find it easier to use a symmetrical balanced design rather than the asymmetrical design used by many newspapers. Recall, however, that balance does not mean you must have equal amounts of text to text or art to art. All elements of design have weight, including white space and color (see Figure 12-14).

It is helpful to think of proportion, a ratio or relationship measure, in terms of larger and smaller elements on a page. For example, in an article with accompanying art, if the copy and headline consume two-thirds of the space assigned to the story, the art and cutline, if in proportion, would take one-third of the space. Conversely, if a large photograph takes two-thirds of the assigned space,

Figure 12-14
All design elements on a page have weight and are used to achieve a balanced layout.

the proportional amount of body copy, including headline, would take the remaining one-third of the space.

With the overall look of the newsletter in mind, editors develop specifications for such design elements as type size and family for body copy and headlines, borders, art, typographical devices, and use of white space and color. Of the many considerations, one of the most important is the basic grid for the newsletter: the number of columns and the widths of external and gutter margins.

Most newsletters have three columns because of the flexibility the design affords. The three-column format allows editors to give primary emphasis to a story by using a one-, two- or three-column headline. With a two-column format, article emphasis can be more difficult because the headline and story widths are limited to either one or two columns (see Figure 12-15). A one-column format with a wide margin is another functional newsletter layout (see Figure 12-16). Four columns are rarely used for an 8½-inch by 11-inch page size because the narrow column width causes excessive end-of-line hyphenation. A five-column format is typically reserved for tabloid-sized newsletters.

Once the name for the newsletter is decided, the next task is to design a nameplate to showcase it. Typically, a newsletter nameplate has a unique design. Achieving the simplicity of an attractive, attention-getting design is extremely difficult, a job best left to a graphic designer. Although perfectly acceptable nameplates have been designed by editors, the extra expense of hiring a graphic artist to create a nameplate is money well spent.

A newsletter's distribution method also influences its design and layout. When newsletters are designed as self-mailers and not distributed within companies and organizations or inserted in an envelope, editors face the additional restrictions of folding, address and postal requirements. For example, you will need to decide where to place the address on your newsletter. As a general rule, select an area that meets postal regulations but consumes as little space as possible. For example, rather than leaving half a page of a folded, 8½-inch by 11-inch newsletter for an address, consider two folds, which reduces the address space to a third of a page.

Figure 12-15
Two- and three-column grids are the most common in newsletters.

Figure 12-16
Another functional newsletter design has a single column and a wide margin, which can be left blank or used for graphics, headlines, pull quotes or other content. This is the format used for the pages of this textbook.

Once determined, design specifications should remain constant from issue to issue. A consistent corporate or organizational image allows readers to more quickly identify with the organization or company. Readers take pleasure in the ability to recognize their newsletter from all others and to find their favorite features or opinion columns quickly in each issue.

Production considerations

Type of paper, use of color and frequency and method of distribution all affect the cost of a newsletter. To reduce expenses, you should consider the following questions:

- Can your newsletters go third class, not first class? Although third class is slower and special postal restrictions apply, postage is cheaper.

- Can the newsletter qualify for bulk mailing or presorting discounts? Check with the postal service and consider these options.

- Can you use a cheaper, lighter-weight paper, or does the overall newsletter appearance and organizational image require a more expensive, heavier-weight paper? Paper weight affects mailing costs.

- Can your newsletter be a self-mailer? Envelopes add to the cost.

- Can the newsletter be distributed through interoffice mail or left at predetermined dropoff points? Does it have to be mailed?

- Can you achieve the desired effect with colored paper stock or a dark ink other than black? An added color necessitates an additional press run, increasing printing costs.

- Can your newsletter be a two-fold rather than a three-fold? Every fold requires additional time and money.

- Can you publish once a month instead of every two or three weeks? How timely does the newsletter need to be?

Challenges of corporate communications   **By Michelle Medley**

LET me tell you a story about eagles, chickens and the newspaper business. A man found an eagle egg and wanted to protect it, so he put it in a hen's nest. The eagle hatched along with a brood of chickens, and he grew up with the chickens. In fact, the eagle thought he was a chicken. He learned to scratch the earth for worms and insects, clucked and cackled, and occasionally would spread his wings and fly a few feet off the ground. Years passed, and the eagle grew old. One day, he saw a magnificent bird far above the clear blue sky, gliding in graceful majesty. The old eagle looked up in awe and asked, "Who is that? What is that?"

"That's the golden eagle, king of the birds; he belongs to the sky," said one of the chickens. "We're just chickens; we belong to the earth."

The eagle lived and died as a chicken because that's all he thought he ever was.*

In the news business, as in the corporate world, there are eagles and there are chickens. The most successful newspapers know that it's not enough to scratch out a living every day with readers, selling information at 50 cents a copy. To be able to soar with the eagles, newspapers have to communicate well inside the company, to sell themselves— their beliefs, personalities and commitments—to the people who drive the company's success through their service to customers.

As editor of the monthly employee magazine at the Dallas Morning News, my job was to figure out how best to support the exchange of information between management and employees. Like other editors in their respective industries, I had two key obligations to my company: to support its objectives and policies, and to meet the needs of employees. These obligations can work in opposition to each other; there is often a conflict between what management wants to say and what employees want to hear.

Just a generation ago, workplace cultures were so rigid that employees wouldn't have thought of challenging management's decisions on how much information to exchange. Today, employees wouldn't think of *not* challenging management's decisions. That's a significant turnaround. A public relations professional has to help both sides exchange information smoothly.

Sometimes I see my reporting job from the employee point of view. Employees say they want to read more about where the company is going, how the company is doing,

---

*Source unknown: story retold by John Ward, ABC, Albuquerque, N.M. Essay reprinted by permission.

Michelle Medley, ABC, worked with news organizations for 20 years before starting her own public relations firm in Dallas. At The Dallas Morning News she helped edit the newspaper's first Pulitzer Prize–winning story. Later she became editor of Intercom, the employee magazine of The Dallas Morning News.

After graduating magna cum laude from the University of Tennessee, she joined the Columbus Enquirer in Columbus, Ga. She worked briefly in Pan Am's aerospace division before going to Cocoa Today (now Florida Today). Medley achieved accreditation from the International Association of Business Communicators in 1993 and has won numerous awards from IABC, Editor and Publisher, the Dallas Press Club and Women in Communications, Inc. She says the awards are great but it's even more fun to get into such access-limited venues as a White House press conference, a prêt-à-porter fashion show in Paris or the home of Dallas millionaire Dick Bass, the first man to reach the summit on the world's highest peaks on all seven continents.

Michelle Medley

what their role is in the company's success. That's when I start advocating for more stories about company direction and workplace issues: stories about the Internet and its impact on the print industry, workplace violence, downsizing, flexible schedules, part-time benefits, wrist injuries caused by writing too much on a computer, all of the high-impact material that gives management pause. Sometimes management listens to me, sometimes not.

Here are the "10 Commandments of Employee Publications." Companies that follow these commandments are no chickens. They are the eagles. I try to fly by these rules.

No. 1 *Always know what your job is, and get a written description of it.* You need to understand the job description because you're going to be evaluated against it. Is your job solely to publish a newsletter, or is it broader than that? Will you be expected to write a communication plan for the company, or measure the effectiveness of all employee materials? Know what's expected. As a corollary, know the rules of the game at your company. Figure out how to deal with your boss and with the approval process. The rules will change with every new boss or every new vice president who comes aboard. Be prepared for them. How? Set some rules and get them in writing. Have everyone sign off on them. Most important, learn how to "fail fast, fix it and race on." This idea comes from Price Pritchett's book *Work Habits for a Radically Changing World*. Change is happening so fast, Pritchett says, that top management won't be able to run things the old way, even if it desperately wants to. It has to make adjustments to keep up with emerging trends. So if you're going to fail on a particular assignment, learn how to do it fast, fix the problem and race on to the next situation.

No. 2 *If your job is primarily to edit an employee publication, always know what your management wants in print.* Make an appointment to visit with the key officers. Ask for the company's vision and direction. If management can't tell you what it wants, then you'll have to create stories you think your management should want. Study lifestyles and business news sections to see what the newspaper is reporting as emerging issues and trends. Propose coverage of these areas inside your company's publication.

No. 3 *Always remember who your audience is.* Our newspaper publisher says that too many employee publications are edited for audiences other than employees, like for other colleagues. They're edited for competitions, for peers, for consultants, for the people who will say nice things about them. Get to know who your audience is by walking around and meeting people. Follow the trail of a grapevine and see where it leads. Learn names and faces. Invite yourself to meetings. Attend those company events.

No. 4 *Always remember what your message is.* Employee publications must help employees understand what the company is about—its values, culture, goals, aspirations, what the expectations are, what the benefits are, the reward systems. It ought to answer questions or reservations people have about management. Try to eat more burritos than chocolate. Think from management's point of view. This leads to No. 5.

No. 5 *Always remember who the publication works for.* It's an organ of the company; it's not USA Today or the Columbia Journalism Review. It must allow communication between management and employees in a way that is useful to both. If you meet that test, your publication will have a lifespan. Just remember that the opposite of "useful" is "useless," and you don't want that!

No. 6 *Always strive for credibility.* Tell the truth, and encourage management that telling the truth is in the best interests of employees. Report the bad news along with the good. Employees won't always like the bad news, but they want to have it. As one sage once said, people can take bad news but they can't stand uncertainty. Provide details. And tell important news at least simultaneously with release in the newspaper.

The next four commandments were written by Kathi Woods, who's the editor of a terrific publication for Meredith Corp. called Insider Magazine.

No. 7 *Plan ahead.* Write a strategic plan with goals and objectives. Send a copy to everyone up the line. Do a progress report at six months, and make sure everyone gets a copy. Do a 12-month evaluation that demonstrates your success. Show management the value of what you're doing with communications.

No. 8 *Stick to a budget.* Although it's probably true that "numbers people" can't write, we can't let the opposite be true and suggest to anyone that writers can't do numbers. Better still, show management a list of ways you intend to save money during the year, such as taking photos yourself instead of hiring out, or switching to a less-expensive printer.

No. 9 *Know when to back down.* You will be criticized, evaluated and turned down on a number of occasions. Your work is among the most visible in the organization, and that makes it ripe for ongoing criticism. You must filter the comments and decide which ones deserve more attention. Pick your battles carefully. You can't afford to alienate those above you or below you.

No. 10 *Communicate regularly.* Everyone hates surprises, especially hard-core business types. Let them know what you're planning and why. Send out a tentative plan for what you hope to be covering in your publication for the next several months—but not for the whole year. It's too much for management to digest.

As a final note, Kathi suggests being a know-it-all, being the expert in two areas—your company and your profession. Cultivate relationships in all areas of the organization. Invite yourself to meetings and events within the organization. Read industry publications, for your company's industry as well as the communications industry. Participate in professional organizations such as IABC, PRSA and WICI. Take classes and courses to continue to educate yourself. Learn for life.

Does any of this count if print publications go away and we all switch to communication on the Internet? You bet it does. The Internet gives editors a new tool for delivering their information; they still have to be credible, knowledgeable and believable in every aspect of their communications internally with employees and externally with customers and shareholders.

Suggestions for additional reading

Bivins, Thomas H. *Fundamentals of Successful Newsletters.* Lincolnwood, Ill.: NTC Business Books, 1994.

Green, Chuck. *The Desktop Publisher's Idea Book,* 2nd ed. New York: Random House, 1997.

Kramer, Felix and Maggie Lovass. *Desktop Publishing Success.* Homewood, Ill.: Business One/Irwin, 1991.

Lichty, Tom. *Design Principles for Desktop Publishers.* New York: HarperCollins, 1989.

Pocket Pal: A Graphic Arts Production Handbook, 17th ed. New York: International Paper, 1997.

Smith, Ronald D. *Becoming a Public Relations Writer.* New York: HarperCollins College Publishers, 1996.

Exercises

1. Compare the layout and design of two fliers you have selected. What differences do you notice? Which flier is more likely to attract the attention of the intended audience? Why?

2. Randomly select four fliers that you have seen posted on campus or in your community. Assume that these fliers were developed by your organization and that your boss has asked you to critique them. Provide your analysis in a written report, using as a guide the writing and design checklist provided in this textbook. In your report, be sure to include ways in which each flier might be improved.

3. Refer to the flier below:

a. Write a headline that will grab the attention of the audience.

b. Rewrite the flier copy so that it is concise and to the point. Eliminate unnecessary information. Use strong verbs.

c. Insert a call to action.

d. Now, reconsider the art. Suggest art that might more appropriately enhance your headline and message. Recall that art includes photographs, illustrations and type.

4. Prepare a flier about an upcoming event for an organization of which you are a member. The event will be in the Student Center from 3 p.m. to 5 p.m. on April 15. Refreshments will be provided by the organization.

   Write the headline and body copy about the event and, if you plan to use art, provide a complete written description of the artwork. Then copy the layout of the flier onto a dummy sheet or provide a printed layout you developed using a software program.

5. Select four brochures that you have seen in your community. Include brochures with different formats, from pamphlets with two folds that were produced from letter-sized paper, to a brochure with three or four folds produced from legal-sized paper, to a booklet containing six to eight pages.

   a. Identify the target audience and desired communication outcome for each brochure.

   b. Review and edit the body copy of each brochure for errors in grammar, style and spelling. Indicate corrections that will need to be made or information that will need to be updated or replaced before the brochure is reprinted.

   c. Prepare an alternative design and layout for one of the smaller brochures.

   d. Prepare an alternative design and layout for the booklet cover.

6. The safety and security department at your university would like you to prepare an informational brochure on drinking. It is up to you to research the topic, define the target audience and determine the desired communication outcome. The format of the brochure is your choice. Complete this task in one week.

   a. After completing the above steps, prepare a draft of the brochure concept for approval by the safety and security office. You may assume that the concept document will be sent as an attachment to a letter from you to the department head. Complete this task in one week.

   b. On the basis of the comments you received from the instructor who reviewed your concept document, prepare a draft of the brochure copy. Complete this task in one week.

   c. Exchange your draft brochure copy with draft brochure copy prepared by a classmate. Edit the classmate's copy for style and content. Prepare a preliminary design and layout for the brochure. Be sure the layout indicates the width of margins, columns and gutters, as well as placement of the body copy, headlines you have written and art. Special graphic considerations such as bold or italic type, drop caps, screens, reverses, rules and boxes should also be indicated on the layout. If actual art is unavailable, you should attach a typed, detailed description of the suggested art. A style sheet that includes your recommended type font and sizes for headlines, subheads, cutlines and body copy should be incorporated on the layout or attached. The preliminary layout should be prepared on dummy sheets that are the actual size of the brochure pages or proportional. The edited body copy and the preliminary design and layout should be returned to the classmate when completed. This task should be completed in one week.

   d. On the basis of the copy editing and preliminary design and layout prepared by your classmate, prepare the final camera-ready pages of your brochure. Complete this task in one week.

7. Select two newsletters sent to your home or available in the community where you live. After analyzing each newsletter, prepare a typed report on your findings. (You may need to look at more than one issue of each newsletter before preparing your report.)

   a. On the basis of your analysis, determine each newsletter's purpose, audience and publishing frequency. From your content analysis list the features that appear regularly in the newsletter and describe the broad categories of stories, such as company information, personnel benefits and competitor activities.

   b. For each broad category you have identified, provide a reasonable estimate of the percent of content for each category and regular feature. To determine the category percent, you must first determine the total amount of space available for text. In arriving at your total, exclude the space occupied by the nameplate or flag on Page One, which gives the name of the publication, date, issue and volume, and the masthead. Also exclude stylized headings for regular features such as columns, editorials or news briefs.

8. Select one edition of one newsletter and edit the copy for errors in style, grammar and spelling.

9. The communications department or college at your university would like you to prepare a design, including all design specifications, for an alumni newsletter. (If one exists at your school, assume you have been asked to redesign the publication.) It is up to you to prepare a mockup of the newsletter's exterior and interior pages. In addition to the design specifications, prepare a typewritten statement about the newsletter's purpose, content and method and frequency of distribution. Your statement should also include your justification for content selection and for the method and frequency of distribution.

Appendix: Frequently Misused Words

ON the next several pages are words that often are misused in both written and spoken English. A few are homonyms that are unlikely to be confused; others are word substitutions that people commonly but erroneously make. A few of these words have fallen into such common misusage that even the experts debate the merits of maintaining the original distinctions. But to professional writers and editors who want to say exactly and concisely what they mean, the distinctions are important. Exercises 5 through 12 at the end of Chapter 3 test your knowledge of these words.

according to It is better to avoid *according to* as an attribution unless the intent is to cast doubt on the speaker's credibility: "According to Jones, he was at home in bed at the time of the crime."

adverse, averse *Adverse* means unfavorable: "Adverse weather delayed our departure." *Averse* means opposed or reluctant and is used with *to:* "She was averse to her daughter's choice of friends."

advice, advise *Advice* is a noun: "His advice was to study harder." *Advise* is a verb: "He advised the student to study harder."

affect, effect *Affect* is a verb: "His illness affected company policy." *Effect* is a noun: "The effect of his illness is unclear." *Effect* may also be used as a verb meaning to bring about: "His illness effected change in the company's insurance costs."

afterward Preferred usage in the United States. The British use *afterwards.*

aggravate, irritate The distinction between these two words seems to be lost, and most authorities say they are interchangeable. Traditionally, *aggravate* means to make an existing situation or condition worse, and *irritate* means to annoy or to provoke to anger: "He aggravated his knee injury and was unable to play football. That irritated him."

altar, alter An *altar* is a table or platform used for sacred ceremonies; *alter* means to change: "They said their wedding vows at the altar. They altered the traditional wedding vows."

annual Something that happens every year. It is incorrect to write *first annual.*

appraise, apprise *Appraise* means to set a value on: "The bank wants to appraise the property before granting a loan." *Apprise* means to notify or inform: "Please apprise me of your progress on the project."

ascent, assent A climb is an *ascent;* the verb form is *ascend:* "They will ascend the stairs"; "The trip to the top of the hill was a steep ascent." *Assent* is a noun or verb meaning "an agreement" or "to agree to": "I want their assent before I continue this program."

awhile, a while *Awhile* is an adverb and *a while* is an article plus a noun: "We fished for a while, but the fish weren't biting, so we swam awhile."

bail, bale *Bail* refers to dipping water out of something or posting a bond. To *bale* something is to tie it into bundles, as to bale old newspapers to take them to a recycling plant.

balance, remainder Do not use these words interchangeably. Use *balance* in fiscal contexts to report the equality of debits and credits or the difference between them. Use *remainder* for what is left when a part is taken away.

baloney, bologna *Baloney* refers to nonsense; *bologna* is lunch meat.

bazaar, bizarre One might buy odd *(bizarre)* items at a *bazaar.*

beach, beech One vacations at the *beach. Beach* may also be used as a verb meaning to run aground (as in beaching a ship). *Beech* trees are not associated with beach areas.

because of, due to *Due to* is an adjective and should modify a noun: "The accident was due to carelessness." *Because of* explains why something happened: "Because of my good work, I received a salary increase."

berth, birth A resting place is a *berth:* "The captain guided the boat into its berth." *Birth* is the act of bringing forth offspring or of being born: "She gave birth to a girl."

beside, besides "The cat lay beside her." *Besides* means in addition to: "Besides the professional musicians, the show will include high school choirs."

better, bettor One who gambles is a *bettor.* It is *better* not to gamble.

biannual, biennial Something that happens twice a year is *biannual;* a *biennial* event occurs once in two years.

bloc, block A *bloc* is a coalition of people or a group with a single purpose or goal: "Farmers were a powerful voting bloc in the last election." *Block* is a different word, with about 40 dictionary definitions.

boar, boor, bore A male hog is a *boar.* An insensitive person is a *boor:* "His behavior at the party shows that he is a boor." *Bore* refers to someone who is boring; *bore* as a verb means to drill: "We like our neighbors, but they are such bores that it is difficult to stay awake when visiting with them."

born, borne A baby is *born. Borne* is the participle of the verb *bear,* meaning "carry": "She has borne great responsibilities during her husband's illness"; "She has borne three children."

bouillon, bullion *Bouillon* refers to broth; *bullion* is gold or silver that has been cast into bars or some other convenient shape: "After working with the bullion all morning, the workers stopped for a lunch of chicken bouillon and sandwiches."

breadth, breath, breathe *Breadth* means width: "The river's breadth is nearly a quarter mile." *Breath* is a noun meaning air taken into the lungs and then let out; *breathe* is the verb form: "I took a deep breath"; "It is unpleasant to breathe smoke-filled air."

Britain, Briton The country is Great Britain; an inhabitant of Britain is a Briton. *Britain* is acceptable usage for reference to Great Britain, which is an island comprising England, Scotland and Wales. The United Kingdom is Great Britain plus Northern Ireland. *The British Isles* applies to the United Kingdom and the islands around it: Scilly to the southwest, the Isle of Man to the west, the Channel Islands to the east, and the Orkneys and the Shetlands to the north of Scotland.

broach, brooch To *broach* is to start a discussion or to make a hole in so as to let out liquid; as a noun, *broach* can refer to a tapered bit for drilling holes. A *brooch* is a large ornamental pin with a clasp: "She wore her favorite brooch that night because she planned to broach the subject of their future together."

burro, burrow A *burro* is a donkey. *Burrow* as a noun refers to a hole in the ground, usually dug by an animal; as a verb, *burrow* means to dig a hole in the ground.

callous, callus Both words come from the same Latin word meaning "hard skin." A *callous* person is one who is unfeeling, who is hardened. *Callus* refers to a thickened place on the skin: "The guitar player has calluses on his fingers."

Calvary, cavalry *Calvary* is the biblical place where Jesus was crucified. *Cavalry* means combat troops mounted originally on horses but now often on motorized armored vehicles.

canvas, canvass *Canvas* is a type of cloth. To *canvass* is to go through places or among people to ask for votes, opinions or orders: "We will canvass this neighborhood in support of our political candidate."

capital, capitol The city is the *capital;* the building is the *capitol*. *Capital* means principal or chief and also refers to money. A capital letter should be used when writing about specific state capitols, such as the Tennessee Capitol, or about the Capitol in Washington, D.C.

cement, concrete *Cement* is a powdered substance made of lime and clay that is mixed with water and sand or gravel to make *concrete*. Most cement is portland cement, so named by its inventor because it resembled stone quarried on the Isle of Portland. The term is a generic and is not capitalized. *Cement* may also be used as a verb.

cemetery Not *cemetary*.

censor, censure, censer *Censor* and *censure* both come from a Latin word meaning to judge, and both can be used as either nouns or verbs. *Censor* means to prohibit or suppress; *censure* means to disapprove or sharply criticize. A book or film may be censored (suppressed, prohibited) or censured (sharply criticized), but a person is censured, not censored: "The Senate formally censured Sen. John Doe." *Censer,* unrelated to the other two words, is a noun meaning "a container in which incense is burned."

cession, session A *cession* is a ceding or giving up to another: "The treaty provided for the cession of individual rights to the territory." A *session* is a period of activity of some kind. A legislative session, for example, might include many meetings and extend for several weeks or months.

childish, childlike *Childish* is a disparaging description of an adult who is silly or foolish: "His childish behavior was inappropriate at the office." *Childlike* means of or like a child in the sense of innocent and trusting: "Her childlike manner made her a delightful companion."

chord, cord A *chord* is a combination of three or more tones sounded together in harmony. *Cord* refers to a string or a measure of wood; it is also the word to apply to vocal cords or the spinal cord.

cite, sight, site One *cites* (quotes) a source or receives a citation ordering a court appearance. *Sight* refers to seeing: "It was a beautiful sight"; "The man was out of my range of sight"; "He carefully aligned the rifle sights with the target." A *site* is a place: "This is the site for our new house."

climactic, climatic *Climactic* refers to the final culminating element in a series, the highest point of interest or the turning point of action: "The climactic scene in the movie was the death of the title character." *Climatic* pertains to weather, as in climatic conditions.

collide Two objects must both be in motion before they can collide. A car might smash into or hit a fence but not collide with it.

commensurate, commiserate *Commensurate* means equal in measure or size: "She wants a salary commensurate with her value to the company." To *commiserate* is to feel or show pity for, to condole: "We commiserate with the family during this sad time."

compare with, compare to *Compare with* means to note both differences and similarities, and this is usually the intended meaning: "Jim compared his report card with John's." *Compare to* means to note similarities alone.

complacent, complaisant One who is *complacent* is self-satisfied: "She was complacent with her life." A complaisant person is willing to please or obliging: "He was *complaisant* regarding his mother's wishes."

complement, compliment As a verb, *complement* means to complete; as a noun it refers to that which completes or perfects: "The sauce complemented the main dish." *Compliment* means praise, and it, too, can be used as either a verb or a noun: "He complimented her on her outstanding work"; "He gave her a compliment on her work."

complementary, complimentary These are the adjective forms of *complement* and *compliment:* "The service department is complementary to the sales department." *Complimentary* can also mean free or given as a courtesy: "He received complimentary tickets."

comprehensible, comprehensive That which is *comprehensible* is understandable: "Now that I know the whole story, his actions are comprehensible." *Comprehensive* means inclusive, wide in scope: "The exam at the end of the semester will be comprehensive."

connotation, denotation A word's *connotation* is its suggested or implied meaning; the *denotation* is the actual meaning or dictionary definition of a word: "The denotation of this word is neutral, but it has a negative connotation."

conscience, conscious, consciousness *Conscience* is an awareness of right and wrong: "Let your conscience be your guide." *Conscious* is an adjective meaning awake; *consciousness* is a noun meaning awareness: "He was conscious throughout the ordeal"; "She regained consciousness after a few minutes."

contagious, infectious A *contagious* disease is spread by contact, whereas an *infectious* disease is transmitted by the presence in the body of certain micro-organisms. An infectious disease may also be contagious.

contemptible, contemptuous A *contemptible* thing deserves scorn or contempt: "His behavior was contemptible." Something is *contemptuous* when it expresses contempt, as a contemptuous remark.

continual, continuous Something that is repeated often at intervals (intermittent) is *continual:* "The rain today was continual" (meaning that it rained off and on during the day). *Continuous* means going on without interruption, or incessant action: "The rain was continuous today" (meaning that it never stopped raining today).

council, counsel, consul A *council* is a group called together for discussion, as in a city council. A *counsel* is one who gives advice or is a lawyer. A *consul* is a diplomat.

councilor, counselor A *councilor* is a member of a council. A *counselor* is an adviser or a lawyer.

couple of The *of* is necessary: "A couple of dollars should be enough for a hamburger."

crochet, crotchet, crotchety *Crochet* is a type of needlework; to crochet is to do such needlework. *Crotchet* is a noun meaning "a particular whim or stubborn notion"; thus a crotchety person is one who is stubborn or cranky.

croquet, croquette, coquette *Croquet* is an outdoor game. A *croquette* is a small meat or fish patty. *Coquette* is a French word meaning a girl or woman flirt.

cue, queue A *cue* is a stick used in billiards or pool to strike a ball. A *queue* is a pigtail or, in Britain, a line, as of persons waiting to be served: "The queue was quite long when we arrived at the restaurant." *Queue* is also used as an intransitive verb with *up,* as in "We queued up to wait for a table at the restaurant."

currant, current A *currant* is a small seedless raisin from the Mediterranean area. *Current* means at the present time or circulating (as electricity): "On our current visit to the Mediterranean, we have been enjoying the currants."

cymbal, symbol A musician uses a *cymbal,* a circular brass plate that makes a ringing sound when hit. A *symbol* is an object used to represent something abstract, a mark or letter standing for a quality or process, as in music or chemistry, or an editing mark.

cypress, Cyprus A *cypress* is an evergreen tree. *Cyprus* is the name of an island country in the east end of the Mediterranean. A citizen of Cyprus is a Cypriot.

defective, deficient Something that has imperfections or is faulty is *defective:* "The car had defective brakes." *Deficient* means lacking in some essential, incomplete or inadequate in amount: "The doctor said her diet was deficient in vitamin C."

demolish, destroy These words mean that something is done away with completely, so it is redundant to say *completely demolished* or *totally destroyed.*

demur, demure To *demur* is to hesitate because of doubts or to have objections; *demur* is also a noun meaning an objection: "The lawyer filed a demur with the court." To be *demure* is to be affectedly modest or coy: "She wore a demure dress for her appearance in court."

deprecate, depreciate To *deprecate* is to express disapproval of, to belittle: "He deprecated her efforts." To *depreciate* is to lessen in value: "A car depreciates rapidly."

desert, dessert To *desert* is to abandon, to forsake, as to leave a military post without permission and with no intent to return. *Desert* also refers to a dry, barren, sandy region, such as the Sahara Desert. A *dessert* is the final course of a meal.

detract, distract To *detract* is to take away: "An unkept lawn detracts from the appearance of a house." To *distract* is to draw the mind in another direction, to divert, to confuse or bewilder: "The child's crying distracted the man from his work."

different from Not *different than:* "Mary's political views are different from those of her sister." *Differ with* indicates disagreement: "I differ with her political views."

dilemma A choice between two alternatives, both bad. *Dilemma* should not be used to mean a choice from among more than two or a choice between a good alternative and a bad one: "To leave the car and walk toward town during the blizzard or to wait for help that wasn't likely to come before daybreak: that was his dilemma."

disapprove, disprove To *disapprove* is to have or express an unfavorable opinion: "She disapproved of John's work." To *disprove* is to prove to be false: "He disproved the belief that the earth is flat."

disburse, dispense, disperse To *disburse* is to pay out, as in disbursing wages. To *dispense* is to give out or distribute, as with medicine or justice: "The judge will dispense justice; the nurse will dispense pills." *Disperse* means to break up and scatter: "They attempted to disperse the oil that had spilled into the bay."

disinterested, uninterested One who is *disinterested* is impartial or unbiased, as in a disinterested judge. An *uninterested* person is indifferent or lacks interest. The distinction between these two words is being lost in common usage, so a writer or speaker might prefer to use *impartial* instead of *disinterested.*

distinctive, distinguished Something that is *distinctive* is different or characteristic. It is not necessarily good or bad, just different. *Distinguished* means excellent, outstanding. A teacher who wears unusual clothes, stands on her desk and shouts at students can be said to have a distinctive teaching style, but it may or may not be considered distinguished: "He had a distinctive speaking style. Later he became a distinguished diplomat."

dose, doze A *dose* is an amount of medicine to be taken at one time; to *doze* is to sleep lightly or nap: "He took a dose of medicine and then sat in front of the television set to doze."

drier, dryer *Drier* is the comparative form of *dry:* "A desert is drier than a river valley." A *dryer* is a person or thing that dries, such as an appliance for drying clothes.

drown Should not have an auxiliary or helping verb unless the victim was helped in the drowning. Just say "He drowned," not "He was drowned."

drunk, drunken Use *drunken* as a modifier before a noun, as in drunken driver. Use *drunk* as a predicate adjective, as in "He was drunk."

dual, duel *Dual* means something composed of two, a double, as in "The car has dual headlights." A *duel* is a prearranged fight between two persons armed with deadly weapons.

each other, one another The consensus among grammatical experts is to use these interchangeably instead of applying *each other* when the meaning is limited to two and *one another* when more than two are involved.

eager, anxious Experts are divided about whether these may be properly interchanged. *Anxious* refers to foreboding; *eager* means to look forward to: "She was anxious about the surgery"; "She was eager for the vacation trip."

ecology, environment *Ecology* refers to the relationship between organisms and their environment. It is not a synonym for *environment*.

eek, eke out *Eek* is an exclamatory expression: "Eek! There's a snake!" *Eke out* means to get something with great difficulty: "During the Depression, they barely managed to eke out a living."

elder, eldest; older, oldest Some dictionaries make a distinction, applying *elder* and *eldest* to people and *older* and *oldest* to either things or people. At what age these terms should be applied to people is highly subjective. The AP stylebook cautions that they should not be used to describe anyone younger than 65 and should not be used casually in referring to anyone beyond that age. *Elderly* is appropriate in generic phrases that do not refer to specific individuals, as in concern for the elderly or a home for the elderly. If the intent is to show that an individual's faculties have deteriorated, the AP stylebook says to cite a graphic example: "His memory fades"; "She walks with a cane."

elicit, illicit *Elicit* is a transitive verb meaning to draw forth or evoke (a response): "The teacher sought to elicit answers from her students." *Illicit* is an adjective describing something that is unlawful, improper or prohibited, as in an illicit affair.

emigrant, immigrant One who leaves a country is an *emigrant*; one who comes into a country is an *immigrant*.

ensure, insure The consensus among usage experts is that these terms may be used interchangeably to mean make certain, but AP style is to use *ensure* for that meaning: "Additional testing will ensure quality control." *Insure* is the correct word to mean guarantee against loss, as in to insure your automobile (buy insurance).

envisage, envision Both words mean to form an image in the mind, to visualize, but *envision* has the connotation of less immediacy than *envisage*, which might refer to imagining something not yet in existence.

epithet, epitaph An *epithet* is a word or phrase characterizing a person or thing; in common usage it has come to be associated with derogatory descriptions. An *epitaph* is an inscription, as for a tombstone, in memory of a dead person.

erasable, irascible A pencil mark is *erasable,* meaning that it can be erased or rubbed out. An *irascible* person is one who is easily angered or is hot-tempered.

especially, specially *Especially* means to an outstanding extent or particularly: "I am especially happy about the good news." *Specially* means for a special purpose: "She bought the dress specially for the party."

every day, everyday *Every day* is an adverb: "She wore a suit every day to work." *Everyday* is an adjective meaning usual, common or suitable for everyday use: "She wore an everyday dress rather than her best suit."

evoke, invoke To *evoke* is to call forth, to elicit: "His soothing voice evoked memories of her father." To *invoke* is to call on a higher authority, such as God or the Muses, for blessing or help; to resort to (such as a law or ruling) as pertinent; to conjure, beg for, implore. The noun form is *invocation*.

exalt, exult *Exalt* is to raise in status or dignity, to praise or glorify, to fill with joy or pride, as in exalted ruler. *Exult*, an intransitive verb, means to rejoice greatly or to glory; the noun form is *exultation:* "They exulted in the news of their victory."

excite, incite *Excite* means to make active, to stimulate, to arouse emotionally; *incite* means to urge to action. A speaker might excite a crowd, for example, without inciting the crowd to take action, but generally a crowd will not become incited without first becoming excited: "The sound of a doorbell excites the dog and causes it to bark"; "The dynamic speaker incited the inmates to begin fighting the guards."

exercise, exorcise *Exercise* pertains to physical activity, as in an exercise class to promote good health. *Exorcise* means to expel (such as evil spirits) by incantations or to free from such spirits; noun forms are *exorcism* and *exorcist*.

expose To lay open, generally to something undesirable, such as danger or attack: "The worker was exposed to radiation"; "The revelations exposed the candidate to political attacks from his opponents." *Expose* should not be used in the sense of making known, as in "Our travels abroad exposed us to new cultures."

extant, extent *Extant* means still existing: "This is the oldest extant structure in North America." *Extent* means space, amount, degree to which a thing extends, size, scope, limits: "The child tested the extent of his mother's patience."

facetious, factious, factitious, fictitious *Facetious* means joking or amusing, as in a facetious comment. *Factious* refers to creating dissent, especially in political matters: "The trade legislation was factious in this congressional session." *Factitious* means forced or artificial. *Fictitious* means of or like fiction, imaginary, false, assumed for disguise not necessarily with the intent to deceive, as in a fictitious account or a fictitious title.

fact A reality, a truth. It is redundant to say *true fact, real fact* or *actual fact.*

feat, fete *Feat* describes an accomplishment of unusual daring or skill: "Few of Babe Ruth's feats have been matched." A fete is a festival, entertainment or lavish party: "The fete honored her 100th birthday."

ferment, foment *Ferment* means to undergo fermentation by the addition of some substance, such as yeast: "Grapes ferment to become wine." *Foment* means to stir up (such as trouble), to incite: "He sought to foment trouble among the workers."

fiancé, fiancée Despite efforts toward a gender-neutral language, this distinction remains. General usage and AP style reserves *fiancé* for males and *fiancée* for females.

fiscal, physical *Fiscal* means financial, as in the nation's fiscal policy.

flack, flak *Flack* is a slang term for a press agent or public relations practitioner. It is often used in a derogatory sense. *Flak* was first used during World War II as an acronym for a German antiaircraft gun and the shells fired by the gun. It has come to mean criticism: "He took a lot of flak for his stand on the issue."

flagrant, fragrant *Flagrant* means obviously evident and connotes outrageous or shocking conduct: "He was flagrant in his disregard for rules and regulations." Something that is *fragrant* smells good.

flaunt, flout To *flaunt* means to show off proudly or in an ostentatious manner: "She flaunted her wealth." *Flout* means to defy, mock or scorn: "His behavior flouts authority."

flier, flyer The news-service stylebooks prefer *flier* for both aviators and handbills. Other usage guides prefer *flyer* for handbill. *Flyer* is the proper name for some trains and buses: the Western Flyer.

flounder, founder In addition to denoting a variety of fish, *flounder* means to struggle awkwardly or to speak or act in an awkward, confused manner: "He floundered in the deep snow." *Founder* as a verb means to stumble, fall or go lame, as in "The horse foundered." *Founder* as a verb also means to fill with water and sink, as in to founder a ship.

forbidding, foreboding *Forbidding* is an adjective meaning difficult or looking dangerous or disagreeable, as in a forbidding climb to the top of a mountain. *Foreboding* as a noun means a prediction, usually of something evil: "She believed that the dream was a foreboding of doom."

foregoing, forgoing *Foregoing* is something previously said or written, as in the foregoing paragraph of the speech. *Forgoing* is the present participle form of the verb *forgo*, meaning to do without, to abstain: "He will forgo eating meat."

fortuitous, fortunate *Fortuitous* means happening by luck or chance: "Our meeting here is fortuitous because I want to talk with you." *Fortunate* means having good luck: "She was fortunate throughout her career."

funeral service A redundant phrase. A funeral is a service.

gantlet, gauntlet A *gantlet* was a punishment in which the offender ran between two rows of men who struck him ("running the gantlet"). Now *gantlet* is used to mean a series of troubles. Originally, *gauntlet* meant a knight's armored glove. Throw down the gauntlet meant to challenge to combat. Opinion is divided on whether modern usage correctly allows these terms to be used interchangeably. Several dictionaries indicate that they are the same, with *gauntlet* the preferred spelling.

genteel, gentle *Genteel* means polite or well bred, with modern usage referring to affectedly refined or polite: "His genteel mannerisms seemed out of place in his current state of homelessness on New York City streets." *Gentle* means refined, courteous, tame, not harsh or rough, as in a gentle man or a gentle animal.

gorilla, guerrilla A *gorilla* is the largest and most powerful of the apes native to Africa. A *guerrilla* is a member of a small defensive force of irregular soldiers.

gourmand, gourmet Both terms refer to someone who likes good food and drink, but *gourmand* is used in the sense of eating or drinking to excess, as a glutton would: "John is a gourmand and weighs 350 pounds." *Gourmet* connotes one who is an excellent judge of fine foods and drinks, a connoisseur: "June is a gourmet cook."

grisly, gristly, grizzly *Grisly* means horrible or gruesome, as in a grisly crime. *Gristly* means having gristles, as in gristly meat. *Grizzly* means gray or streaked with gray, having gray hair.

half brother, stepbrother If they have one parent in common, they are *half brothers;* if they are related by the remarriage of parents, they are *stepbrothers.* Because in some cultures it is considered insensitive to identify family members as *half brother, half sister, stepmother* and so on, some newspapers do not specify such family relationships except when germane to a story or specified by the persons involved.

half-mast, half-staff Flags on ships or at naval stations are lowered to or flown at (but not raised to) *half-mast.* Flags in other places are lowered to *half-staff.*

hangar, hanger A *hangar* shelters airplanes. A *hanger* is used to support clothes or other objects.

hardy, hearty *Hardy* is an adjective meaning bold and resolute, robust, or vigorous, as in a hardy species of plants. *Hearty* means warm and friendly, jovial, unrestrained, as in a hearty laugh.

head up Incorrect usage. A person heads a committee, perhaps.

healthful, healthy Something that is conducive to good health is *healthful:* "Exercise is healthful." Something that has good health is *healthy:* "The healthy man exercises daily." Today, *healthy* is commonly used in both senses.

historic, historical *Historic* means important to history, as in a historic battle. *Historical* means of or concerning history: "It is a historical novel."

holey, holy *Holey* means full of holes: "Throw the holey socks in the trash." *Holy* refers to sacred things: "He considered his work to be a holy duty." Neither word should be confused with *wholly,* which means entirely.

hopefully One of the most commonly misused words. It should be used as an adverb to describe the way the subject feels; it should not be used as an adjective. Thus, it is incorrect to write "Hopefully, he will make an A in the course." The correct wording is "He hopes he will make an A." To describe his feelings, write "He looked hopefully at his grade report."

impassable, impassible *Impassable* means not capable of being passed, as in an impassable obstacle. An *impassible* person is one who is incapable of showing emotion: "He was impassible as the judge sentenced him to prison."

inapt, inept *Inapt* (also *unapt*) means inappropriate or not suitable: "To wear a hat at the dining room table is inapt behavior." *Inept* is sometimes used in that sense, but usually it refers to something that is foolish or incompetent: "Mary is a computer expert, but she is inept in diagnosing problems with her car."

incite, insight To *incite* is to urge to action, as in to incite violence (see entry *excite, incite*). *Insight* is a noun meaning the ability to see and understand clearly the inner nature of things, especially by intuition: "She had a keen insight into the situation."

incredible, incredulous Something that is unbelievable is *incredible; incredulous* means skeptical: "I was incredulous when I heard about his feats on the basketball court, but when I saw him perform, I realized that he was capable of incredible plays."

ingenious, ingenuous An *ingenious* person is inventive; an *ingenuous* person is honest or open to the point of being naive: "We know that Benjamin Franklin was ingenious, but he was probably not ingenuous."

insoluble, insolvable, insolvent An *insoluble* substance cannot be dissolved. An *insolvable* problem is one that cannot be solved. A person who cannot pay debts is said to be *insolvent.*

interment, internment To *inter* is to put into a grave or tomb, so *interment* is a burial. *Internment* means detention, as in internment camp.

interstate, intrastate *Interstate* means between states: "The truck was used for interstate commerce along the eastern coast." *Intrastate* means within a single state.

intestate Not having a will: "He died intestate."

into, in to The preposition *into* is not interchangeable with the adverb *in* followed by the preposition *to*: "The firefighter ran into the burning building"; "The escaped convict turned himself in to the police."

irrespective An adjective meaning regardless. Do not use *irregardless.*

judicial, judicious *Judicial* refers to a judge or court or their functions, as in a judicial system or the judicial branch of government. *Judicious* means having or showing sound judgment: "His actions demonstrate that he is judicious."

lam, lamb *Lam* is a slang expression for a headlong flight, as in fleeing. A person in this situation is said to be on the lam. A *lamb* is a baby sheep.

lama, llama A priest or monk in Tibet or Mongolia is a *lama.* A *llama* is an animal found in the South American Andes.

leach, leech To *leach* is to wash a solid substance with a filtering liquid or to extract from some material. A *leech* is a bloodsucker, originally a bloodsucking worm; now the term is also applied to a person who clings to another to get what he or she can.

leak, leek *Leak* is a verb meaning to let fluid in or out accidentally or, as a noun, meaning a hole: "The boat had a leak"; "Water leaked into the boat." A *leek* is an onionlike vegetable.

lie, lay See Rule 31 in Chapter 2.

lightening, lightning *Lightening* means making something less heavy or less dark, as in lightening the color of paint or lightening the load. *Lightning* is a flash of light in the sky caused by the discharge of atmospheric electricity.

like, as *As* is a conjunction; *like* is a verb or a preposition: "She looks like her sister"; "The two women look as though they might be sisters." *Though* or *if* is needed with *as* when what follows is a clause; a conjunction, not a preposition, is needed to join the dependent clause and the main clause.

linage, lineage *Linage* is the number of written or printed lines on a page. In journalism, advertising linage refers to the number of lines of advertising matter in an issue. *Lineage* means descent from an ancestor: "She traced her lineage to the Pilgrims."

loath, loathe *Loath* is an adjective meaning reluctant; the expression *is loath to*: "She is loath to give a speech before a large audience." *Loathe* means to dislike intensely: "She loathed her boss because of his sexist behavior."

locate To fix the position of, to situate or become situated, to discover. *Locate* is not a synonym for *find;* "She located her car keys" is incorrect. Correct usage: "The city council decided to locate the new city hall at Fourth and Main streets."

Magna Carta, Magna Charta In the United States, *Magna Carta* is the preferred spelling.

majority, plurality More than half is a majority. A plurality is less than half but is the largest number. For example, if the votes of 11 people were 5 for, 4 against, and 2 undecided, you could say that a plurality voted in favor. At least 6 of 11 people would have to vote the same way before there would be a majority. Do not use *majority* in place of most or many or where numbers are not involved. Do not use *majority* in the comparative sense, as in greater majority or greatest majority.

marshal, marshall *Marshal* is the correct word for the verb form (marshal the forces) or the noun (fire marshal, parade marshal). *Marshall* is the usual spelling for a proper noun (John Marshall).

masterful, masterly *Masterful* means domineering: "She feared her masterful teacher." *Masterly* means skillful or expert: "It was a masterly performance." *Masterful* is often misused in the latter sense, perhaps because there is no adverbial form of *masterly.*

may be, maybe *May be* is a verb, as in "I may be selected for the job." *Maybe* means perhaps, as in "Maybe I will be selected for the job." *Maybe* should not be used as an adjective: a maybe fun party.

mean, median *Mean* is a synonym for average, referring to the sum of all components divided by the number of components. The *median* is the middle number, meaning that half the components are larger and half are smaller: "The test scores were 95, 85, 70, for a mean of 83.33, but the median grade was 85." Some authorities object to using *average* to mean common or ordinary, as in an average person.

media, medium *Media* is plural: "The media are business enterprises." *Medium* is singular: "The artist's medium was watercolor."

motor, engine An *engine* develops its own power, usually through internal combustion or the pressure of air, steam or water passing over vanes attached to a wheel: an airplane engine, an automobile engine, a jet engine, a missile engine, a steam engine, a turbine engine. A *motor* receives power from an outside source: an electric motor, a hydraulic motor.

nauseated, nauseous A person becomes *nauseated* because of something that is *nauseous,* which means causing nausea. It is wrong to say a person who is ill is nauseous: "While on the trip, she was nauseated because she suffers from motion sickness."

negligent, negligible To be *negligent* is to be careless, inattentive or neglectful: "This place will shelter the children of negligent parents." *Negligible* refers to that which can be disregarded, a trifling: "At the end of the week, the amount of work left to do on the house was negligible."

odious, odorous *Odious* means hateful, disgusting or offensive, as in an odious task. Something fragrant is *odorous,* as in odorous flowers.

palate, palette, pallet The *palate* is the roof of the mouth. Although the taste buds are not located there, in common usage the word *palate* applies to taste. An artist uses a *palette* for mixing paints. A *pallet* is a small, simple bed or a low platform for moving and stacking materials, as at a warehouse.

parlay, parley To *parlay* is to bet an original wager plus its earnings on another race or game: "He parlayed $10 into $1,000." *Parley* comes from the French word for speak and means to confer, especially with an enemy.

partially, partly Most dictionaries list these words as synonyms in the sense of part of the whole. *Partially* can also mean showing favoritism. If there is room for ambiguity, use *partly:* "The work was partly done."

pedal, petal, peddle You *pedal* a bicycle. A flower has *petals.* When selling something, you *peddle* it.

pendant, pendent A *pendant* is an ornamental hanging object, such as a locket or earring: "She wore a silver pendant." *Pendent* means suspended, overhanging, undecided or pending.

peremptory, pre-emptory *Peremptory* comes from a Latin word meaning to destroy. In a legal sense, *peremptory* means barring further action or final, as in a peremptory challenge. *Pre-emptory* means prior: "That television show will pre-empt the one I wanted to see."

perquisite, prerequisite A *perquisite* is something in addition to the regular pay for one's work: "A perquisite of the position is the use of a health club." A short form of *perquisite* is *perk*. A *prerequisite* is something required beforehand as a necessary condition. In education, for example, a student must complete basic courses as prerequisites to more advanced courses.

persecute, prosecute To *persecute* is to afflict constantly so as to injure or distress, particularly for reasons of race or religion: "The Jewish people were persecuted by the Nazis." To *prosecute* is to conduct legal proceedings against one accused of a crime: "The state will prosecute those arrested for selling illegal drugs."

perspective, prospective *Perspective* refers to the appearance of objects as determined by their relative distance and position; it also refers to a sense of proportion: "The artist's paintings had unusual perspective." It has come to be used as a synonym of viewpoint: "What is your perspective on this matter?" *Prospective* is an adjective meaning expected or likely: "Jones is the prospective candidate for the job."

persuade, convince People are *persuaded to*, meaning they are talked into or induced. People may become *convinced*, meaning that they feel secure about a decision or principle. *Convince* should not be followed by an infinitive. People are convinced that it is so or convinced of a fact: "She persuaded her father to allow her to attend the party"; "He was convinced that it was the right thing to do."

podium, lectern A speaker stands on a *podium* or dais. The speaker stands behind a *lectern*.

populous, populace A thickly populated place is *populous:* "The cost of living usually is high in such populous places as New York City." *Populace* refers to the common people, the masses: "The politician was admired by the populace."

precede, proceed To *precede* is to go ahead of something or someone: "The attendants will precede the bride down the aisle." *Proceed* means to continue some action: "He proceeded to read the newspaper." The plural noun *proceeds* refers to the yield derived from a commercial or fund-raising venture.

predominant, predominate *Predominant* is an adjective; *predominate* is a verb. Both refer to having influence over others or being dominant in frequency: "The New York Yankees were the predominant baseball team during the 1950s"; "The teams predominated the American League."

prescribe, proscribe *Prescribe* means to order, as a medicine is prescribed by a doctor. *Proscribe* means to prohibit, outlaw or denounce: "Drunken driving is proscribed behavior."

pretense, pretext A *pretense* is a false show, an overt act intended to conceal personal feelings: "My profuse compliments were a pretense." A *pretext* is a motive or reason for action offered in place of the true one: "She was accused of tardiness, but that was only a pretext for sexism."

principle, principal A guiding rule or basic truth is a *principle* (a noun): "He followed the principle 'live and let live.'" *Principal*, which can be used as either a noun or an adjective, means first, dominant or leading thing. A memory aid taught to schoolchildren is "The principal is your pal," because the dominant person at most schools is the principal. In the early years of a home mortgage, most of the monthly payments are applied to the interest on the loan, rather than the *principal* (the dominant amount).

reckless Heedless or rash. It is *reckless* (not wreckless) driving that often causes automobile accidents.

recur, reoccur Copperud *(American Usage and Style)* found that most experts see no distinction between these forms. Of the language authorities he consulted, only one said that *reoccur* suggests a single repetition. The consensus is that *recur* and *recurrence* are preferred.

refute To argue successfully, to prove to be false or mistaken. *Disprove* is a correct substitute for *refute*. Do not use *refute* if there is any question about the success of the argument. *Deny, contradict, reject, rebut* and *dispute* are appropriate words to indicate that disagreement took place. "He refuted the argument" means that he disproved the argument. "He rejected/denied/disputed/contradicted/rebutted the argument" means that he disagreed with the argument, but it does not mean that he proved the argument wrong.

regardless Not *irregardless*.

reluctant, reticent *Reluctant* means that someone does not want to act: "She was reluctant to audition for the play." *Reticent* means disposed to keep silent: "He was reticent about his failed marriage."

remediable, remedial Something that can be fixed is *remediable*. Something that is meant to be a remedy is *remedial:* "The student enrolled in remedial reading."

repairable, reparable Both words mean that something can be repaired. *Repairable* is used for physical items: "The child's toy is repairable." *Reparable* is used with non-physical things: "I hope that the damage to the group's morale is reparable."

rise, raise See Rule 31 in Chapter 2.

rye, wry *Rye* is grass. *Wry*, from an Old English word meaning to turn, is used in the sense of twisted, distorted or ironic, as in wry humor.

say, said The most serviceable words of attribution. Other verbs of attribution, including *stated, declared, admitted, screamed, yelled, shouted* and *cried*, have meanings different from *said* and should not be used unless they accurately describe the speaker's demeanor. Sources don't *grin, frown, smile* or *giggle* their comments to a reporter.

seasonable, seasonal *Seasonable* means timely, suitable to the season: "A wool suit is seasonable for winter." *Seasonal* means depending on the season: "Fresh vegetables are seasonal."

shear, sheer *Shear* means to cut off, as in shear wool from sheep. *Sheer* as a verb means to turn aside or cause to turn aside, to swerve: "The truck sheered from the mountainside." As an adjective, *sheer* refers to very thin, transparent material, as in sheer curtains. It can also mean absolute or utter, as in sheer folly.

similar to Not *similar with*.

sit, set See Rule 31 in Chapter 2.

sleight, slight *Sleight* means skill with the hands, especially in deceiving onlookers, as in magic: sleight of hand. To *slight* is to treat as unimportant; as a noun *slight* can refer to the condition of being treated as unimportant: "The slight was unintentional." As an adjective, *slight* can mean light, slender in build, frail or fragile, as in the slight man.

sniffle, snivel *Sniffle* means the act or sound of sniffling or, as a verb, to sniff repeatedly. *Snivel* means to cry and sniffle or to complain and whine.

spade, spayed A *spade* is a shovel. To *spay* is to sterilize a female animal by removing the ovaries. *Spayed* is the past tense of *spay*.

strop, strap The leather band for sharpening razors is a razor *strop*, not *strap*.

supersede To replace or succeed: "The agency issued guidelines that supersede those adopted in 1988." *Supersede* is often misspelled. It is the only word in the English language that ends in *sede*. Three words end in *ceed: succeed, exceed* and *proceed*. The others end in *cede*.

supposed to The correct form (not *suppose to*) in the sense of *expected to*: "I am supposed to attend training sessions this week."

tack, tact In addition to being a short nail, a *tack* is a course of action or the direction a ship goes in relation to the position of the sails: "He decided to use a different tack to reach his goals." *Tact* means a delicate perception of the right thing to say or do without offending: "Mending the relationship will require tact." *Tactful* is the adjective form, as in a tactful person.

teem, team *Teem* means to be prolific, to abound, to swarm. The present participle form is *teeming*, not *teaming*: "The room was teeming with flies."

tempera, tempura *Tempera* is used in painting, *tempura* in cooking.

temperatures They get higher or lower, but they don't get cooler or warmer.

tenant, tenet A *tenant* is one who pays rent to occupy land or a building. A *tenet* is a principle, doctrine or belief held as a truth: "Doing unto others as you would have them do unto you is a tenet of Christianity."

that, which See Rule 18 in Chapter 2.

there Generally, sentences should not begin with *there*, as in there is, there was, there were. Rather than writing "There were four touchdowns scored in the game," write "The team scored four touchdowns." Get to the real subject rather than using a false subject. Examples abound of good writing with sentences beginning with *there*, especially where the idea is to downplay the true subject, but more often in common usage *there* at the beginning is a signal of lazy thinking.

tort, torte *Tort* is a legal term referring to a wrongful act or damage not involving a breach of contract for which a civil action can be brought: "Libel is an example of a tort." A *torte* is a rich cake.

toward Correct usage in the United States; the British prefer *towards*.

translucent, transparent When looking through something that is *translucent*, one can see light but cannot see objects on the other side; one would be able to see through a *transparent* glass or fabric: "He installed translucent windows in the office to provide privacy."

trooper, trouper A *trooper* is a member of the cavalry, a mounted police officer or a state police officer. A *trouper* is a member of a troop of actors or singers. *Trouper* is also used to refer to a veteran entertainer.

type Use as a noun, not an adjective. Incorrect: "He is a studious type person." Instead, say "He is a studious type." *Type* with a hyphen is acceptable in technical uses, as in B-type blood.

unique Something that is unique is one of a kind, so expressions like *more unique, most unique* and *very unique* should be avoided.

up Avoid its use as part of a verb, as in *stood up, beat up, paired up* and *stirred up*.

venal, venial *Venal* means open to or characterized by corruption or bribery, as in a venal government official. *Venial* means that which may be forgiven or is pardonable, as in a venial sin.

veracious, voracious To be *veracious* is to be habitually truthful or honest: "A veracious person is not likely to become a thief." *Voracious* comes from a Latin word meaning devour. It means greedy, ravenous or very eager, as in a voracious reader.

viral, virile *Viral* means of or caused by a virus, which is an organism that causes certain diseases: "He is ill with a viral disease" (not with a virus). *Virile* means of or characteristic of a man's ability to function sexually. Alternatives to *virile* that can refer to both sexes include *energetic, vigorous, strong, dynamic* or *bold*.

waist, waste *Waist* is correct for referring to part of the human body: "He put his arm around her waist."

wangle, wrangle To *wangle* is to get or cause by contrivance or tricks: "Can you wangle an invitation to the party?" To *wrangle* is to argue or quarrel. As a noun, *wrangle* means an angry, noisy dispute. A *wrangler* is a ranch hand who herds livestock, especially saddle horses.

well-known, widely known Journalistic usage prefers *widely known* to describe someone whose name or work is known by many people: "The actor Paul Newman is widely known, but few of his fans have ever met him, so they do not know him well."

who's, whose See Rule 17 in Chapter 2.

wholly Entirely: "The incorporated village was wholly within the city."

wreak, wreck *Wreak* means to inflict: "The storm will wreak havoc on our new plants." To *wreck* is to damage.

Index